LOVE MAN

LET US KNOW WH

AVAILABLE ONLINE
VIZ.COM/MANGASURVEY

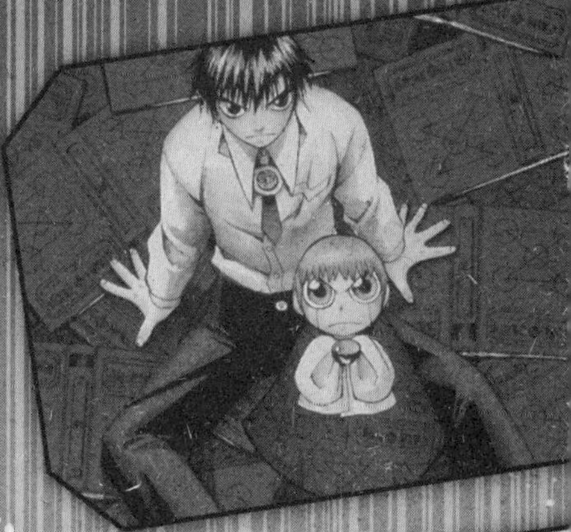

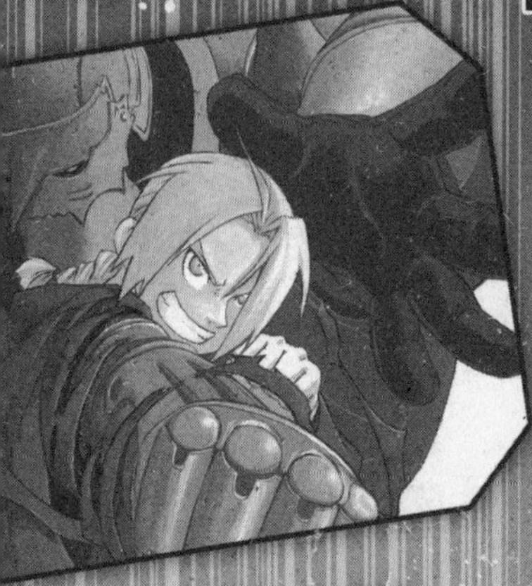

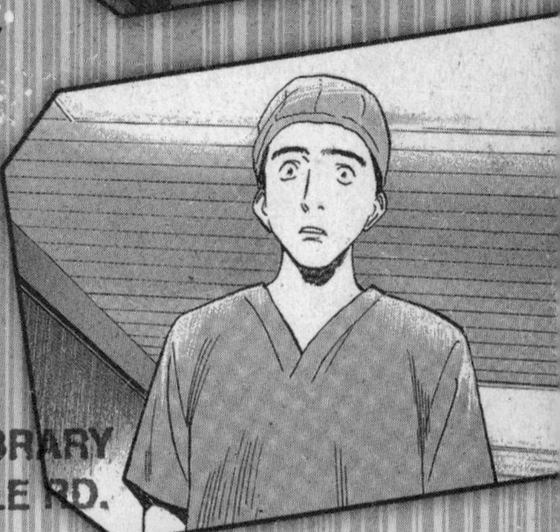

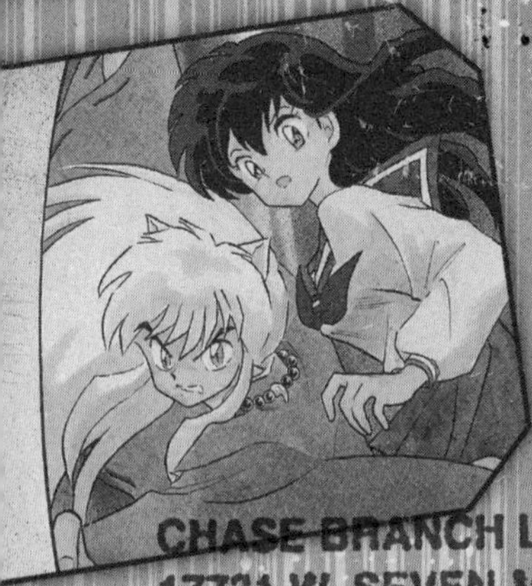

HELP US MAKE THE MANGA YOU LOVE BETTER!

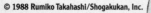

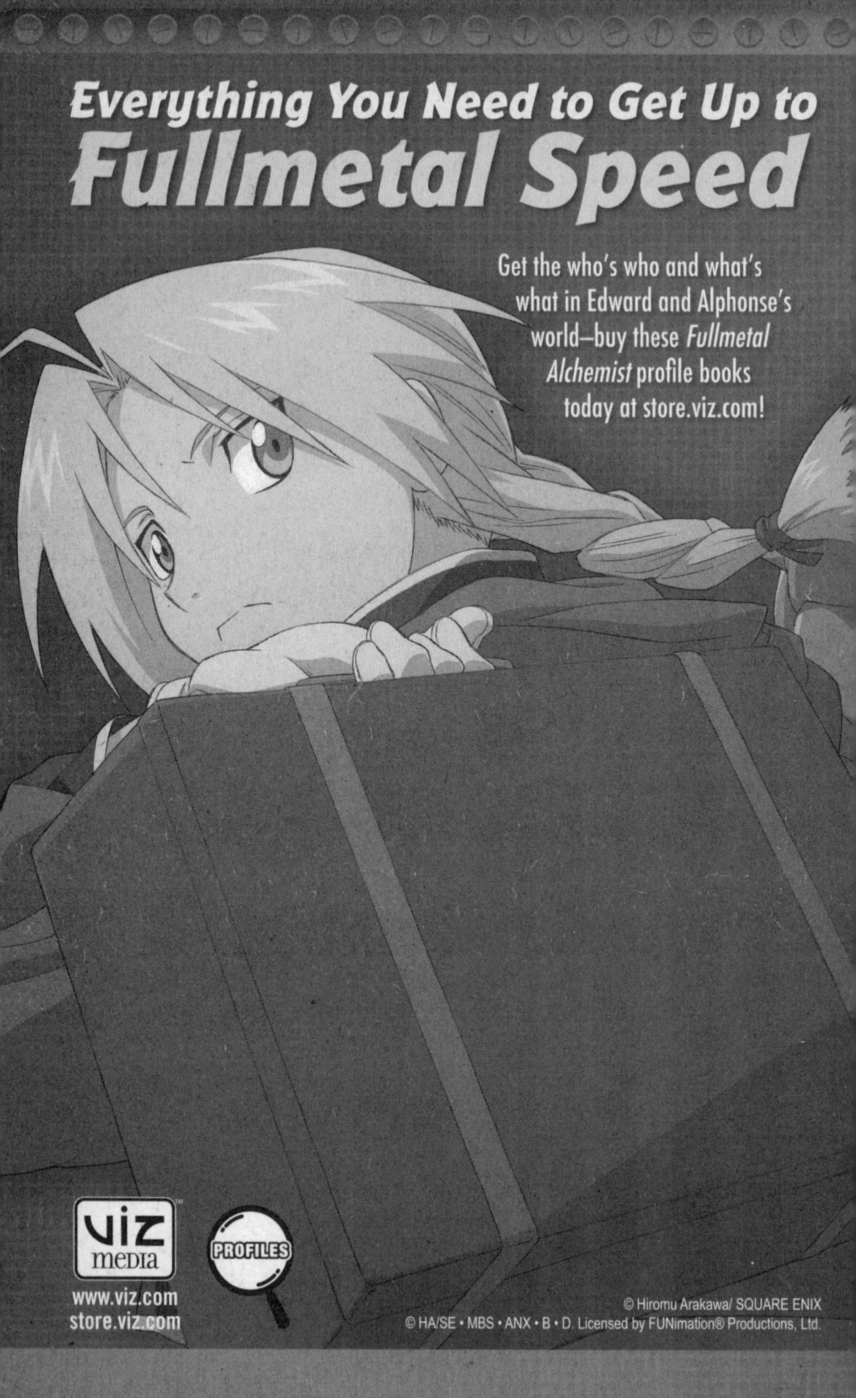
Everything You Need to Get Up to
Fullmetal Speed
Get the who's who and what's what in Edward and Alphonse's world—buy these Fullmetal Alchemist profile books today at store.viz.com!
viz media
PROFILES
www.viz.com
store.viz.com
© Hiromu Arakawa/ SQUARE ENIX
© HA/SE • MBS • ANX • B • D. Licensed by FUNimation® Productions, Ltd.

Fullmetal Alchemist Profiles

Get the background story and world history of the manga, plus:

- Character bios
- New, original artwork
- Interview with creator Hiromu Arakawa
- Bonus manga episode only available in this book

Fullmetal Alchemist Anime Profiles

Stay on top of your favorite episodes and characters with:

- Actual cel artwork from the TV series
- Summaries of all 51 TV episodes
- Definitive cast biographies
- Exclusive poster for your wall

Freshly Baked from Japan!
It's 16-year-old Kazuma Azuma's dream to use his otherworldly baking powers to create Ja-pan, the national bread of the land of the rising sun. But in a nation known for rice and seafood delicacies, the stakes are high. Can Kazuma rise to the occasion before his dreams fall flat?
Find out in Yakitate!! Japan—buy the manga today!
Yakitate!! Japan™
Yakitate!! Japan 1
JAPAN
STORY & ART BY Takashi Hashiguchi
$9.99
© 2002 Takashi HASHIGUCHI/Shogakukan Inc.
www.viz.com
viz media

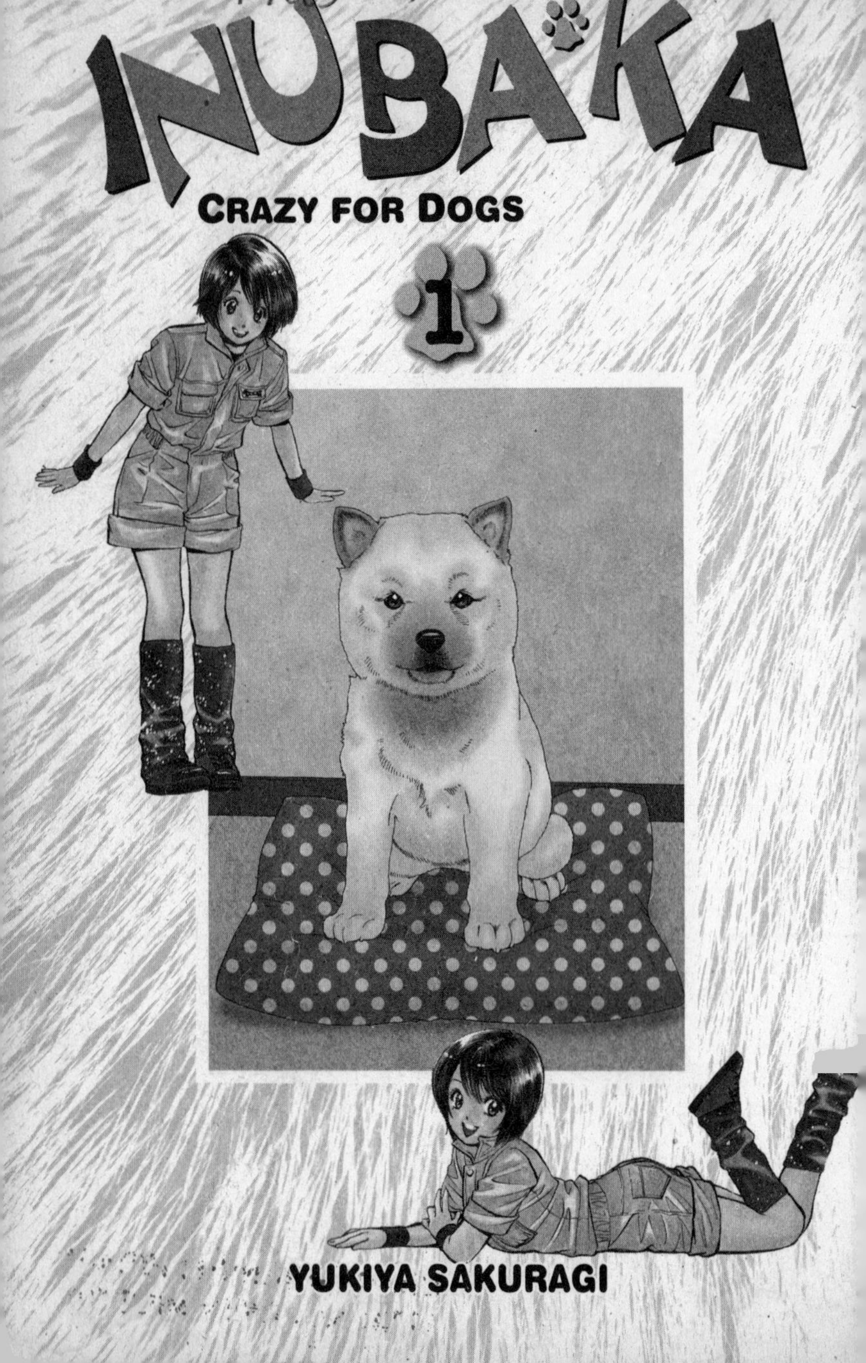
INUBAKA
CRAZY FOR DOGS
1
YUKIYA SAKURAGI

Contents

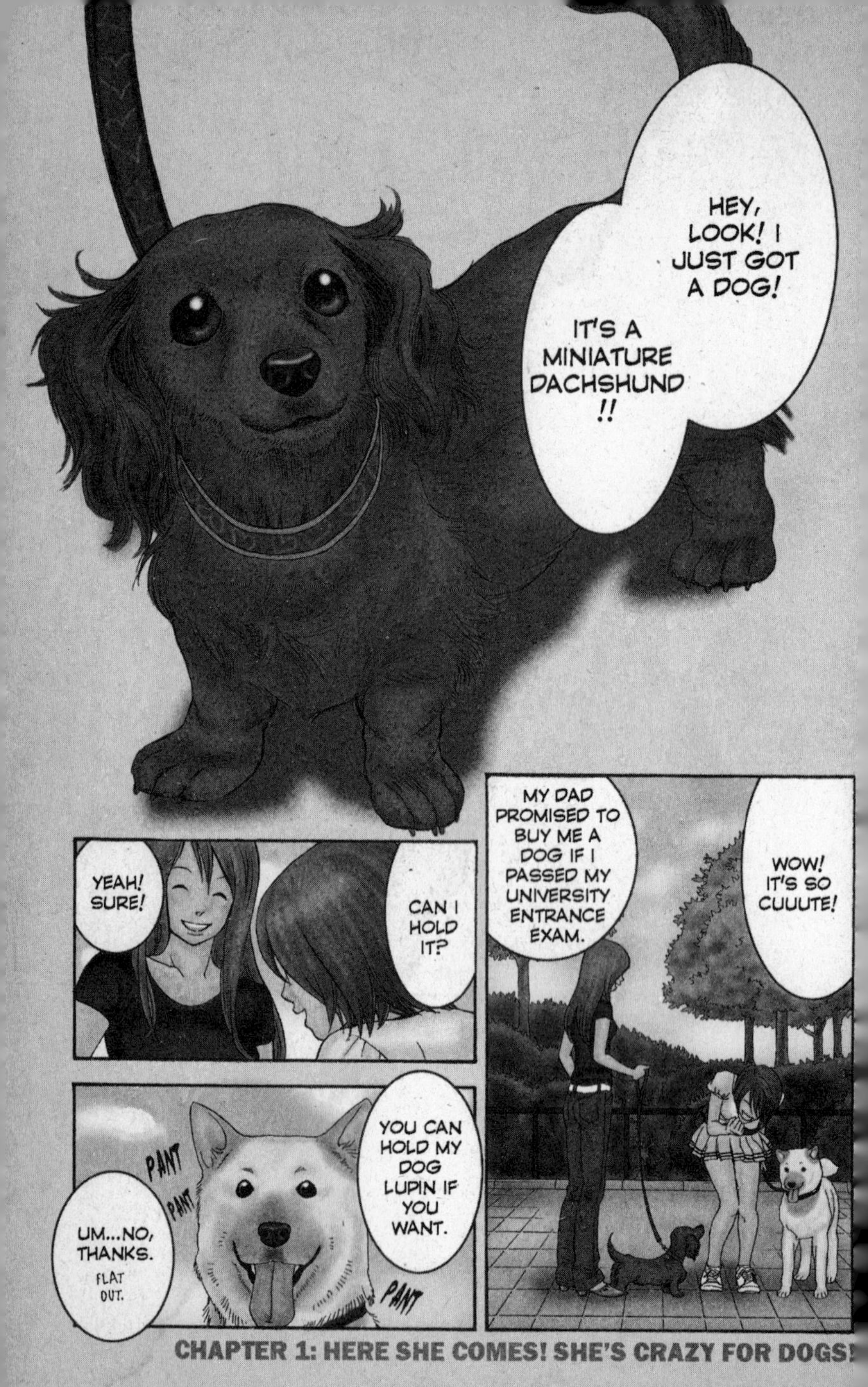
HEY, LOOK! I JUST GOT A DOG!
IT'S A MINIATURE DACHSHUND!!
WOW! IT'S SO CUUUTE!
MY DAD PROMISED TO BUY ME A DOG IF I PASSED MY UNIVERSITY ENTRANCE EXAM.
CAN I HOLD IT?
YEAH! SURE!
YOU CAN HOLD MY DOG LUPIN IF YOU WANT.
PANT
PANT
UM...NO, THANKS.
FLAT OUT.
PANT

CHAPTER 1: HERE SHE COMES! SHE'S CRAZY FOR DOGS!

CHAPTER 1:
HERE SHE COMES! SHE'S CRAZY FOR DOGS!

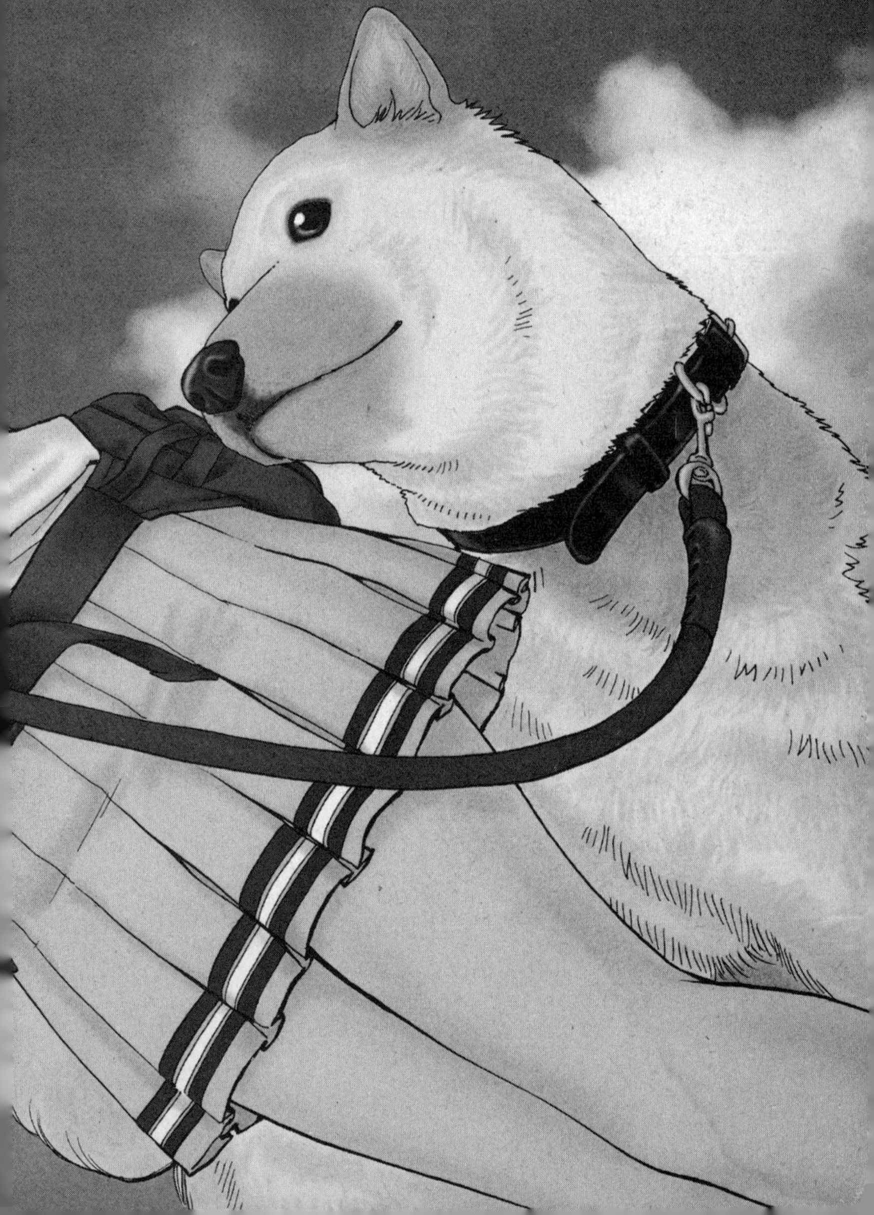

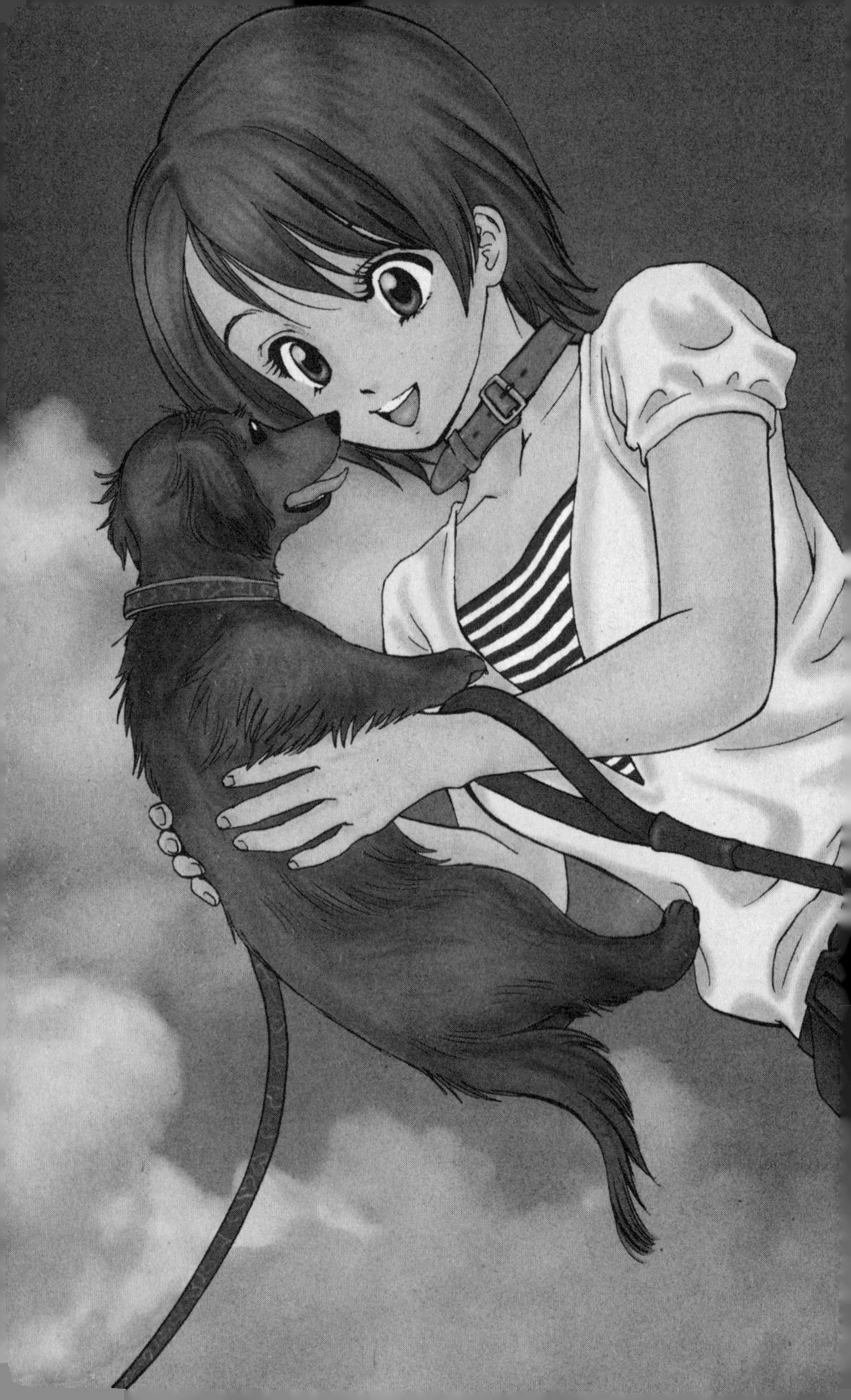

INUBAKA

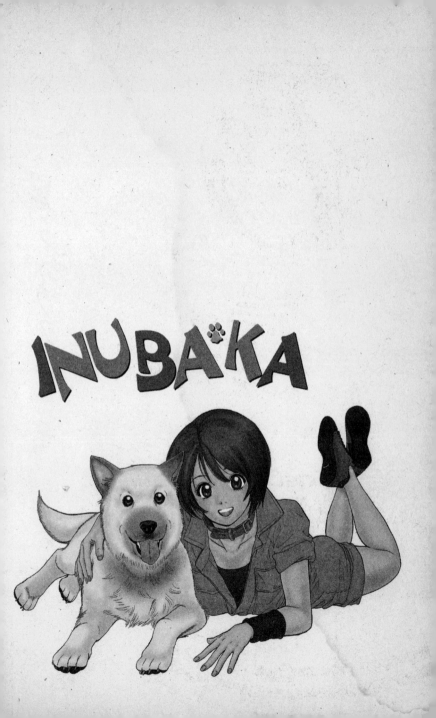

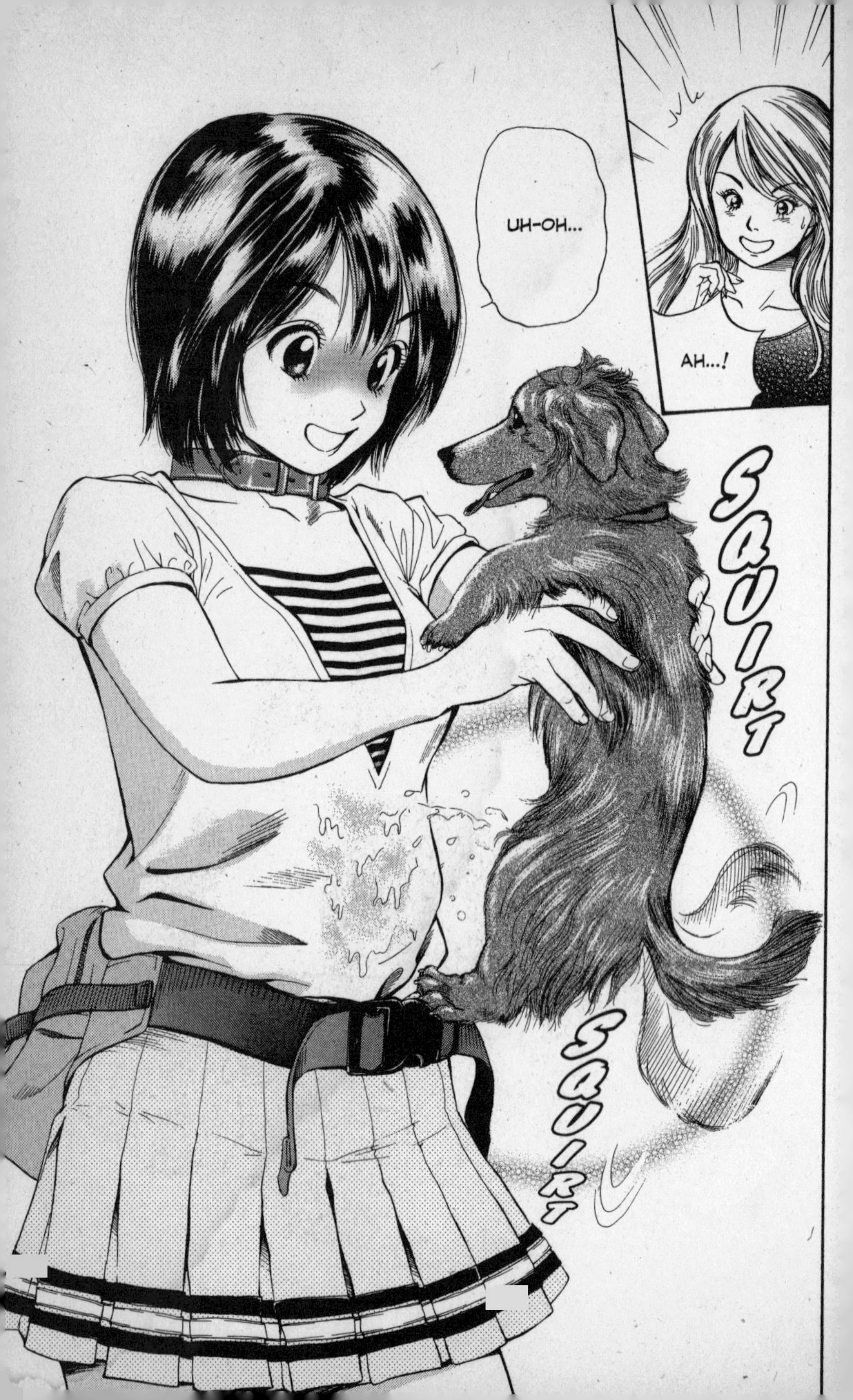
AH...!
UH-OH...
SQUIRT
SQUIRT

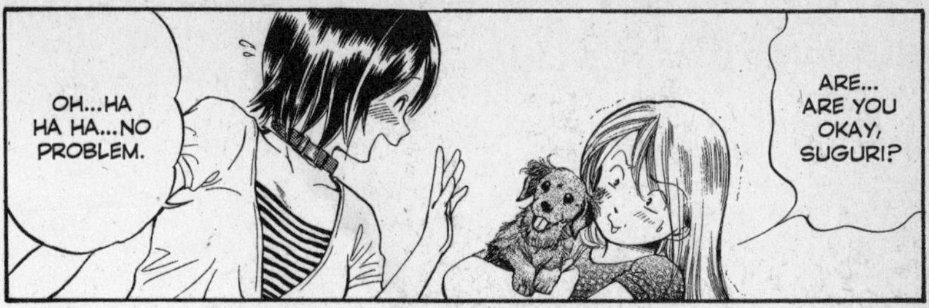
ARE... ARE YOU OKAY, SUGURI?
OH...HA HA HA...NO PROBLEM.
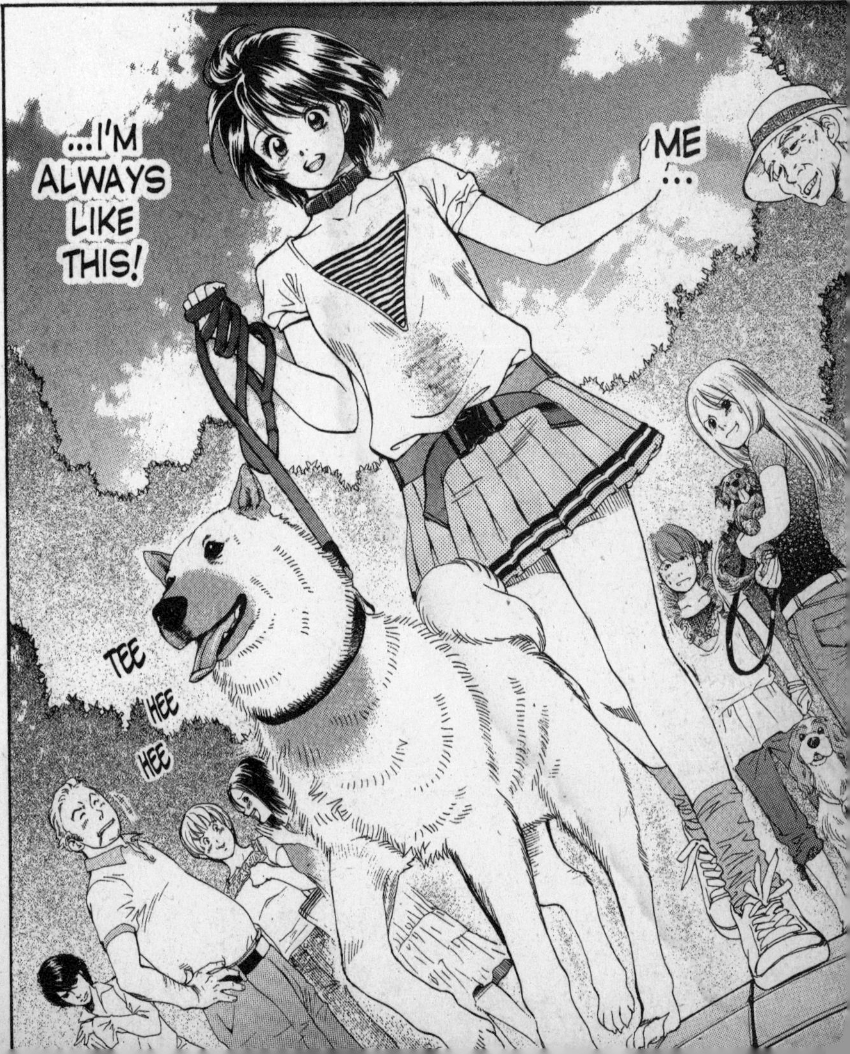
ME...
...I'M ALWAYS LIKE THIS!
TEE HEE HEE

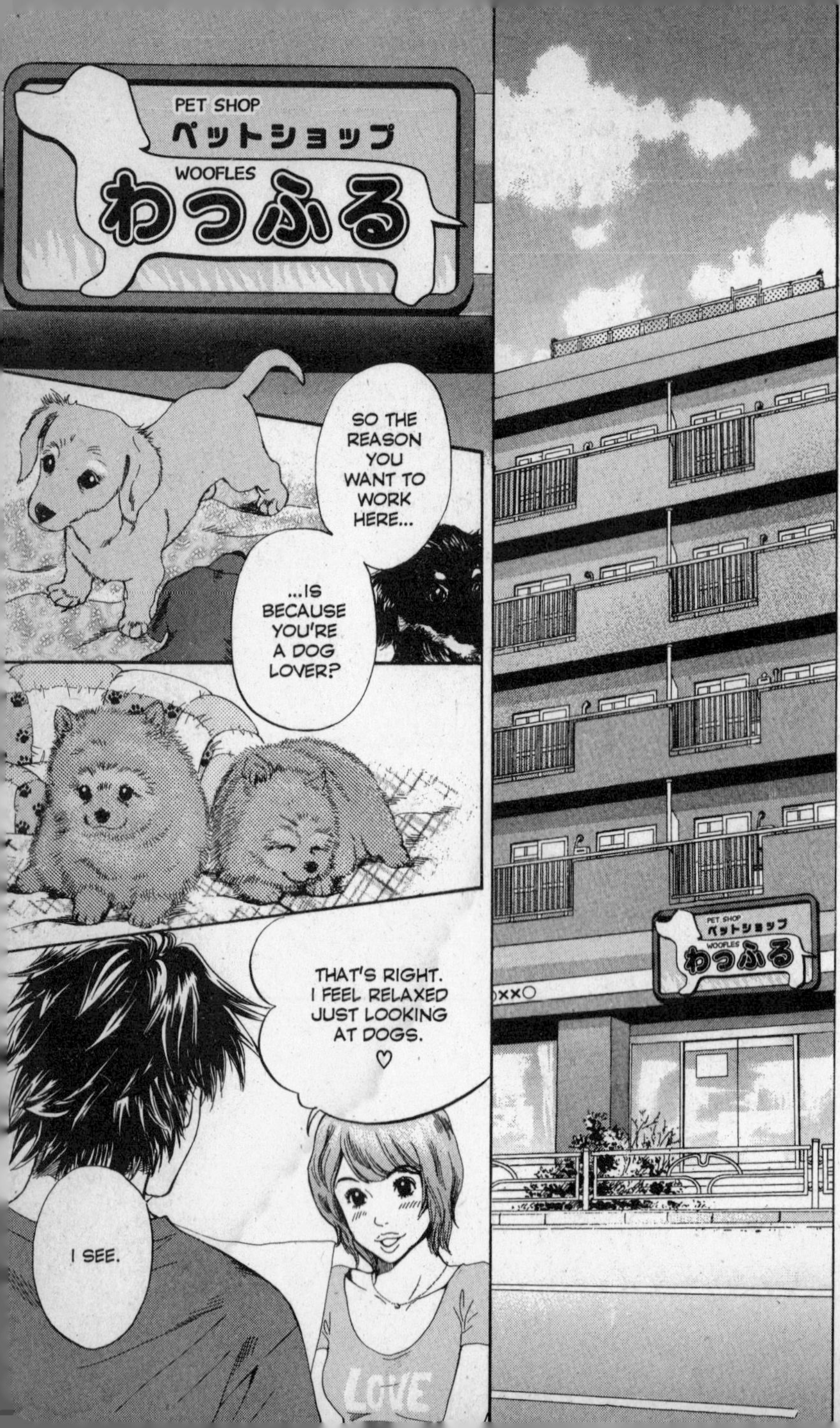
PET SHOP
ペットショップ
WOOFLES
わっふる
○××○
PET SHOP
ペットショップ
WOOFLES
わっふる
SO THE REASON YOU WANT TO WORK HERE...
...IS BECAUSE YOU'RE A DOG LOVER?
THAT'S RIGHT. I FEEL RELAXED JUST LOOKING AT DOGS. ♡
I SEE.
LOVE

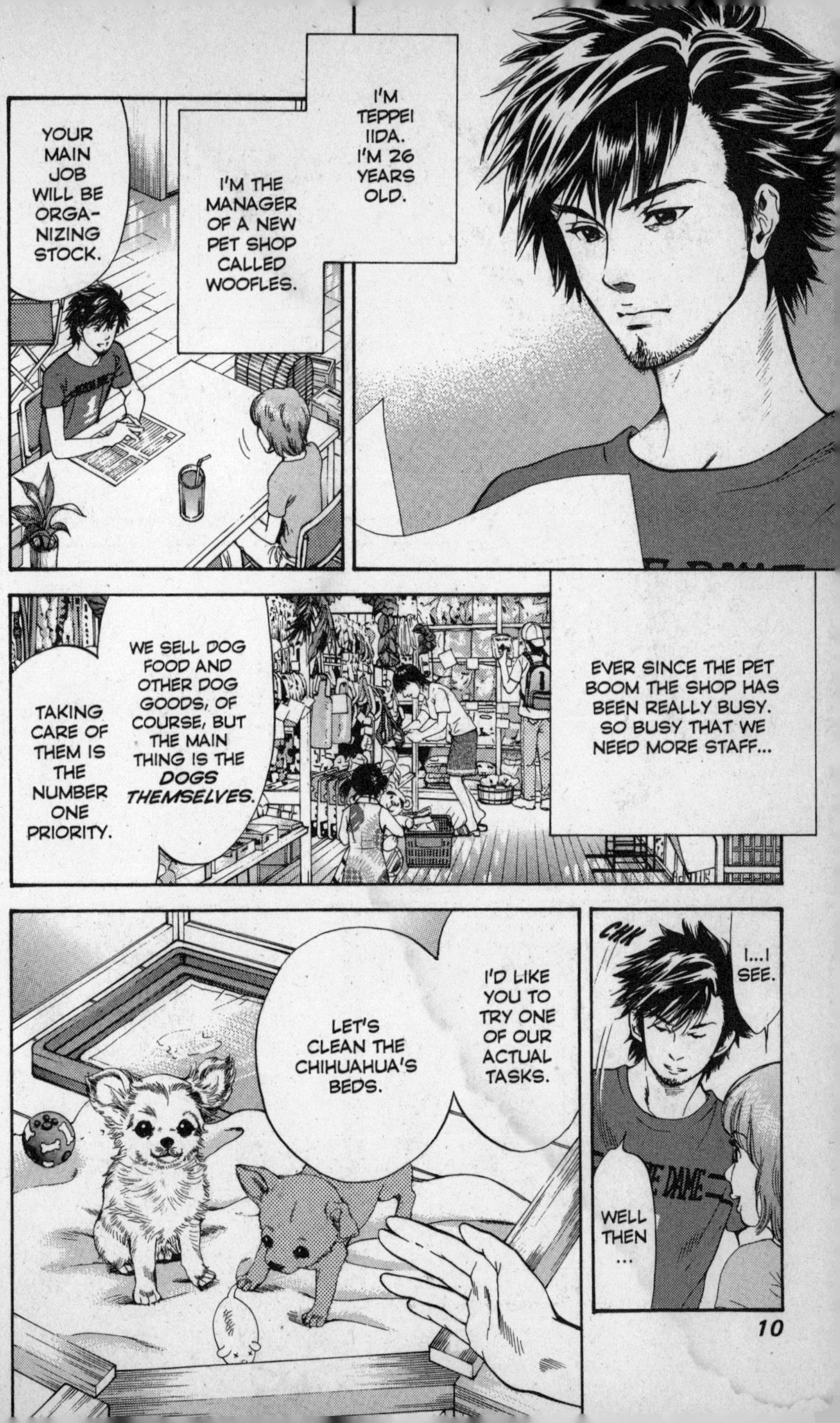
I'M TEPPEI IIDA. I'M 26 YEARS OLD.
I'M THE MANAGER OF A NEW PET SHOP CALLED WOOFLES.
YOUR MAIN JOB WILL BE ORGA-NIZING STOCK.
EVER SINCE THE PET BOOM THE SHOP HAS BEEN REALLY BUSY. SO BUSY THAT WE NEED MORE STAFF...
WE SELL DOG FOOD AND OTHER DOG GOODS, OF COURSE, BUT THE MAIN THING IS THE *DOGS THEMSELVES*.
TAKING CARE OF THEM IS THE NUMBER ONE PRIORITY.
CHK
I...I SEE.
WELL THEN ...
I'D LIKE YOU TO TRY ONE OF OUR ACTUAL TASKS.
LET'S CLEAN THE CHIHUAHUA'S BEDS.

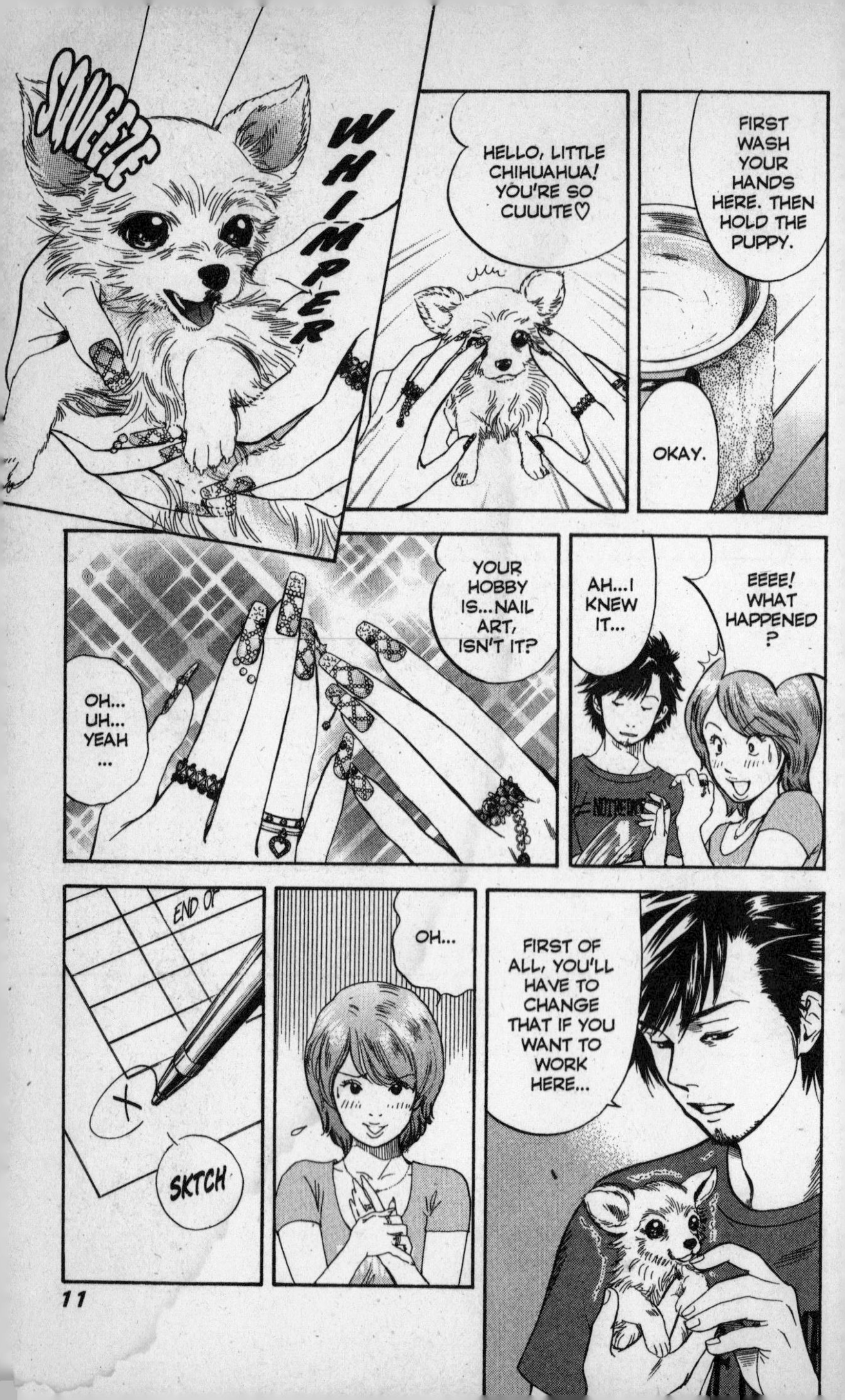
FIRST WASH YOUR HANDS HERE. THEN HOLD THE PUPPY.
OKAY.
HELLO, LITTLE CHIHUAHUA! YOU'RE SO CUUUTE♡
SQUEEZE
WHIMPER
EEEE! WHAT HAPPENED?
AH...I KNEW IT...
YOUR HOBBY IS...NAIL ART, ISN'T IT?
OH... UH... YEAH ...
FIRST OF ALL, YOU'LL HAVE TO CHANGE THAT IF YOU WANT TO WORK HERE...
OH...
END OF
SKTCH

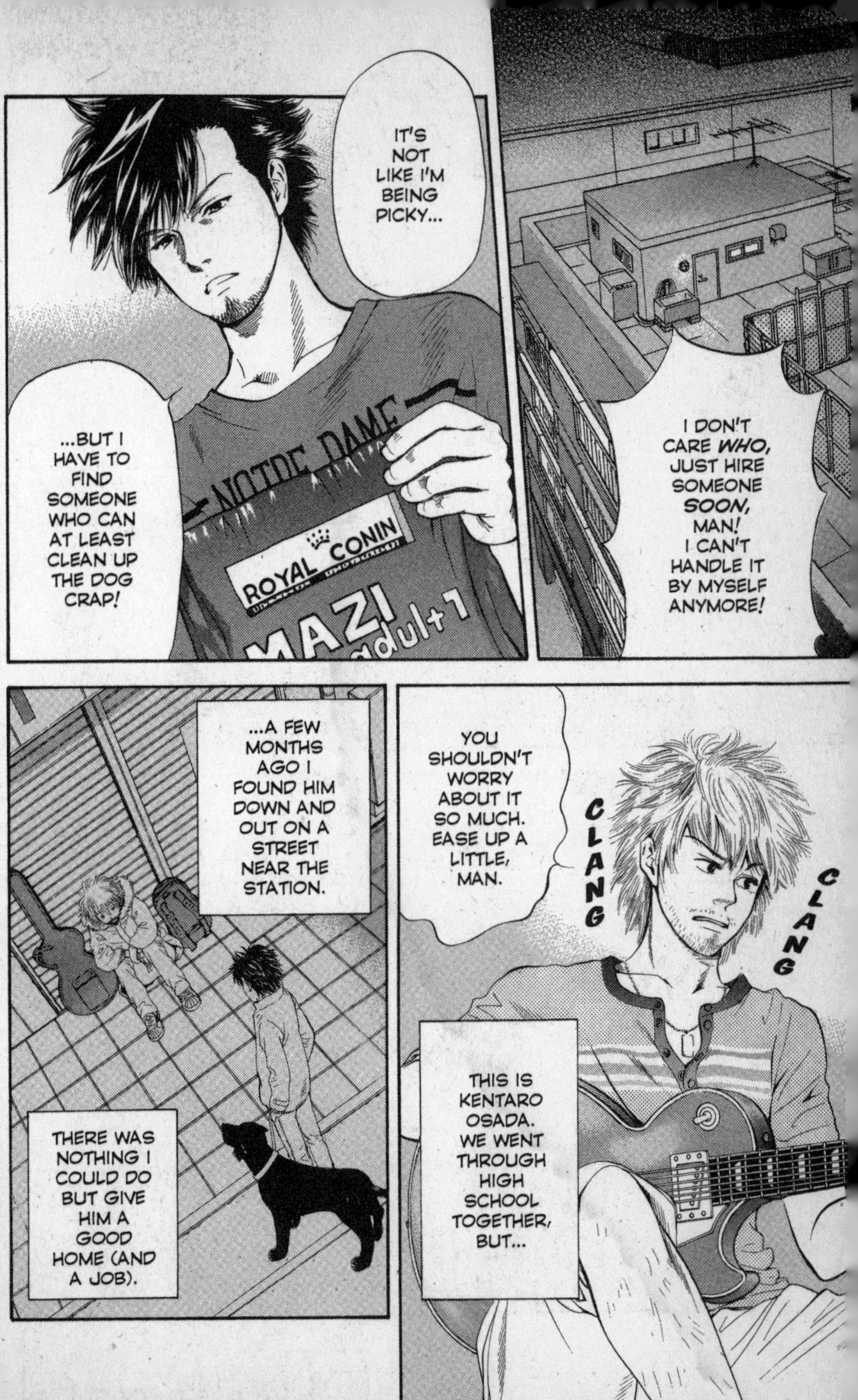
I DON'T CARE WHO, JUST HIRE SOMEONE SOON, MAN! I CAN'T HANDLE IT BY MYSELF ANYMORE!
IT'S NOT LIKE I'M BEING PICKY...
...BUT I HAVE TO FIND SOMEONE WHO CAN AT LEAST CLEAN UP THE DOG CRAP!
NOTRE DAME
ROYAL CONIN
YOU SHOULDN'T WORRY ABOUT IT SO MUCH. EASE UP A LITTLE, MAN.
CLANG
CLANG
THIS IS KENTARO OSADA. WE WENT THROUGH HIGH SCHOOL TOGETHER, BUT...
...A FEW MONTHS AGO I FOUND HIM DOWN AND OUT ON A STREET NEAR THE STATION.
THERE WAS NOTHING I COULD DO BUT GIVE HIM A GOOD HOME (AND A JOB).

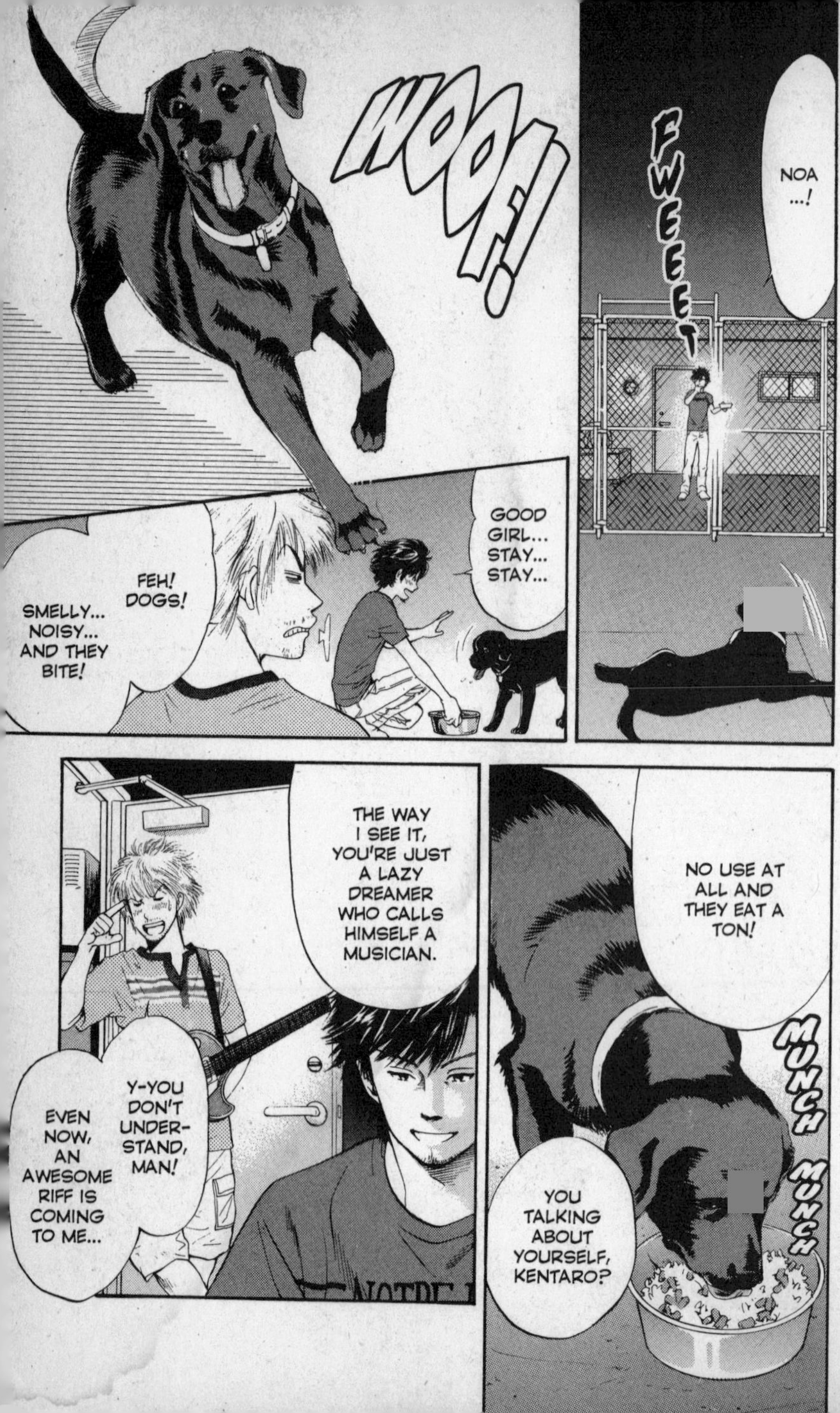
NOA ...!
FWEEET
WOOF!!
GOOD GIRL... STAY... STAY...
FEH! DOGS!
SMELLY... NOISY... AND THEY BITE!
NO USE AT ALL AND THEY EAT A TON!
MUNCH MUNCH
YOU TALKING ABOUT YOURSELF, KENTARO?
THE WAY I SEE IT, YOU'RE JUST A LAZY DREAMER WHO CALLS HIMSELF A MUSICIAN.
Y-YOU DON'T UNDER-STAND, MAN!
EVEN NOW, AN AWESOME RIFF IS COMING TO ME...

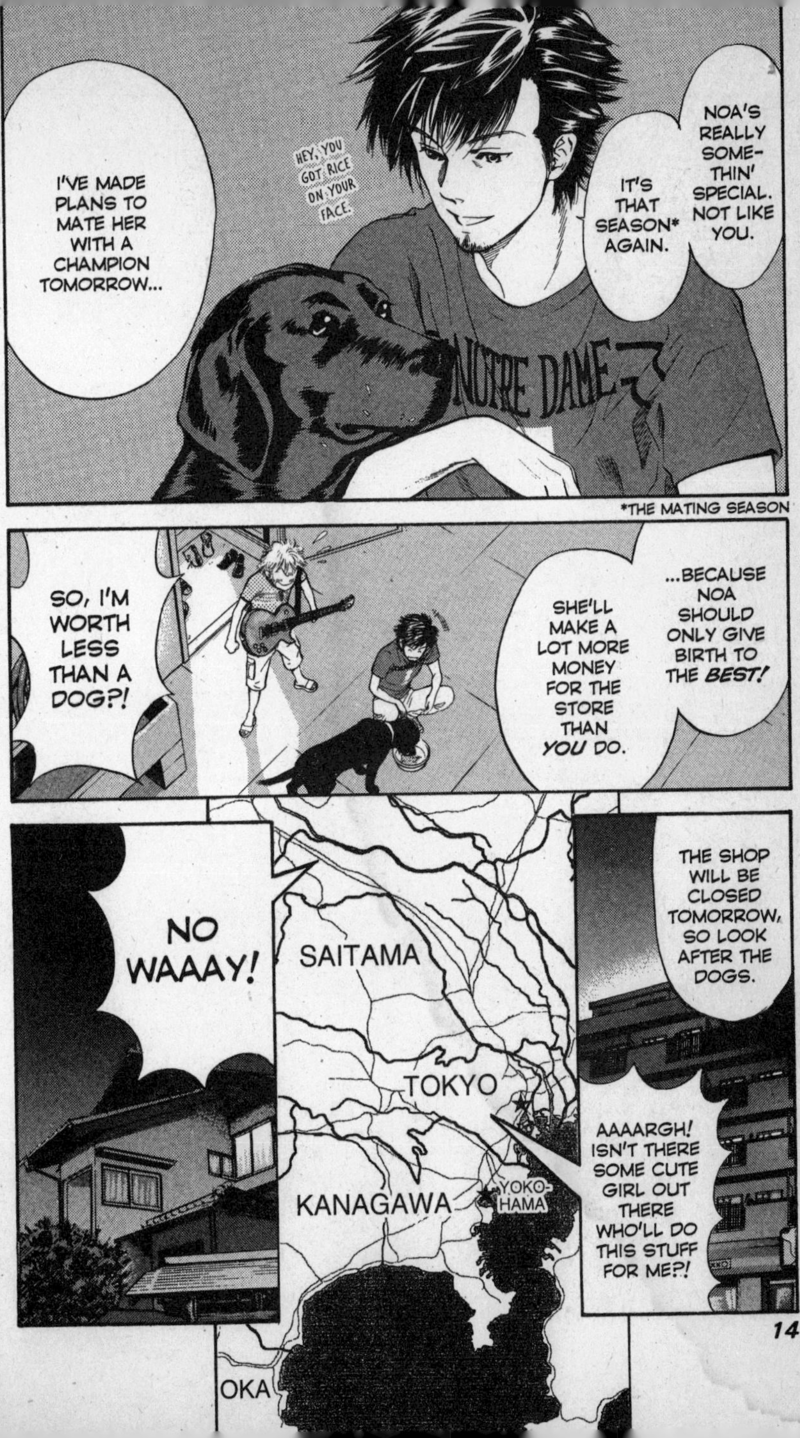
NOA'S REALLY SOME-THIN' SPECIAL. NOT LIKE YOU.
IT'S THAT SEASON* AGAIN.
HEY, YOU GOT RICE ON YOUR FACE.
I'VE MADE PLANS TO MATE HER WITH A CHAMPION TOMORROW...
...BECAUSE NOA SHOULD ONLY GIVE BIRTH TO THE *BEST!*
SHE'LL MAKE A LOT MORE MONEY FOR THE STORE THAN *YOU* DO.
SO, I'M WORTH LESS THAN A DOG?!
THE SHOP WILL BE CLOSED TOMORROW, SO LOOK AFTER THE DOGS.
AAAARGH! ISN'T THERE SOME CUTE GIRL OUT THERE WHO'LL DO THIS STUFF FOR ME?!
SAITAMA
TOKYO
KANAGAWA
YOKO-HAMA
OKA
NO WAAAY!
*THE MATING SEASON

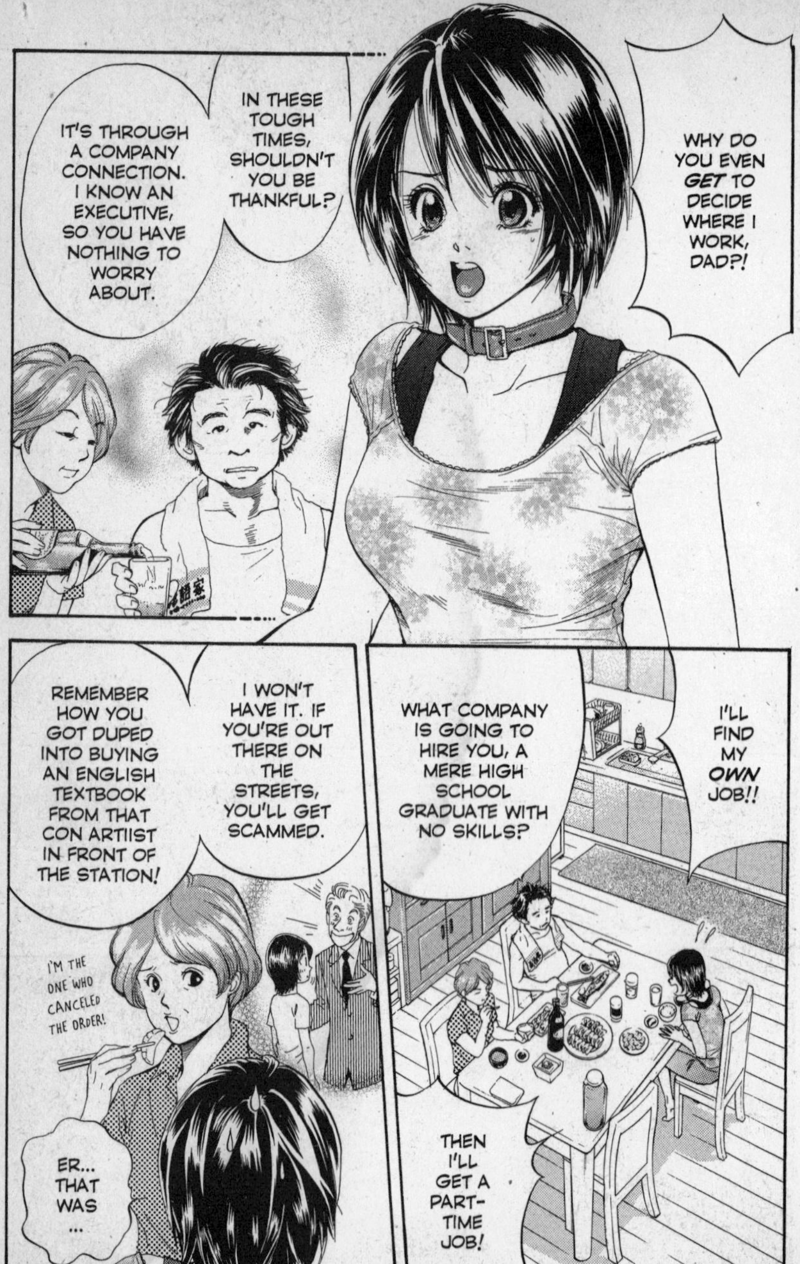
WHY DO YOU EVEN *GET* TO DECIDE WHERE I WORK, DAD?!
IN THESE TOUGH TIMES, SHOULDN'T YOU BE THANKFUL?
IT'S THROUGH A COMPANY CONNECTION. I KNOW AN EXECUTIVE, SO YOU HAVE NOTHING TO WORRY ABOUT.
I'LL FIND MY *OWN* JOB!!
WHAT COMPANY IS GOING TO HIRE YOU, A MERE HIGH SCHOOL GRADUATE WITH NO SKILLS?
THEN I'LL GET A PART-TIME JOB!
I WON'T HAVE IT. IF YOU'RE OUT THERE ON THE STREETS, YOU'LL GET SCAMMED.
REMEMBER HOW YOU GOT DUPED INTO BUYING AN ENGLISH TEXTBOOK FROM THAT CON ARTIIST IN FRONT OF THE STATION!
I'M THE ONE WHO CANCELED THE ORDER!
ER... THAT WAS ...

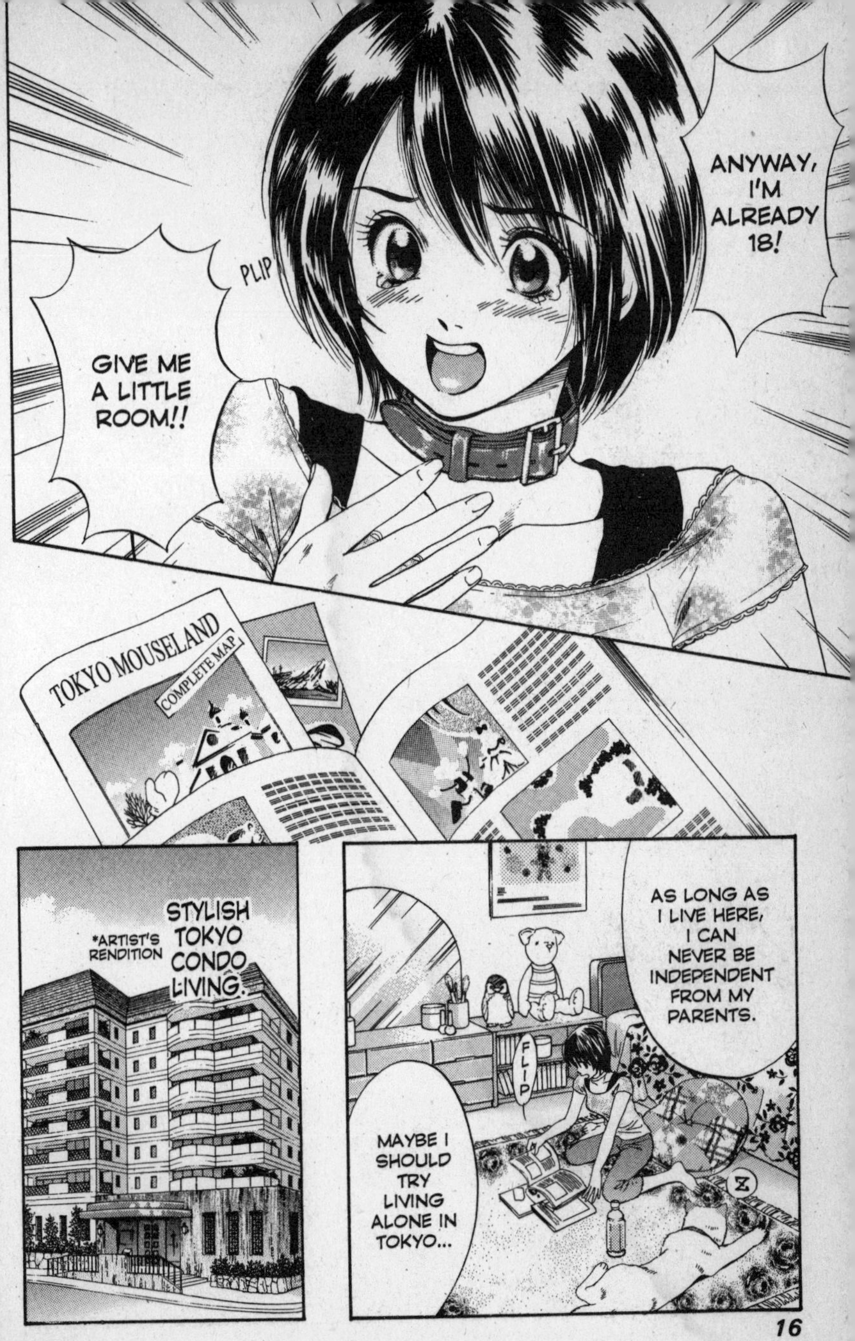
ANYWAY, I'M ALREADY 18!
PLIP
GIVE ME A LITTLE ROOM!!
TOKYO MOUSELAND
COMPLETE MAP
AS LONG AS I LIVE HERE, I CAN NEVER BE INDEPENDENT FROM MY PARENTS.
FLIP
MAYBE I SHOULD TRY LIVING ALONE IN TOKYO...
STYLISH TOKYO CONDO LIVING.
*ARTIST'S RENDITION

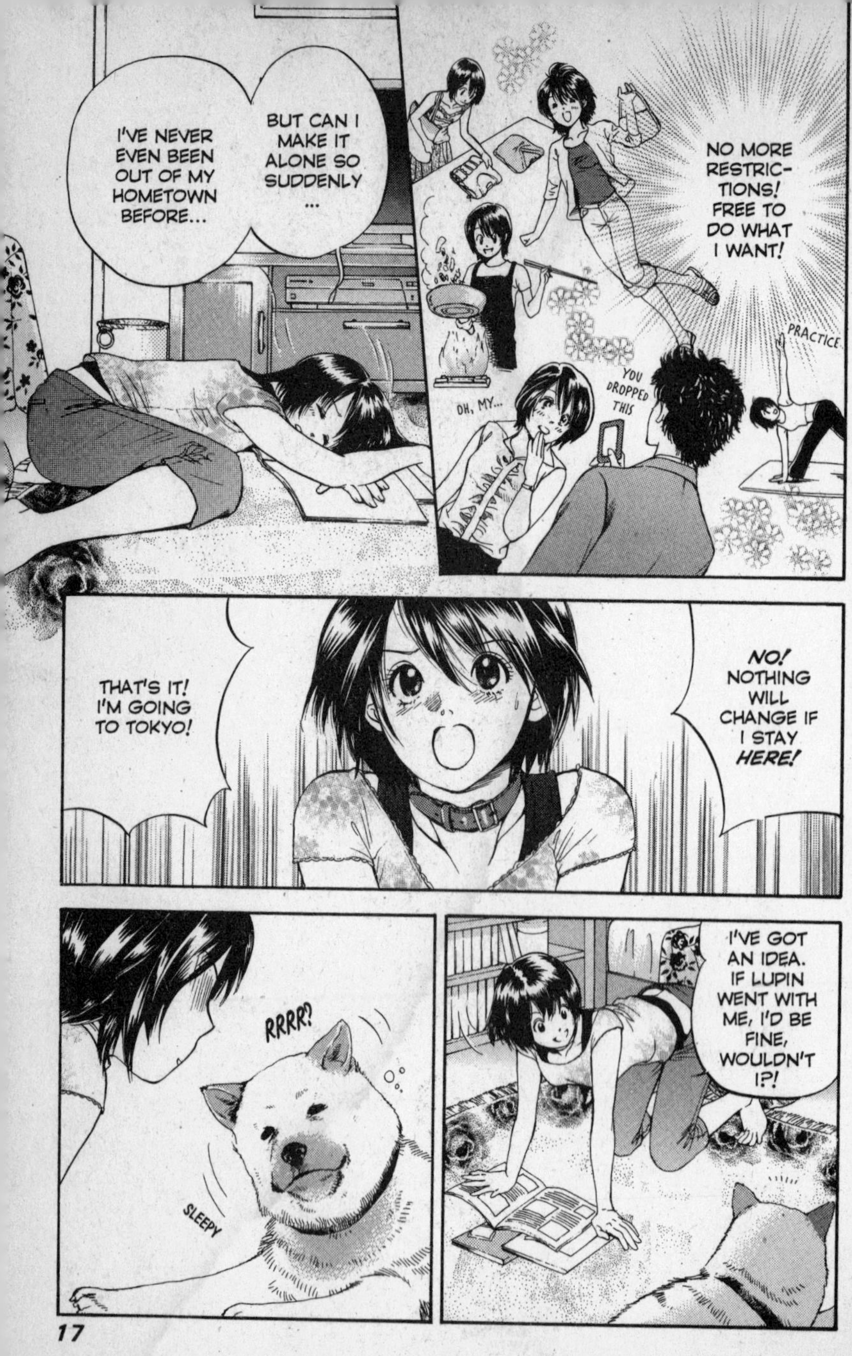
NO MORE RESTRICTIONS! FREE TO DO WHAT I WANT!
PRACTICE
YOU DROPPED THIS
OH, MY...
BUT CAN I MAKE IT ALONE SO SUDDENLY ...
I'VE NEVER EVEN BEEN OUT OF MY HOMETOWN BEFORE...
NO! NOTHING WILL CHANGE IF I STAY HERE!
THAT'S IT! I'M GOING TO TOKYO!
I'VE GOT AN IDEA. IF LUPIN WENT WITH ME, I'D BE FINE, WOULDN'T I?!
RRRR?
SLEEPY

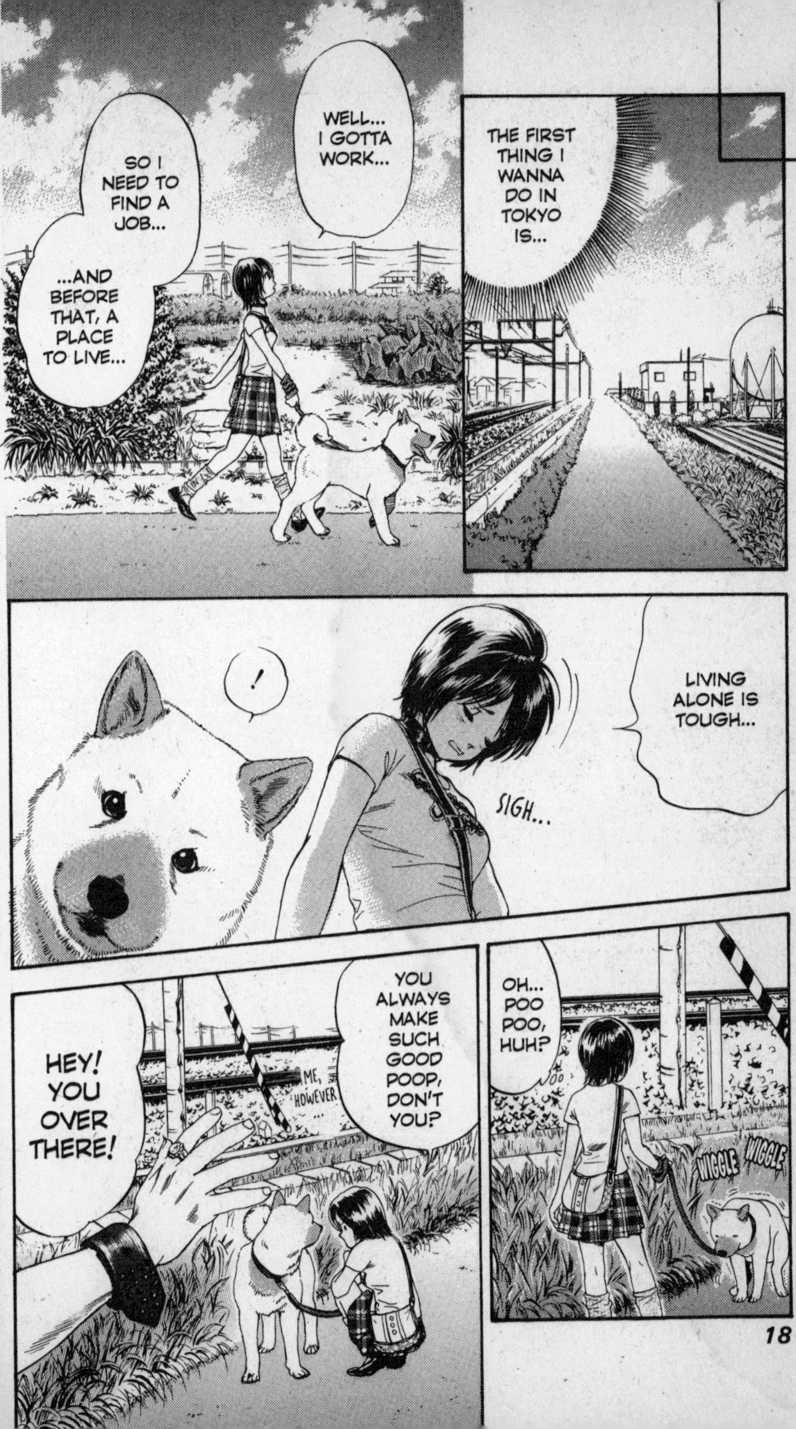
THE FIRST THING I WANNA DO IN TOKYO IS...
WELL... I GOTTA WORK...
SO I NEED TO FIND A JOB...
...AND BEFORE THAT, A PLACE TO LIVE...
LIVING ALONE IS TOUGH...
SIGH...
!
OH... POO POO, HUH?
WIGGLE WIGGLE
YOU ALWAYS MAKE SUCH GOOD POOP, DON'T YOU?
ME, HOWEVER ...
HEY! YOU OVER THERE!

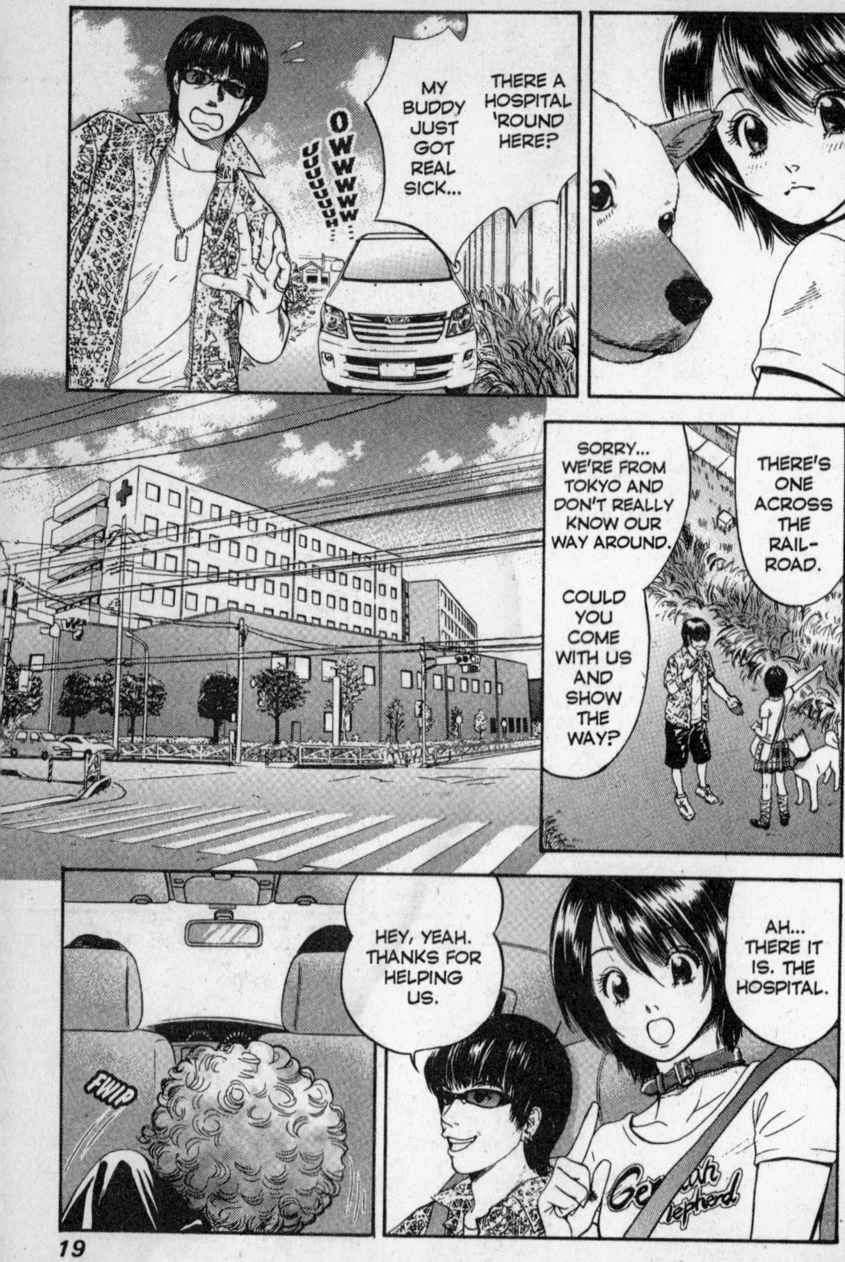
MY BUDDY JUST GOT REAL SICK... THERE A HOSPITAL 'ROUND HERE?
OWWWWW... UUUUUUUH...
THERE'S ONE ACROSS THE RAIL-ROAD.
SORRY... WE'RE FROM TOKYO AND DON'T REALLY KNOW OUR WAY AROUND.
COULD YOU COME WITH US AND SHOW THE WAY?
AH... THERE IT IS. THE HOSPITAL.
HEY, YEAH. THANKS FOR HELPING US.
FWIP

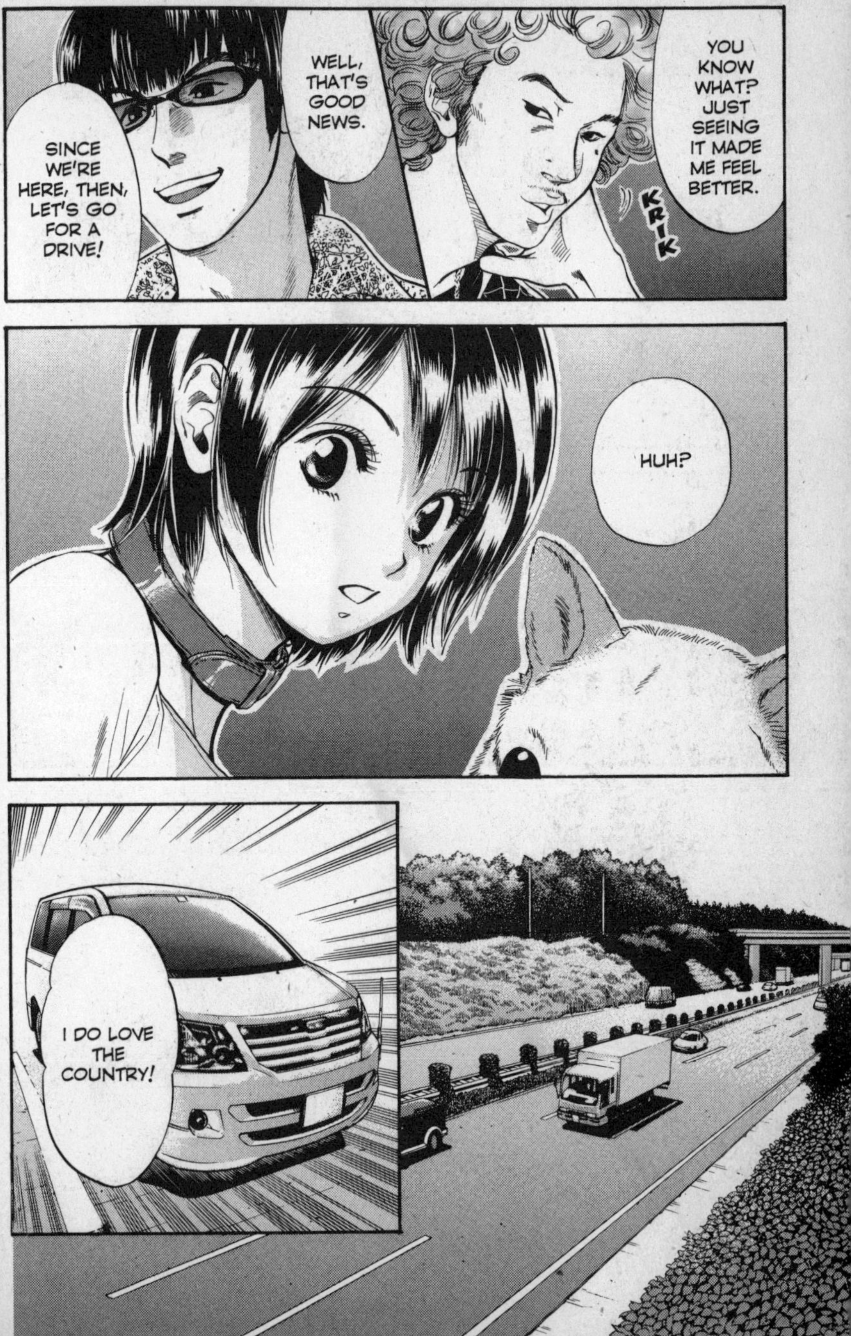
YOU KNOW WHAT? JUST SEEING IT MADE ME FEEL BETTER.
KRIK
WELL, THAT'S GOOD NEWS.
SINCE WE'RE HERE, THEN, LET'S GO FOR A DRIVE!
HUH?
I DO LOVE THE COUNTRY!

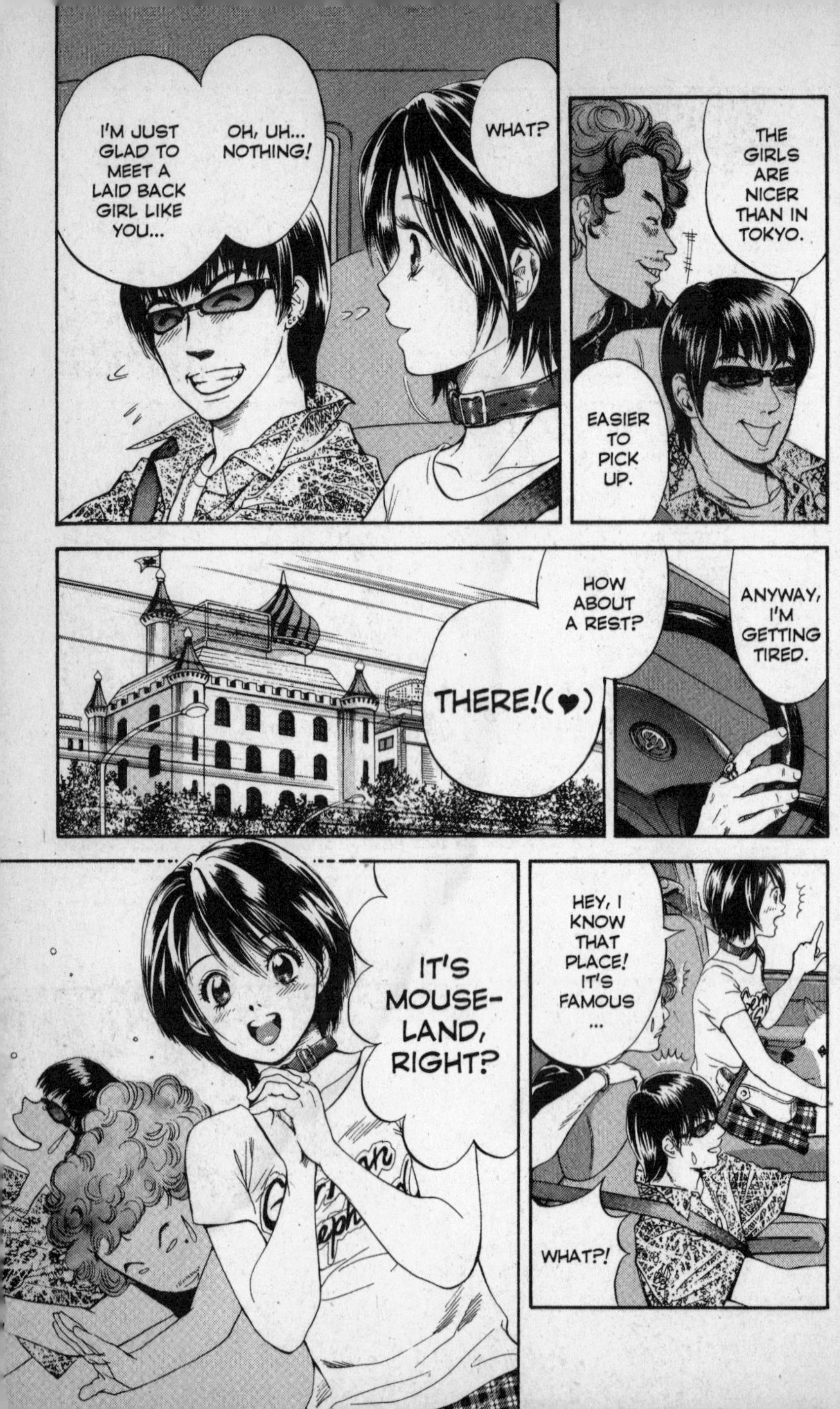
THE GIRLS ARE NICER THAN IN TOKYO.
EASIER TO PICK UP.
WHAT?
OH, UH... NOTHING!
I'M JUST GLAD TO MEET A LAID BACK GIRL LIKE YOU...
ANYWAY, I'M GETTING TIRED.
HOW ABOUT A REST?
THERE!(♥)
HEY, I KNOW THAT PLACE! IT'S FAMOUS ...
WHAT?!
IT'S MOUSE-LAND, RIGHT?

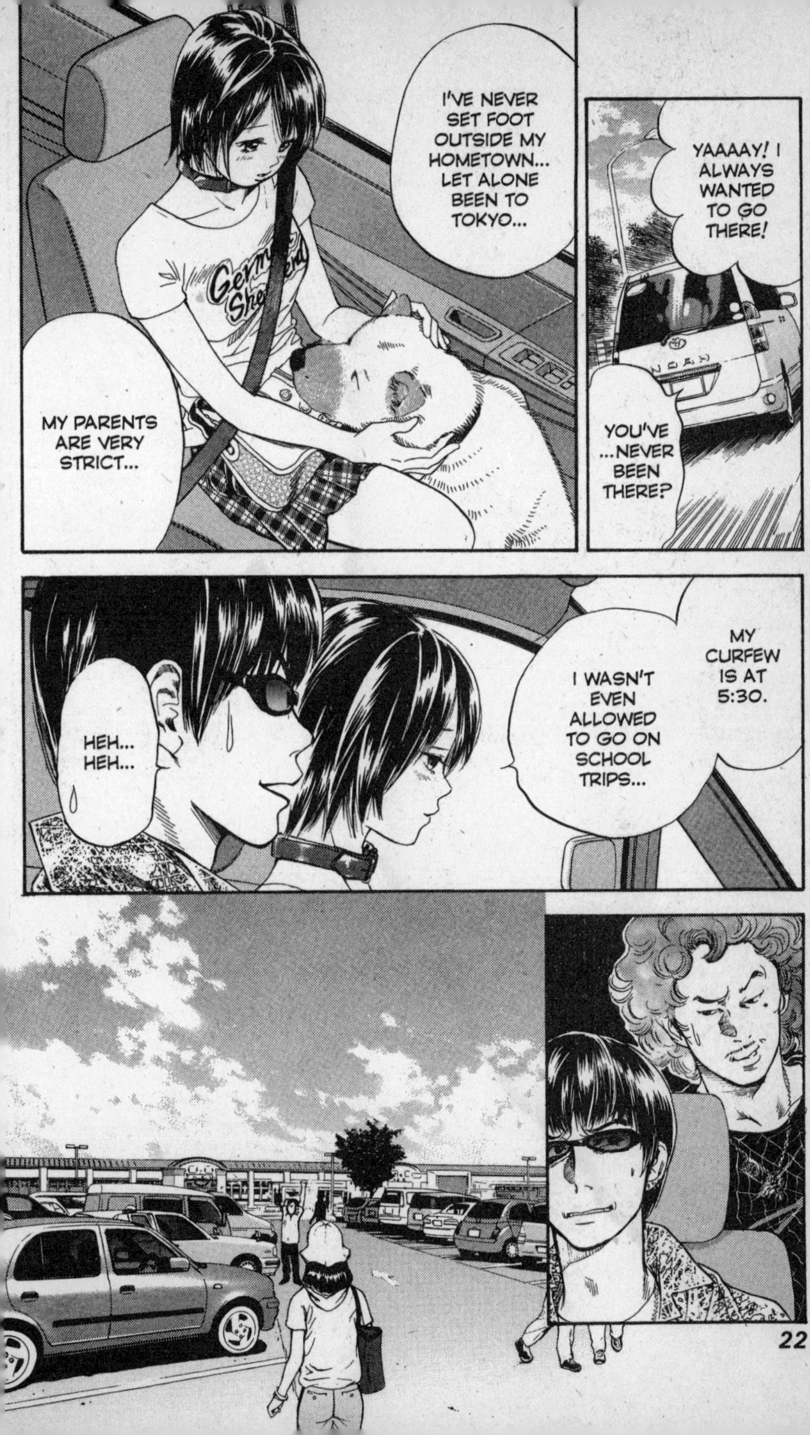
YAAAAY! I ALWAYS WANTED TO GO THERE!
YOU'VE ...NEVER BEEN THERE?
I'VE NEVER SET FOOT OUTSIDE MY HOMETOWN... LET ALONE BEEN TO TOKYO...
MY PARENTS ARE VERY STRICT...
MY CURFEW IS AT 5:30.
I WASN'T EVEN ALLOWED TO GO ON SCHOOL TRIPS...
HEH... HEH...

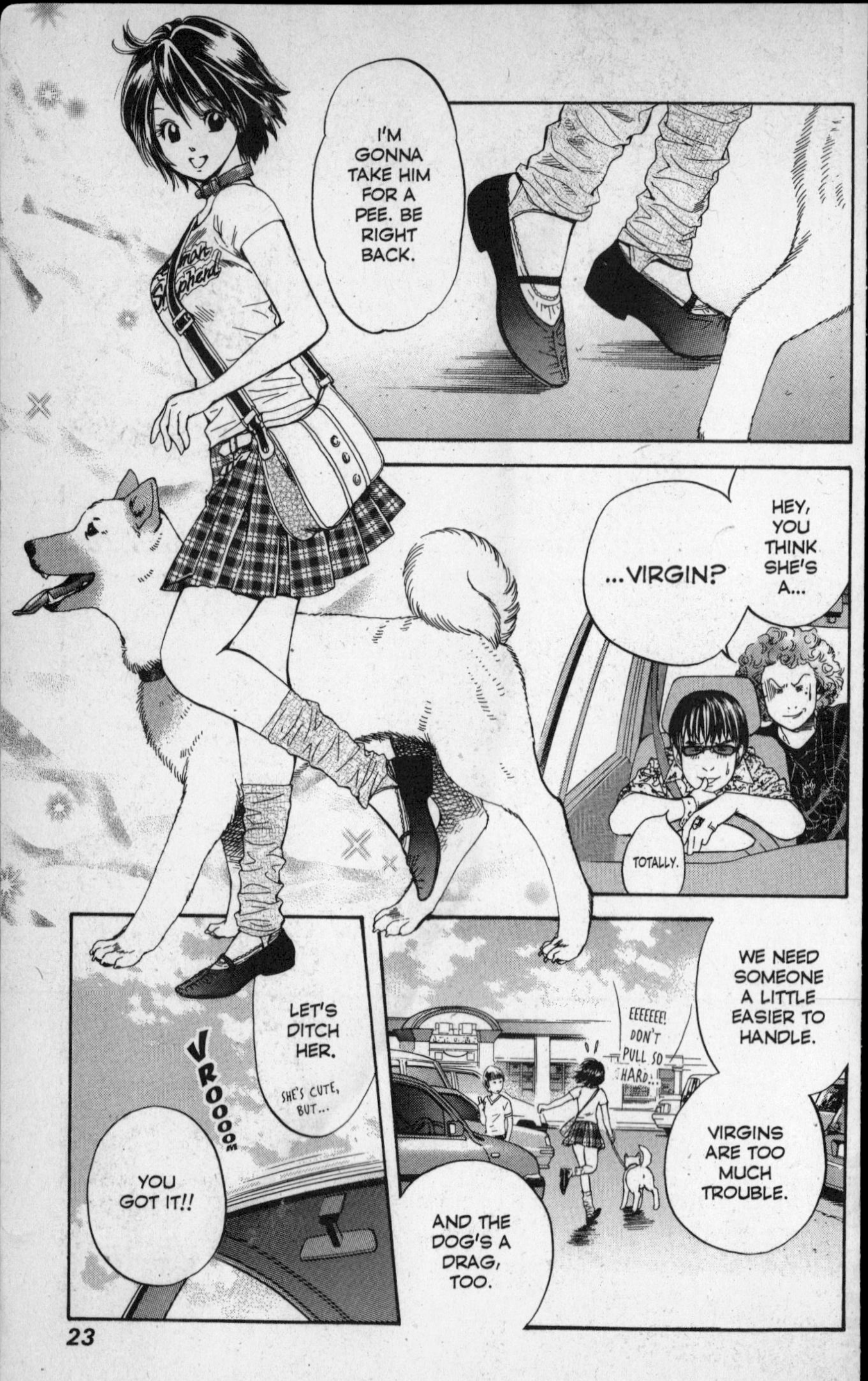
I'M GONNA TAKE HIM FOR A PEE. BE RIGHT BACK.
HEY, YOU THINK SHE'S A...
...VIRGIN?
TOTALLY.
WE NEED SOMEONE A LITTLE EASIER TO HANDLE.
EEEEEEE! DON'T PULL SO HARD...
VIRGINS ARE TOO MUCH TROUBLE.
AND THE DOG'S A DRAG, TOO.
LET'S DITCH HER.
SHE'S CUTE, BUT...
VROOOOOM
YOU GOT IT!!

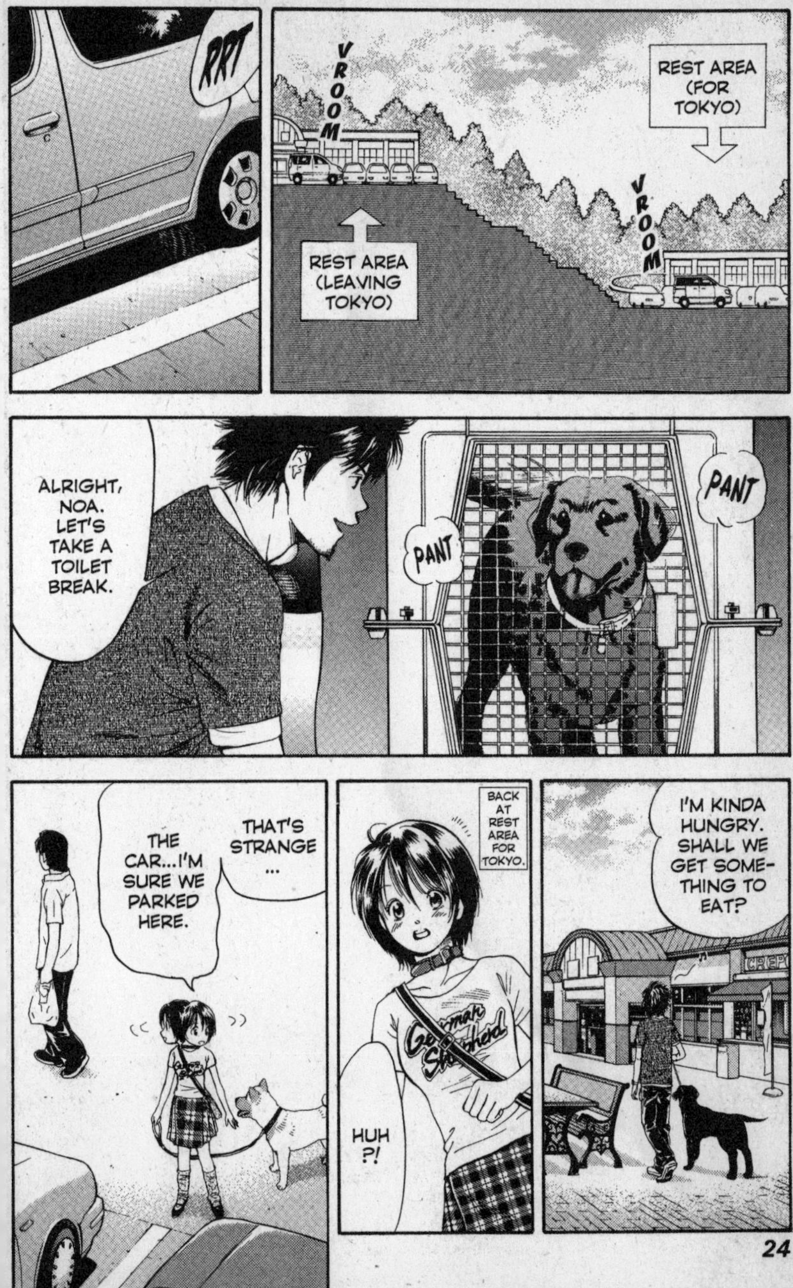
REST AREA (FOR TOKYO)
VROOM
VROOM
REST AREA (LEAVING TOKYO)
RRT
PANT
PANT
ALRIGHT, NOA. LET'S TAKE A TOILET BREAK.
I'M KINDA HUNGRY. SHALL WE GET SOME-THING TO EAT?
CREP
BACK AT REST AREA FOR TOKYO.
German Shepherd
HUH ?!
THAT'S STRANGE ...
THE CAR...I'M SURE WE PARKED HERE.

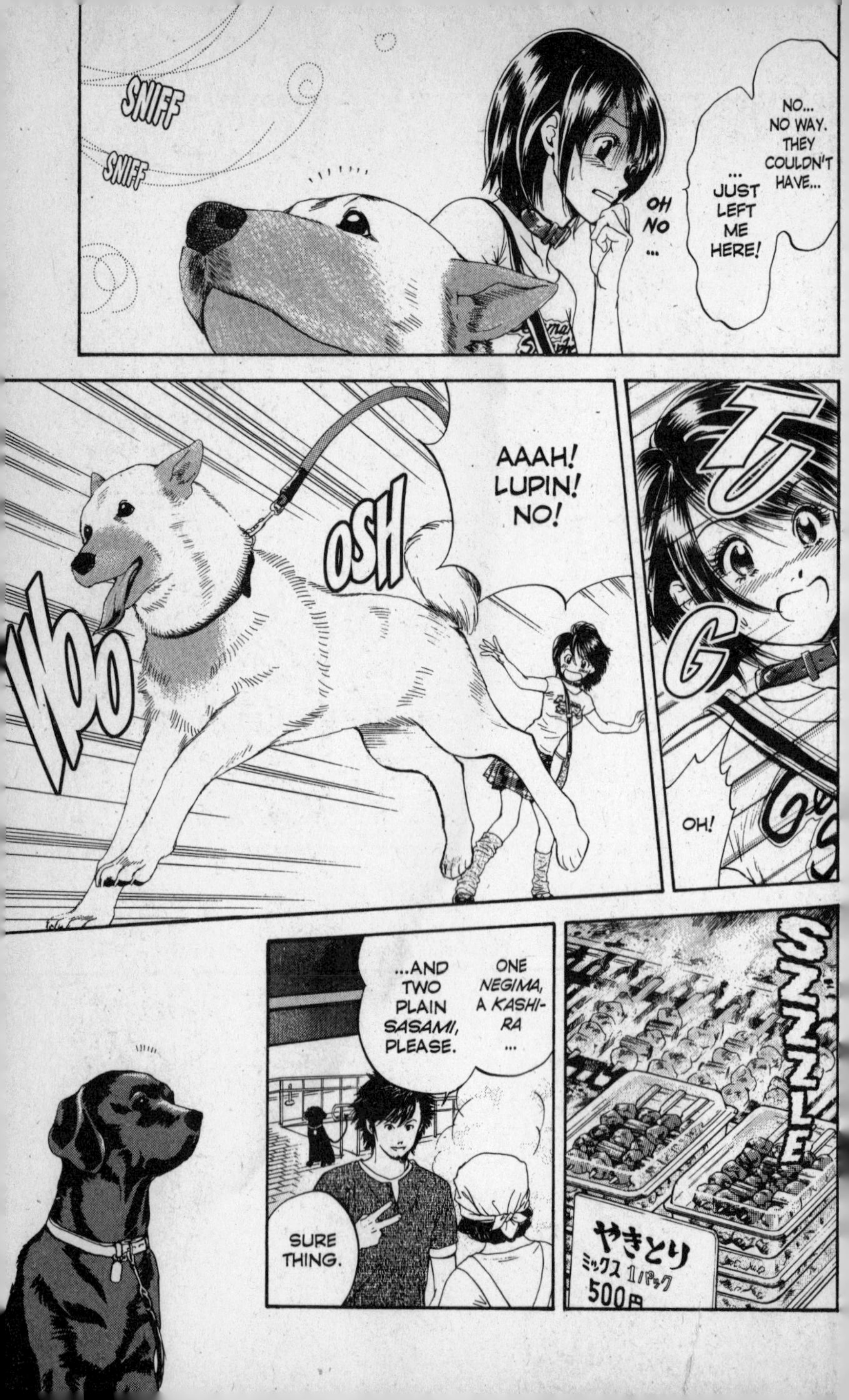
SNIFF
SNIFF
NO... NO WAY. THEY COULDN'T HAVE...
... JUST LEFT ME HERE!
OH NO ...
TUG
OH!
AAAH! LUPIN! NO!
WHOO
OSH
SIZZLE
やきとり ミックス 1パック 500円
ONE NEGIMA, A KASHIRA ...
...AND TWO PLAIN SASAMI, PLEASE.
SURE THING.

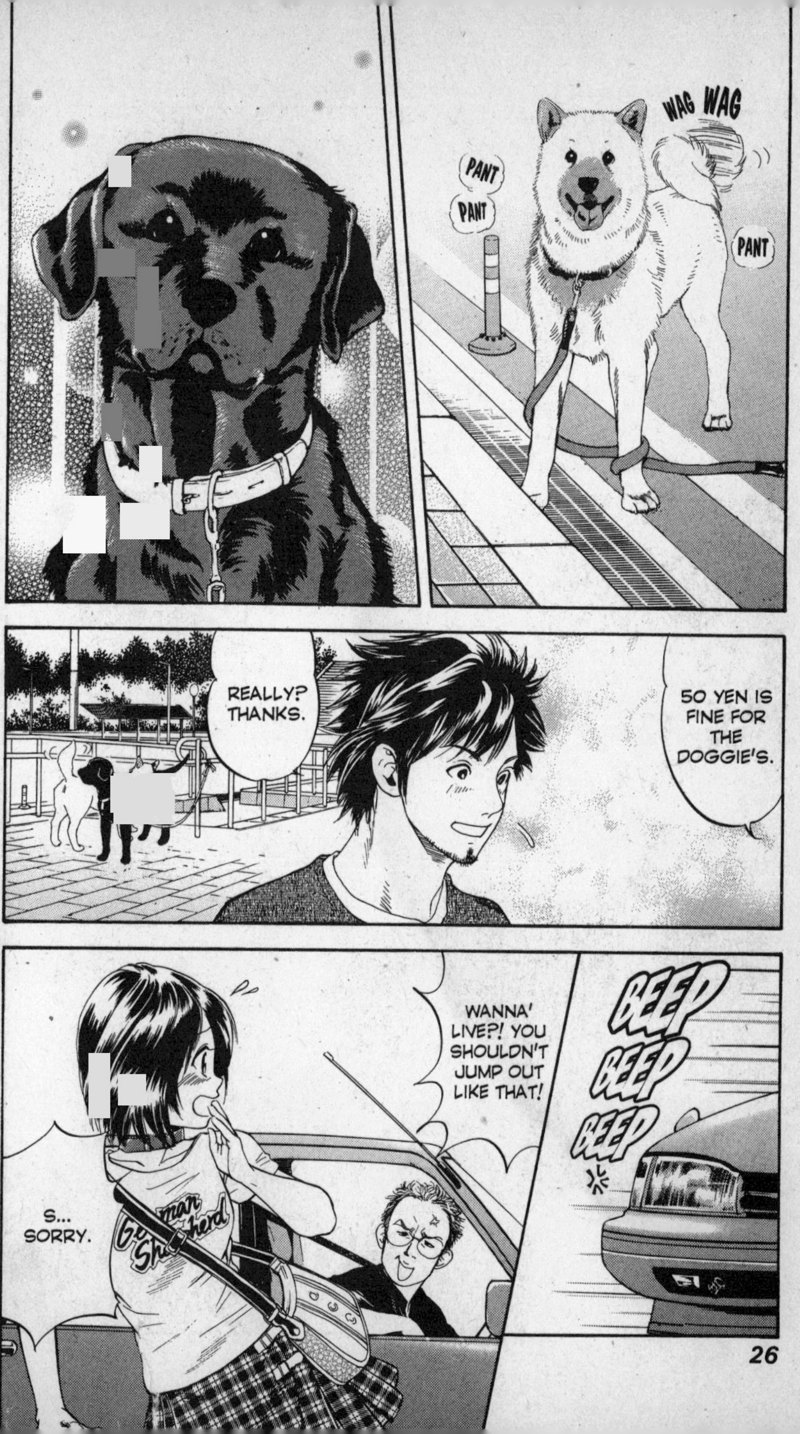
WAG WAG
PANT
PANT
PANT
50 YEN IS FINE FOR THE DOGGIE'S.
REALLY? THANKS.
BEEP BEEP BEEP
WANNA' LIVE?! YOU SHOULDN'T JUMP OUT LIKE THAT!
S... SORRY.

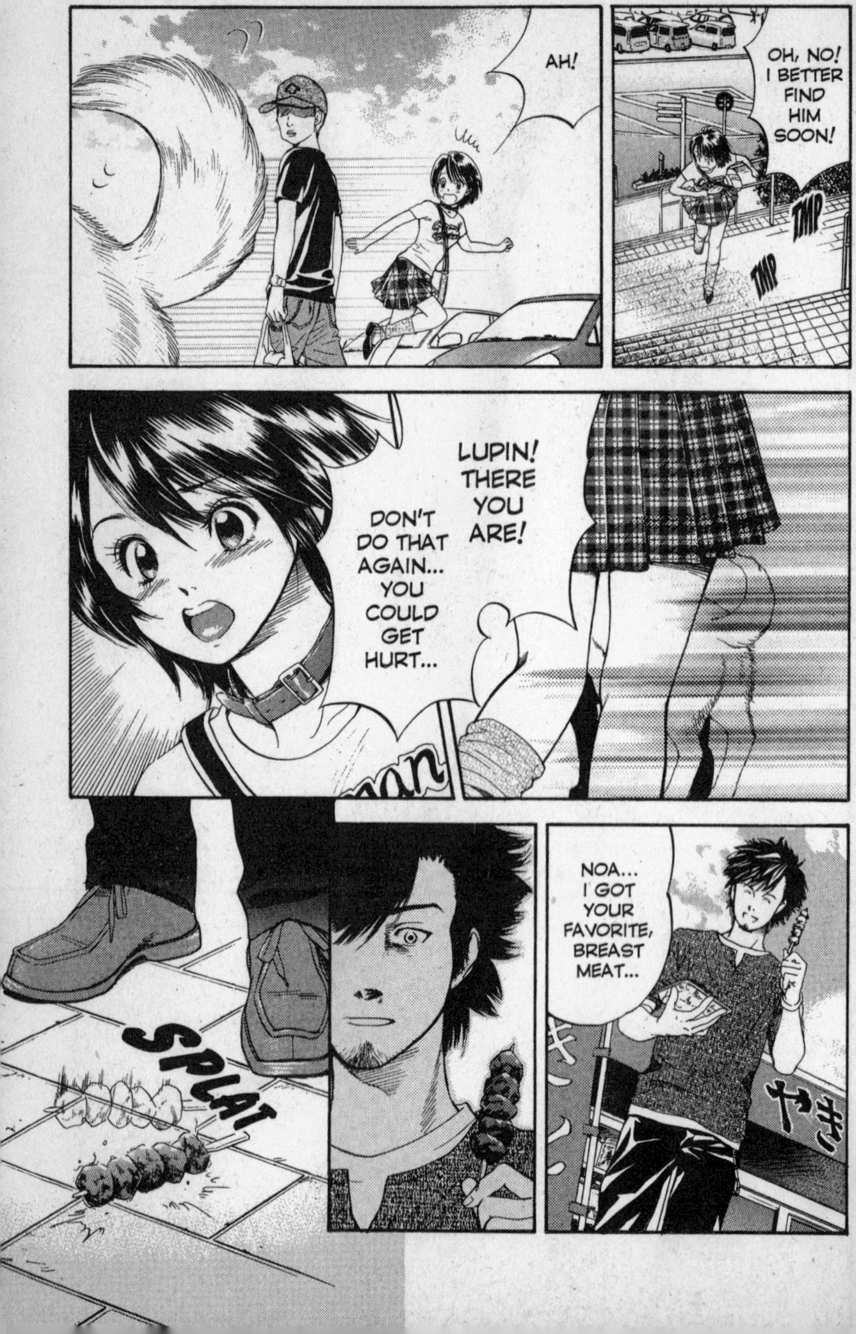
OH, NO! I BETTER FIND HIM SOON!
TMP
TMP
AH!
LUPIN! THERE YOU ARE!
DON'T DO THAT AGAIN... YOU COULD GET HURT...
NOA... I GOT YOUR FAVORITE, BREAST MEAT...
やき
SPLAT

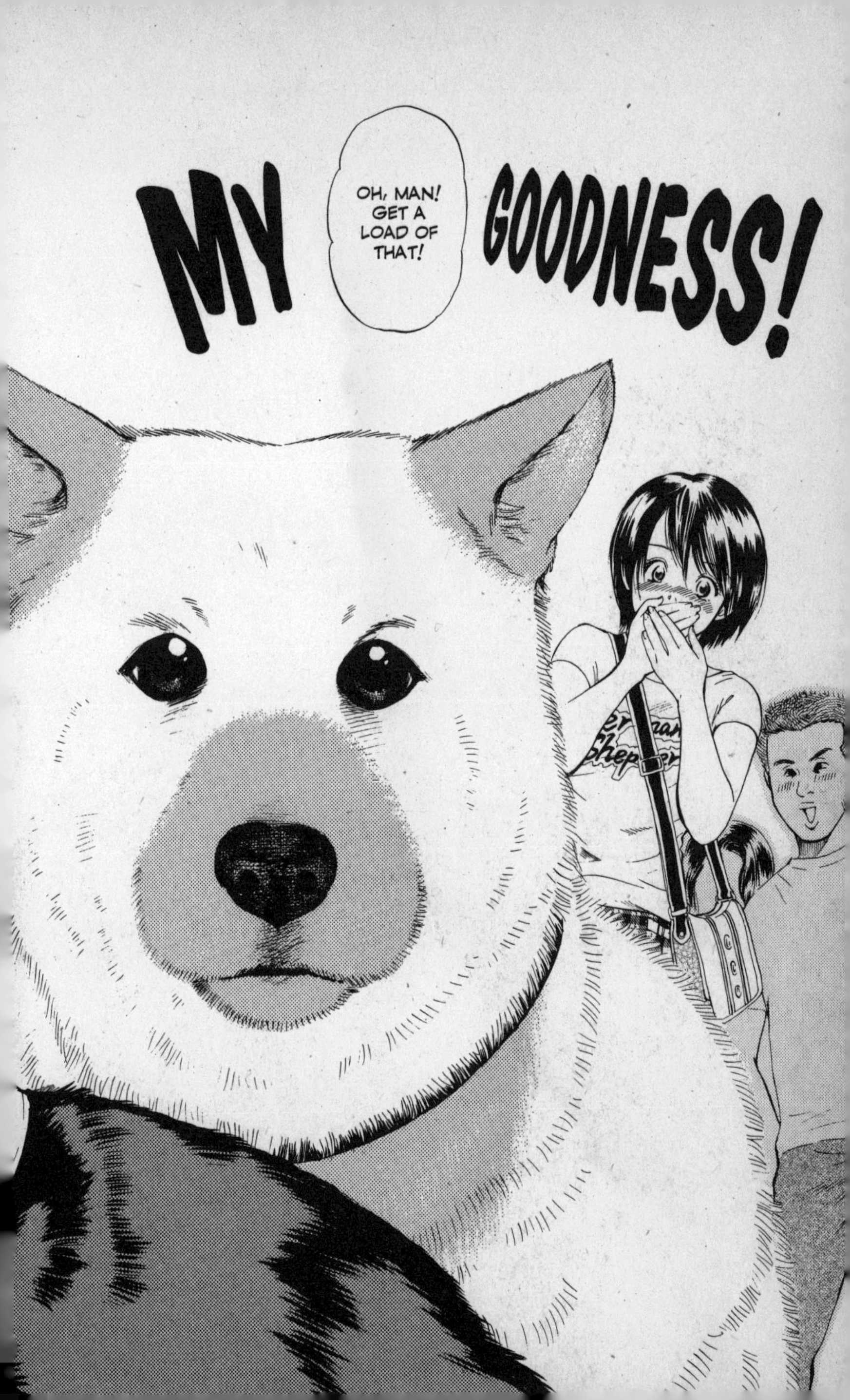
MY GOODNESS!
OH, MAN! GET A LOAD OF THAT!

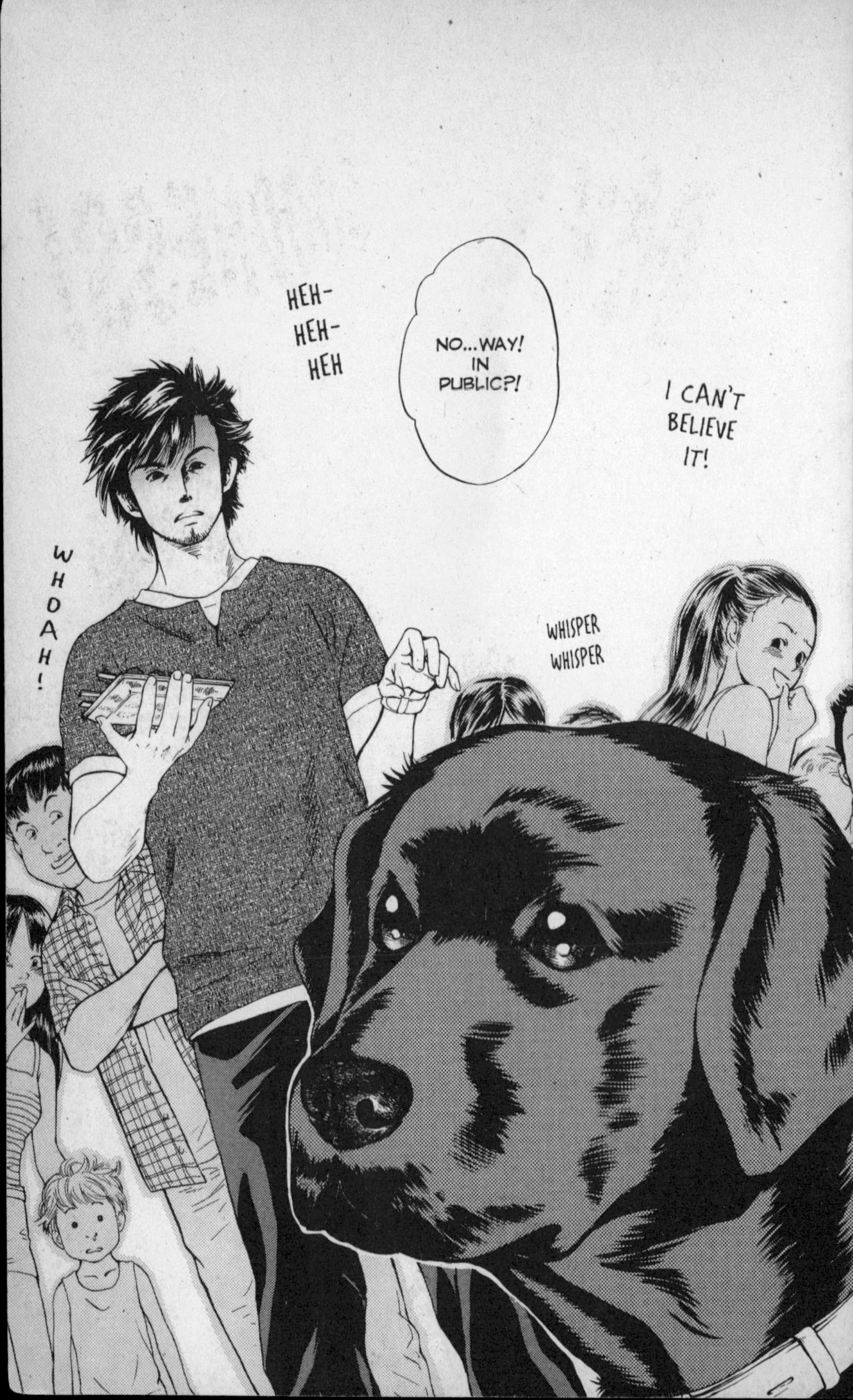
I CAN'T BELIEVE IT!
NO...WAY! IN PUBLIC?!
HEH-HEH-HEH
WHISPER WHISPER
WHOAH!

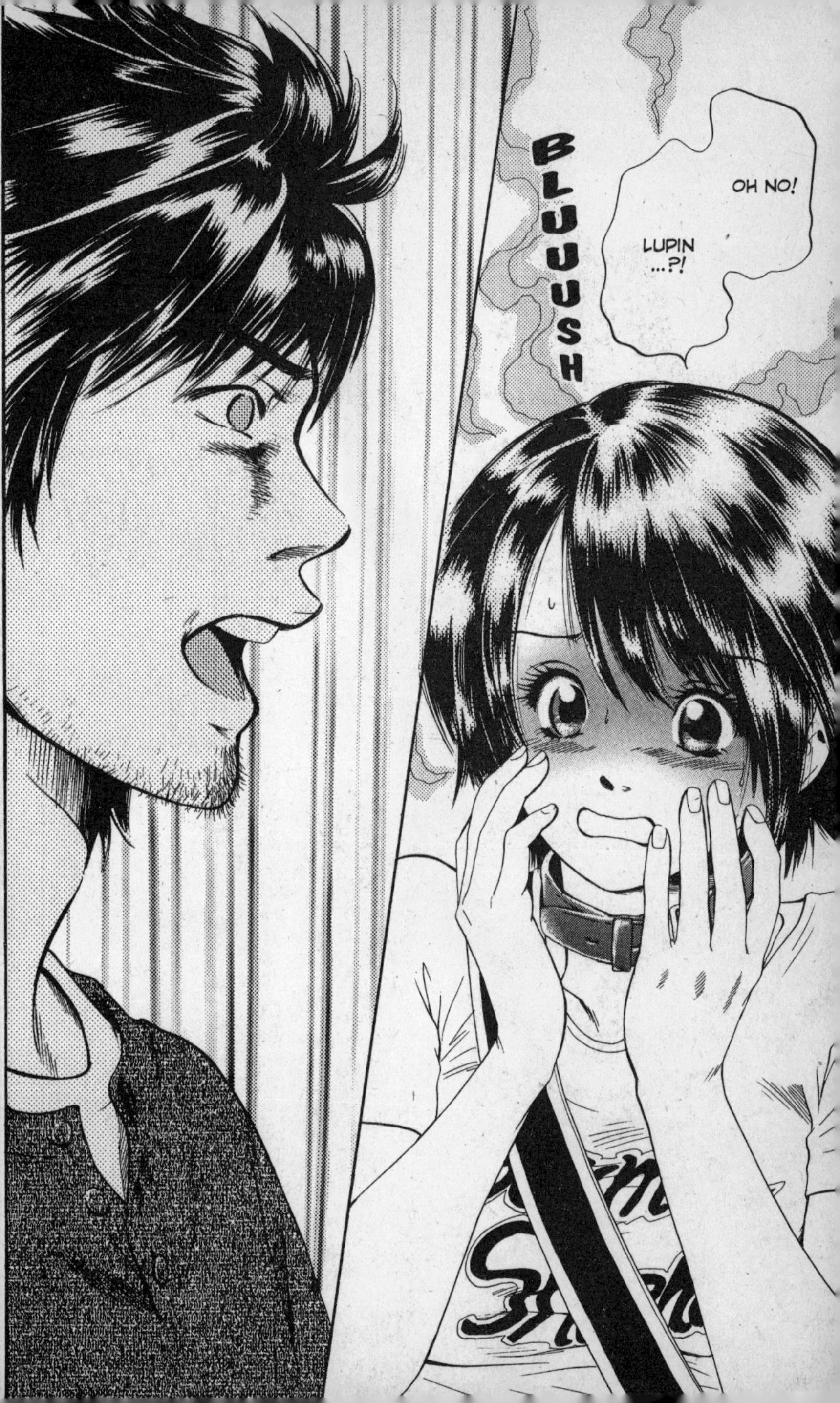
OH NO!
LUPIN ...?!
BLUUUSH

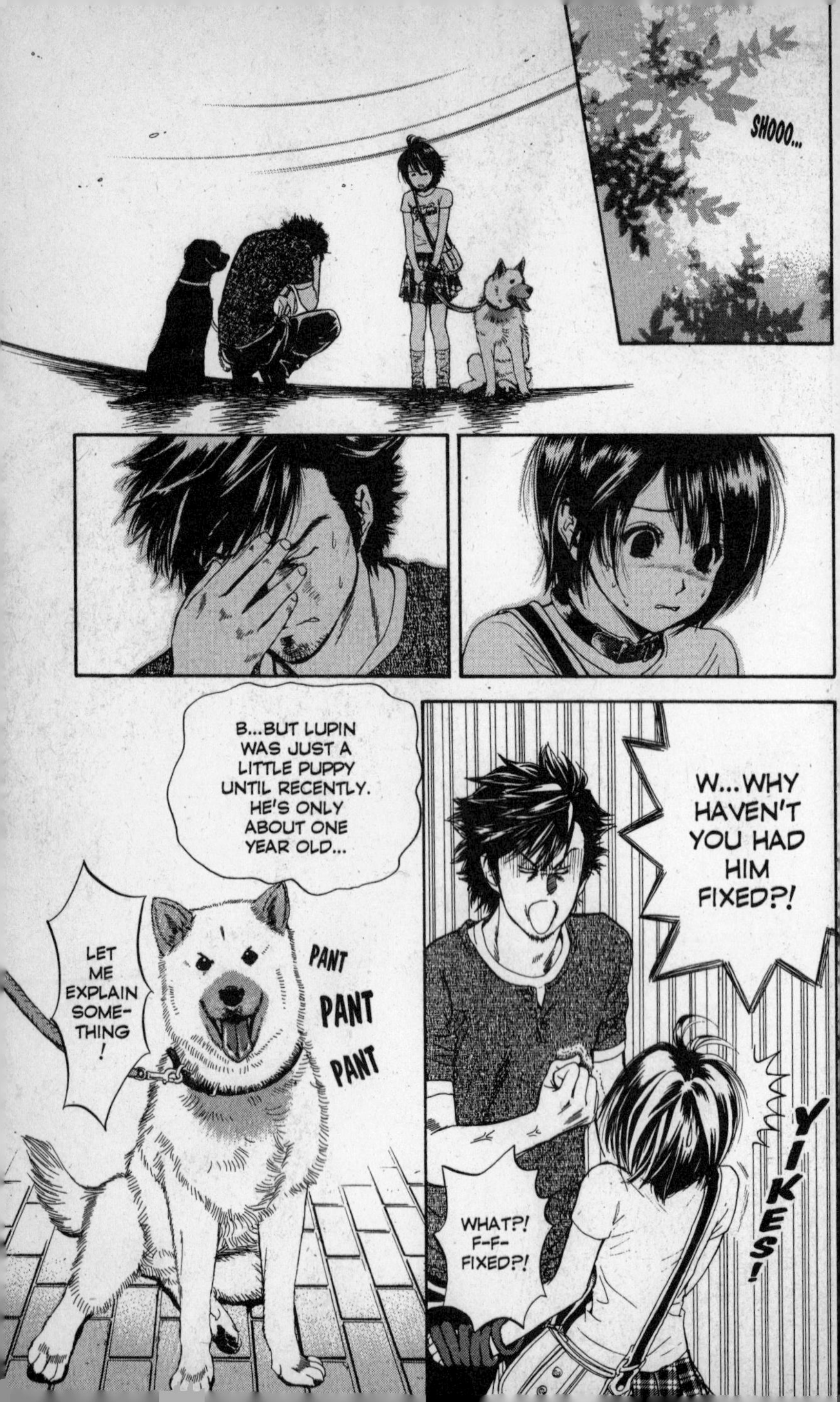
SHOOO...
W...WHY HAVEN'T YOU HAD HIM FIXED?!
YIKES!
WHAT?! F-F-FIXED?!
B...BUT LUPIN WAS JUST A LITTLE PUPPY UNTIL RECENTLY. HE'S ONLY ABOUT ONE YEAR OLD...
LET ME EXPLAIN SOME-THING!
PANT
PANT
PANT

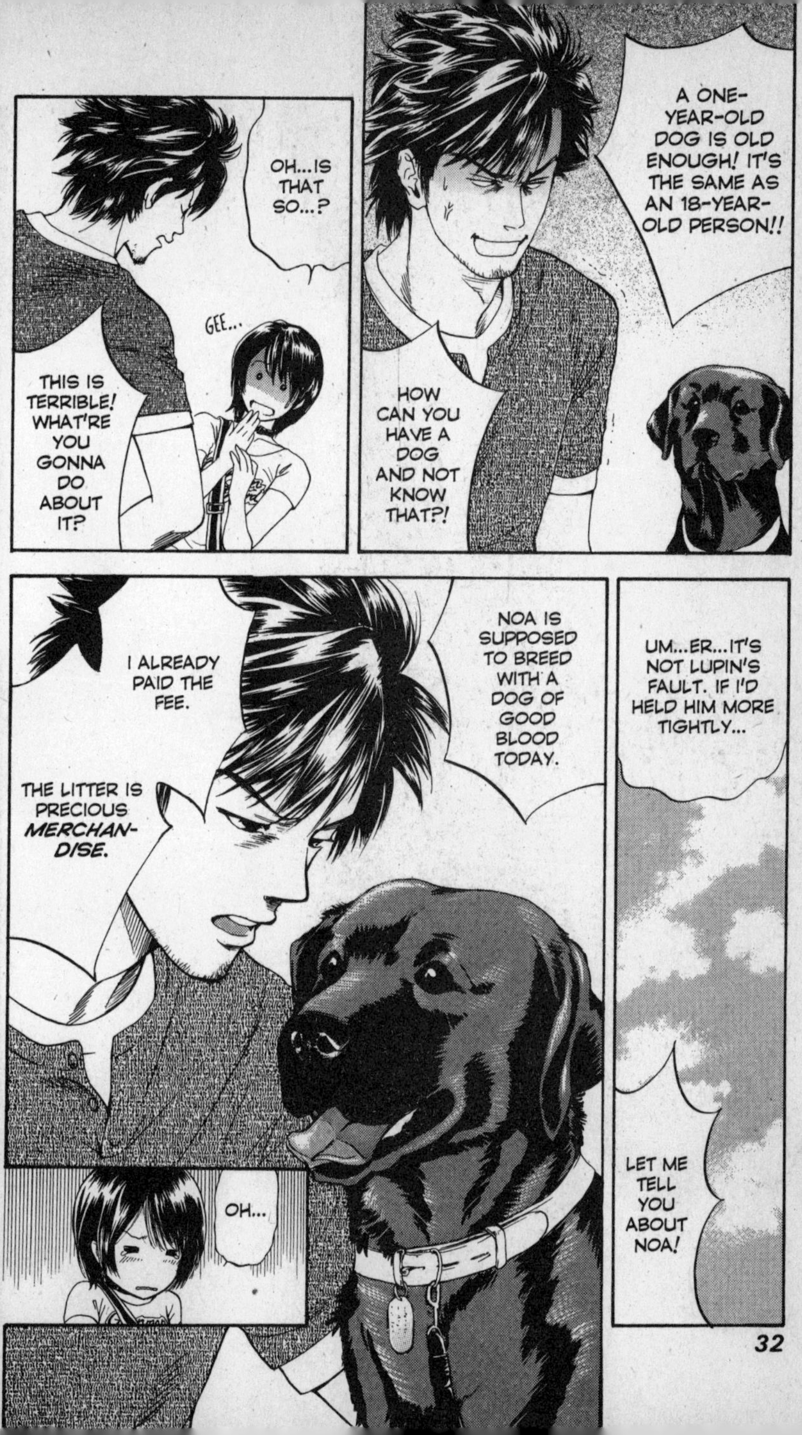
A ONE-YEAR-OLD DOG IS OLD ENOUGH! IT'S THE SAME AS AN 18-YEAR-OLD PERSON!!
HOW CAN YOU HAVE A DOG AND NOT KNOW THAT?!
OH...IS THAT SO...?
GEE...
THIS IS TERRIBLE! WHAT'RE YOU GONNA DO ABOUT IT?
UM...ER...IT'S NOT LUPIN'S FAULT. IF I'D HELD HIM MORE TIGHTLY...
LET ME TELL YOU ABOUT NOA!
NOA IS SUPPOSED TO BREED WITH A DOG OF GOOD BLOOD TODAY.
I ALREADY PAID THE FEE.
THE LITTER IS PRECIOUS *MERCHANDISE.*
OH...

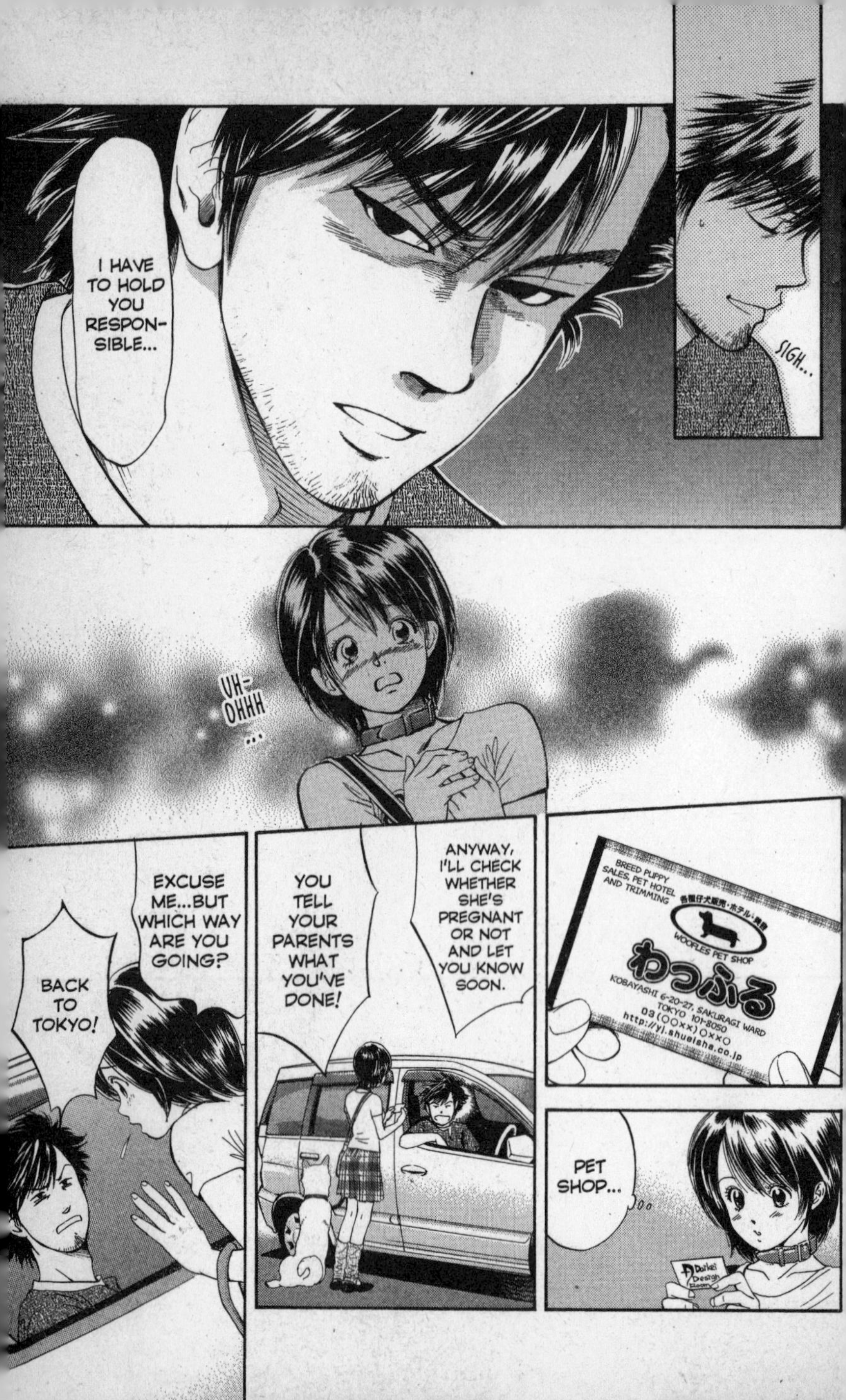
SIGH...
I HAVE TO HOLD YOU RESPONSIBLE...
UH-OHHH...
BREED PUPPY SALES, PET HOTEL AND TRIMMING
WOOFLES PET SHOP
わっふる
KOBAYASHI 6-20-27, SAKURAGI WARD TOKYO 101-8050
03(○○xx)○xx○
http://yj.shueisha.co.jp
PET SHOP...
Daikei Design Room
ANYWAY, I'LL CHECK WHETHER SHE'S PREGNANT OR NOT AND LET YOU KNOW SOON.
YOU TELL YOUR PARENTS WHAT YOU'VE DONE!
EXCUSE ME...BUT WHICH WAY ARE YOU GOING?
BACK TO TOKYO!

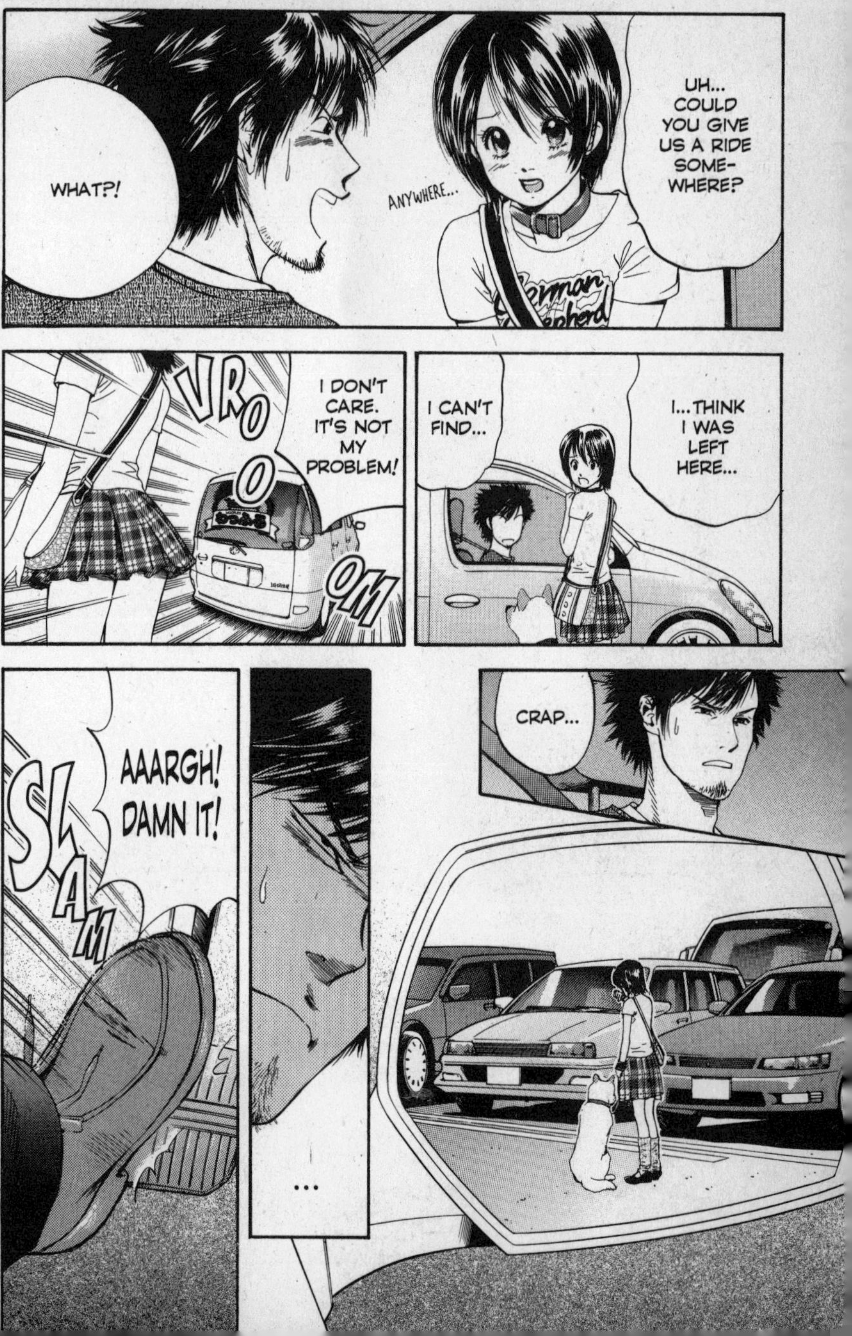
UH... COULD YOU GIVE US A RIDE SOME-WHERE?
ANYWHERE...
WHAT?!
I...THINK I WAS LEFT HERE...
I CAN'T FIND...
I DON'T CARE. IT'S NOT MY PROBLEM!
VROOOOM
CRAP...
...
AAARGH! DAMN IT!
SLAM

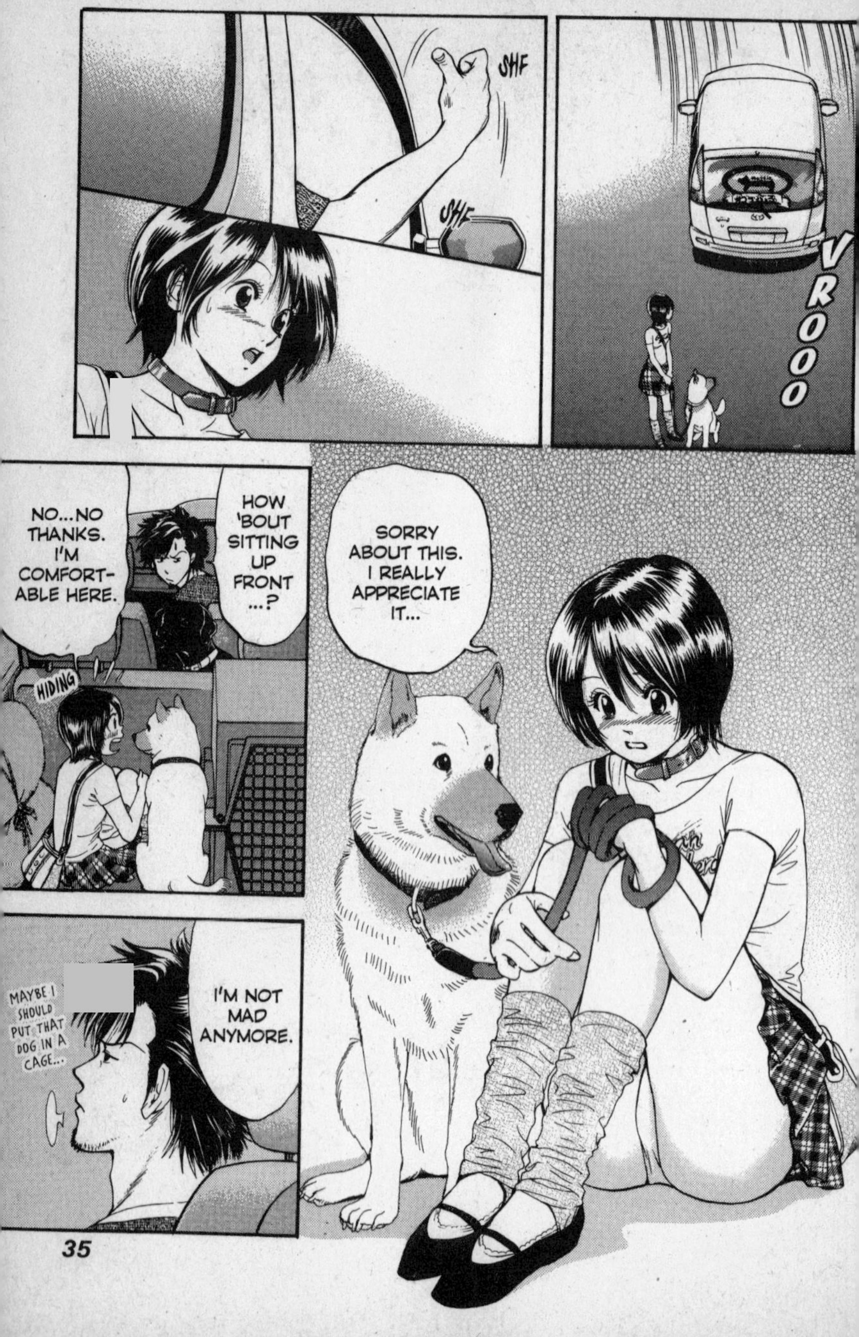
VROOOO
SHF
SHF
SORRY ABOUT THIS. I REALLY APPRECIATE IT...
HOW 'BOUT SITTING UP FRONT ...?
NO...NO THANKS. I'M COMFORTABLE HERE.
HIDING
I'M NOT MAD ANYMORE.
MAYBE I SHOULD PUT THAT DOG IN A CAGE...

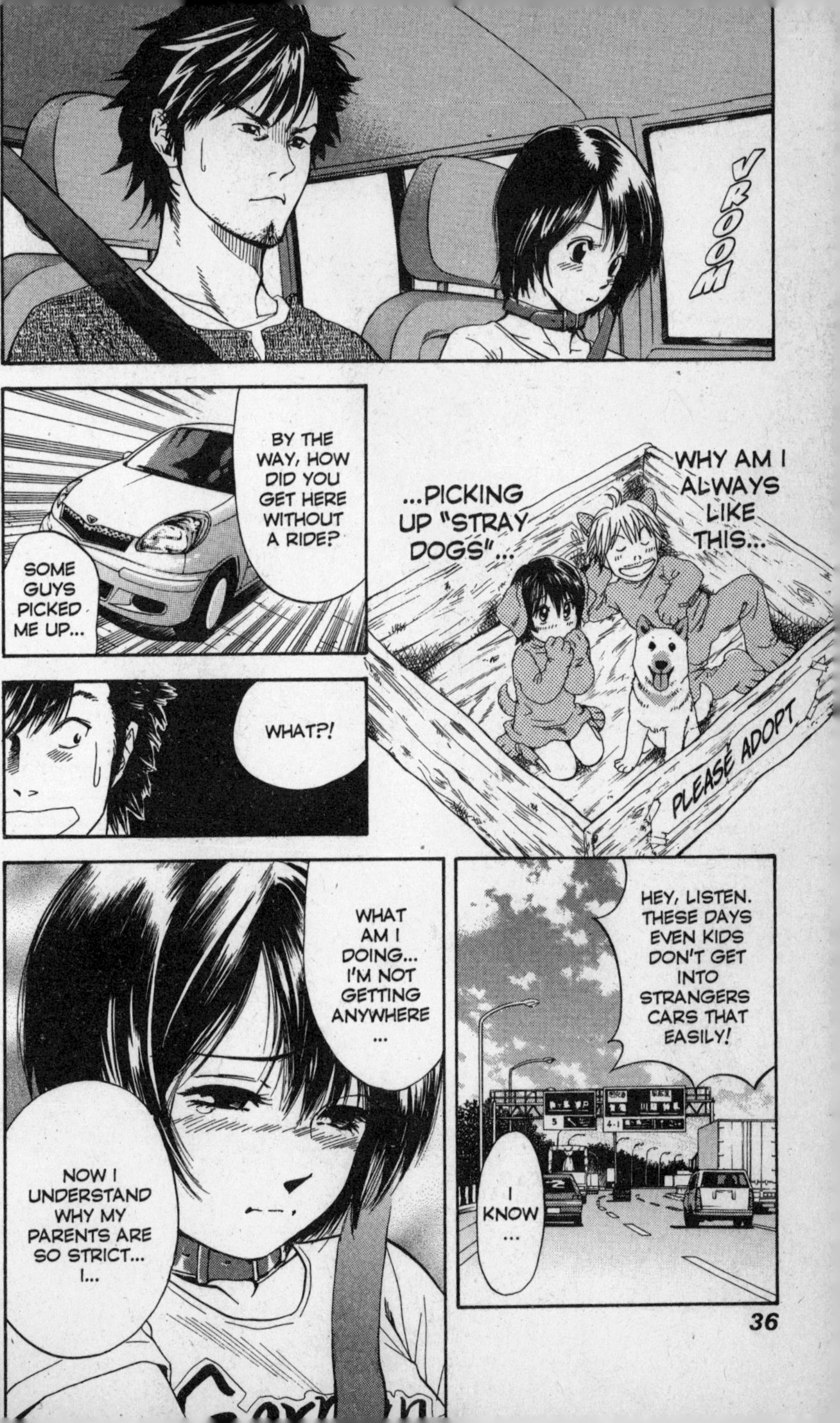
VROOM
WHY AM I ALWAYS LIKE THIS...
...PICKING UP "STRAY DOGS"...
PLEASE ADOPT
BY THE WAY, HOW DID YOU GET HERE WITHOUT A RIDE?
SOME GUYS PICKED ME UP...
WHAT?!
HEY, LISTEN. THESE DAYS EVEN KIDS DON'T GET INTO STRANGERS CARS THAT EASILY!
I KNOW...
WHAT AM I DOING... I'M NOT GETTING ANYWHERE...
NOW I UNDERSTAND WHY MY PARENTS ARE SO STRICT... I...

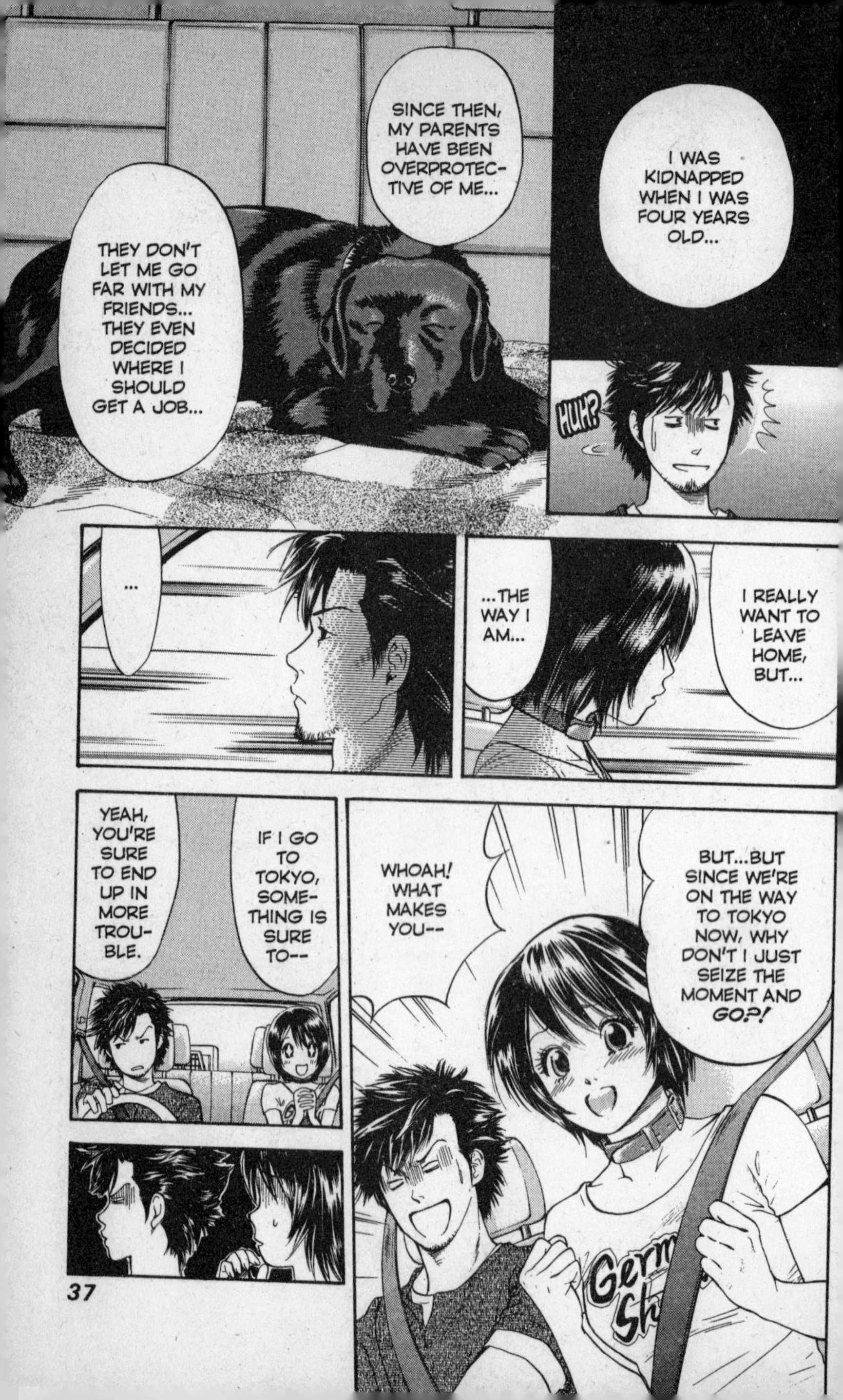
I WAS KIDNAPPED WHEN I WAS FOUR YEARS OLD...
HUH?
SINCE THEN, MY PARENTS HAVE BEEN OVERPROTECTIVE OF ME...
THEY DON'T LET ME GO FAR WITH MY FRIENDS... THEY EVEN DECIDED WHERE I SHOULD GET A JOB...
I REALLY WANT TO LEAVE HOME, BUT...
...THE WAY I AM...
...
BUT...BUT SINCE WE'RE ON THE WAY TO TOKYO NOW, WHY DON'T I JUST SEIZE THE MOMENT AND GO?!
WHOAH! WHAT MAKES YOU--
IF I GO TO TOKYO, SOMETHING IS SURE TO--
YEAH, YOU'RE SURE TO END UP IN MORE TROUBLE.

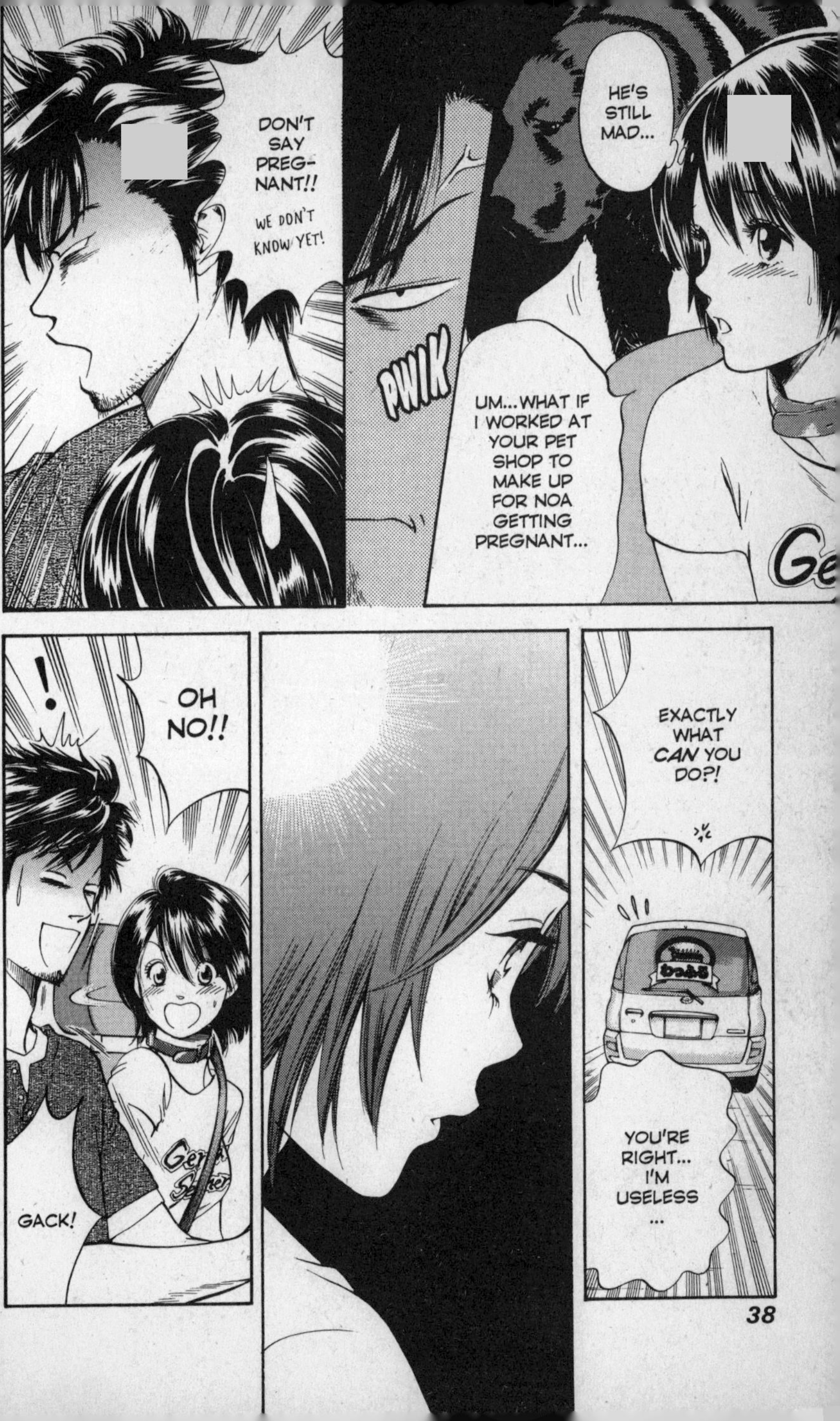
HE'S STILL MAD...
PWIK
UM...WHAT IF I WORKED AT YOUR PET SHOP TO MAKE UP FOR NOA GETTING PREGNANT...
DON'T SAY PREGNANT!!
WE DON'T KNOW YET!
EXACTLY WHAT *CAN* YOU DO?!
YOU'RE RIGHT... I'M USELESS ...
!
OH NO!!
GACK!

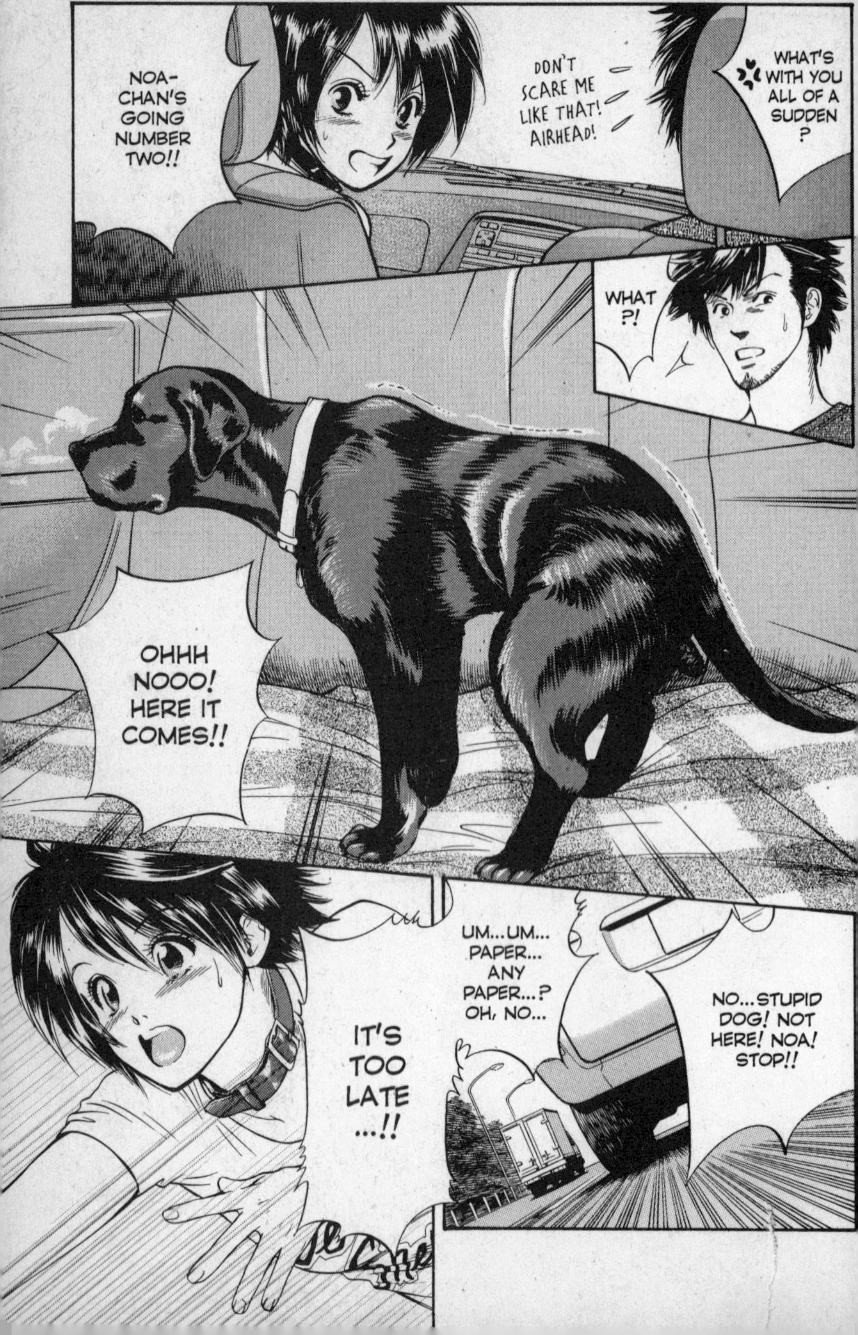
WHAT'S WITH YOU ALL OF A SUDDEN?
DON'T SCARE ME LIKE THAT! AIRHEAD!
NOA-CHAN'S GOING NUMBER TWO!!
WHAT?!
OHHH NOOO! HERE IT COMES!!
NO...STUPID DOG! NOT HERE! NOA! STOP!!
UM...UM... PAPER... ANY PAPER...? OH, NO...
IT'S TOO LATE...!!

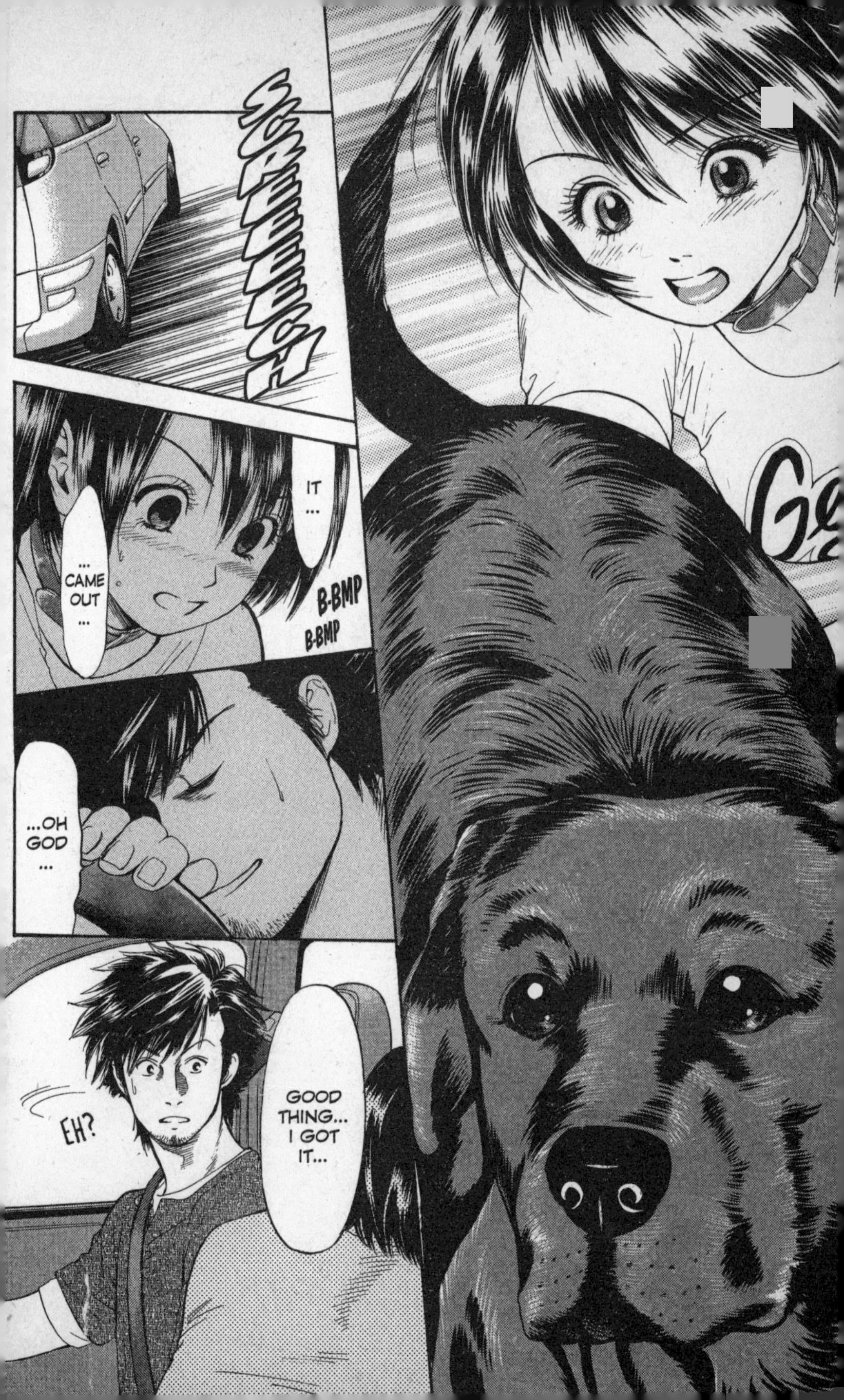
SCREEEEECH
IT ...
... CAME OUT ...
B-BMP
B-BMP
...OH GOD ...
GOOD THING... I GOT IT...
EH?

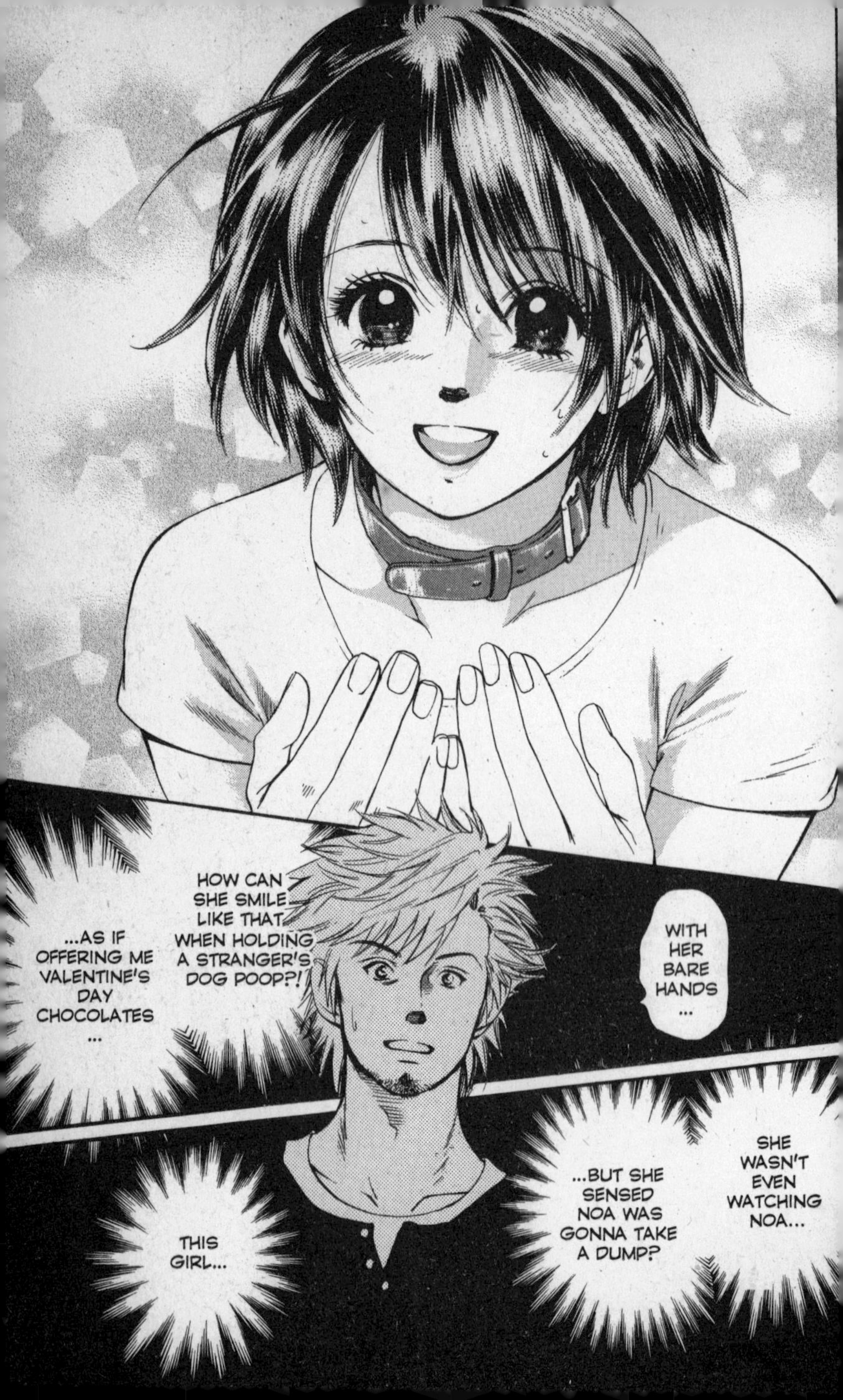
WITH HER BARE HANDS...
HOW CAN SHE SMILE LIKE THAT WHEN HOLDING A STRANGER'S DOG POOP?!
...AS IF OFFERING ME VALENTINE'S DAY CHOCOLATES...
SHE WASN'T EVEN WATCHING NOA...
...BUT SHE SENSED NOA WAS GONNA TAKE A DUMP?
THIS GIRL...

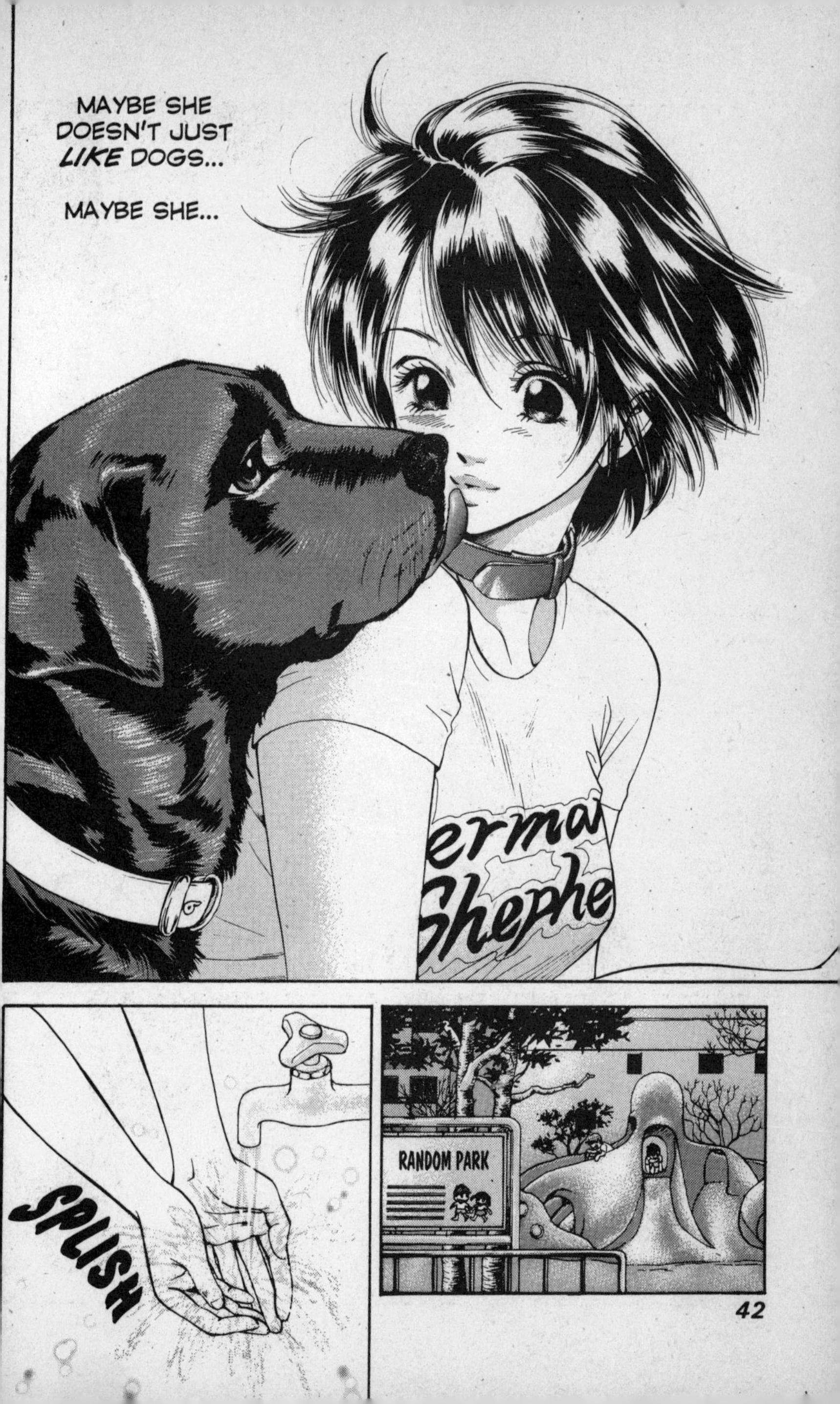
MAYBE SHE DOESN'T JUST *LIKE* DOGS...
MAYBE SHE...
erma
Shephe
RANDOM PARK
SPLISH

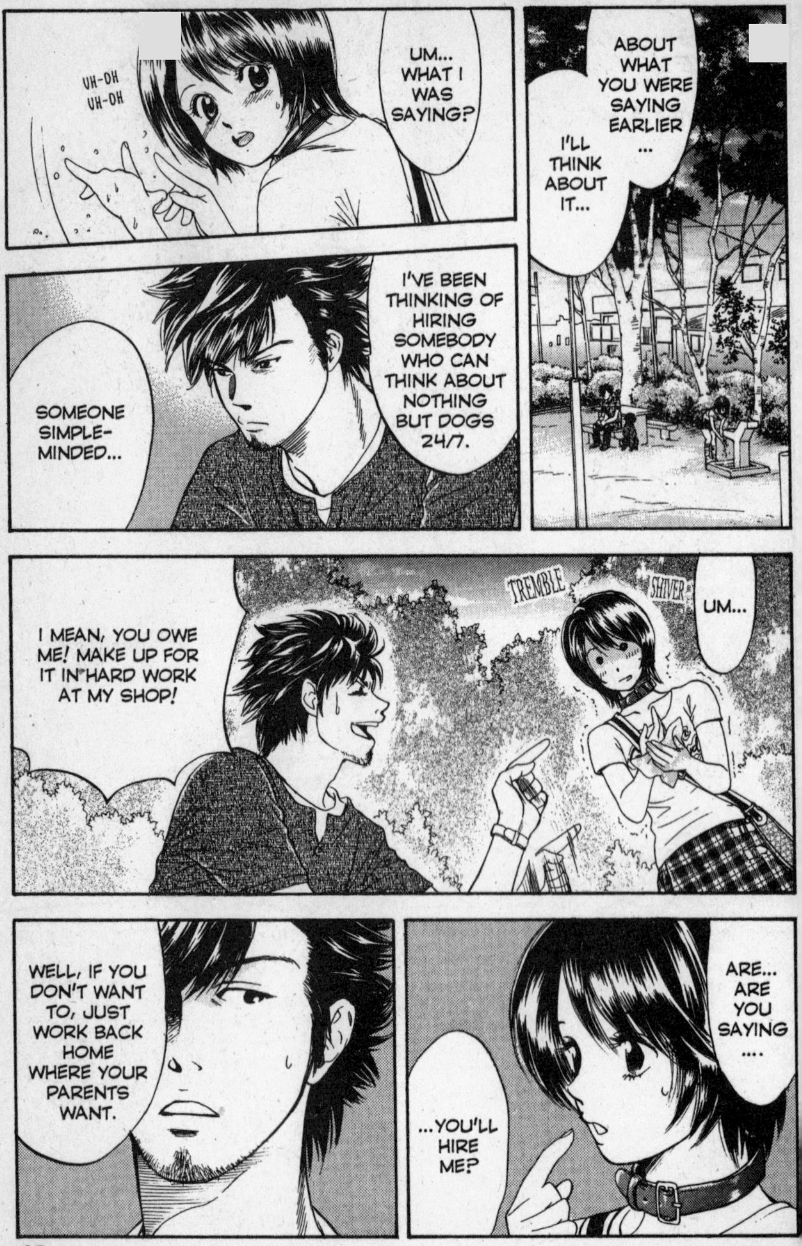
ABOUT WHAT YOU WERE SAYING EARLIER ...
I'LL THINK ABOUT IT...
UM... WHAT I WAS SAYING?
UH-OH UH-OH
I'VE BEEN THINKING OF HIRING SOMEBODY WHO CAN THINK ABOUT NOTHING BUT DOGS 24/7.
SOMEONE SIMPLE-MINDED...
UM...
SHIVER
TREMBLE
I MEAN, YOU OWE ME! MAKE UP FOR IT IN HARD WORK AT MY SHOP!
ARE... ARE YOU SAYING ....
...YOU'LL HIRE ME?
WELL, IF YOU DON'T WANT TO, JUST WORK BACK HOME WHERE YOUR PARENTS WANT.

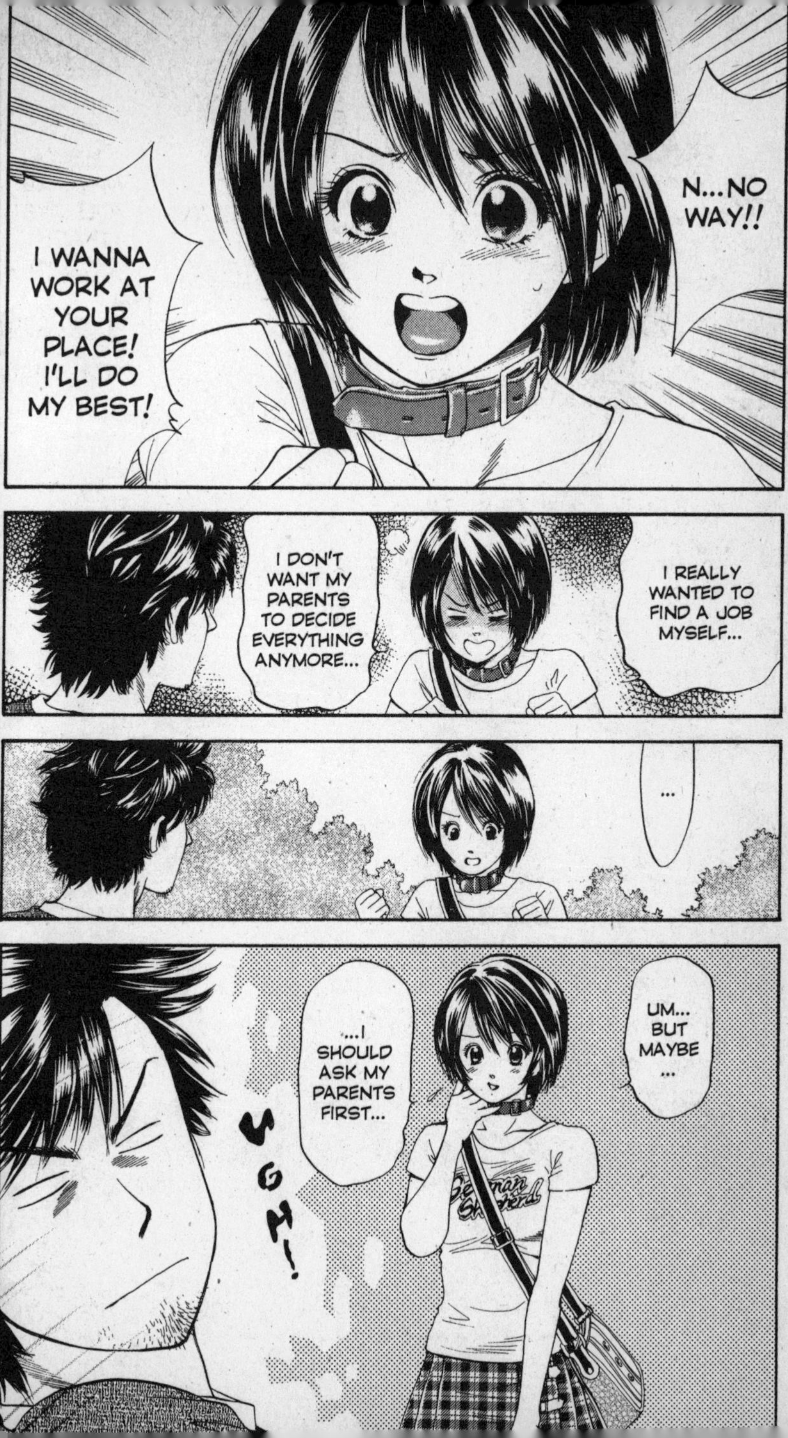
N...NO WAY!!
I WANNA WORK AT YOUR PLACE! I'LL DO MY BEST!
I REALLY WANTED TO FIND A JOB MYSELF...
I DON'T WANT MY PARENTS TO DECIDE EVERYTHING ANYMORE...
...
UM... BUT MAYBE ...
...I SHOULD ASK MY PARENTS FIRST...
UGH!

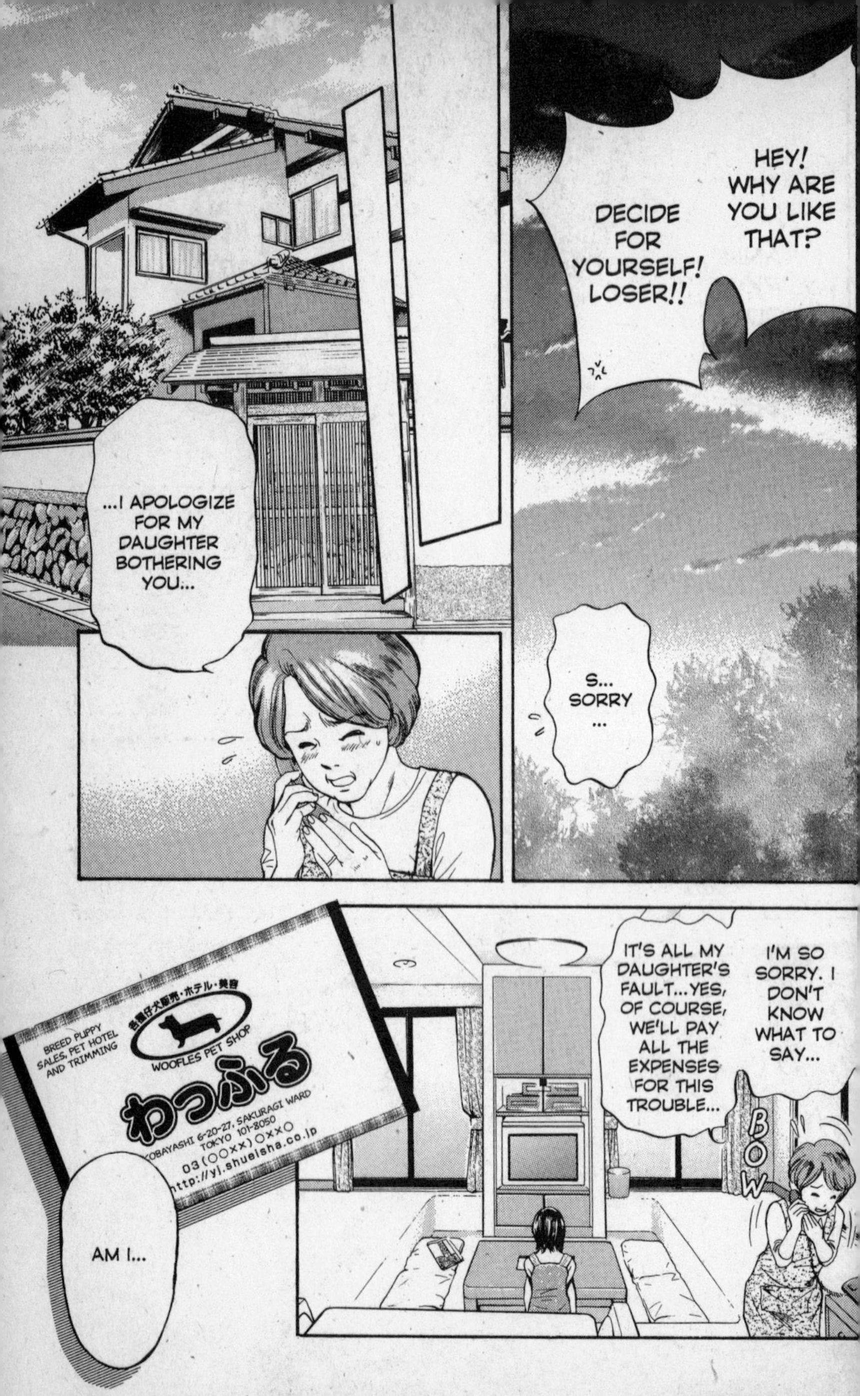

HEY! WHY ARE YOU LIKE THAT?
DECIDE FOR YOURSELF! LOSER!!
S... SORRY ...
...I APOLOGIZE FOR MY DAUGHTER BOTHERING YOU...
I'M SO SORRY. I DON'T KNOW WHAT TO SAY...
IT'S ALL MY DAUGHTER'S FAULT...YES, OF COURSE, WE'LL PAY ALL THE EXPENSES FOR THIS TROUBLE...
BOW
各種仔犬販売・ホテル・美容
BREED PUPPY SALES, PET HOTEL AND TRIMMING
WOOFLES PET SHOP
わっふる
KOBAYASHI 6-20-27, SAKURAGI WARD
TOKYO 101-8050
03(○○××)○××○
http://yj.shueisha.co.jp
AM I...

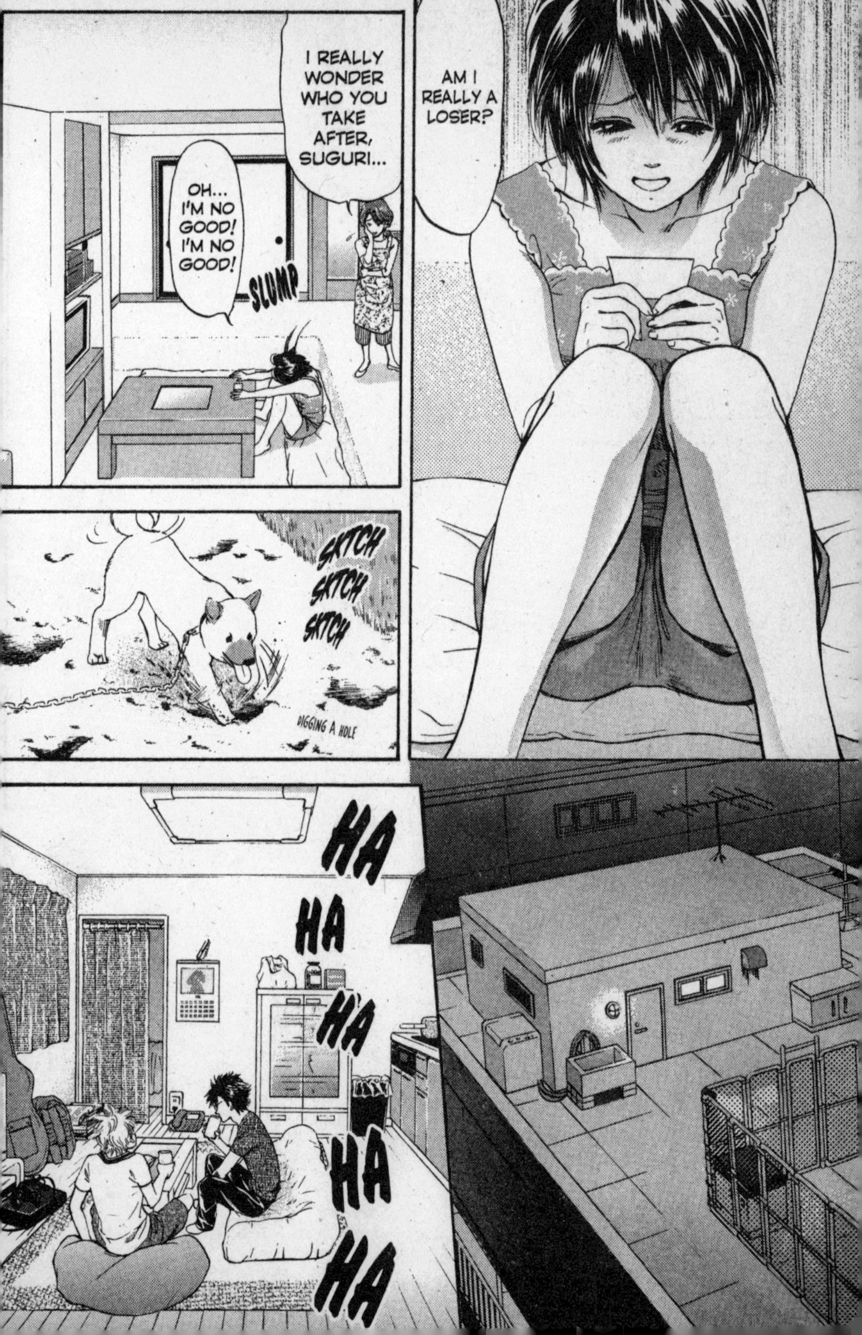
AM I REALLY A LOSER?
I REALLY WONDER WHO YOU TAKE AFTER, SUGURI...
OH... I'M NO GOOD! I'M NO GOOD!
SLUMP
SKTCH SKTCH SKTCH
DIGGING A HOLE
HA HA HA HA HA

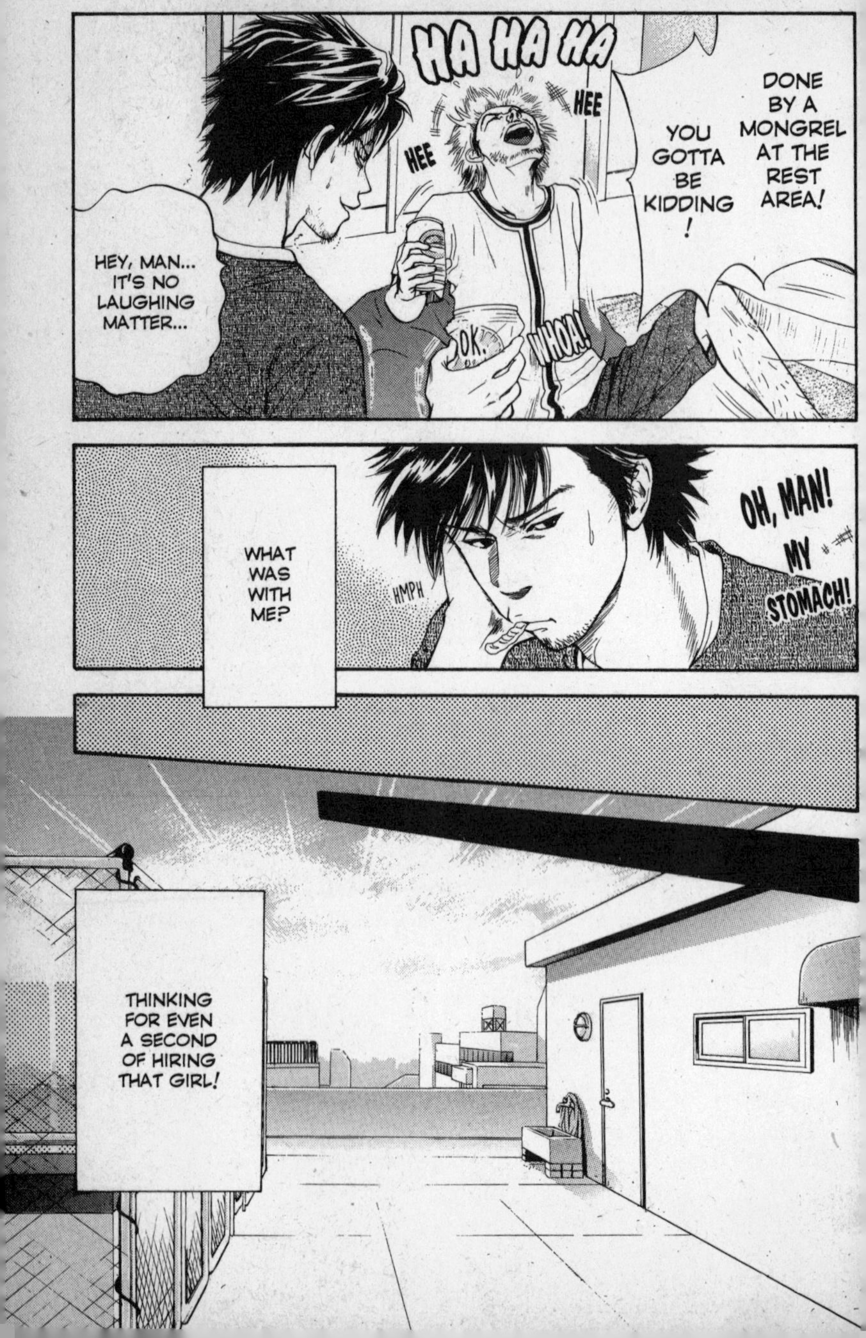
HA HA HA
DONE BY A MONGREL AT THE REST AREA!
YOU GOTTA BE KIDDING!
HEE
HEE
WHOA!
OK.
HEY, MAN... IT'S NO LAUGHING MATTER...
OH, MAN! MY STOMACH!
HMPH
WHAT WAS WITH ME?
THINKING FOR EVEN A SECOND OF HIRING THAT GIRL!

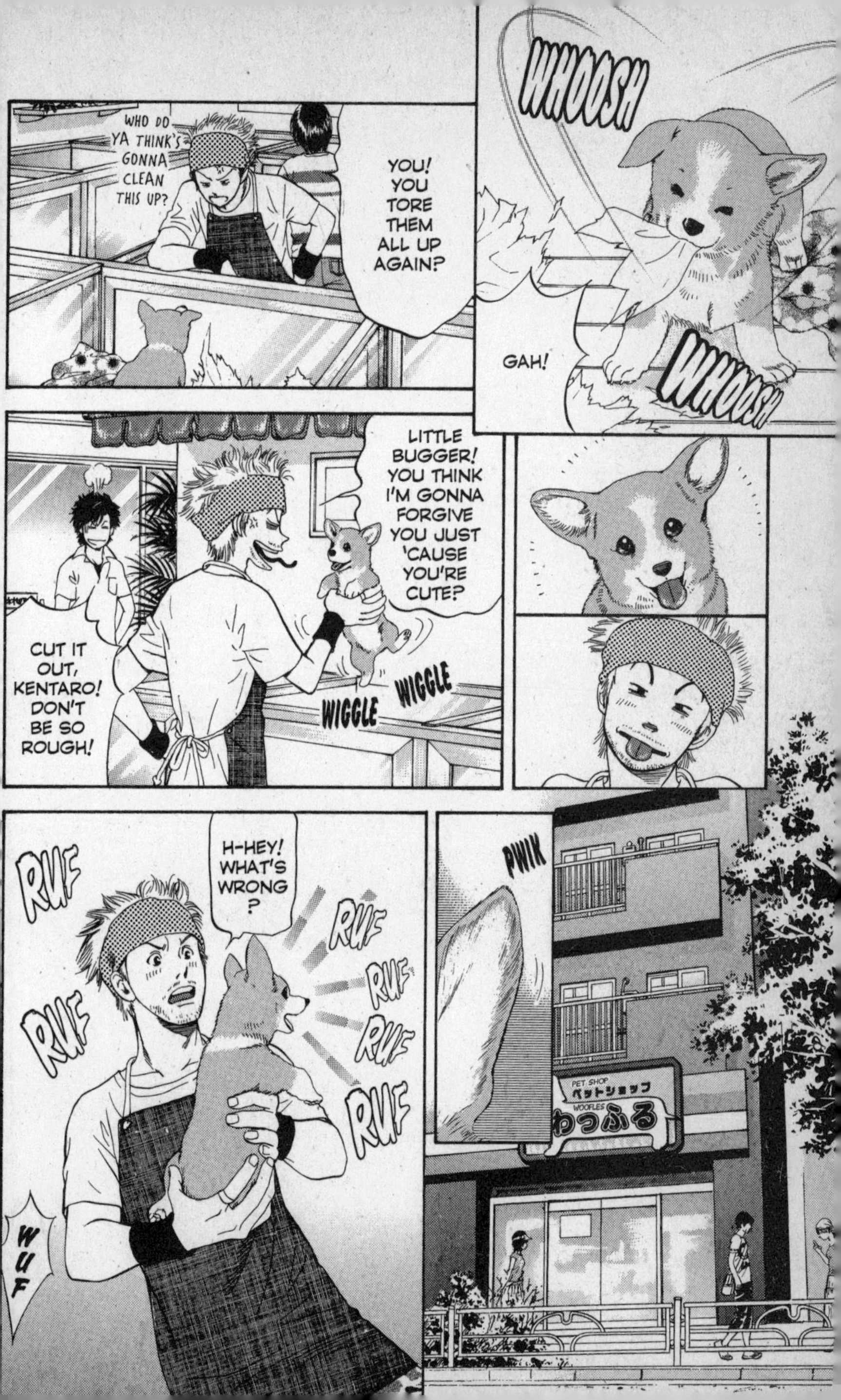
WHOOSH
GAH!
WHOOSH
YOU! YOU TORE THEM ALL UP AGAIN?
WHO DO YA THINK'S GONNA CLEAN THIS UP?
LITTLE BUGGER! YOU THINK I'M GONNA FORGIVE YOU JUST 'CAUSE YOU'RE CUTE?
WIGGLE
WIGGLE
CUT IT OUT, KENTARO! DON'T BE SO ROUGH!
PWIK
PET SHOP
ペットショップ
WOOFLES
わっふる
H-HEY! WHAT'S WRONG?
RUF
RUF
RUF
RUF
RUF
RUF
WUF

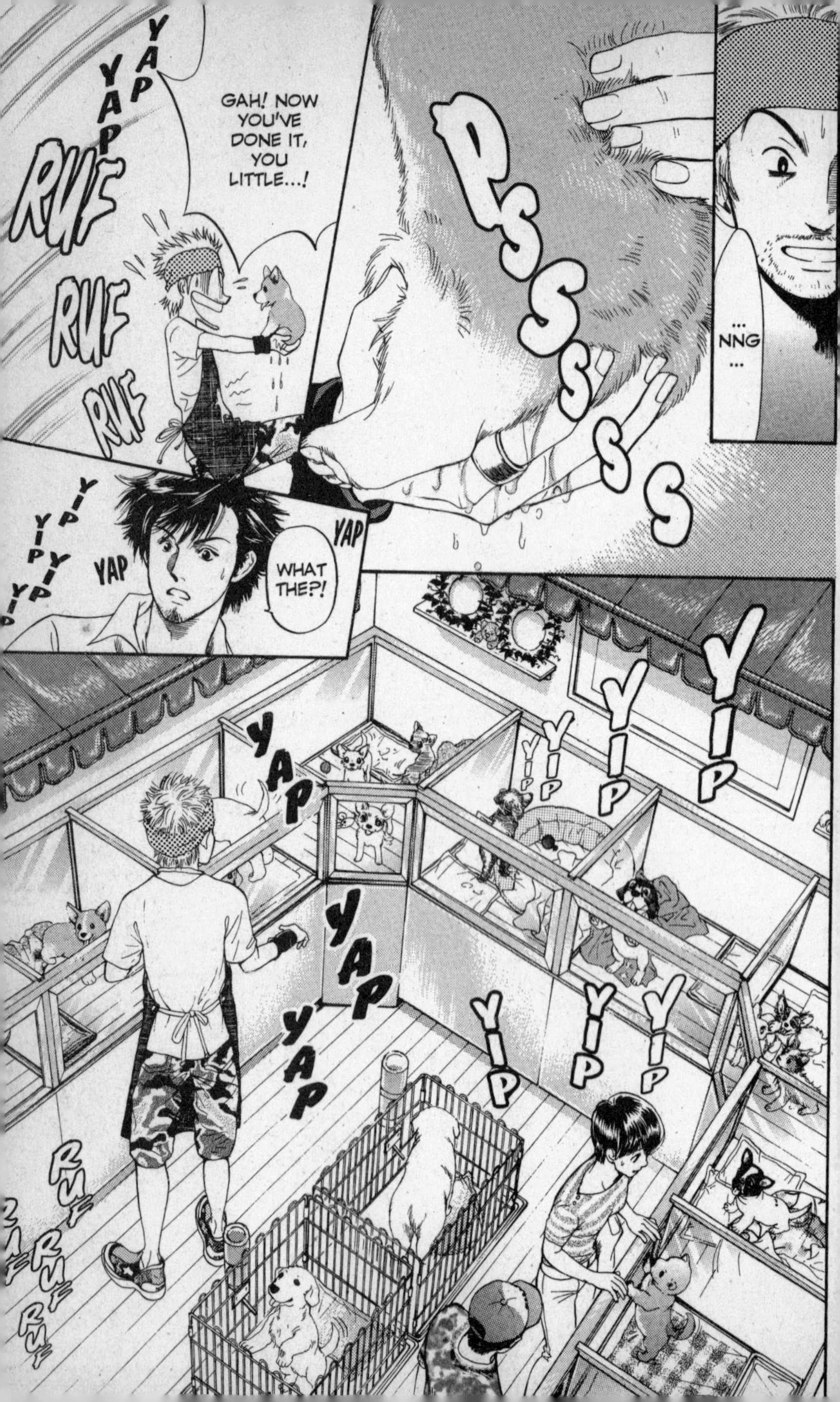
...NNG...
PSSSSSS
YAP YAP YAP
GAH! NOW YOU'VE DONE IT, YOU LITTLE...!
RUF
RUF
RUF
YAP
WHAT THE?!
YAP
YIP YIP YIP YIP
YIP YIP YIP YIP
YAP YAP
YAP YAP YAP YAP
YIP YIP YIP
RUF RUF RUF

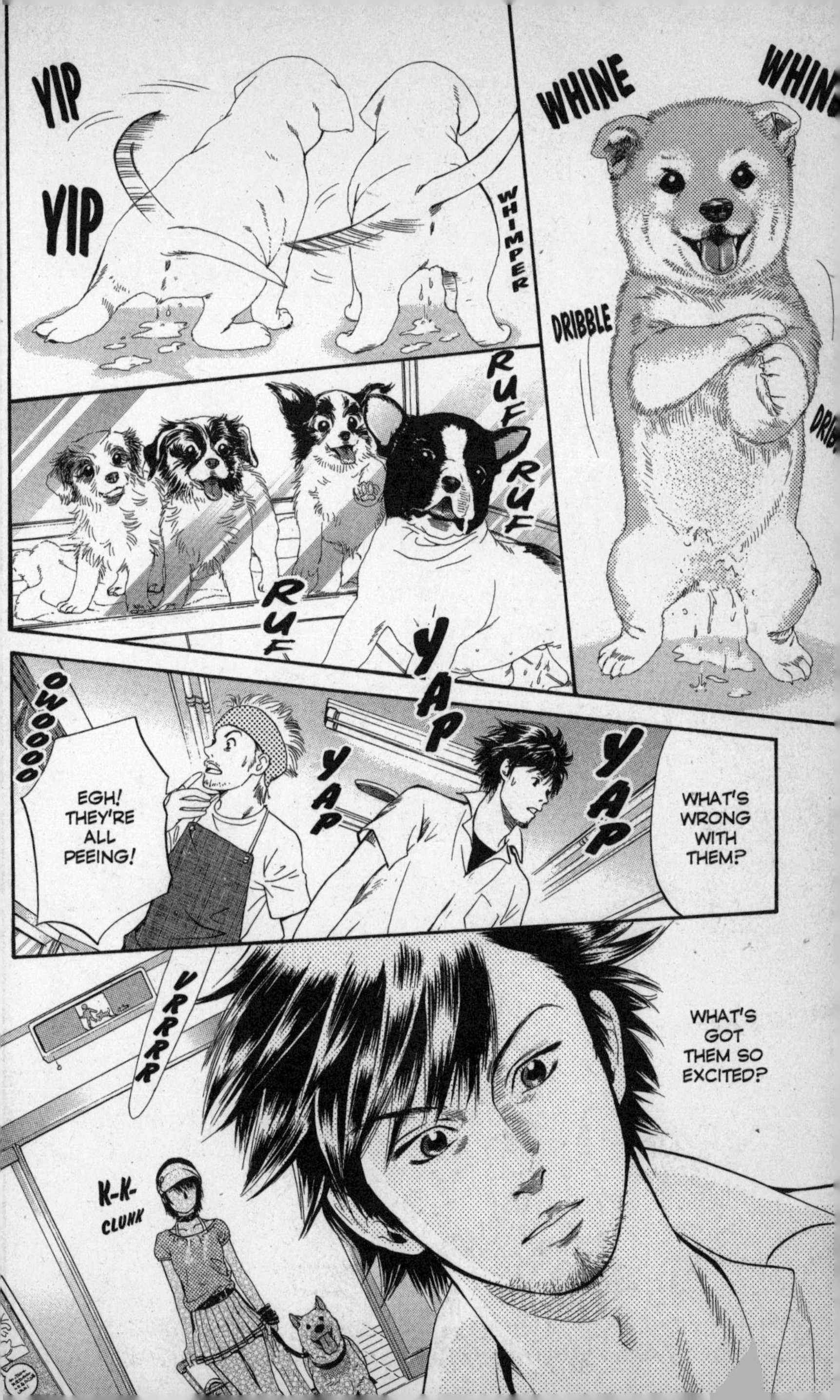
WHINE
DRIBBLE
YIP
YIP
WHIMPER
RUF
RUF
RUF
YAP
WHAT'S WRONG WITH THEM?
YAP
YAP
EGH! THEY'RE ALL PEEING!
OWOOOOO
WHAT'S GOT THEM SO EXCITED?
VRRRRR
K-K-CLUNK

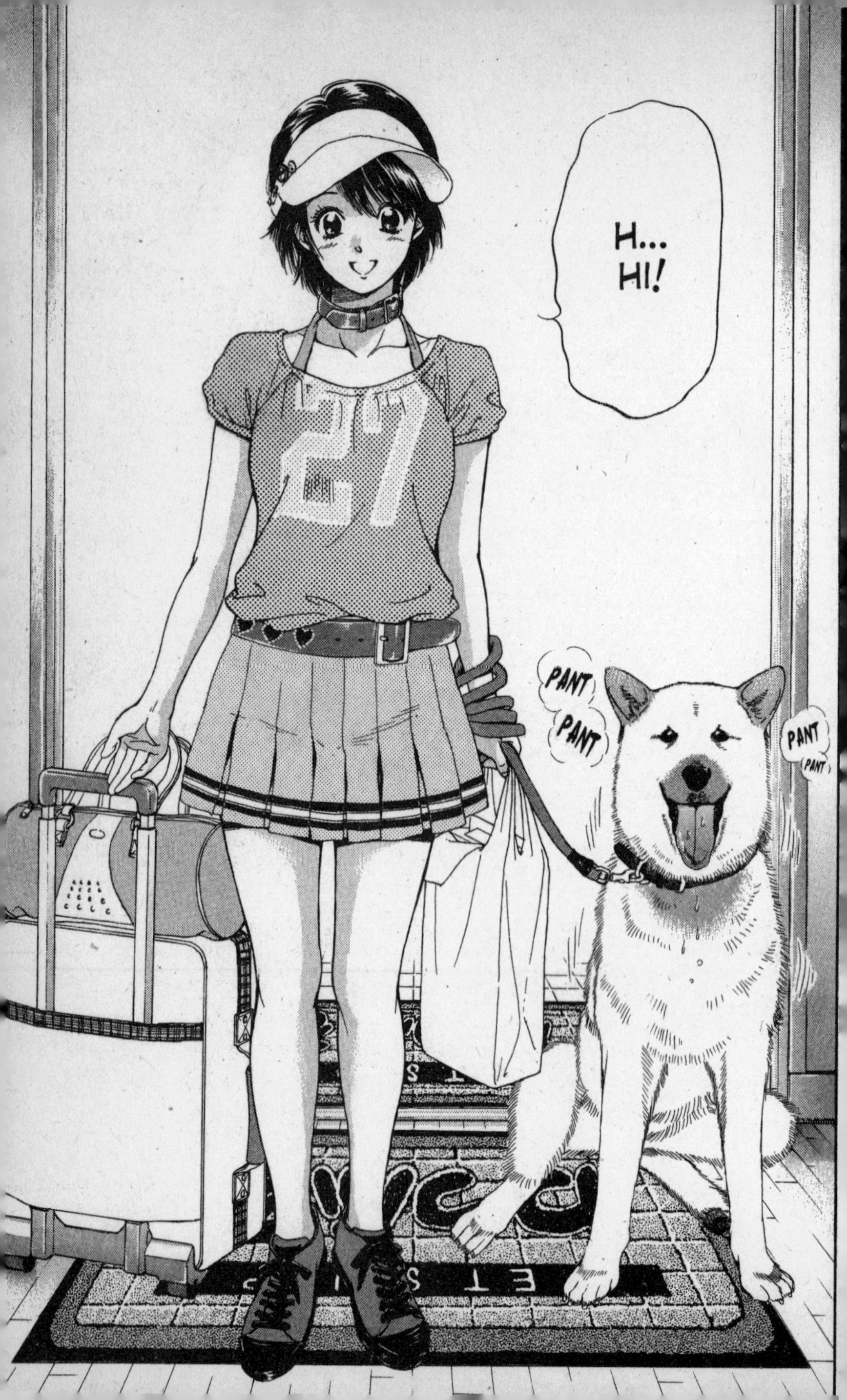
H... HI!
PANT
PANT
PANT
PANT

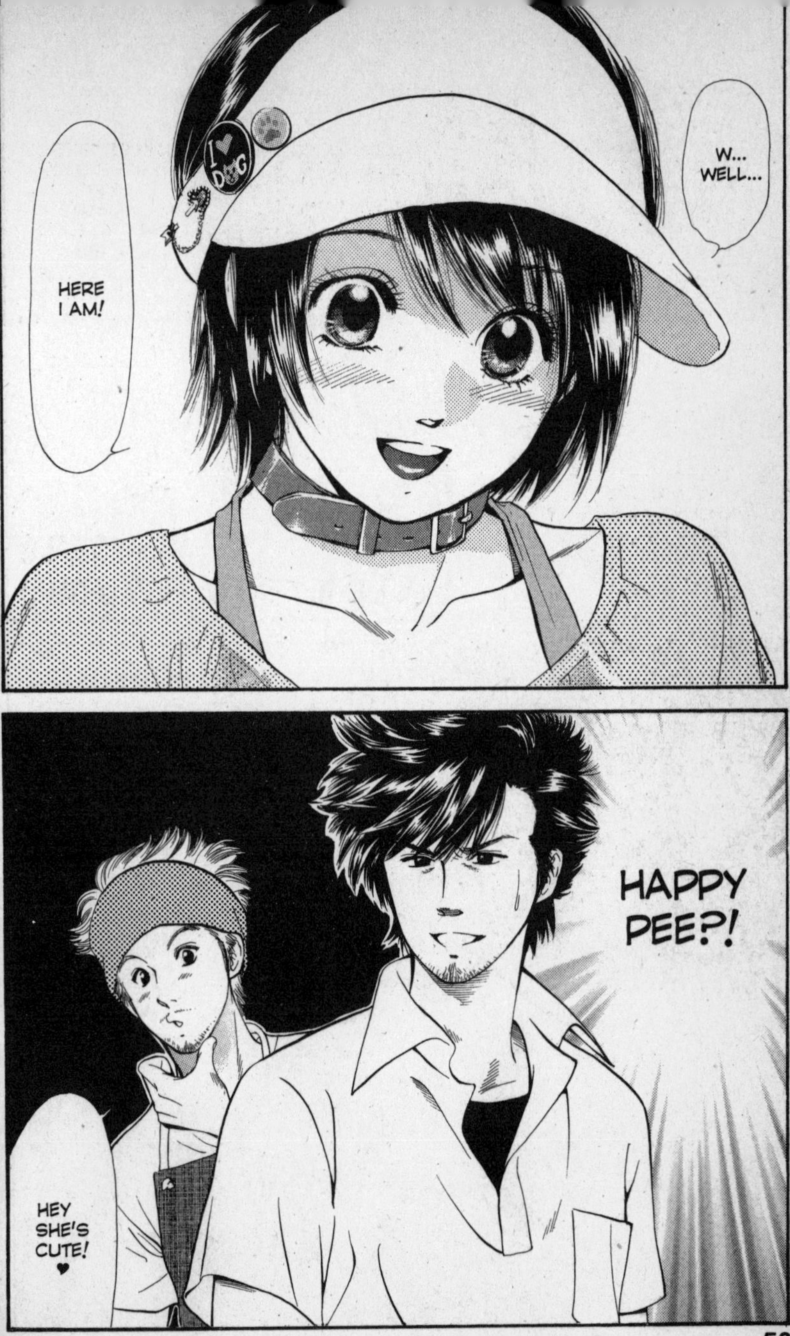
W... WELL...
HERE I AM!
HAPPY PEE?!
HEY SHE'S CUTE! ♥

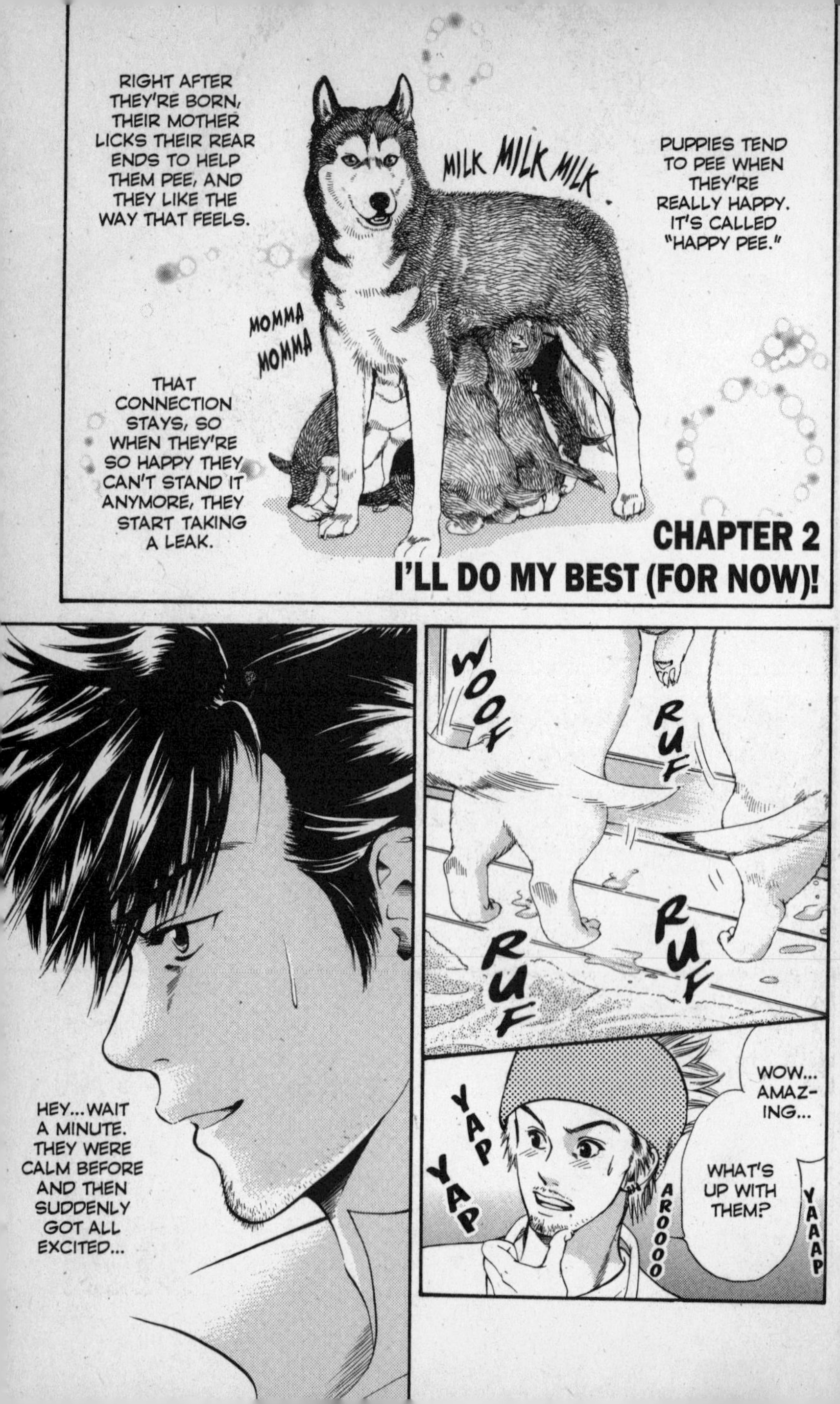
PUPPIES TEND TO PEE WHEN THEY'RE REALLY HAPPY. IT'S CALLED "HAPPY PEE."
MILK MILK MILK
RIGHT AFTER THEY'RE BORN, THEIR MOTHER LICKS THEIR REAR ENDS TO HELP THEM PEE, AND THEY LIKE THE WAY THAT FEELS.
MOMMA MOMMA
THAT CONNECTION STAYS, SO WHEN THEY'RE SO HAPPY THEY CAN'T STAND IT ANYMORE, THEY START TAKING A LEAK.
CHAPTER 2
I'LL DO MY BEST (FOR NOW)!
RUF RUF
RUF RUF
WOOF
RUF RUF
WOW... AMAZ-ING...
YAAAP
WHAT'S UP WITH THEM?
AROOOOO
YAP YAP
HEY...WAIT A MINUTE. THEY WERE CALM BEFORE AND THEN SUDDENLY GOT ALL EXCITED...

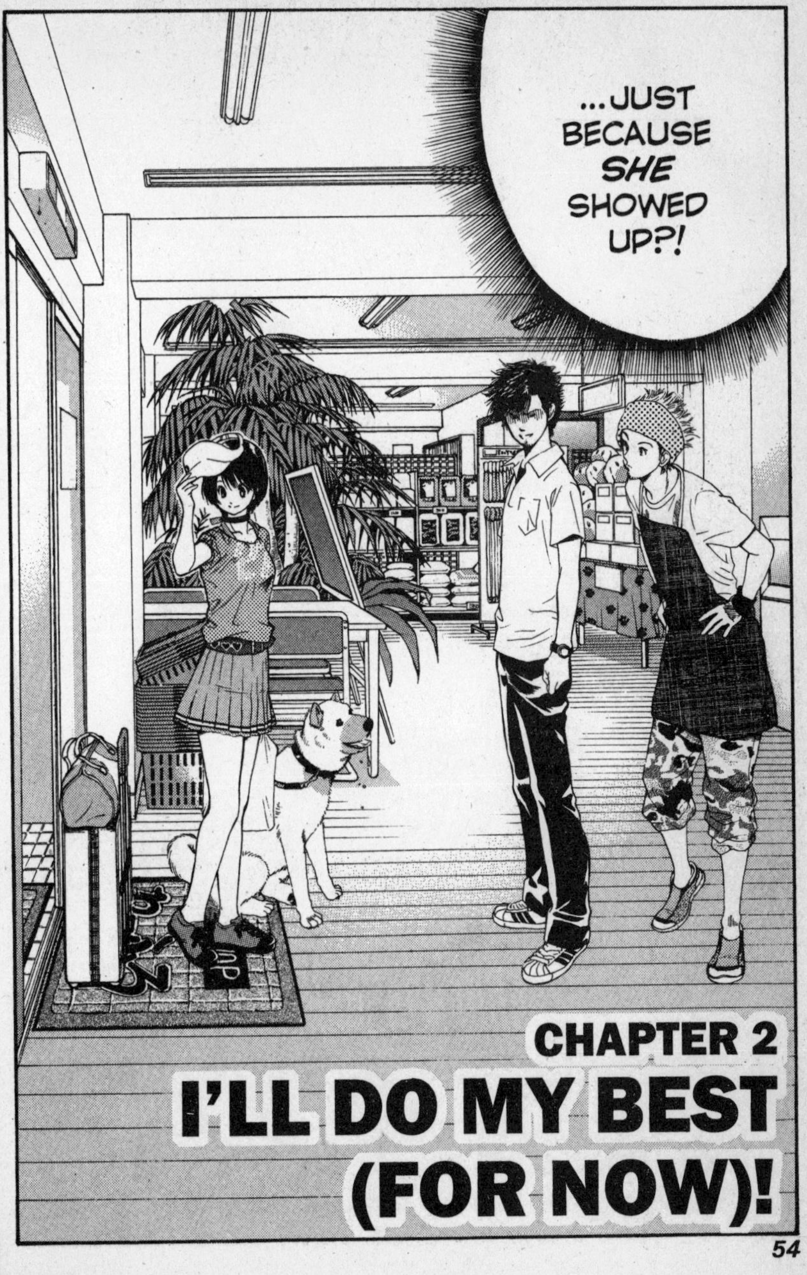
...JUST BECAUSE *SHE* SHOWED UP?!
CHAPTER 2
I'LL DO MY BEST (FOR NOW)!

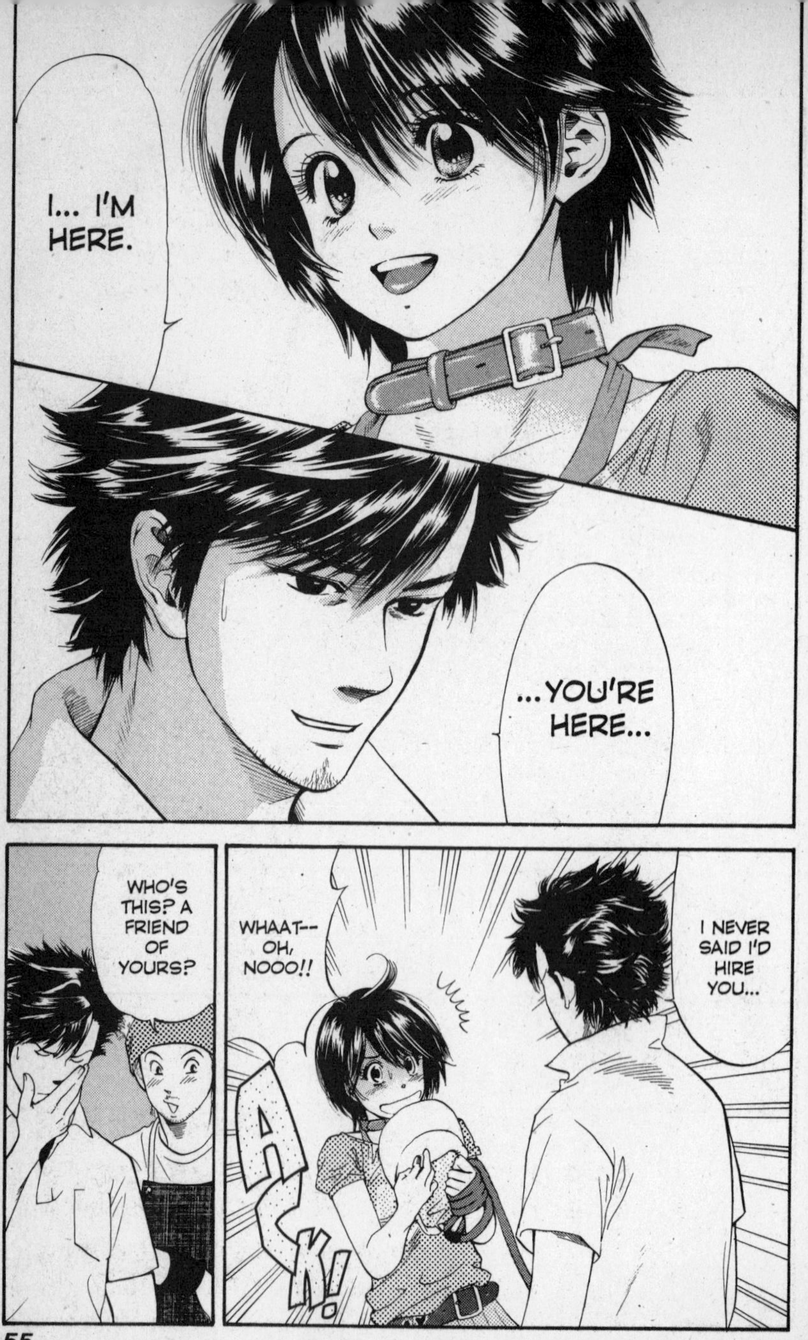
I... I'M HERE.
...YOU'RE HERE...
I NEVER SAID I'D HIRE YOU...
WHAAT-- OH, NOOO!!
ACK!
WHO'S THIS? A FRIEND OF YOURS?

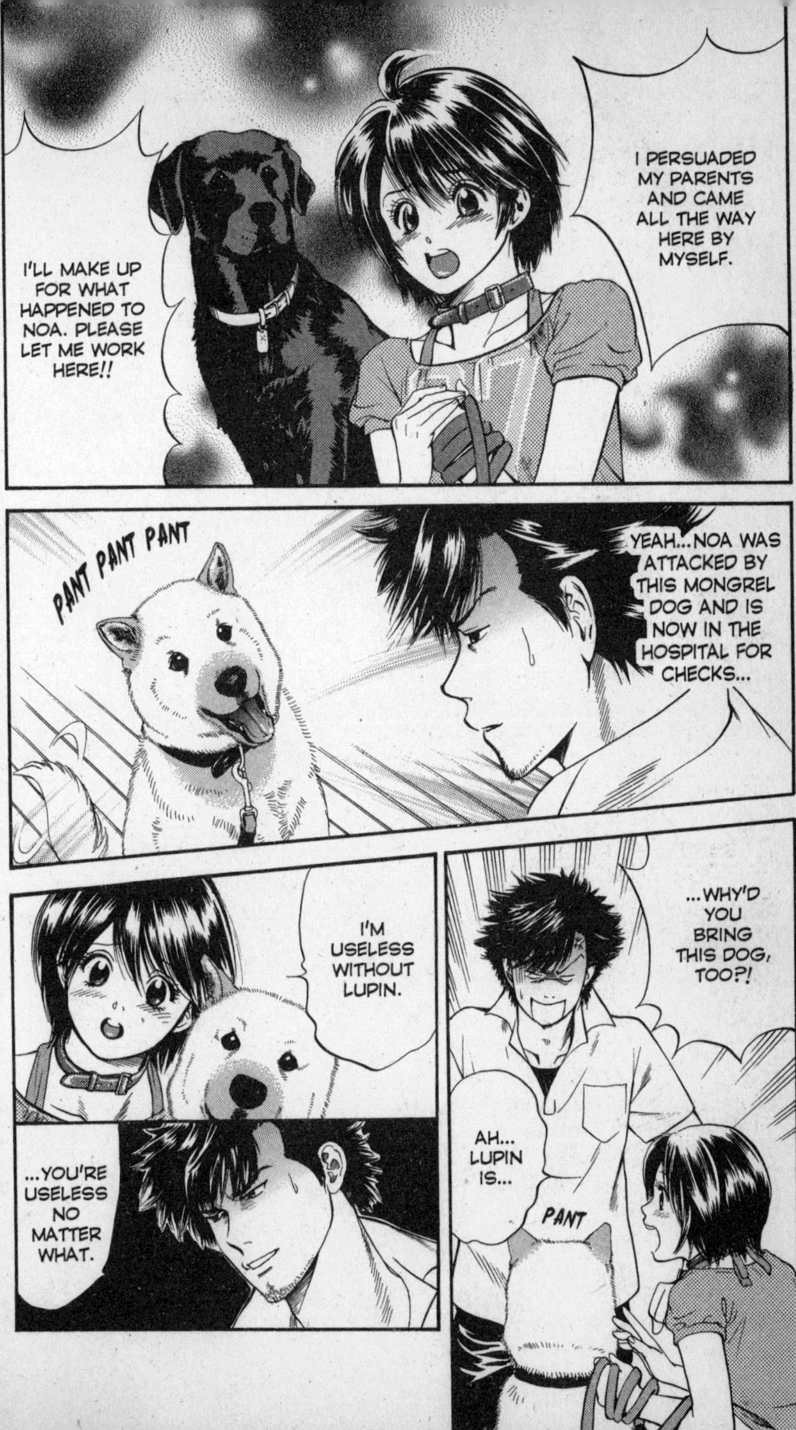
I PERSUADED MY PARENTS AND CAME ALL THE WAY HERE BY MYSELF.
I'LL MAKE UP FOR WHAT HAPPENED TO NOA. PLEASE LET ME WORK HERE!!
YEAH...NOA WAS ATTACKED BY THIS MONGREL DOG AND IS NOW IN THE HOSPITAL FOR CHECKS...
PANT PANT PANT
...WHY'D YOU BRING THIS DOG, TOO?!
AH... LUPIN IS...
PANT
I'M USELESS WITHOUT LUPIN.
...YOU'RE USELESS NO MATTER WHAT.

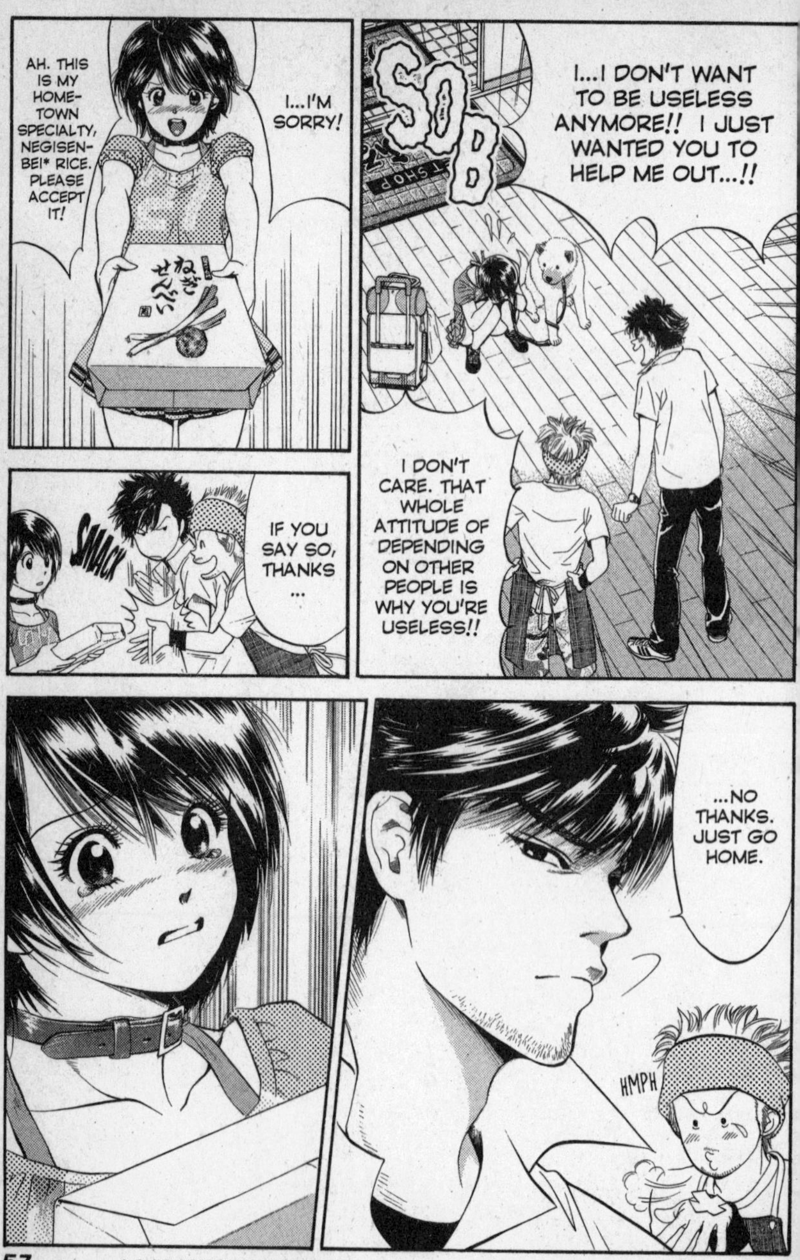

SOB
I...I DON'T WANT TO BE USELESS ANYMORE!! I JUST WANTED YOU TO HELP ME OUT...!!
I DON'T CARE. THAT WHOLE ATTITUDE OF DEPENDING ON OTHER PEOPLE IS WHY YOU'RE USELESS!!
I...I'M SORRY!
AH. THIS IS MY HOME-TOWN SPECIALTY, NEGISEN-BEI* RICE. PLEASE ACCEPT IT!
ねぎせんべい
IF YOU SAY SO, THANKS ...
SMACK
...NO THANKS. JUST GO HOME.
HMPH

* ONION RICE CRACKERS

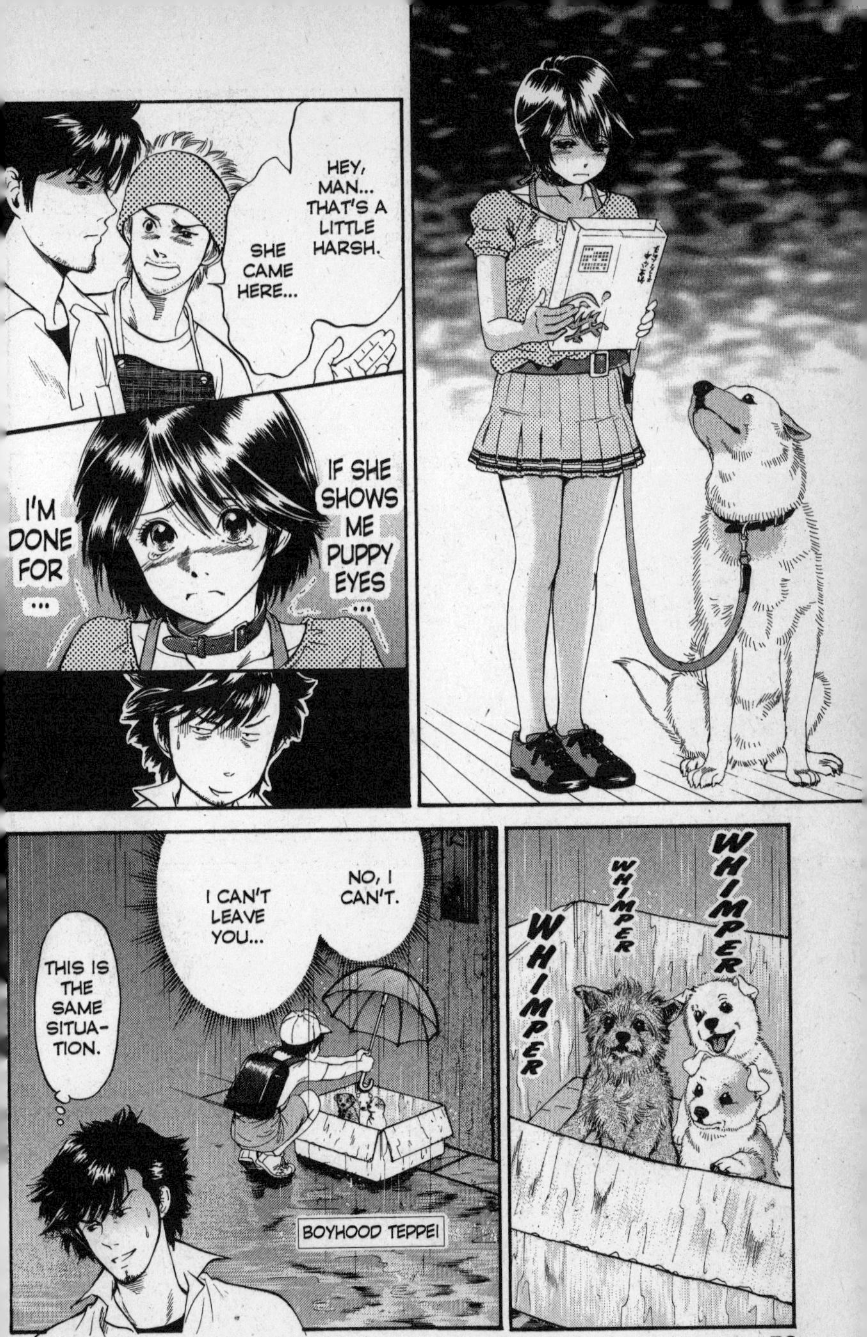
HEY, MAN... THAT'S A LITTLE HARSH.
SHE CAME HERE...
IF SHE SHOWS ME PUPPY EYES ...
I'M DONE FOR ...
WHIMPER
WHIMPER
WHIMPER
NO, I CAN'T.
I CAN'T LEAVE YOU...
BOYHOOD TEPPEI
THIS IS THE SAME SITUATION.

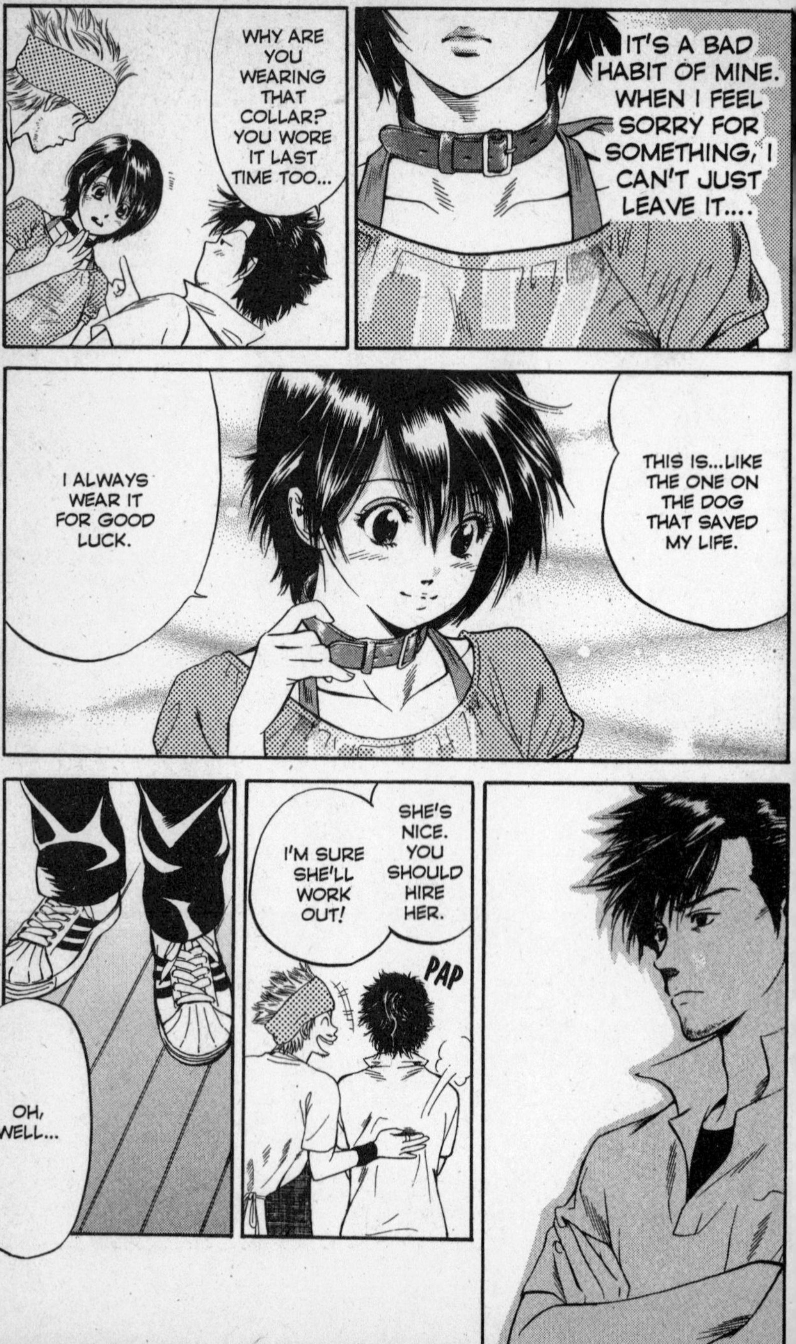
IT'S A BAD HABIT OF MINE. WHEN I FEEL SORRY FOR SOMETHING, I CAN'T JUST LEAVE IT....
WHY ARE YOU WEARING THAT COLLAR? YOU WORE IT LAST TIME TOO...
THIS IS...LIKE THE ONE ON THE DOG THAT SAVED MY LIFE.
I ALWAYS WEAR IT FOR GOOD LUCK.
SHE'S NICE. YOU SHOULD HIRE HER.
I'M SURE SHE'LL WORK OUT!
PAP
OH, WELL...

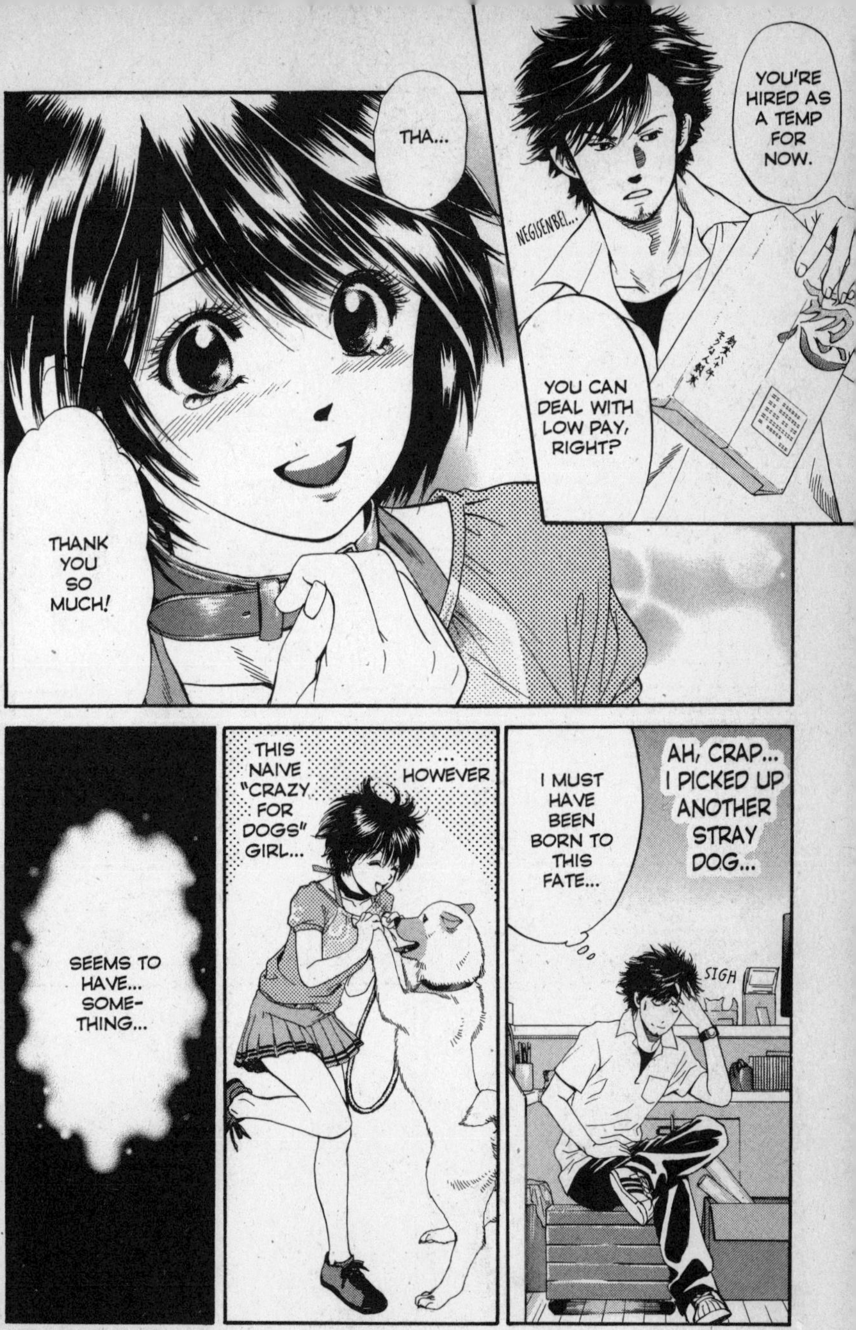
YOU'RE HIRED AS A TEMP FOR NOW.
NEGISENBEI...
YOU CAN DEAL WITH LOW PAY, RIGHT?
THA...
THANK YOU SO MUCH!
AH, CRAP... I PICKED UP ANOTHER STRAY DOG...
I MUST HAVE BEEN BORN TO THIS FATE...
SIGH
... HOWEVER
THIS NAIVE "CRAZY FOR DOGS" GIRL...
SEEMS TO HAVE... SOME-THING...

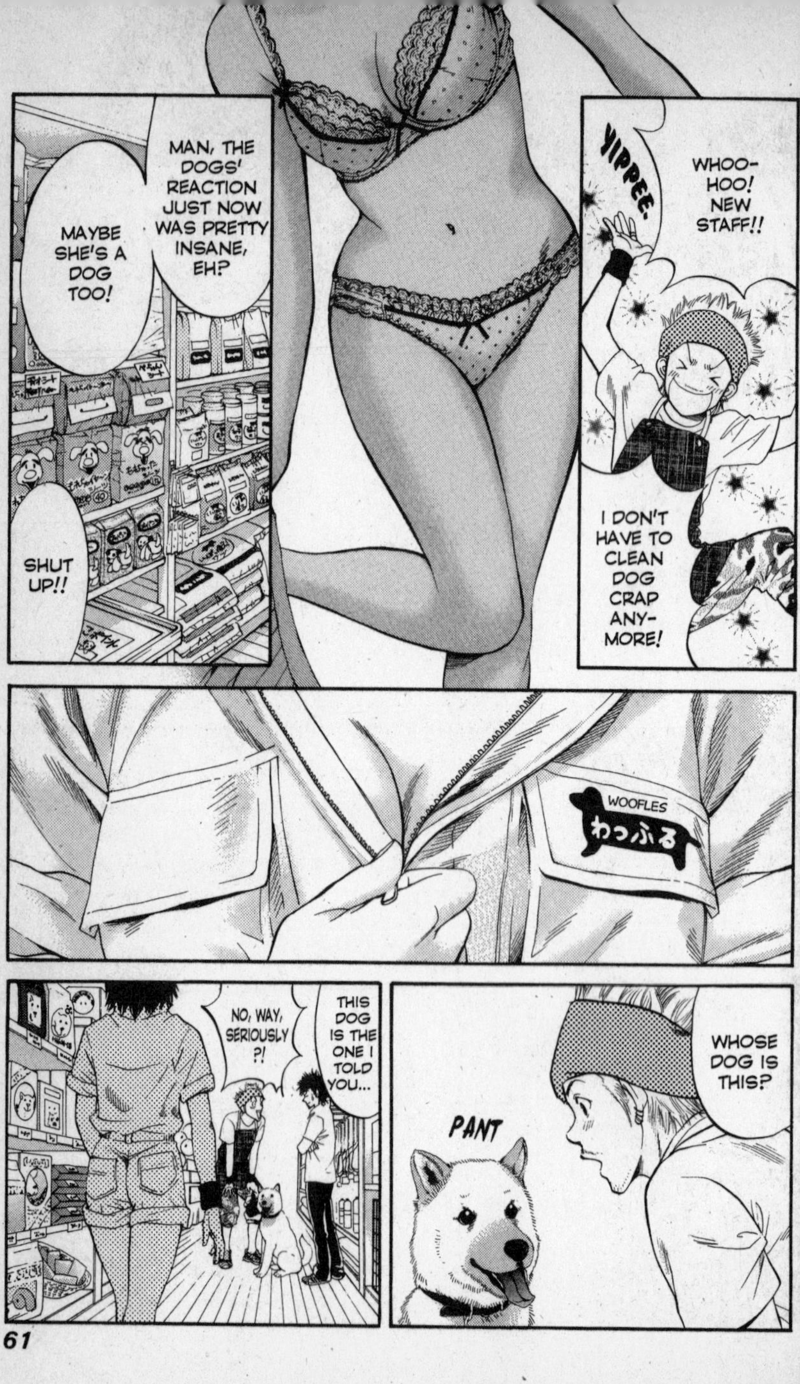

WHOO-HOO! NEW STAFF!!
YIPPEE.
I DON'T HAVE TO CLEAN DOG CRAP ANYMORE!
MAN, THE DOGS' REACTION JUST NOW WAS PRETTY INSANE, EH?
MAYBE SHE'S A DOG TOO!
SHUT UP!!
WOOFLES
わっふる
WHOSE DOG IS THIS?
PANT
THIS DOG IS THE ONE I TOLD YOU...
NO, WAY, SERIOUSLY?!

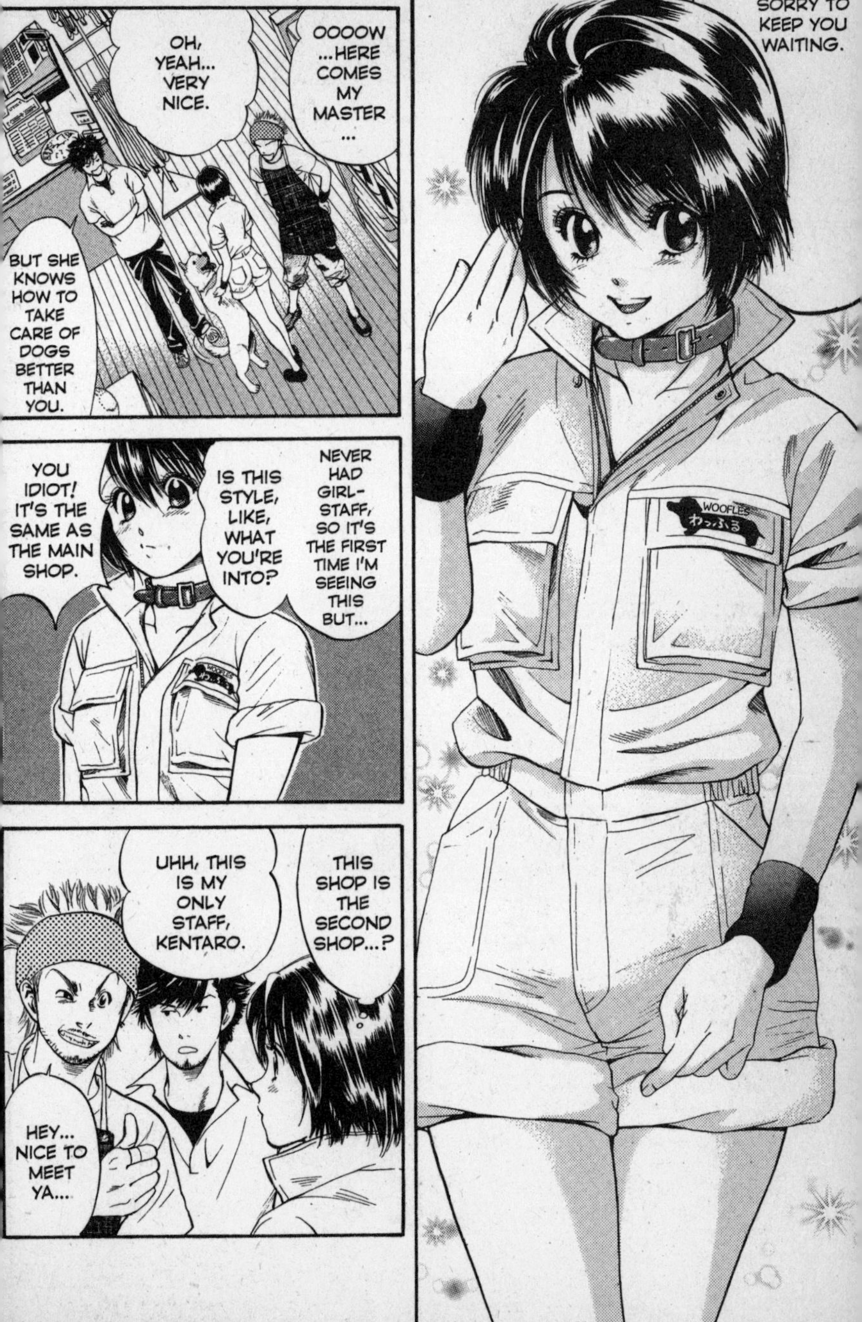
SORRY TO KEEP YOU WAITING.
WOOFLES わっふる
OOOOW ...HERE COMES MY MASTER ...
OH, YEAH... VERY NICE.
BUT SHE KNOWS HOW TO TAKE CARE OF DOGS BETTER THAN YOU.
NEVER HAD GIRL-STAFF, SO IT'S THE FIRST TIME I'M SEEING THIS BUT...
IS THIS STYLE, LIKE, WHAT YOU'RE INTO?
YOU IDIOT! IT'S THE SAME AS THE MAIN SHOP.
THIS SHOP IS THE SECOND SHOP...?
UHH, THIS IS MY ONLY STAFF, KENTARO.
HEY... NICE TO MEET YA...

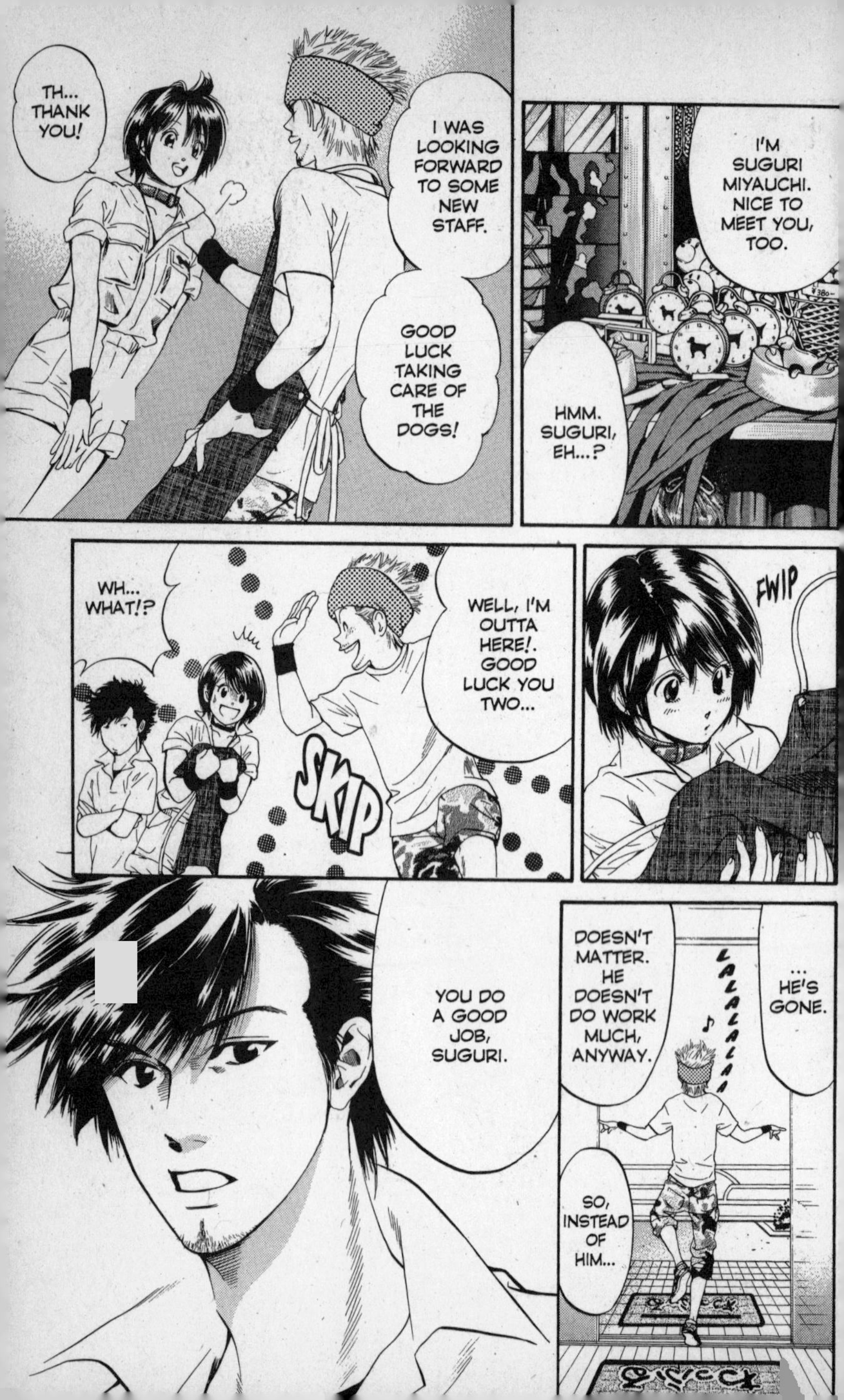
I'M SUGURI MIYAUCHI. NICE TO MEET YOU, TOO.
HMM. SUGURI, EH...?
I WAS LOOKING FORWARD TO SOME NEW STAFF.
GOOD LUCK TAKING CARE OF THE DOGS!
TH... THANK YOU!
FWIP
WELL, I'M OUTTA HERE!. GOOD LUCK YOU TWO...
SKIP
WH... WHAT!?
... HE'S GONE.
LALALALAA ♪
DOESN'T MATTER. HE DOESN'T DO WORK MUCH, ANYWAY.
SO, INSTEAD OF HIM...
YOU DO A GOOD JOB, SUGURI.

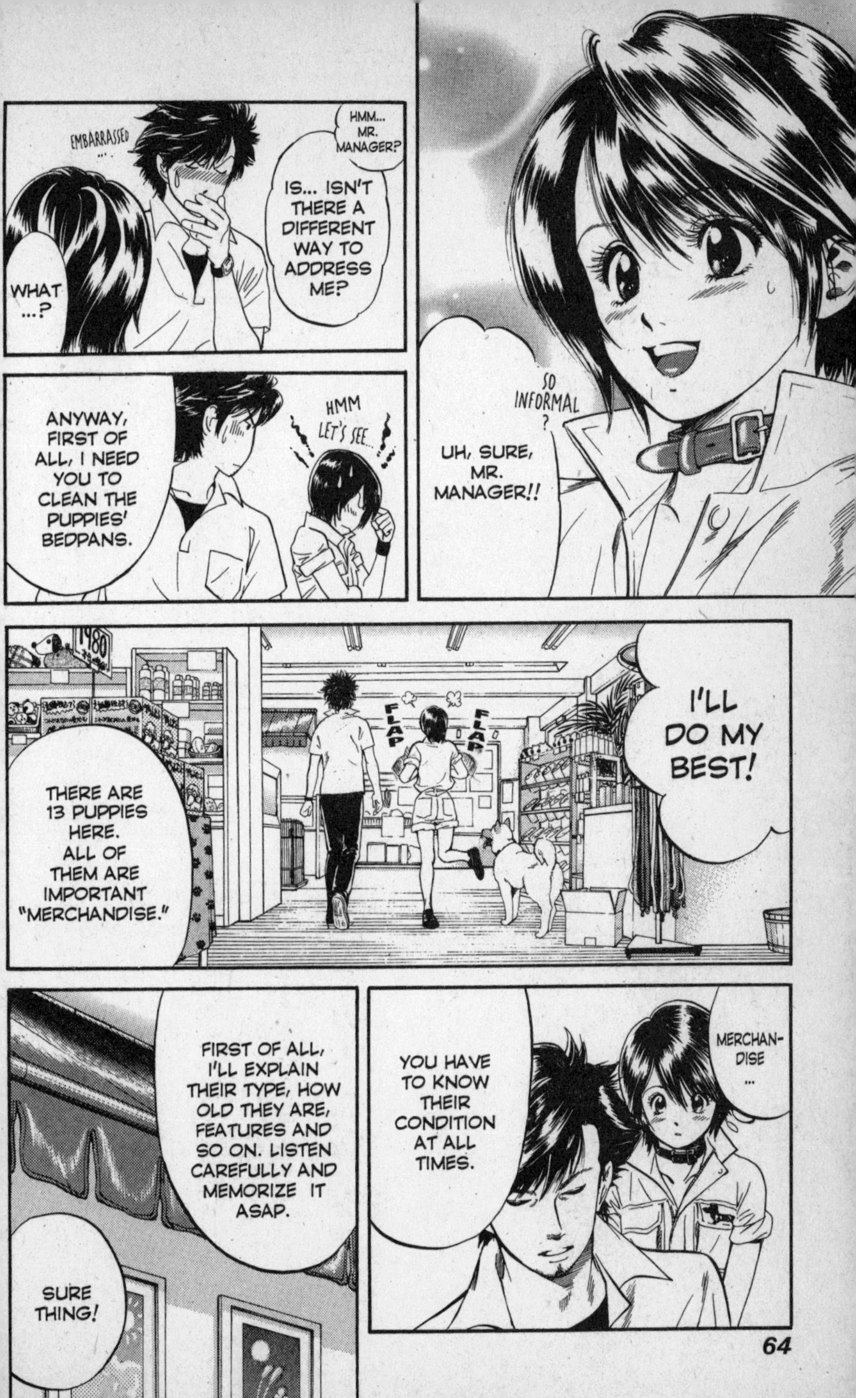
UH, SURE, MR. MANAGER!!
SO INFORMAL ?
HMM... MR. MANAGER?
IS... ISN'T THERE A DIFFERENT WAY TO ADDRESS ME?
EMBARRASSED ...
WHAT ...?
HMM LET'S SEE...
ANYWAY, FIRST OF ALL, I NEED YOU TO CLEAN THE PUPPIES' BEDPANS.
I'LL DO MY BEST!
FLAP
FLAP
1980
THERE ARE 13 PUPPIES HERE. ALL OF THEM ARE IMPORTANT "MERCHANDISE."
MERCHAN-DISE ...
YOU HAVE TO KNOW THEIR CONDITION AT ALL TIMES.
FIRST OF ALL, I'LL EXPLAIN THEIR TYPE, HOW OLD THEY ARE, FEATURES AND SO ON. LISTEN CAREFULLY AND MEMORIZE IT ASAP.
SURE THING!

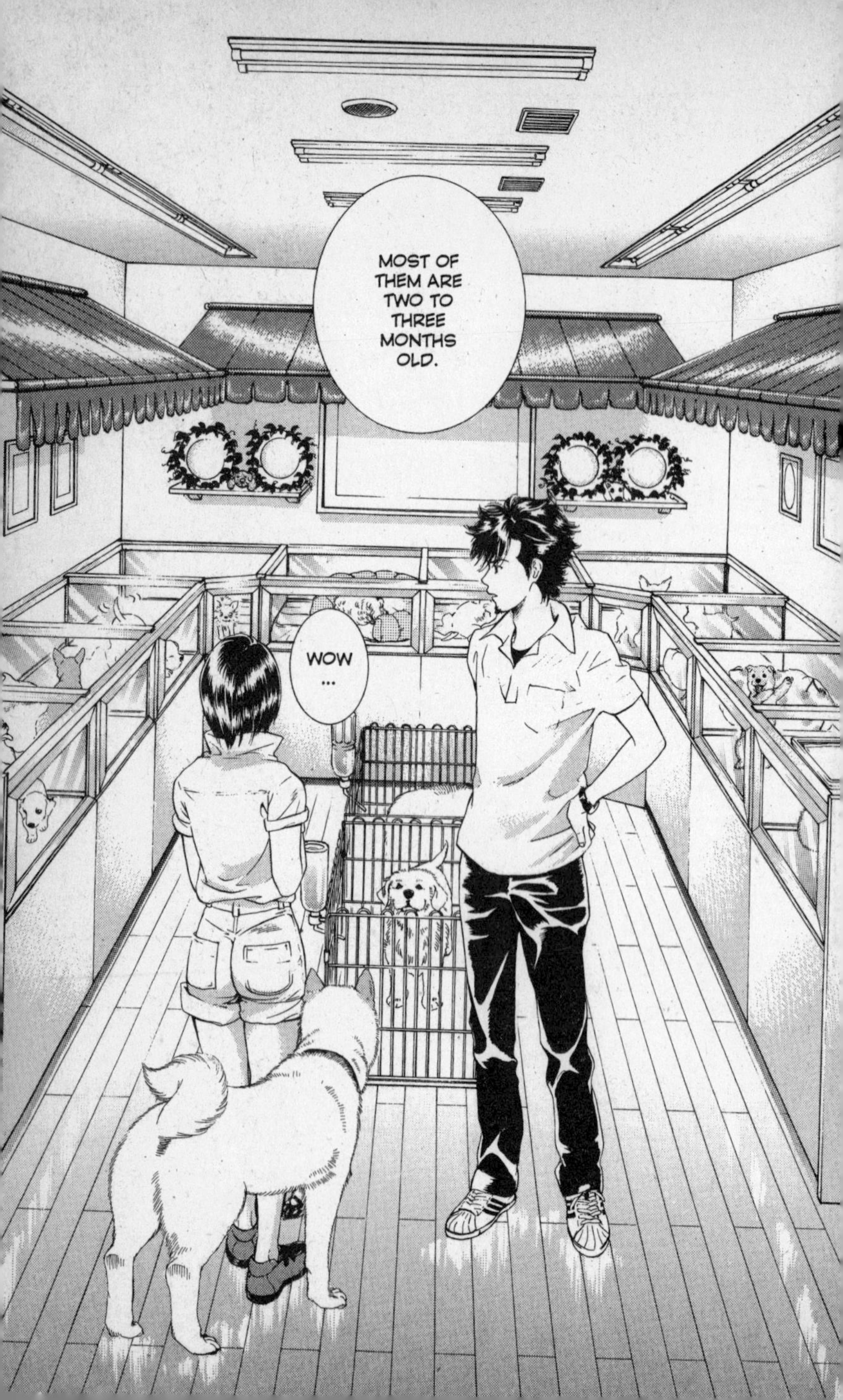
MOST OF THEM ARE TWO TO THREE MONTHS OLD.
WOW ...

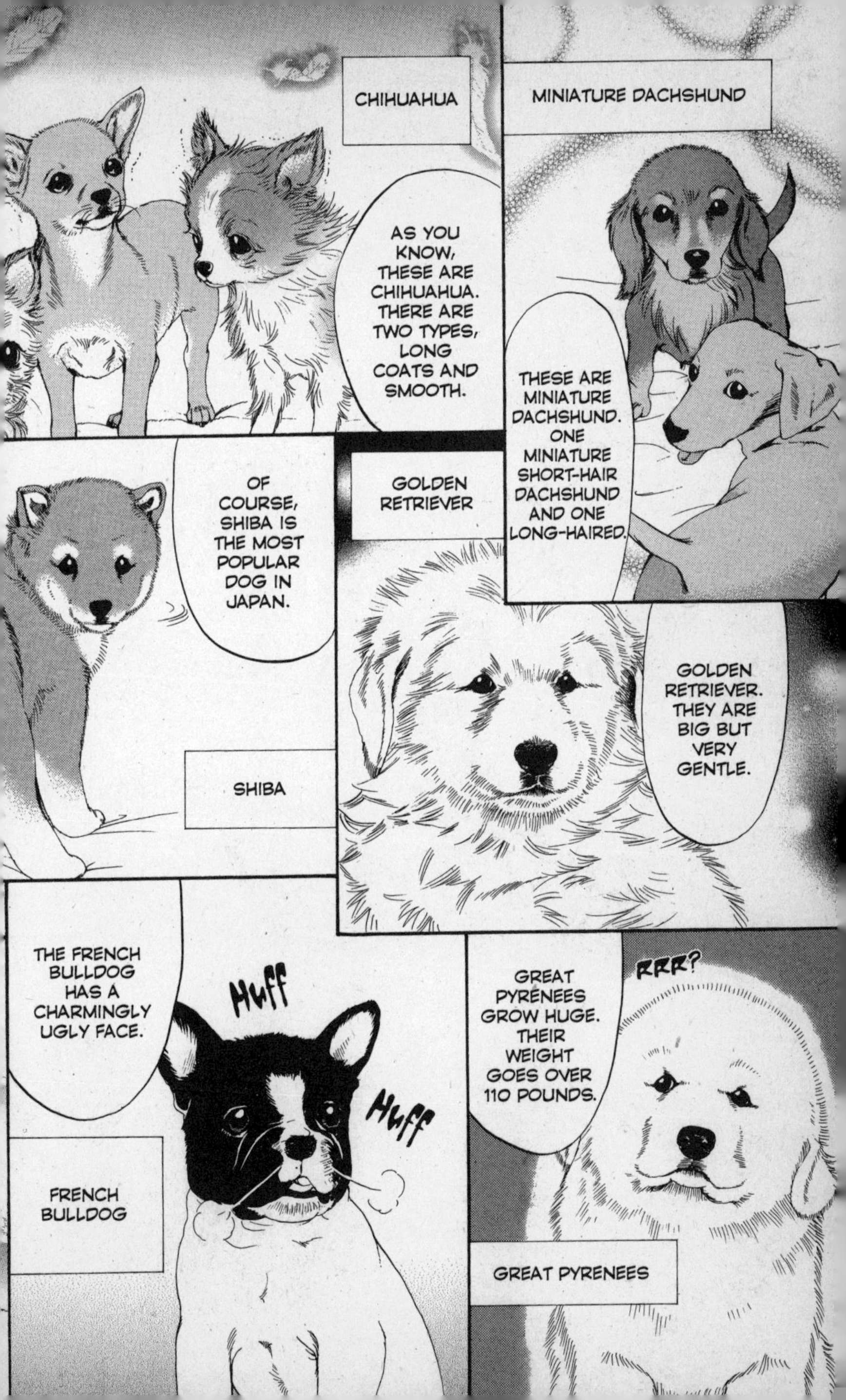
MINIATURE DACHSHUND
THESE ARE MINIATURE DACHSHUND. ONE MINIATURE SHORT-HAIR DACHSHUND AND ONE LONG-HAIRED.
CHIHUAHUA
AS YOU KNOW, THESE ARE CHIHUAHUA. THERE ARE TWO TYPES, LONG COATS AND SMOOTH.
GOLDEN RETRIEVER
GOLDEN RETRIEVER. THEY ARE BIG BUT VERY GENTLE.
OF COURSE, SHIBA IS THE MOST POPULAR DOG IN JAPAN.
SHIBA
RRR?
GREAT PYRENEES GROW HUGE. THEIR WEIGHT GOES OVER 110 POUNDS.
GREAT PYRENEES
THE FRENCH BULLDOG HAS A CHARMINGLY UGLY FACE.
HUFF
HUFF
FRENCH BULLDOG

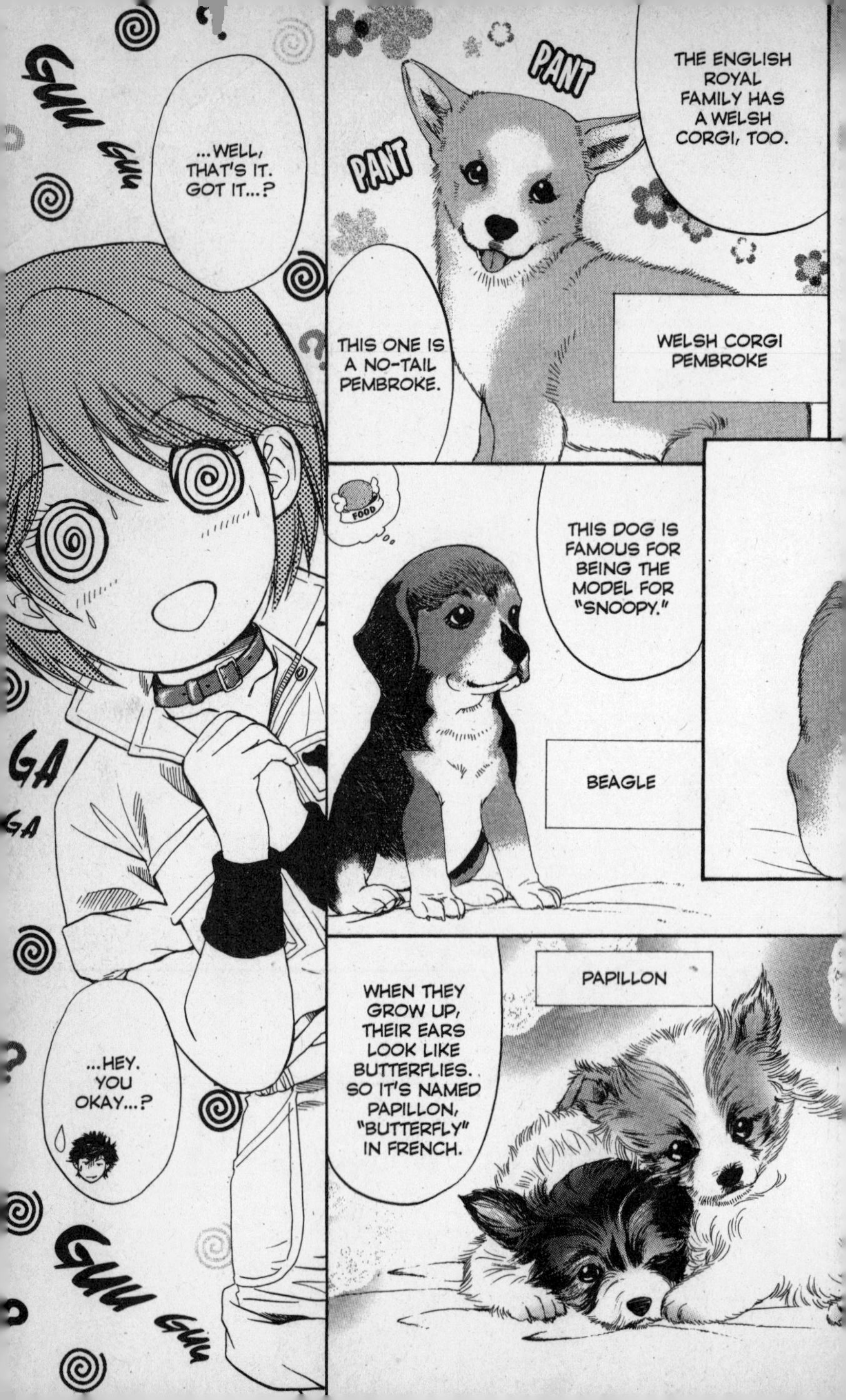
THE ENGLISH ROYAL FAMILY HAS A WELSH CORGI, TOO.
PANT
PANT
WELSH CORGI PEMBROKE
THIS ONE IS A NO-TAIL PEMBROKE.
THIS DOG IS FAMOUS FOR BEING THE MODEL FOR "SNOOPY."
FOOD
BEAGLE
PAPILLON
WHEN THEY GROW UP, THEIR EARS LOOK LIKE BUTTERFLIES. SO IT'S NAMED PAPILLON, "BUTTERFLY" IN FRENCH.
GUU GUU
...WELL, THAT'S IT. GOT IT...?
GA GA
...HEY. YOU OKAY...?
GUU GUU

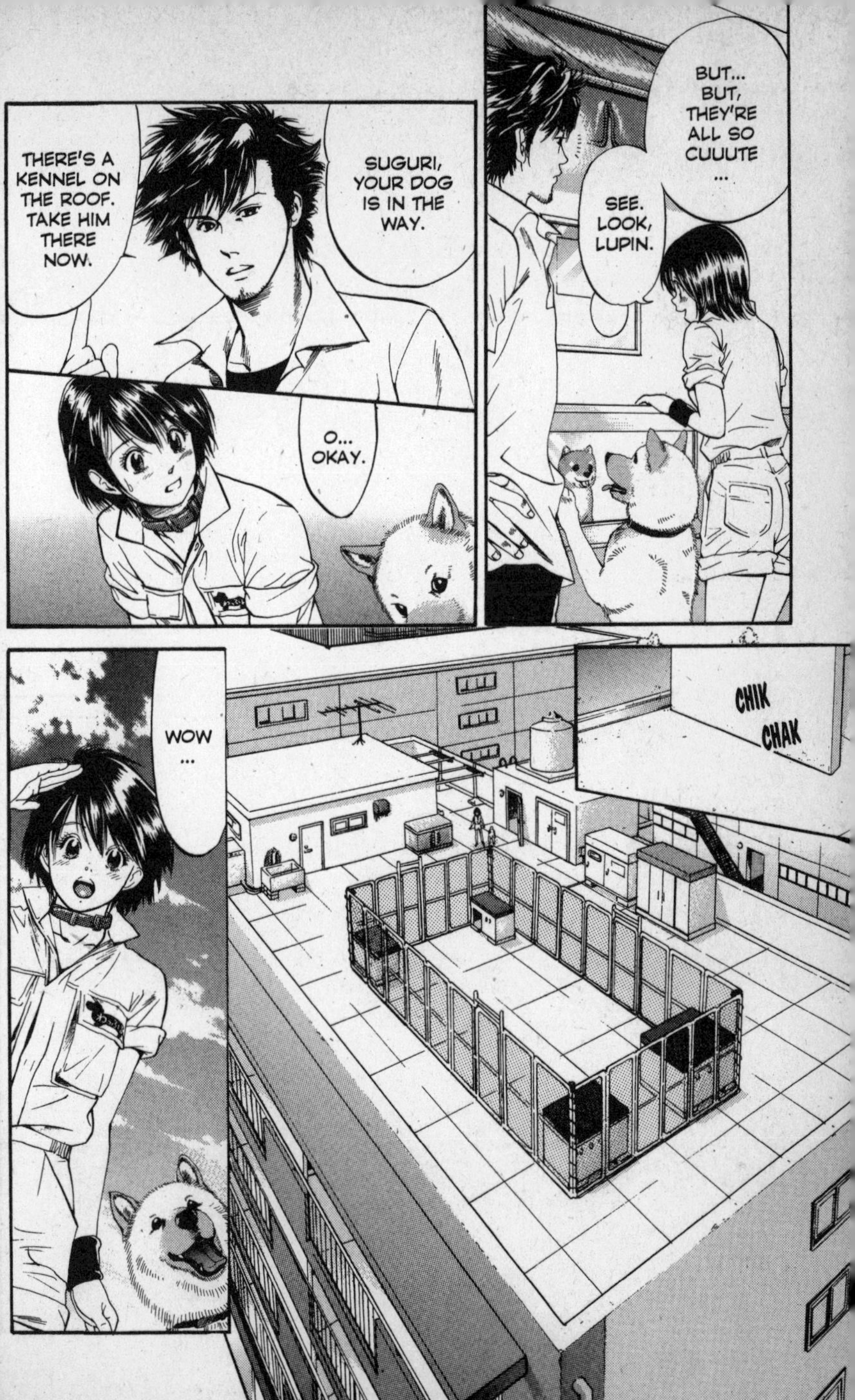
BUT... BUT, THEY'RE ALL SO CUUUTE ...
SEE. LOOK, LUPIN.
SUGURI, YOUR DOG IS IN THE WAY.
THERE'S A KENNEL ON THE ROOF. TAKE HIM THERE NOW.
O... OKAY.
CHIK
CHAK
WOW ...

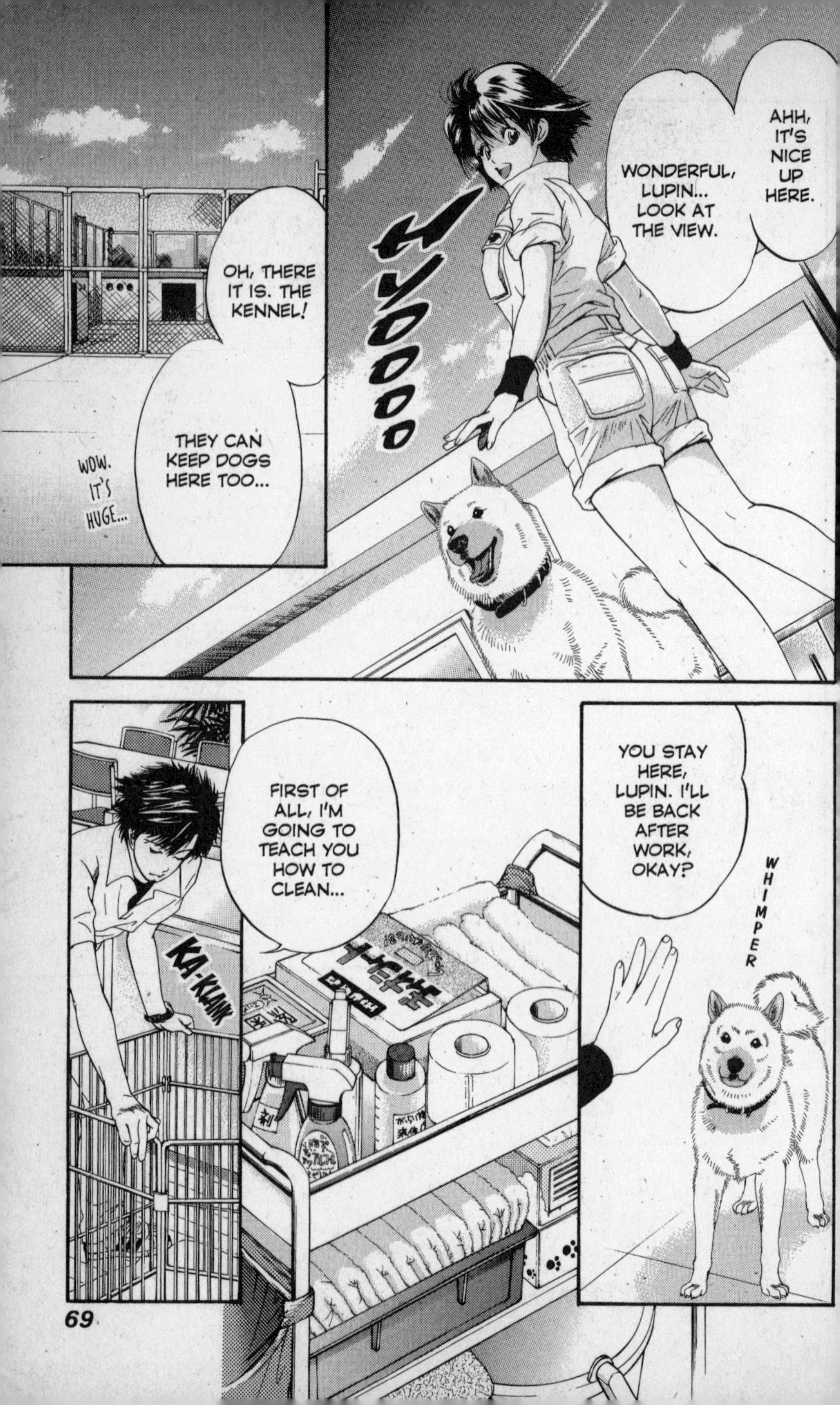
AHH, IT'S NICE UP HERE.
WONDERFUL, LUPIN... LOOK AT THE VIEW.
HYOOOOO
OH, THERE IT IS. THE KENNEL!
THEY CAN KEEP DOGS HERE TOO...
WOW. IT'S HUGE...
YOU STAY HERE, LUPIN. I'LL BE BACK AFTER WORK, OKAY?
WHIMPER
FIRST OF ALL, I'M GOING TO TEACH YOU HOW TO CLEAN...
KA-KLANK

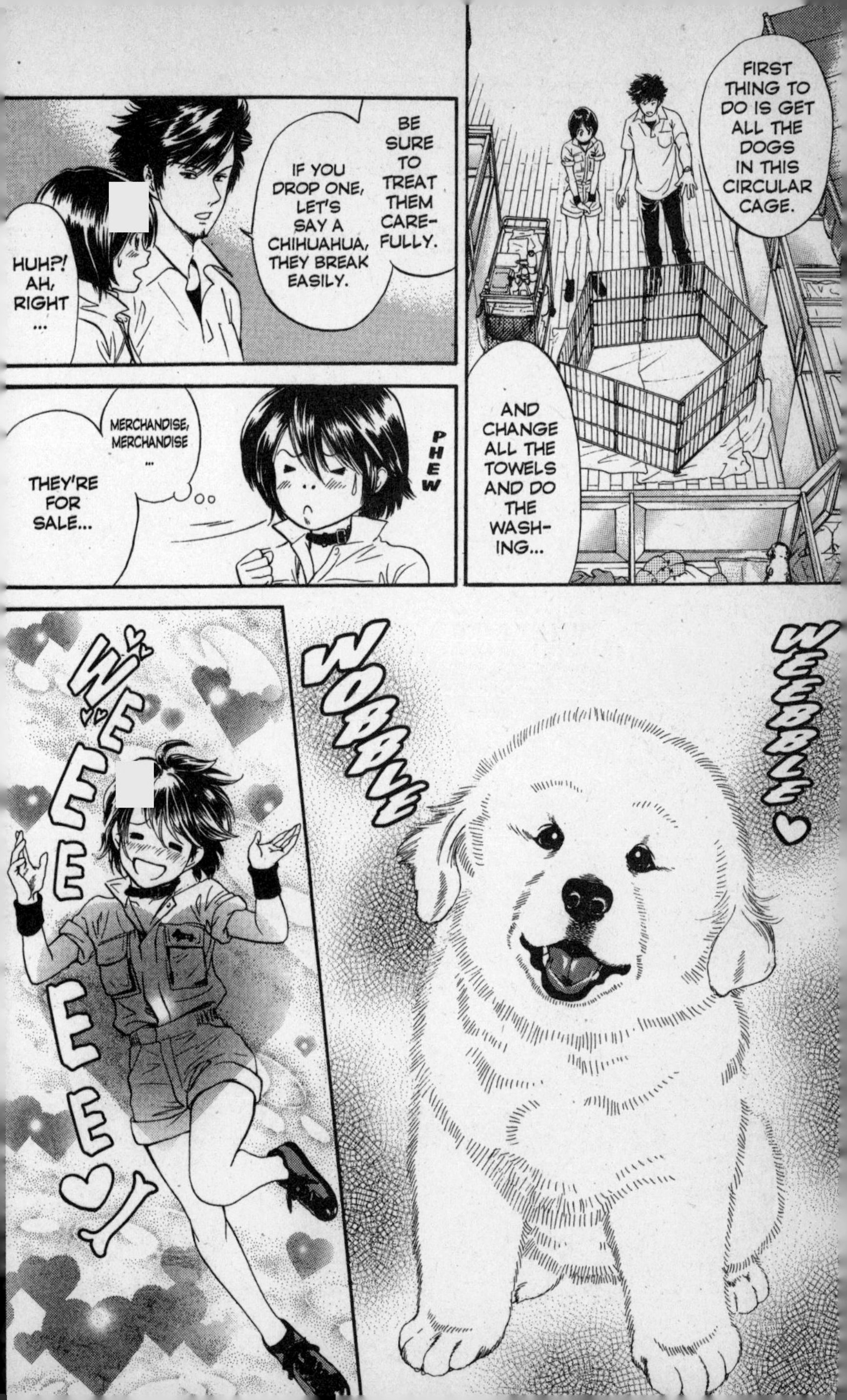
FIRST THING TO DO IS GET ALL THE DOGS IN THIS CIRCULAR CAGE.
AND CHANGE ALL THE TOWELS AND DO THE WASHING...
BE SURE TO TREAT THEM CAREFULLY.
IF YOU DROP ONE, LET'S SAY A CHIHUAHUA, THEY BREAK EASILY.
HUH?! AH, RIGHT...
PHEW
MERCHANDISE, MERCHANDISE...
THEY'RE FOR SALE...
WEEBBLE♥
WOBBLE
WEEEEEE♥!

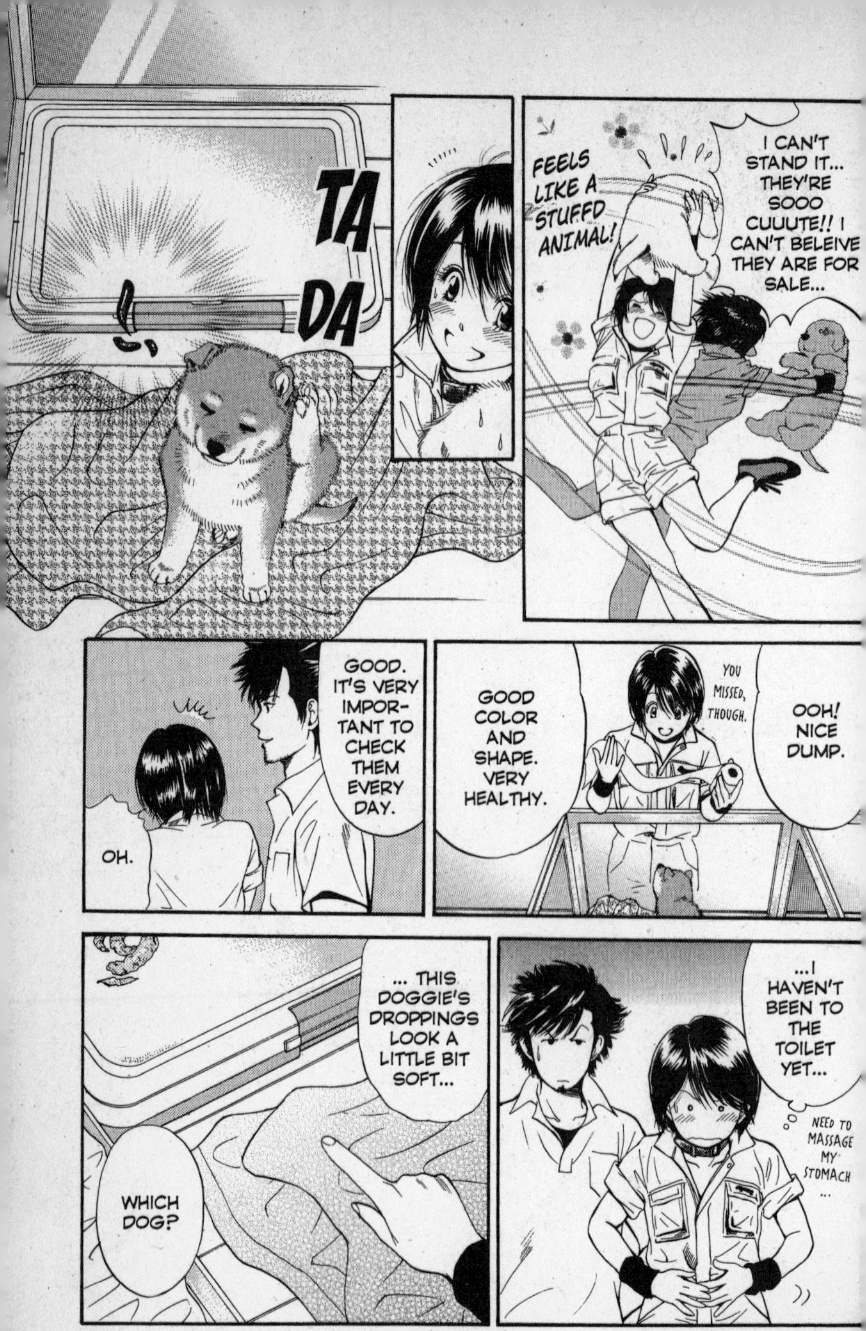

I CAN'T STAND IT... THEY'RE SOOO CUUUTE!! I CAN'T BELEIVE THEY ARE FOR SALE...
FEELS LIKE A STUFFD ANIMAL!
TA DA
OOH! NICE DUMP.
YOU MISSED, THOUGH.
GOOD COLOR AND SHAPE. VERY HEALTHY.
GOOD. IT'S VERY IMPORTANT TO CHECK THEM EVERY DAY.
OH.
...I HAVEN'T BEEN TO THE TOILET YET...
NEED TO MASSAGE MY STOMACH ...
... THIS DOGGIE'S DROPPINGS LOOK A LITTLE BIT SOFT...
WHICH DOG?

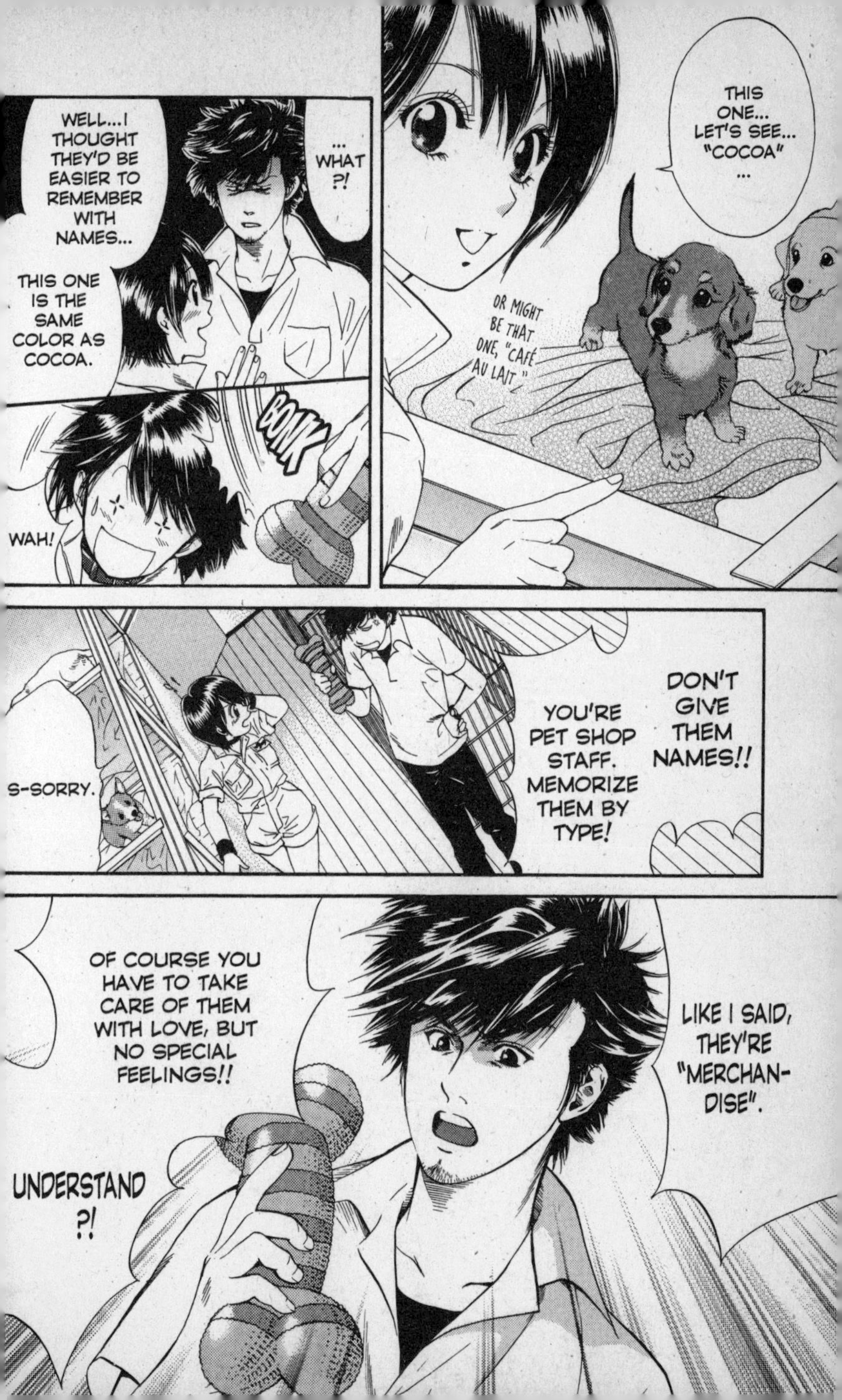
THIS ONE... LET'S SEE... "COCOA" ...
OR MIGHT BE THAT ONE, "CAFÉ AU LAIT"
... WHAT ?!
WELL...I THOUGHT THEY'D BE EASIER TO REMEMBER WITH NAMES...
THIS ONE IS THE SAME COLOR AS COCOA.
BONK
WAH!
DON'T GIVE THEM NAMES!!
YOU'RE PET SHOP STAFF. MEMORIZE THEM BY TYPE!
S-SORRY.
LIKE I SAID, THEY'RE "MERCHANDISE".
OF COURSE YOU HAVE TO TAKE CARE OF THEM WITH LOVE, BUT NO SPECIAL FEELINGS!!
UNDERSTAND ?!

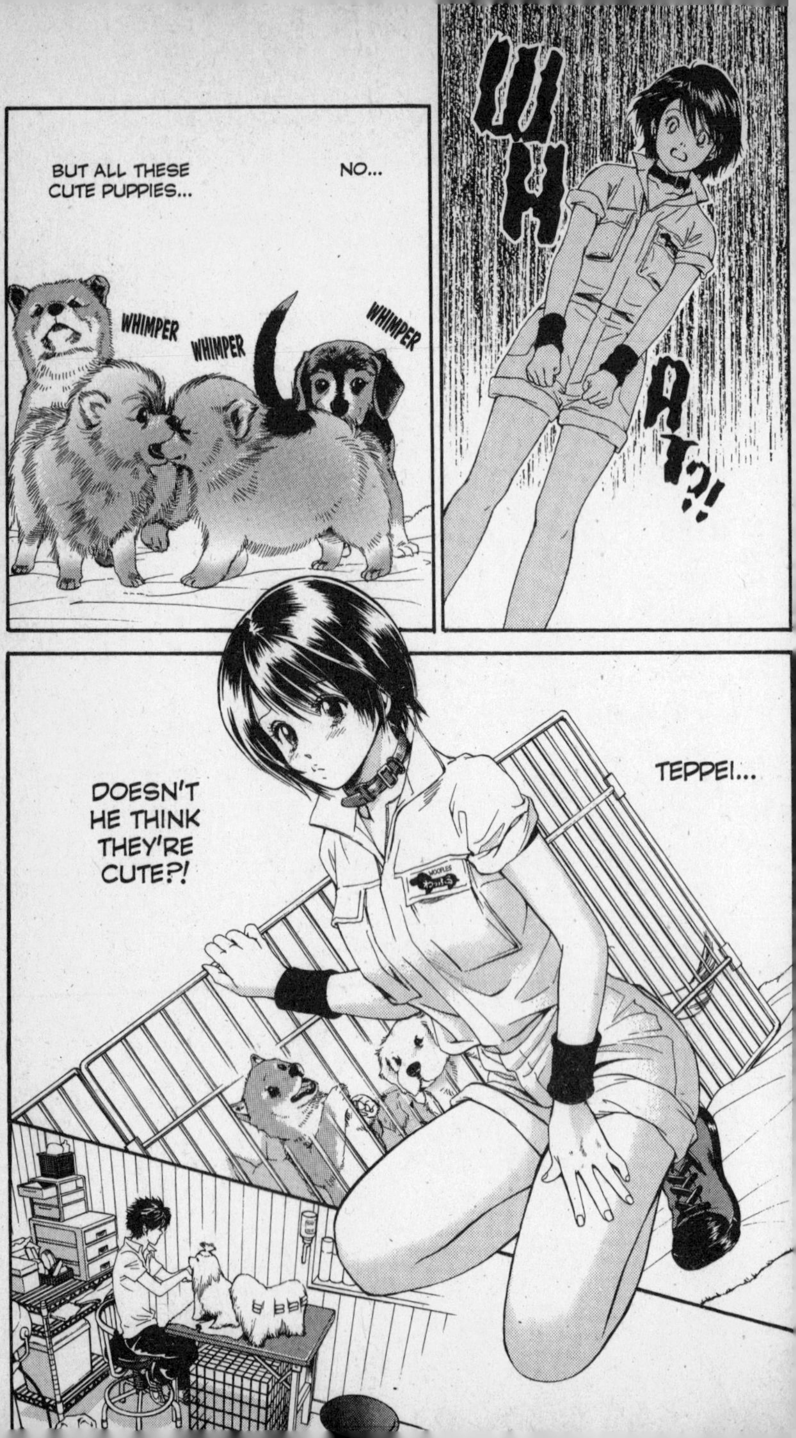

UH
NO...
BUT ALL THESE CUTE PUPPIES...
WHIMPER
WHIMPER
WHIMPER
TEPPEI...
DOESN'T HE THINK THEY'RE CUTE?!

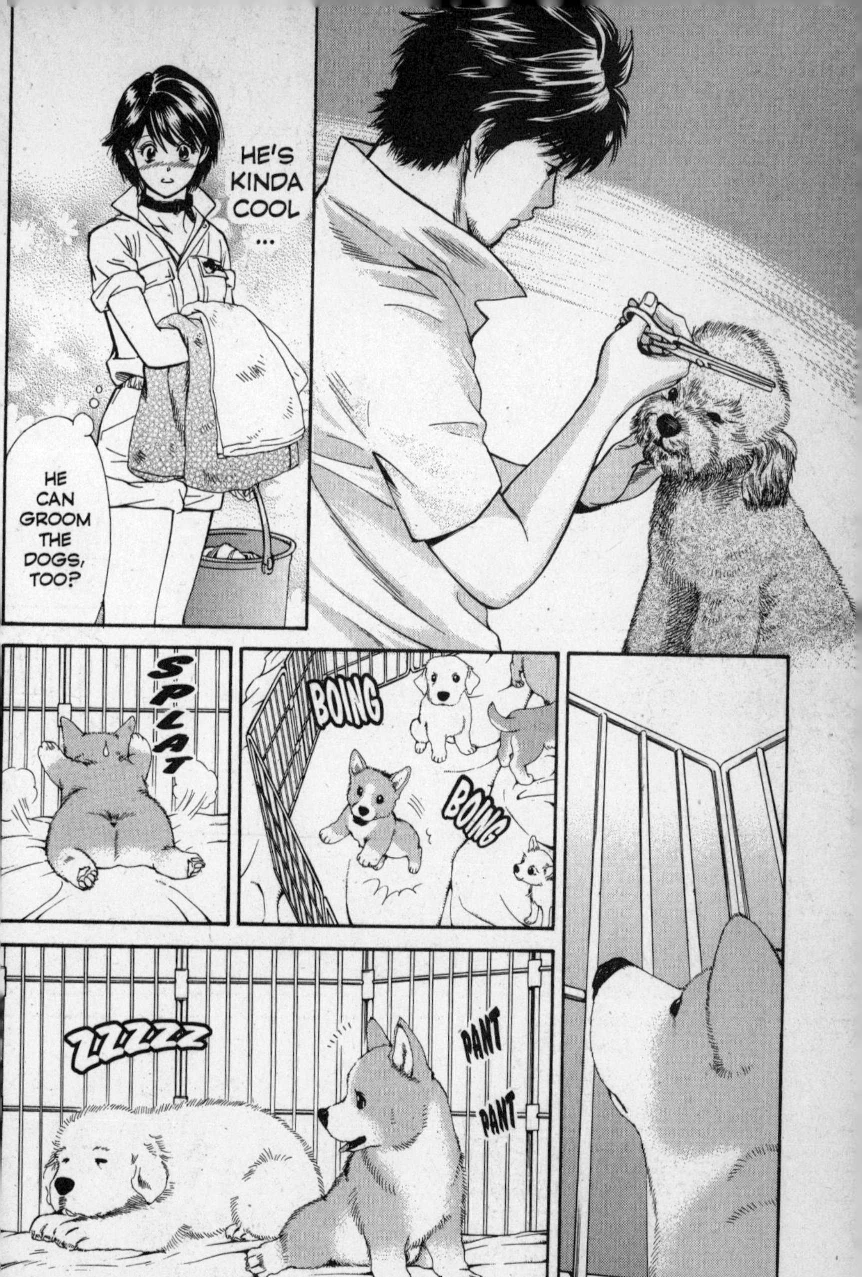
HE'S KINDA COOL ...
HE CAN GROOM THE DOGS, TOO?
BOING
BOING
SPLAT
PANT
PANT
ZZZZZ

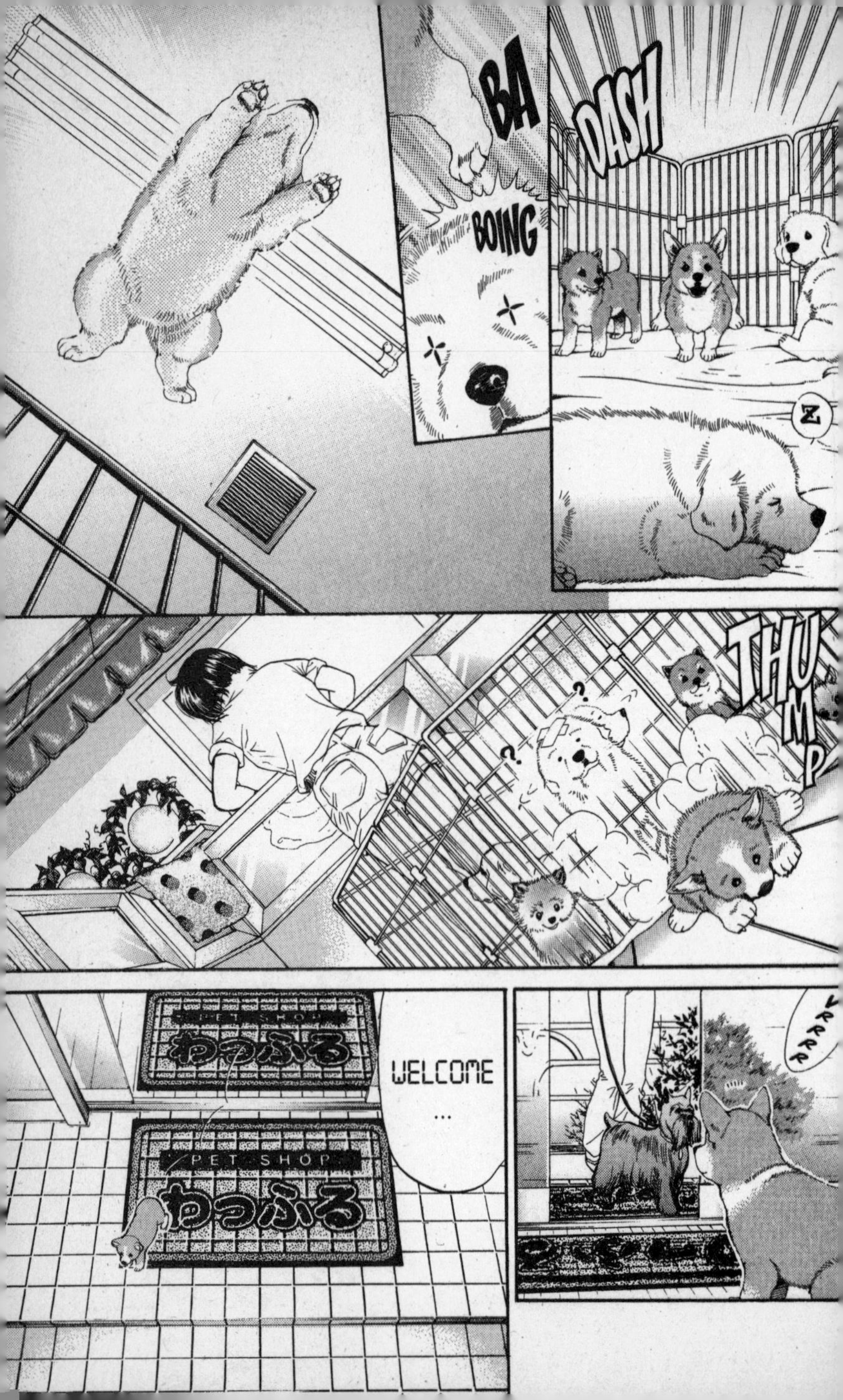
DASH
Z
BA
BOING
THUMP
VRRRR
PET SHOP
わっふる
WELCOME ...
PET SHOP
わっふる

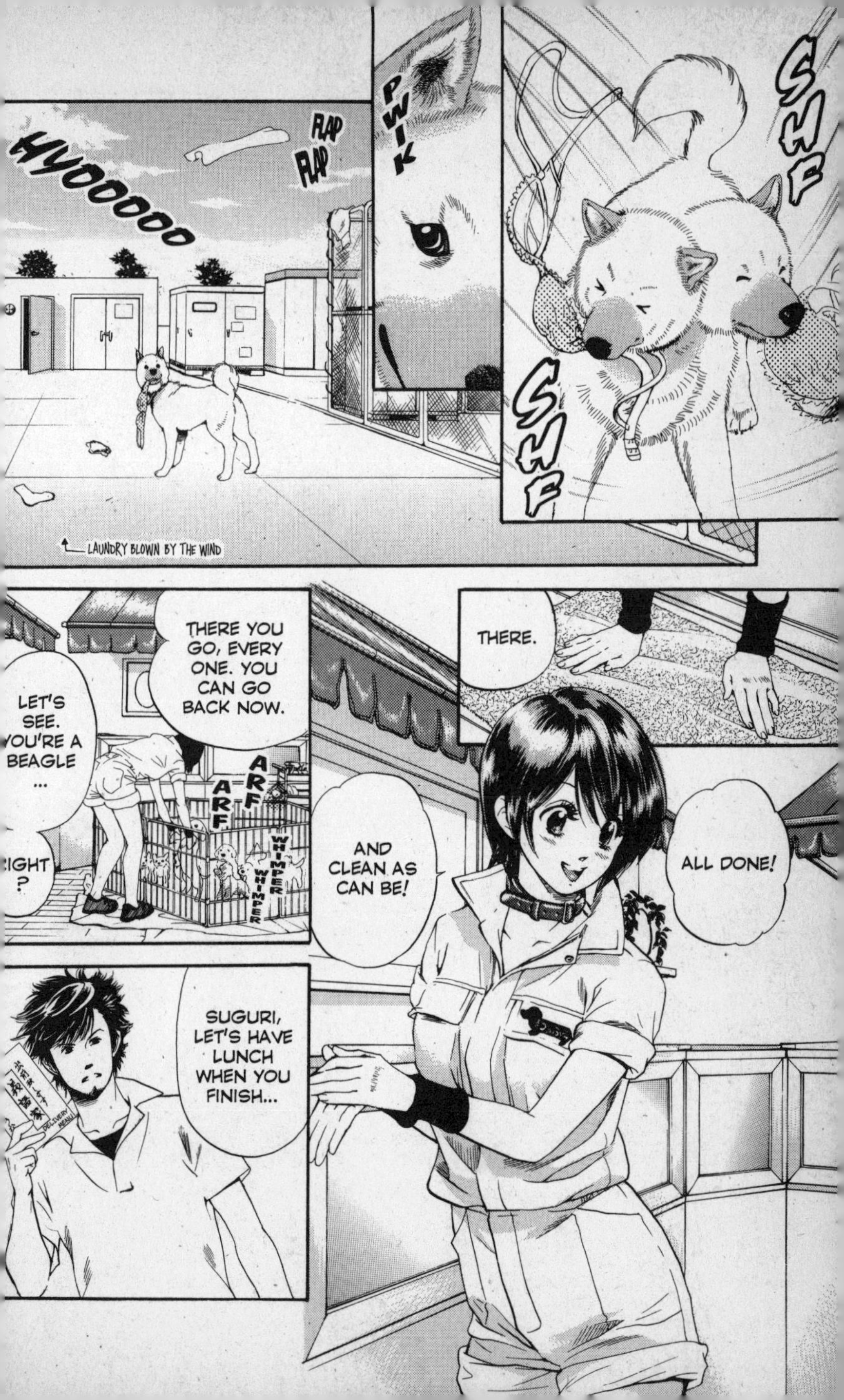
SHF
SHF
PWIK
HYOOOOOO
FLAP
FLAP
LAUNDRY BLOWN BY THE WIND
THERE.
ALL DONE!
AND CLEAN AS CAN BE!
THERE YOU GO, EVERY ONE. YOU CAN GO BACK NOW.
ARF
ARF
WHIMPER
WHIMPER
LET'S SEE. YOU'RE A BEAGLE ...
IGHT ?
SUGURI, LET'S HAVE LUNCH WHEN YOU FINISH...
DELIVERY MENU

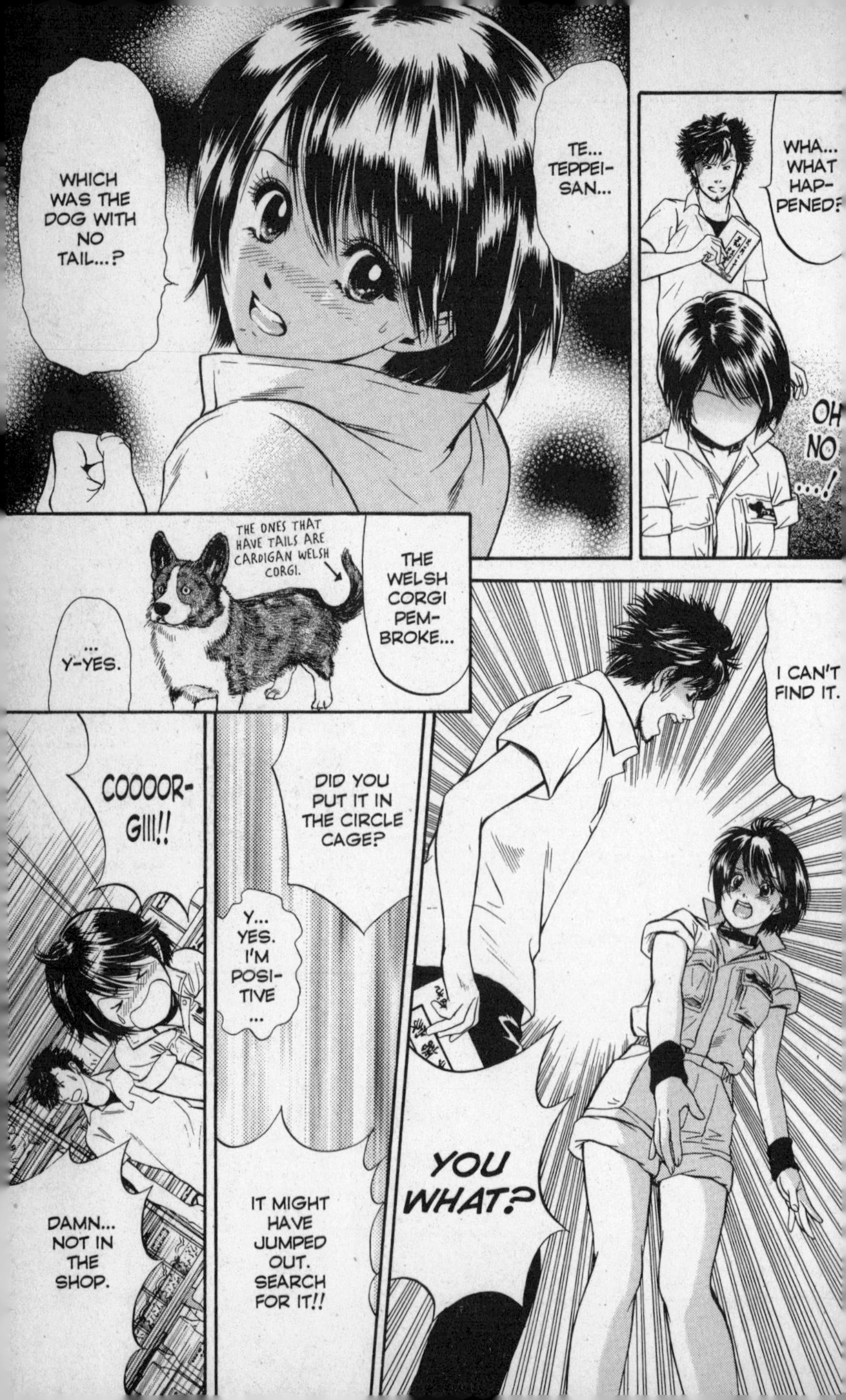
WHA... WHAT HAP-PENED?!
OH NO...!
TE... TEPPEI-SAN...
WHICH WAS THE DOG WITH NO TAIL...?
I CAN'T FIND IT.
YOU WHAT?
THE WELSH CORGI PEM-BROKE...
THE ONES THAT HAVE TAILS ARE CARDIGAN WELSH CORGI.
... Y-YES.
DID YOU PUT IT IN THE CIRCLE CAGE?
Y... YES. I'M POSI-TIVE ...
IT MIGHT HAVE JUMPED OUT. SEARCH FOR IT!!
COOOOR-GIII!!
DAMN... NOT IN THE SHOP.

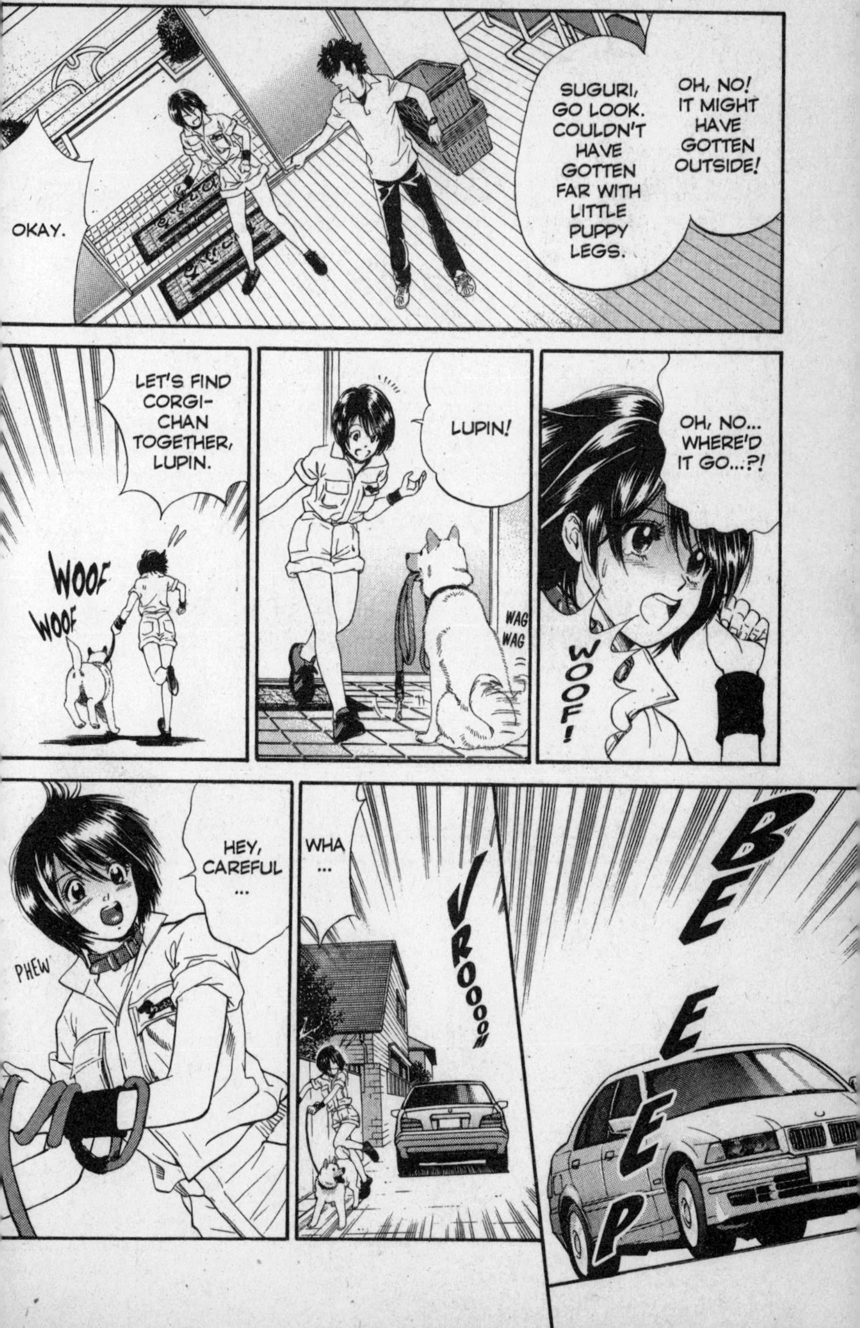
OH, NO! IT MIGHT HAVE GOTTEN OUTSIDE!
SUGURI, GO LOOK. COULDN'T HAVE GOTTEN FAR WITH LITTLE PUPPY LEGS.
OKAY.
OH, NO... WHERE'D IT GO...?!
WOOF!
LUPIN!
WAG WAG
LET'S FIND CORGI-CHAN TOGETHER, LUPIN.
WOOF WOOF
BEEEEP
WHA ...
VROOOOOM
HEY, CAREFUL ...
PHEW

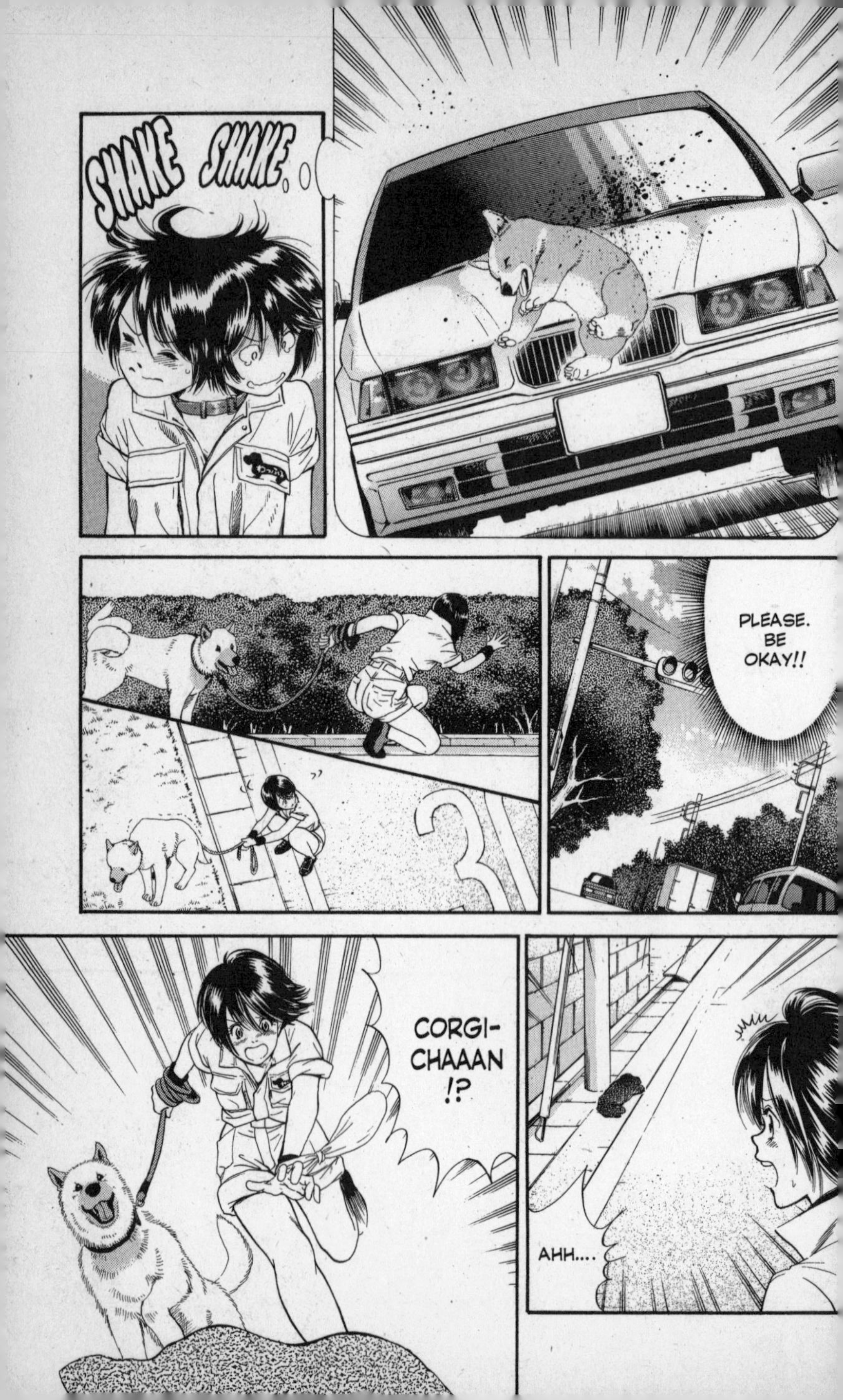
SHAKE SHAKE
PLEASE. BE OKAY!!
CORGI-CHAAAN !?
AHH....

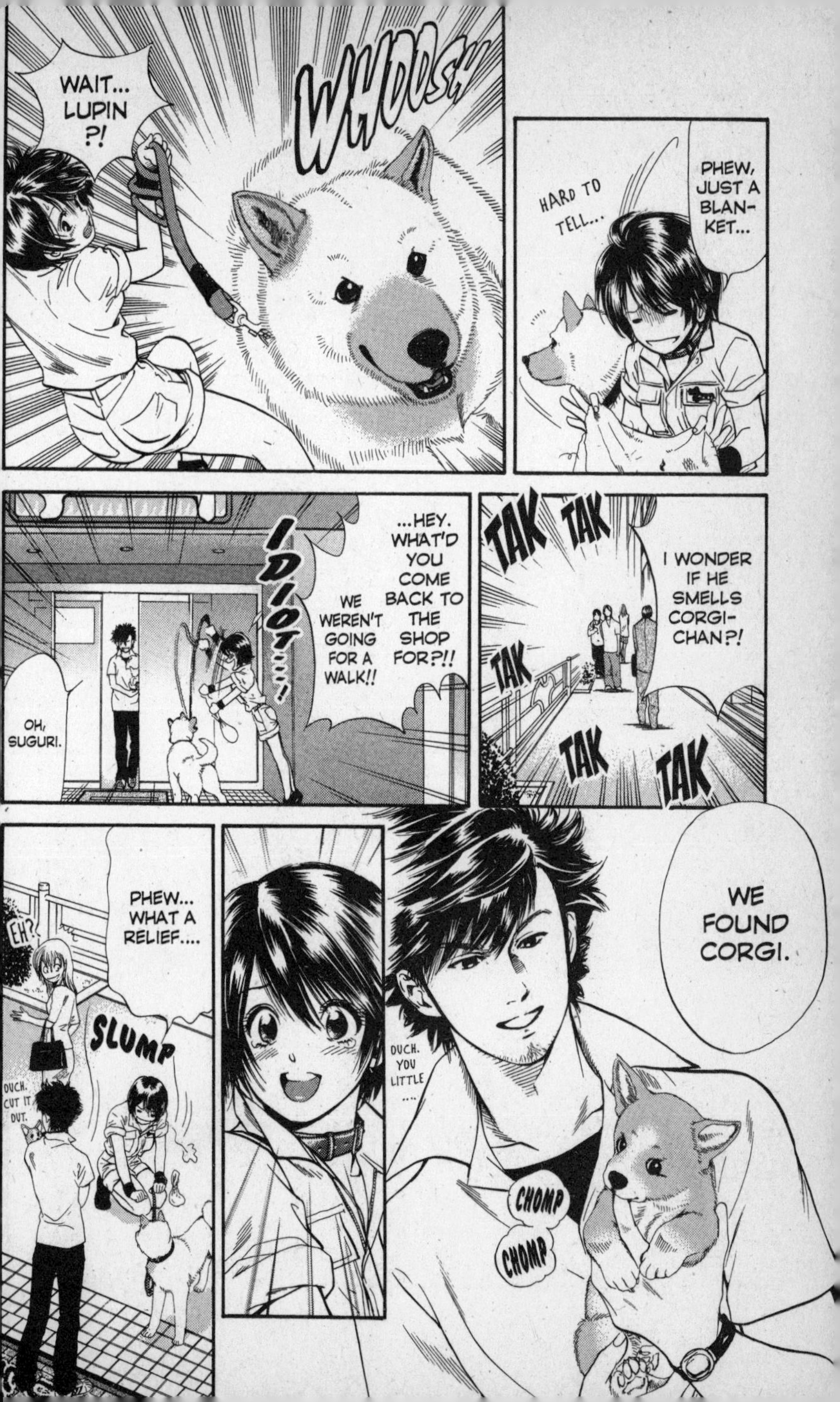
PHEW, JUST A BLANKET...
HARD TO TELL...
WHOOSH
WAIT... LUPIN ?!
TAK TAK
I WONDER IF HE SMELLS CORGI-CHAN?!
TAK
TAK TAK
...HEY. WHAT'D YOU COME BACK TO THE SHOP FOR?!!
WE WEREN'T GOING FOR A WALK!!
IDIOT...!
OH, SUGURI.
WE FOUND CORGI.
OUCH. YOU LITTLE ....
CHOMP
CHOMP
PHEW... WHAT A RELIEF....
EH?
SLUMP
OUCH. CUT IT OUT.

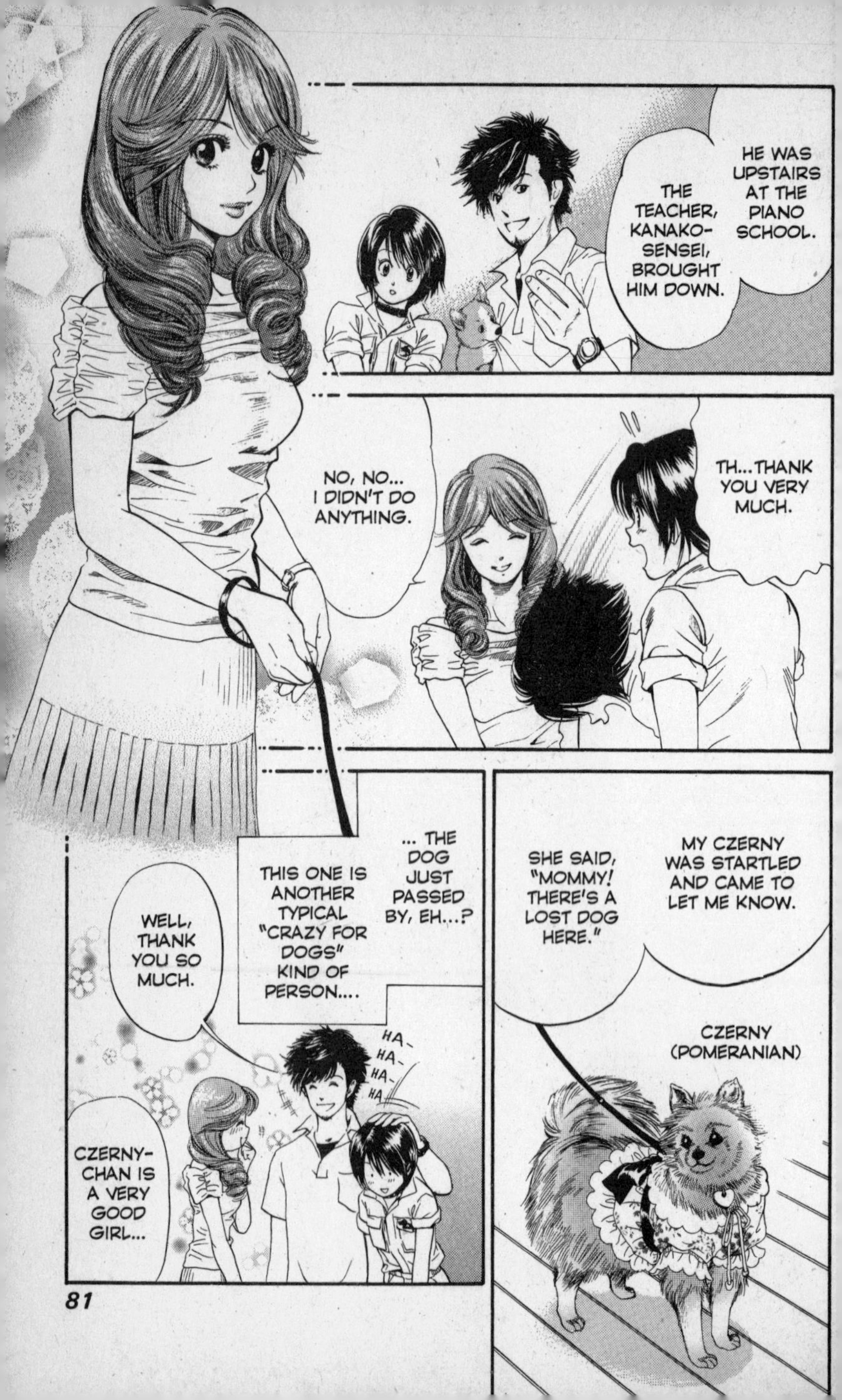
HE WAS UPSTAIRS AT THE PIANO SCHOOL.
THE TEACHER, KANAKO-SENSEI, BROUGHT HIM DOWN.
TH...THANK YOU VERY MUCH.
NO, NO... I DIDN'T DO ANYTHING.
MY CZERNY WAS STARTLED AND CAME TO LET ME KNOW.
SHE SAID, "MOMMY! THERE'S A LOST DOG HERE."
CZERNY (POMERANIAN)
... THE DOG JUST PASSED BY, EH...?
THIS ONE IS ANOTHER TYPICAL "CRAZY FOR DOGS" KIND OF PERSON....
WELL, THANK YOU SO MUCH.
HA-HA-HA-HA
CZERNY-CHAN IS A VERY GOOD GIRL...

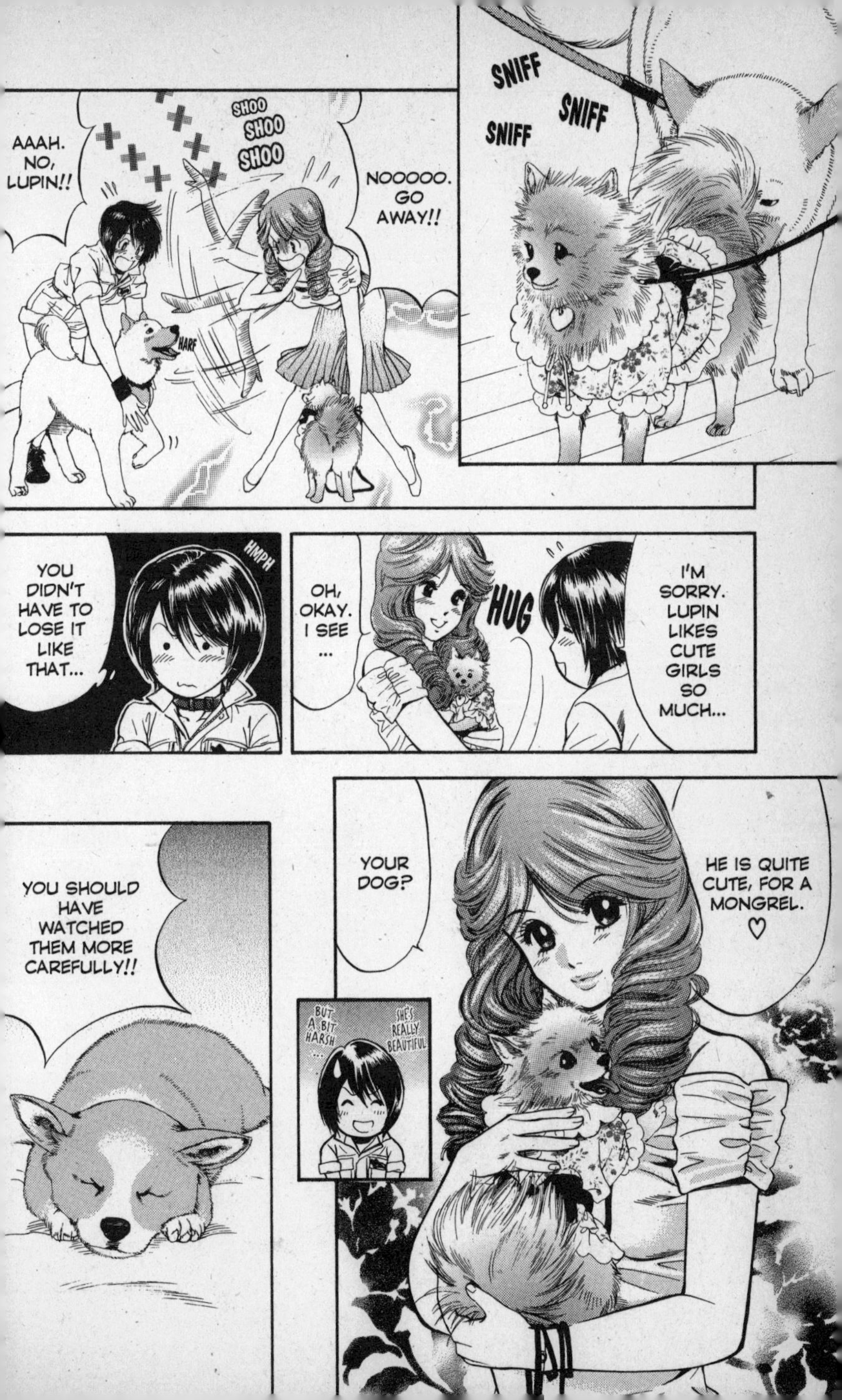
SNIFF
SNIFF
SNIFF
NOOOOO. GO AWAY!!
SHOO SHOO SHOO
AAAH. NO, LUPIN!!
HARF
I'M SORRY. LUPIN LIKES CUTE GIRLS SO MUCH...
HUG
OH, OKAY. I SEE ...
HMPH
YOU DIDN'T HAVE TO LOSE IT LIKE THAT...
HE IS QUITE CUTE, FOR A MONGREL. ♡
YOUR DOG?
SHE'S REALLY BEAUTIFUL
BUT A BIT HARSH ...
YOU SHOULD HAVE WATCHED THEM MORE CAREFULLY!!

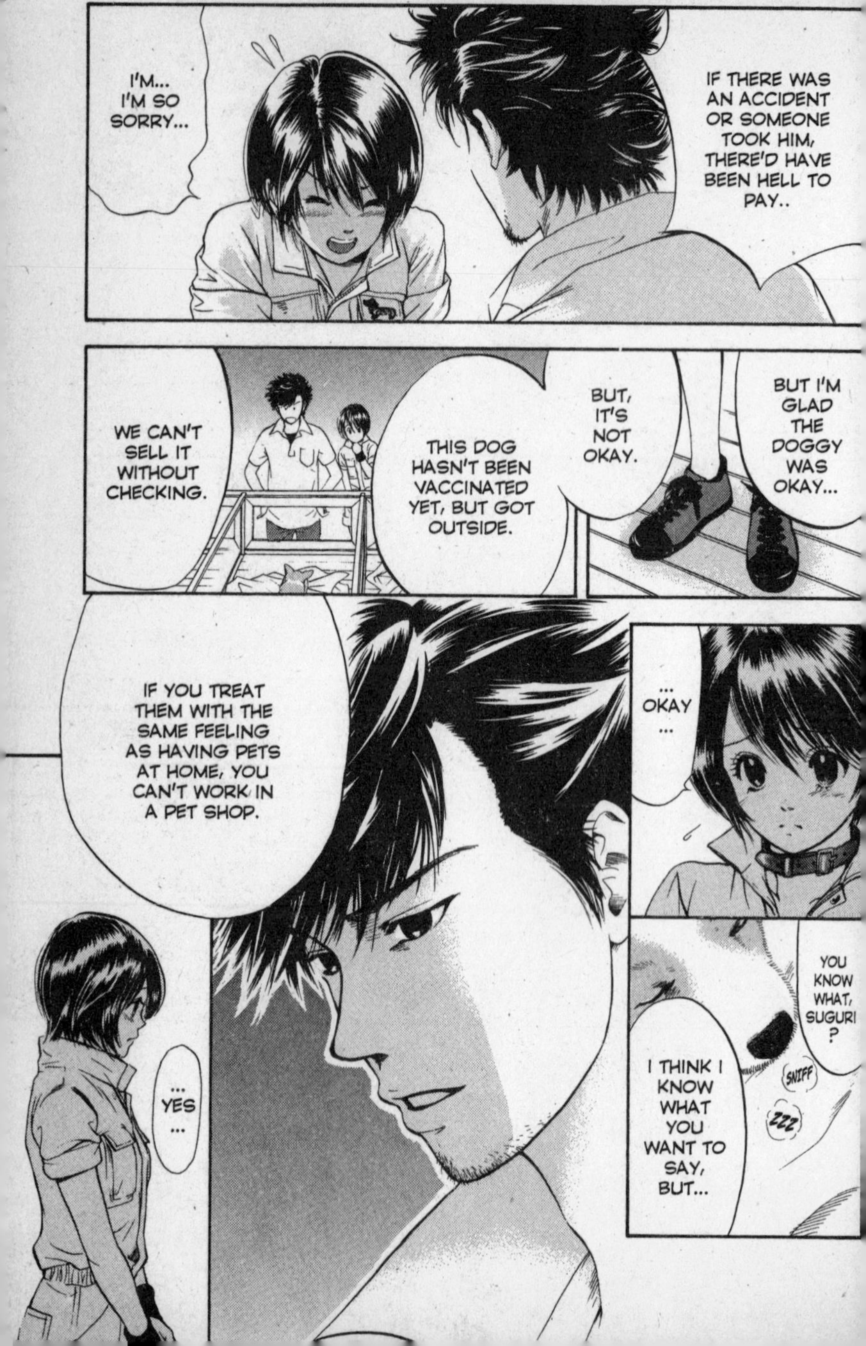
IF THERE WAS AN ACCIDENT OR SOMEONE TOOK HIM, THERE'D HAVE BEEN HELL TO PAY..
I'M... I'M SO SORRY...
BUT I'M GLAD THE DOGGY WAS OKAY...
BUT, IT'S NOT OKAY.
THIS DOG HASN'T BEEN VACCINATED YET, BUT GOT OUTSIDE.
WE CAN'T SELL IT WITHOUT CHECKING.
... OKAY ...
YOU KNOW WHAT, SUGURI?
SNIFF
ZZZ
I THINK I KNOW WHAT YOU WANT TO SAY, BUT...
IF YOU TREAT THEM WITH THE SAME FEELING AS HAVING PETS AT HOME, YOU CAN'T WORK IN A PET SHOP.
... YES ...

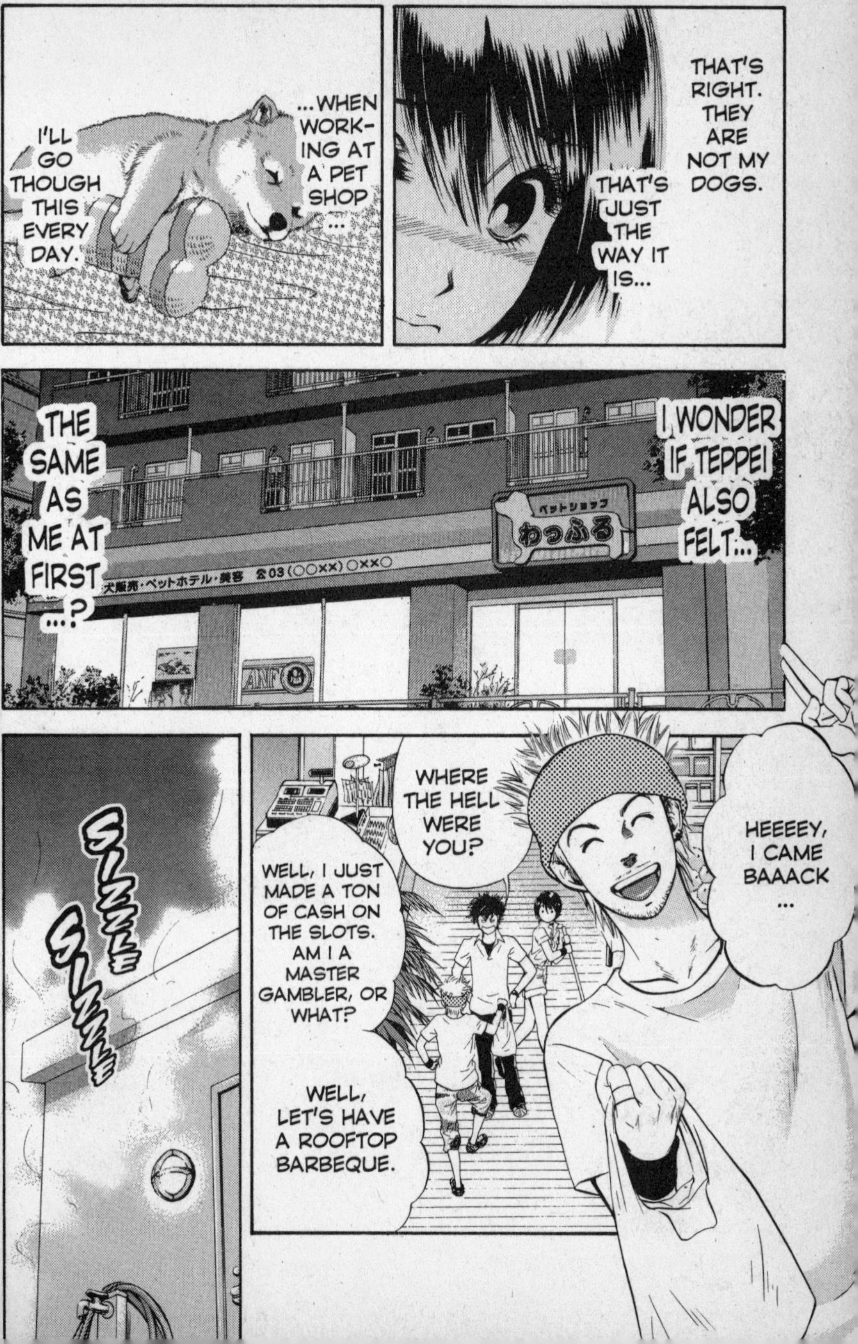
THAT'S RIGHT. THEY ARE NOT MY DOGS.
THAT'S JUST THE WAY IT IS...
...WHEN WORKING AT A PET SHOP ...
I'LL GO THOUGH THIS EVERY DAY.
I WONDER IF TEPPEI ALSO FELT...
ペットショップ
わっふる
犬販売・ペットホテル・美容 ☎03(○○××)○××○
THE SAME AS ME AT FIRST ...?
ANF
HEEEEY, I CAME BAAACK ...
WHERE THE HELL WERE YOU?
WELL, I JUST MADE A TON OF CASH ON THE SLOTS. AM I A MASTER GAMBLER, OR WHAT?
WELL, LET'S HAVE A ROOFTOP BARBEQUE.
SIZZLE SIZZLE

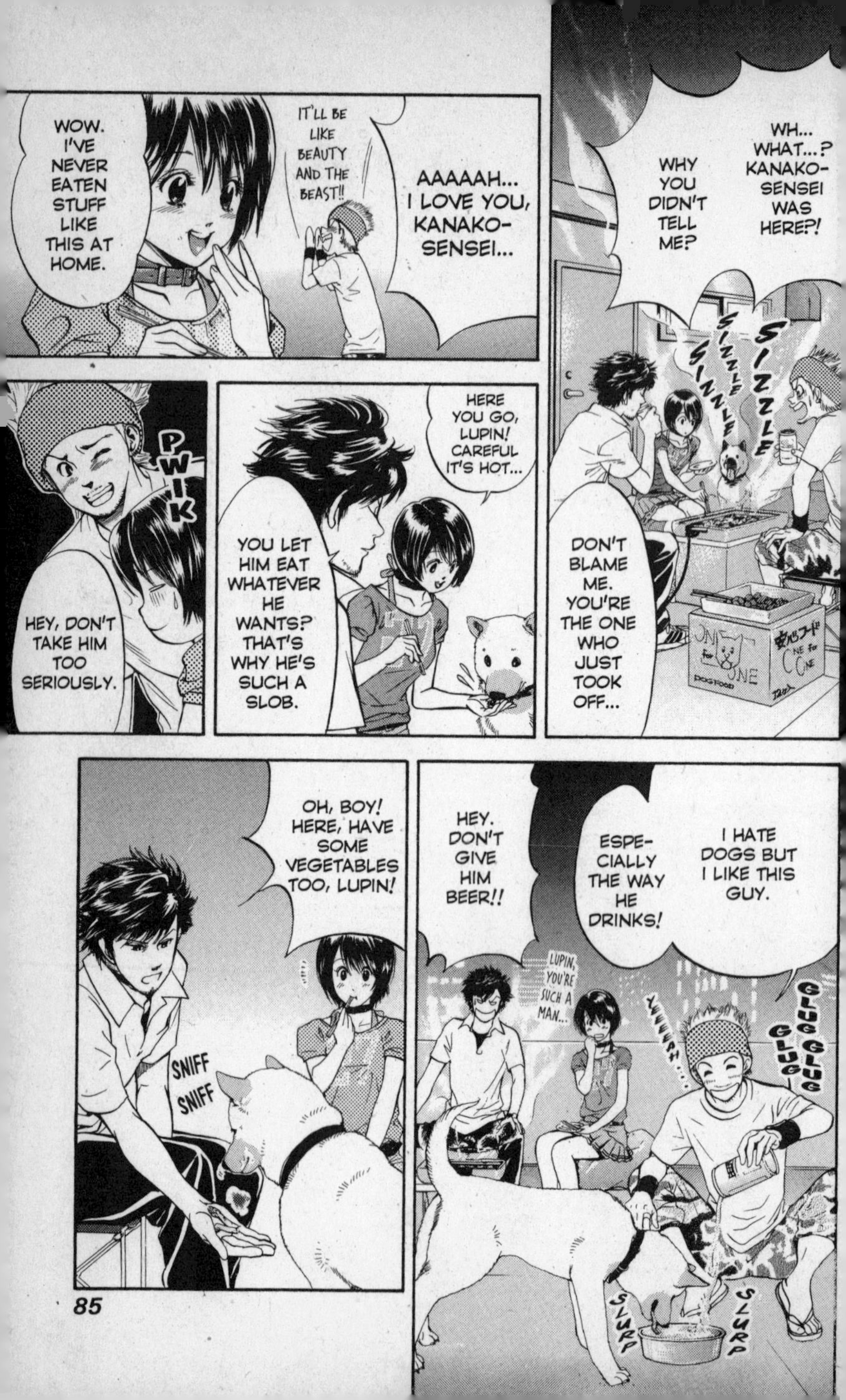
WH... WHAT...? KANAKO-SENSEI WAS HERE?!
WHY YOU DIDN'T TELL ME?
SIZZLE SIZZLE SIZZLE
DON'T BLAME ME. YOU'RE THE ONE WHO JUST TOOK OFF...
ONE for ONE DOGFOOD
ONE for ONE
AAAAAH... I LOVE YOU, KANAKO-SENSEI...
IT'LL BE LIKE BEAUTY AND THE BEAST!!
WOW. I'VE NEVER EATEN STUFF LIKE THIS AT HOME.
HERE YOU GO, LUPIN! CAREFUL IT'S HOT...
YOU LET HIM EAT WHATEVER HE WANTS? THAT'S WHY HE'S SUCH A SLOB.
PWIK
HEY, DON'T TAKE HIM TOO SERIOUSLY.
I HATE DOGS BUT I LIKE THIS GUY.
ESPE-CIALLY THE WAY HE DRINKS!
HEY. DON'T GIVE HIM BEER!!
GLUG GLUG GLUG GLUG
LUPIN, YOU'RE SUCH A MAN...
YEEEAH...
SLURP SLURP
OH, BOY! HERE, HAVE SOME VEGETABLES TOO, LUPIN!
SNIFF SNIFF

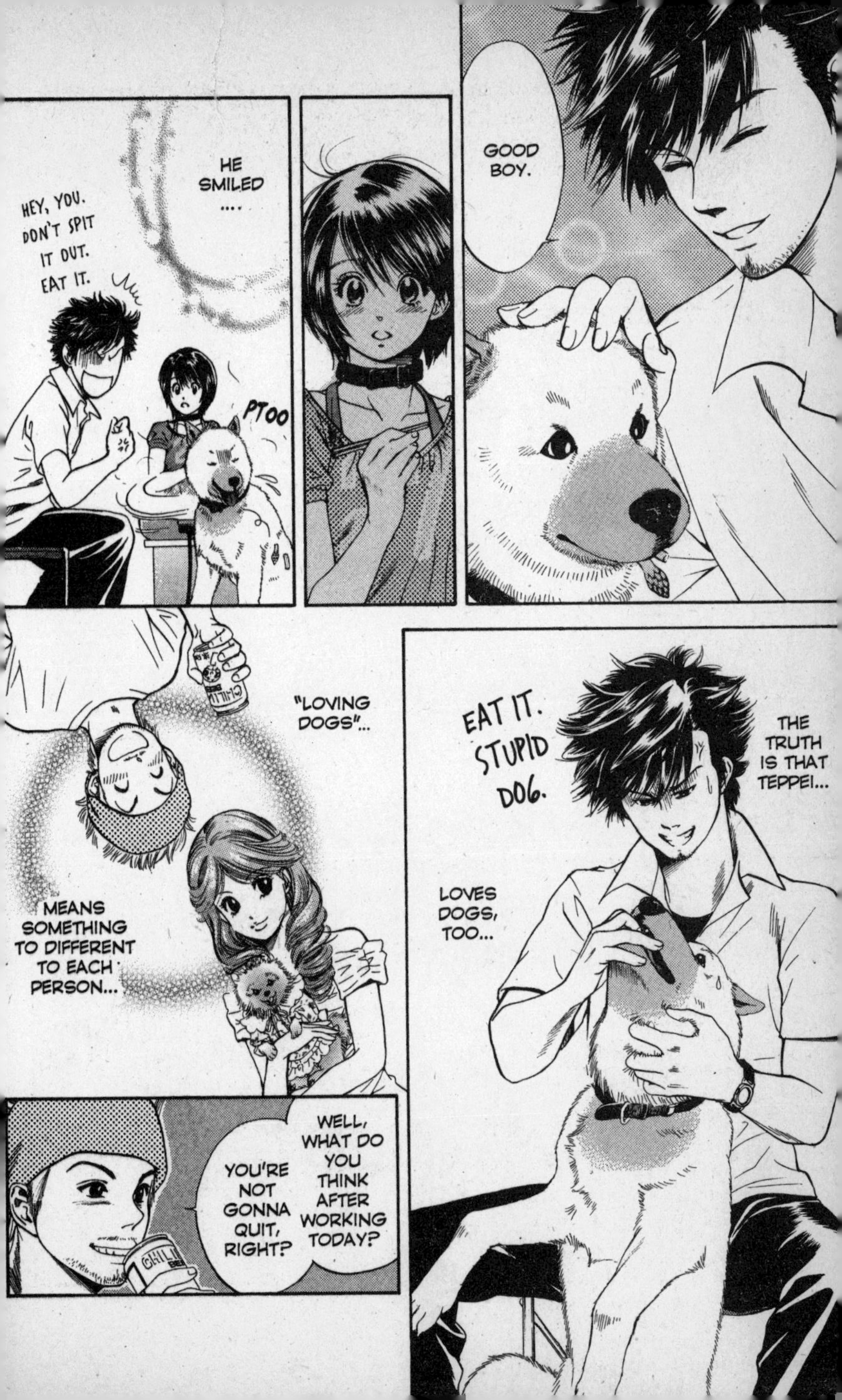
GOOD BOY.
HE SMILED ....
HEY, YOU. DON'T SPIT IT OUT. EAT IT.
PTOO
THE TRUTH IS THAT TEPPEI...
EAT IT. STUPID DOG.
LOVES DOGS, TOO...
"LOVING DOGS"...
MEANS SOMETHING TO DIFFERENT TO EACH PERSON...
WELL, WHAT DO YOU THINK AFTER WORKING TODAY?
YOU'RE NOT GONNA QUIT, RIGHT?

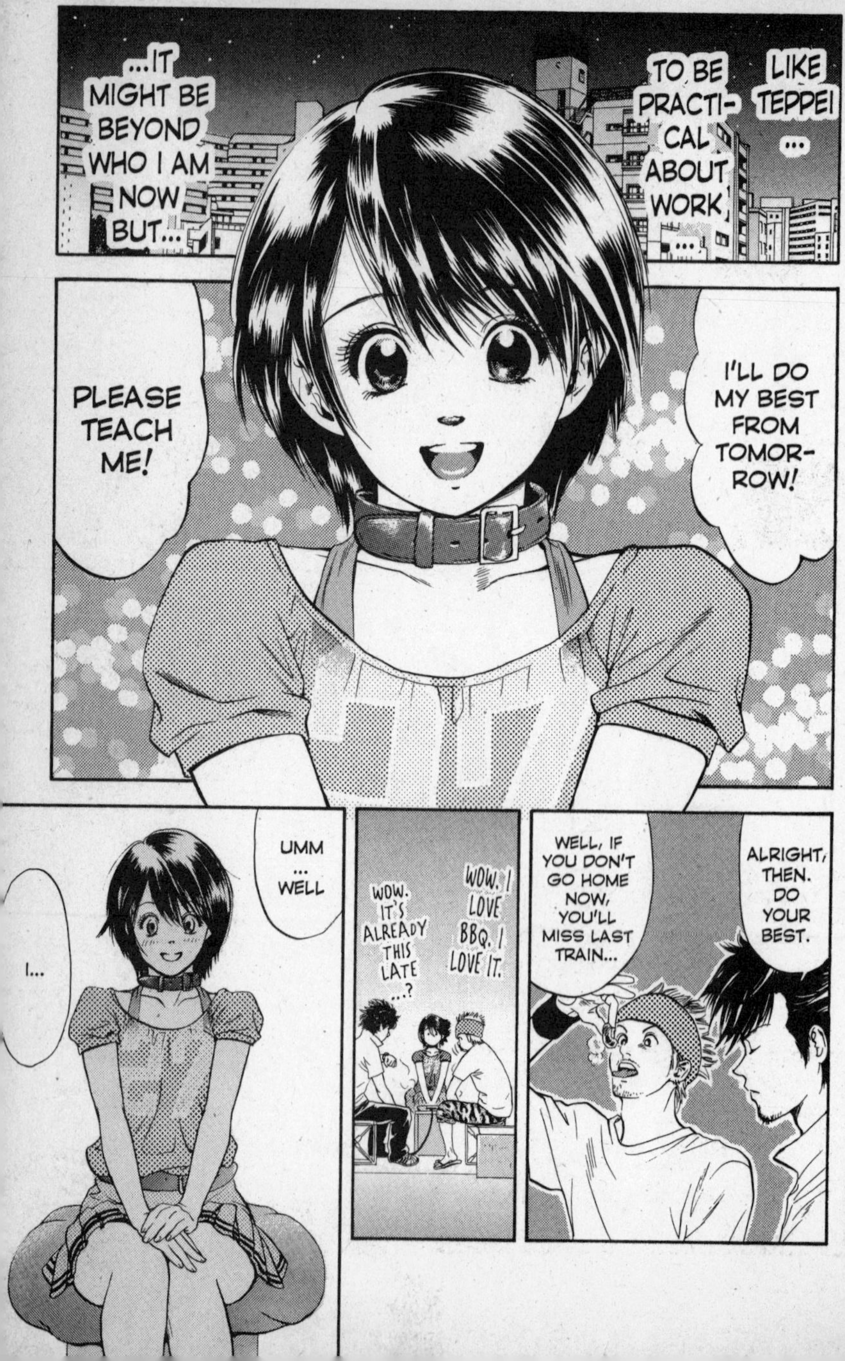
LIKE TEPPEI ...
TO BE PRACTI-CAL ABOUT WORK ....
...IT MIGHT BE BEYOND WHO I AM NOW BUT...
I'LL DO MY BEST FROM TOMOR-ROW!
PLEASE TEACH ME!
ALRIGHT, THEN. DO YOUR BEST.
WELL, IF YOU DON'T GO HOME NOW, YOU'LL MISS LAST TRAIN...
WOW. I LOVE BBQ. I LOVE IT.
WOW. IT'S ALREADY THIS LATE ...?
UMM ... WELL
I...

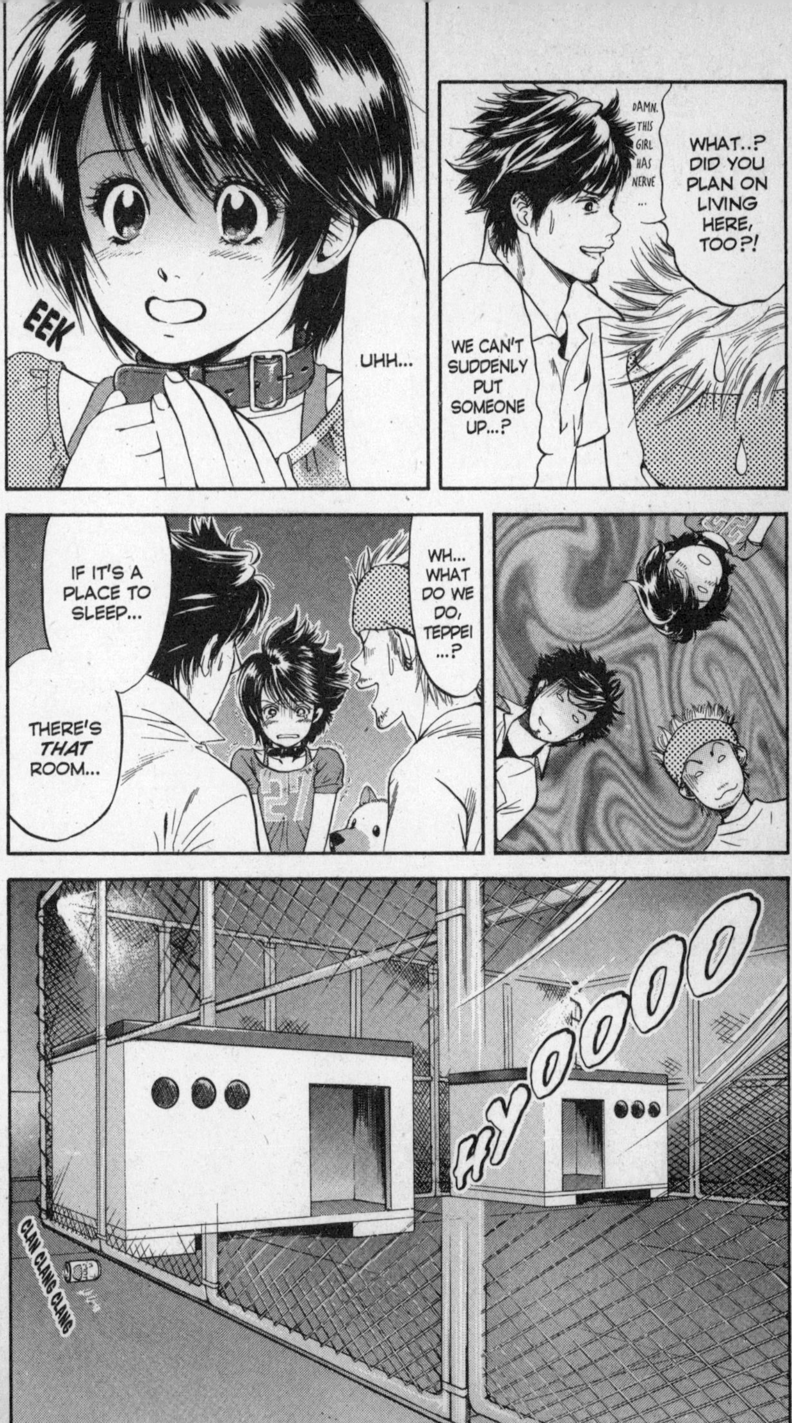
WHAT..? DID YOU PLAN ON LIVING HERE, TOO?!
DAMN. THIS GIRL HAS NERVE ...
WE CAN'T SUDDENLY PUT SOMEONE UP...?
UHH...
EEK
WH... WHAT DO WE DO, TEPPEI ...?
IF IT'S A PLACE TO SLEEP...
THERE'S THAT ROOM...
HYOOOOO
CLAN CLANG CLANG

CHAPTER 3
WHICH ONE TASTES THE BEST?

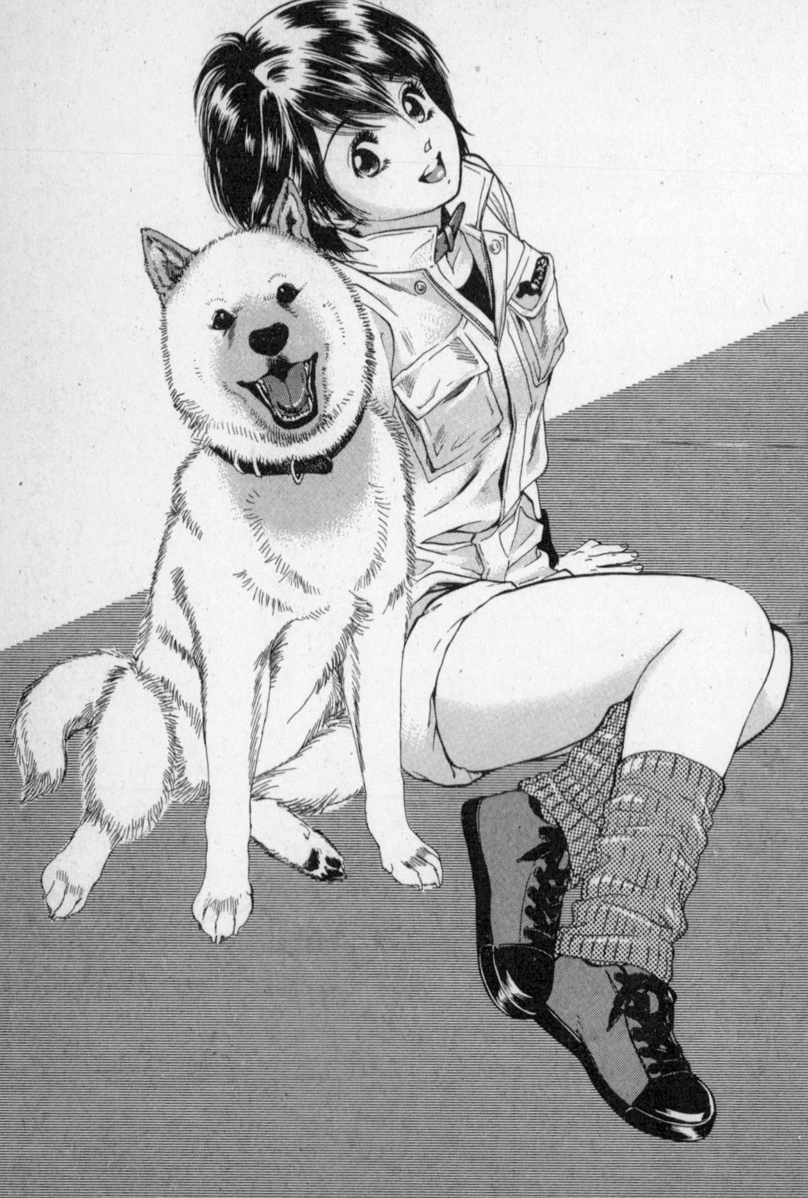

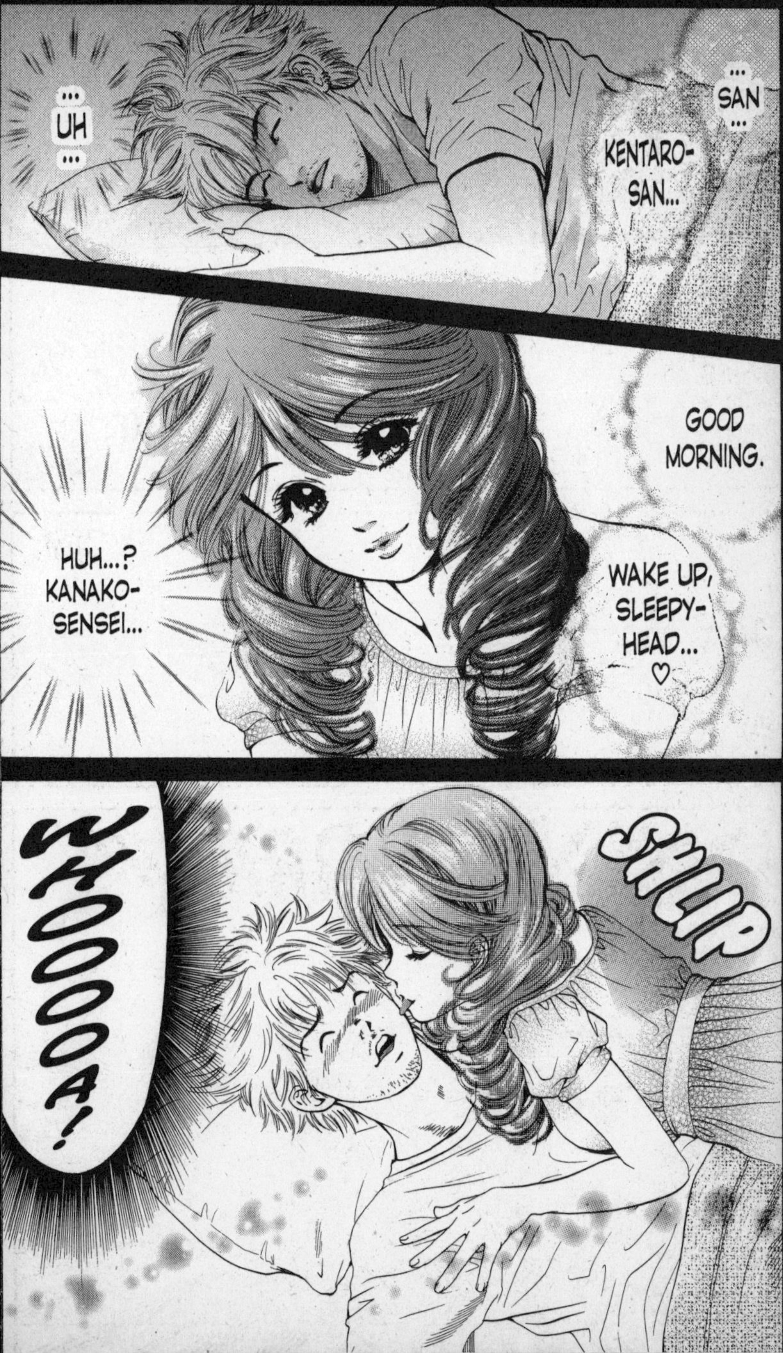
...SAN...
KENTARO-SAN...
...UH...
GOOD MORNING.
WAKE UP, SLEEPY-HEAD... ♡
HUH...? KANAKO-SENSEI...
SHLIP
WHOOOOA!

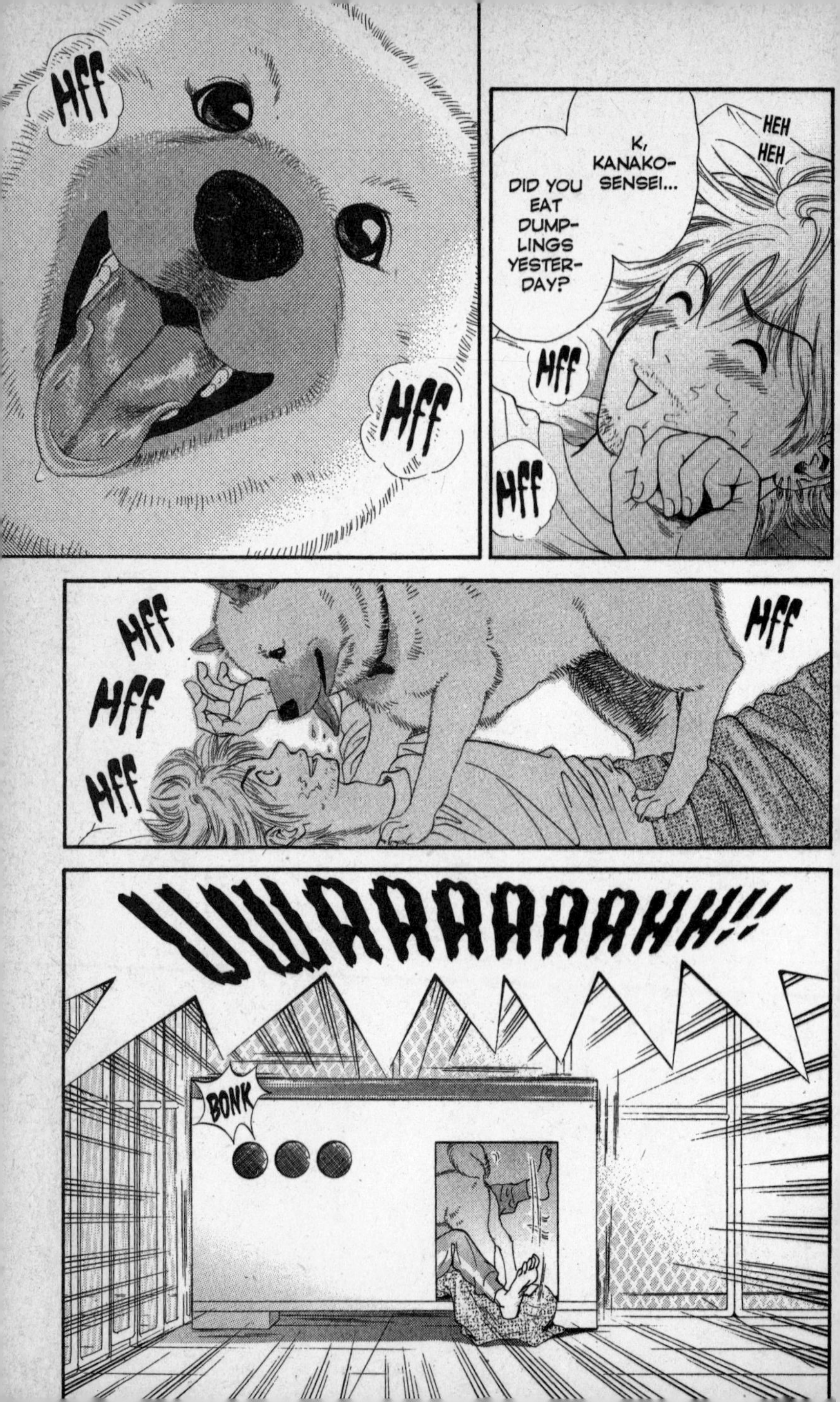
HEH HEH
K, KANAKO-SENSEI... DID YOU EAT DUMPLINGS YESTERDAY?
Hff
Hff
Hff
Hff
Hff
Hff
Hff
Hff
UWAAAAAAHH!!
BONK
• • •

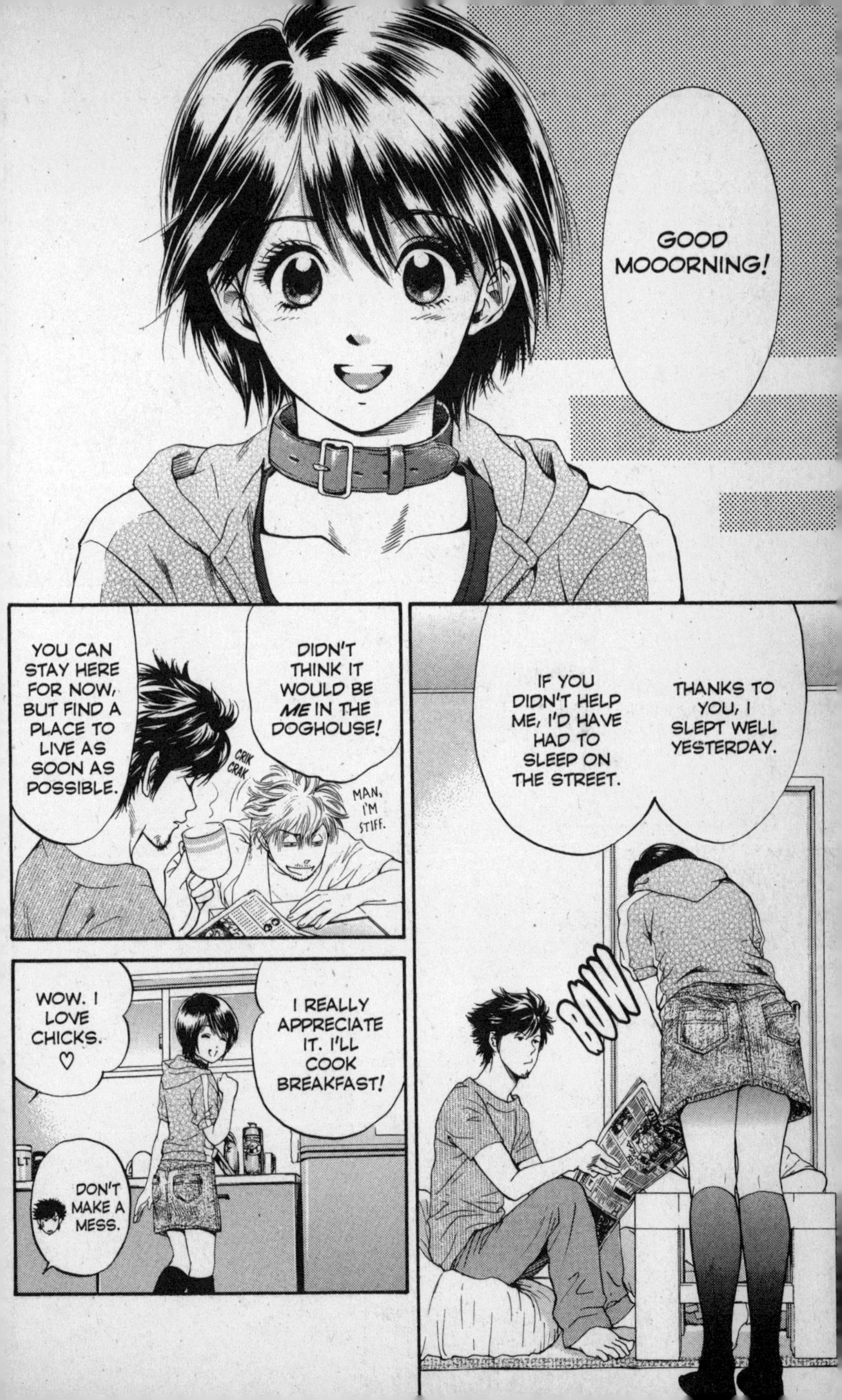
GOOD MOOORNING!
THANKS TO YOU, I SLEPT WELL YESTERDAY.
IF YOU DIDN'T HELP ME, I'D HAVE HAD TO SLEEP ON THE STREET.
BOW
DIDN'T THINK IT WOULD BE *ME* IN THE DOGHOUSE!
YOU CAN STAY HERE FOR NOW, BUT FIND A PLACE TO LIVE AS SOON AS POSSIBLE.
MAN, I'M STIFF.
CRIK CRAK
I REALLY APPRECIATE IT. I'LL COOK BREAKFAST!
WOW. I LOVE CHICKS. ♡
DON'T MAKE A MESS.

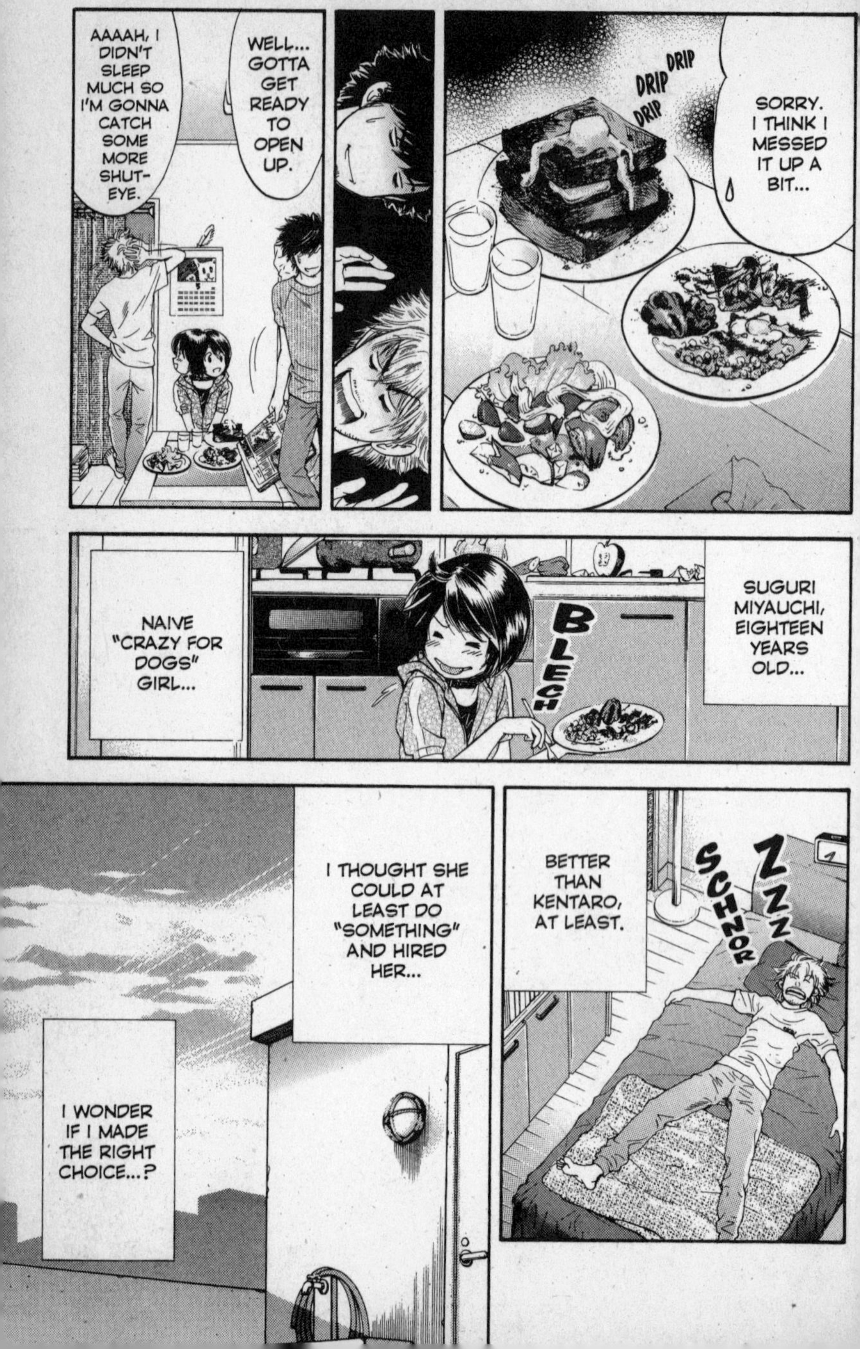
DRIP
DRIP
DRIP
SORRY. I THINK I MESSED IT UP A BIT...
WELL... GOTTA GET READY TO OPEN UP.
AAAAH, I DIDN'T SLEEP MUCH SO I'M GONNA CATCH SOME MORE SHUT-EYE.
SUGURI MIYAUCHI, EIGHTEEN YEARS OLD...
BLECH
NAIVE "CRAZY FOR DOGS" GIRL...
ZZZ
SCHNOR
BETTER THAN KENTARO, AT LEAST.
I THOUGHT SHE COULD AT LEAST DO "SOMETHING" AND HIRED HER...
I WONDER IF I MADE THE RIGHT CHOICE...?

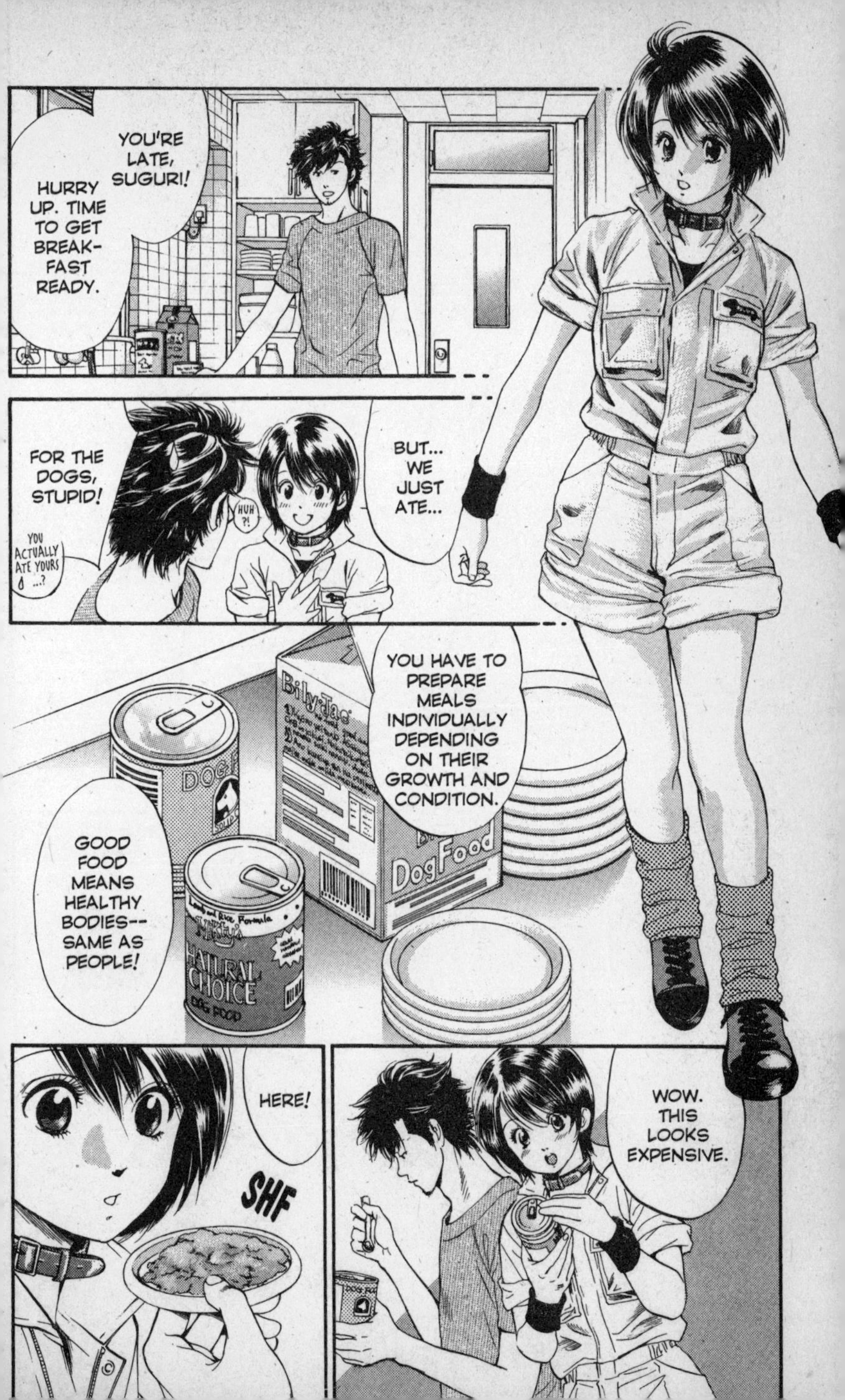

YOU'RE LATE, SUGURI!
HURRY UP. TIME TO GET BREAK-FAST READY.
BUT... WE JUST ATE...
HUH?!
FOR THE DOGS, STUPID!
YOU ACTUALLY ATE YOURS...?
YOU HAVE TO PREPARE MEALS INDIVIDUALLY DEPENDING ON THEIR GROWTH AND CONDITION.
Dog Food
NATURAL CHOICE
DOG FOOD
GOOD FOOD MEANS HEALTHY BODIES-- SAME AS PEOPLE!
WOW. THIS LOOKS EXPENSIVE.
HERE!
SHF

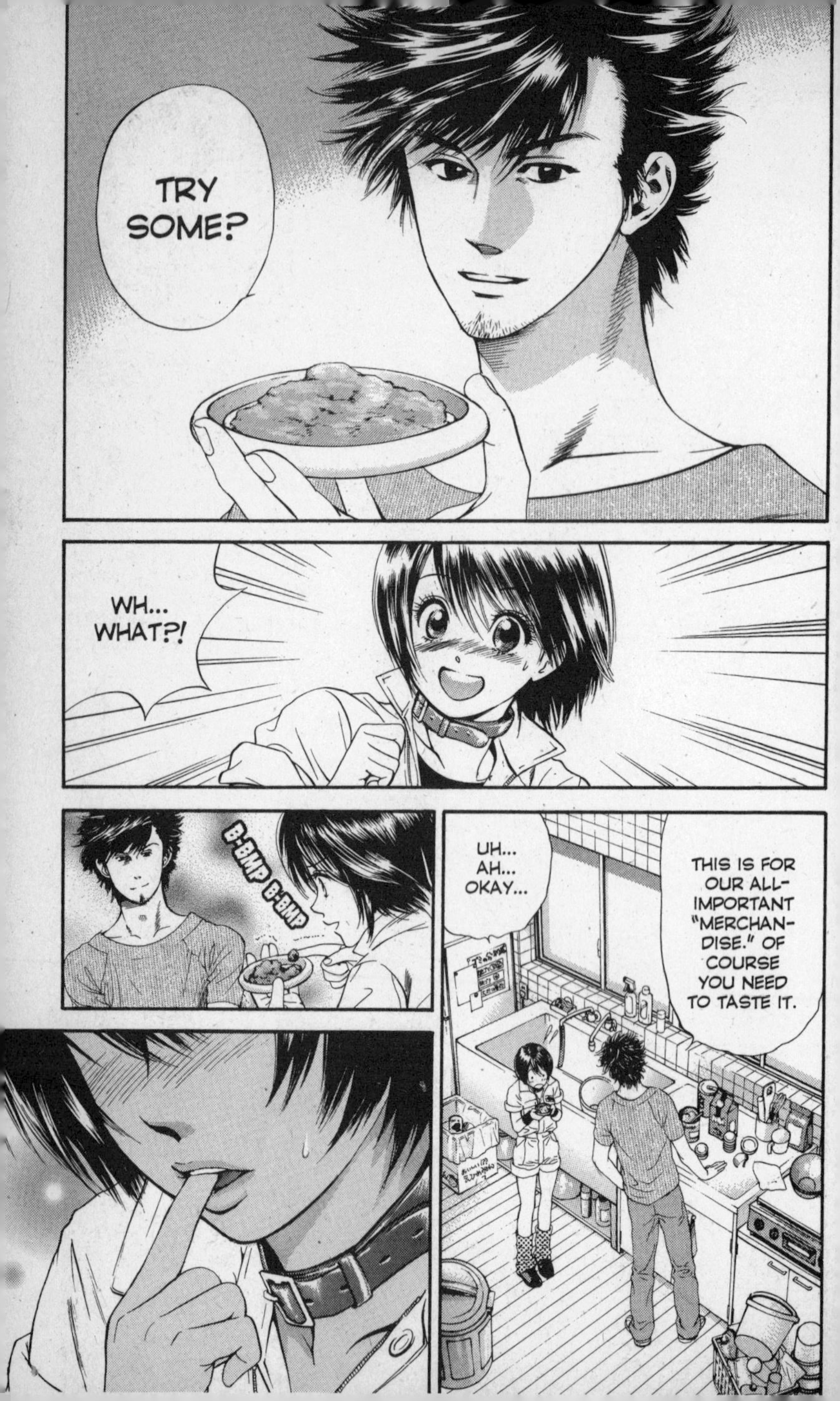
TRY SOME?
WH... WHAT?!
THIS IS FOR OUR ALL-IMPORTANT "MERCHANDISE." OF COURSE YOU NEED TO TASTE IT.
UH... AH... OKAY...
B-BMP B-BMP

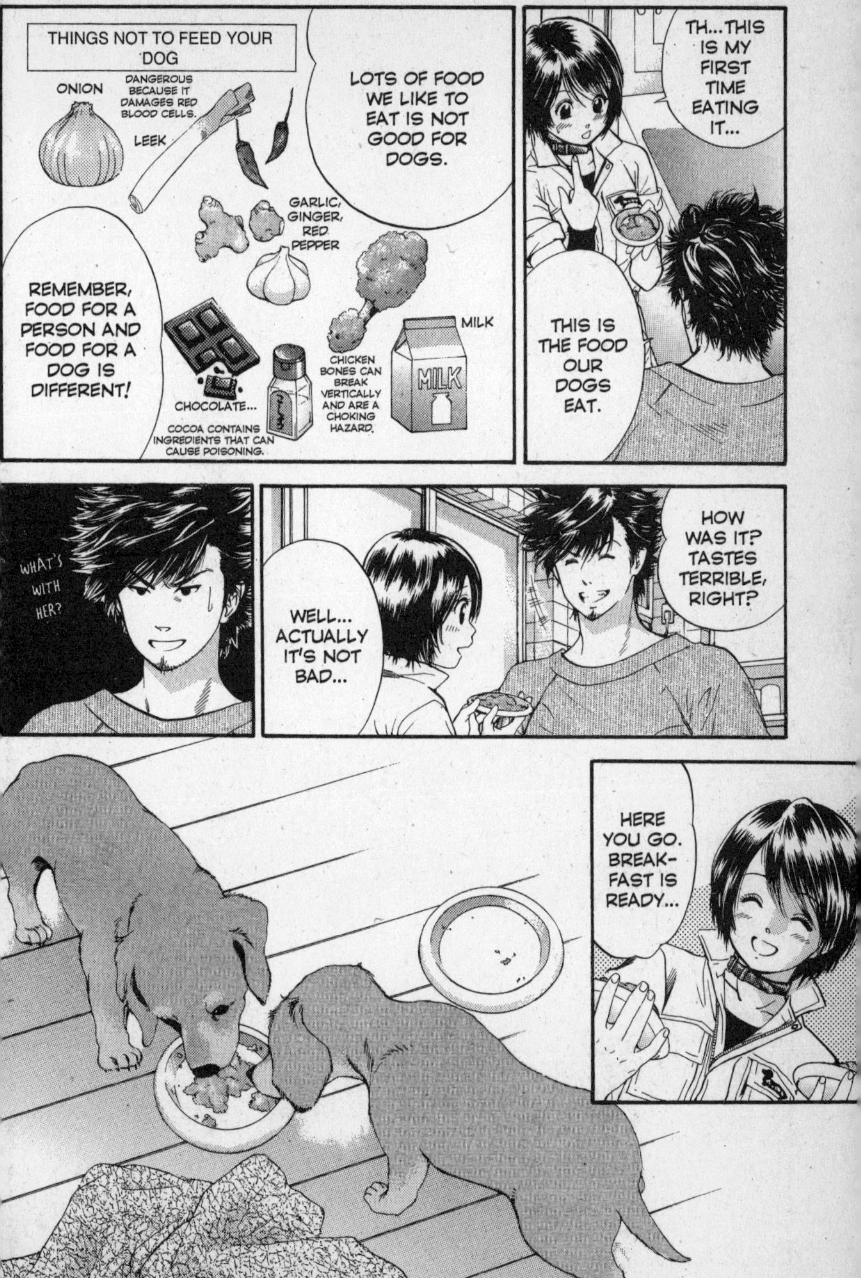
TH...THIS IS MY FIRST TIME EATING IT...
THIS IS THE FOOD OUR DOGS EAT.
LOTS OF FOOD WE LIKE TO EAT IS NOT GOOD FOR DOGS.
THINGS NOT TO FEED YOUR DOG
DANGEROUS BECAUSE IT DAMAGES RED BLOOD CELLS.
ONION
LEEK
GARLIC, GINGER, RED PEPPER
MILK
CHICKEN BONES CAN BREAK VERTICALLY AND ARE A CHOKING HAZARD.
CHOCOLATE...
COCOA CONTAINS INGREDIENTS THAT CAN CAUSE POISONING.
MILK
REMEMBER, FOOD FOR A PERSON AND FOOD FOR A DOG IS DIFFERENT!
HOW WAS IT? TASTES TERRIBLE, RIGHT?
WELL... ACTUALLY IT'S NOT BAD...
WHAT'S WITH HER?
HERE YOU GO. BREAK-FAST IS READY...

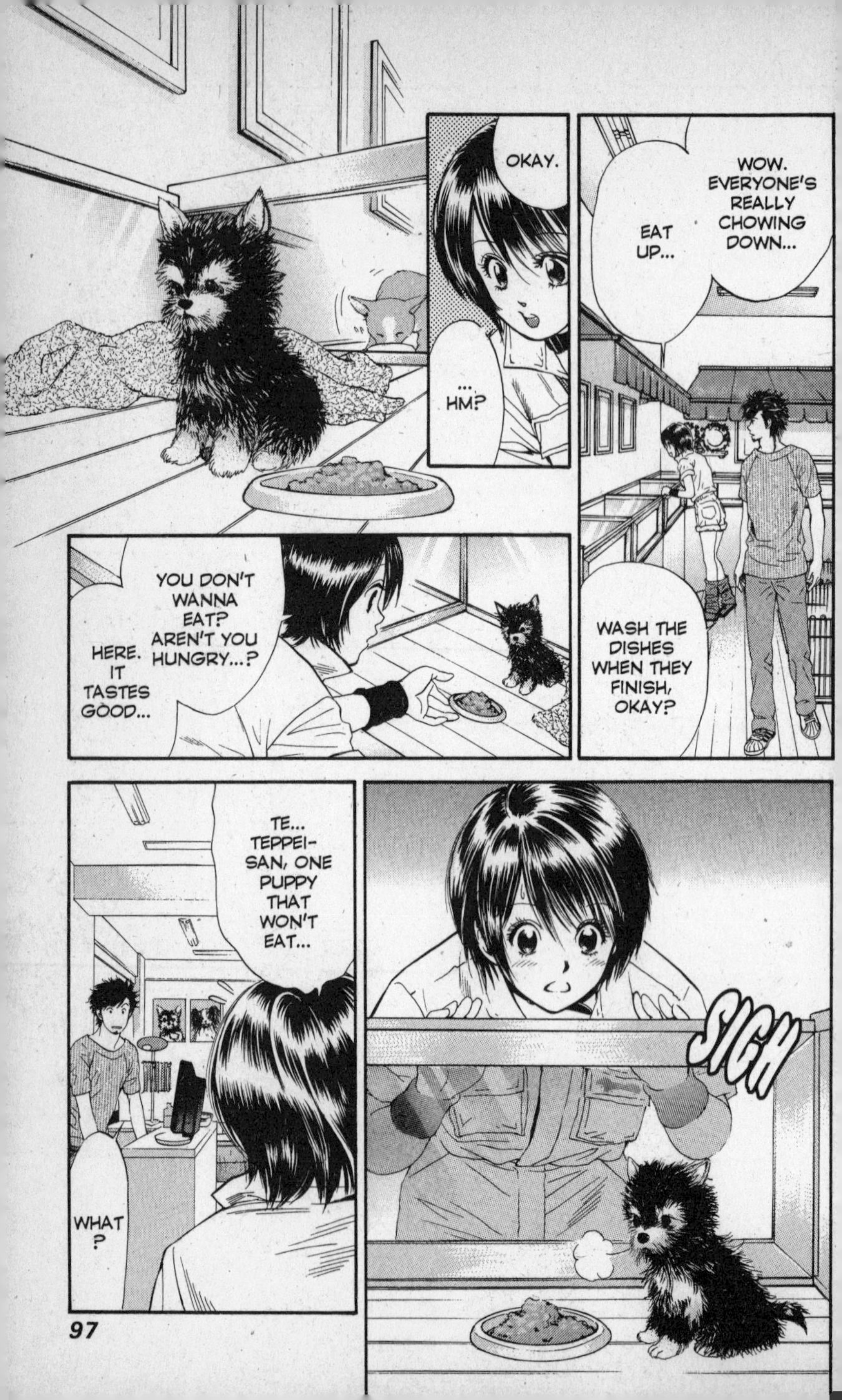

WOW. EVERYONE'S REALLY CHOWING DOWN...
EAT UP...
WASH THE DISHES WHEN THEY FINISH, OKAY?
OKAY.
... HM?
YOU DON'T WANNA EAT? AREN'T YOU HUNGRY...?
HERE. IT TASTES GOOD...
SIGH
TE... TEPPEI-SAN, ONE PUPPY THAT WON'T EAT...
WHAT?

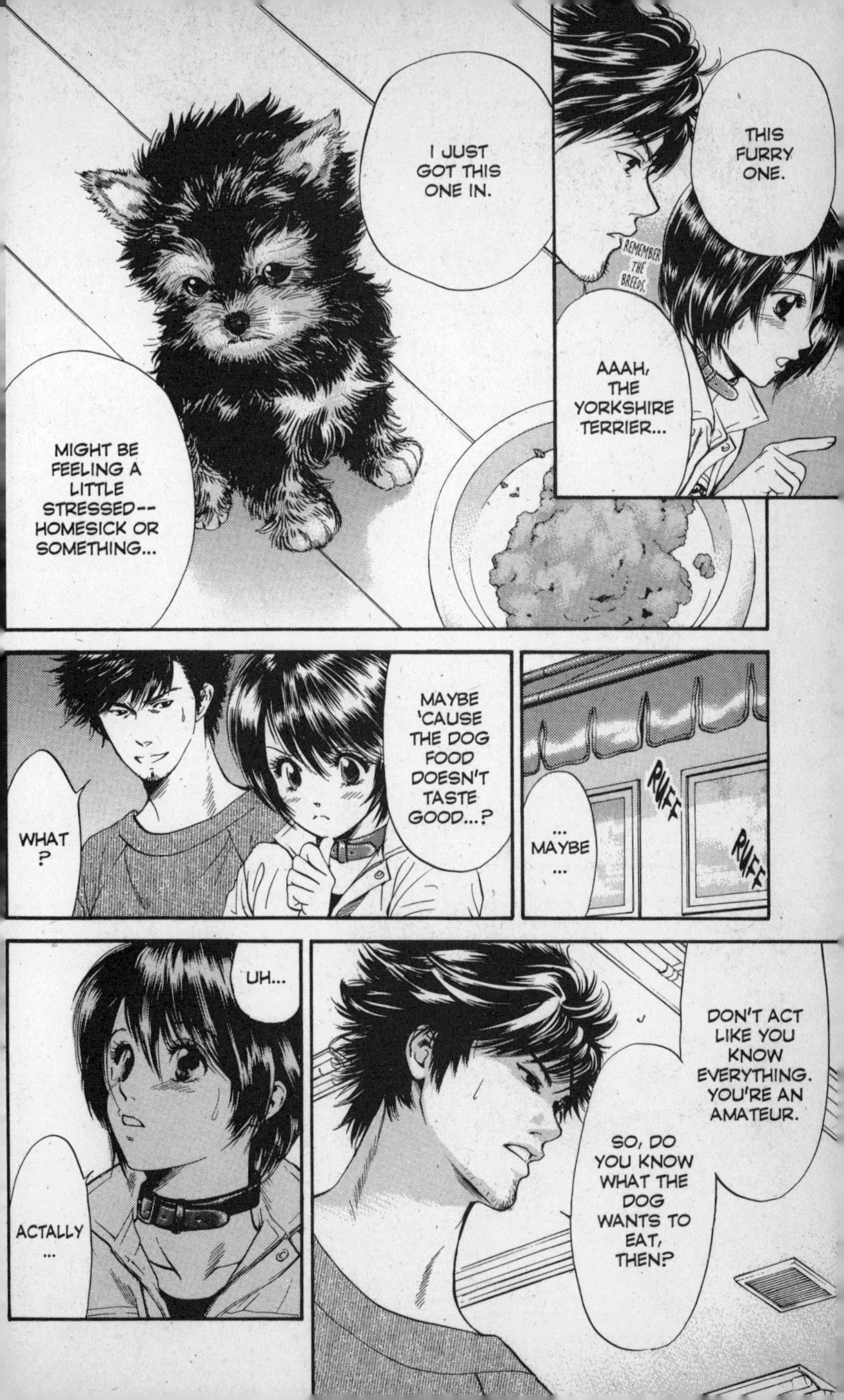
THIS FURRY ONE.
REMEMBER THE BREEDS.
AAAH, THE YORKSHIRE TERRIER...
I JUST GOT THIS ONE IN.
MIGHT BE FEELING A LITTLE STRESSED--HOMESICK OR SOMETHING...
...MAYBE...
RUFF
RUFF
MAYBE 'CAUSE THE DOG FOOD DOESN'T TASTE GOOD...?
WHAT?
DON'T ACT LIKE YOU KNOW EVERYTHING. YOU'RE AN AMATEUR.
SO, DO YOU KNOW WHAT THE DOG WANTS TO EAT, THEN?
UH...
ACTALLY...

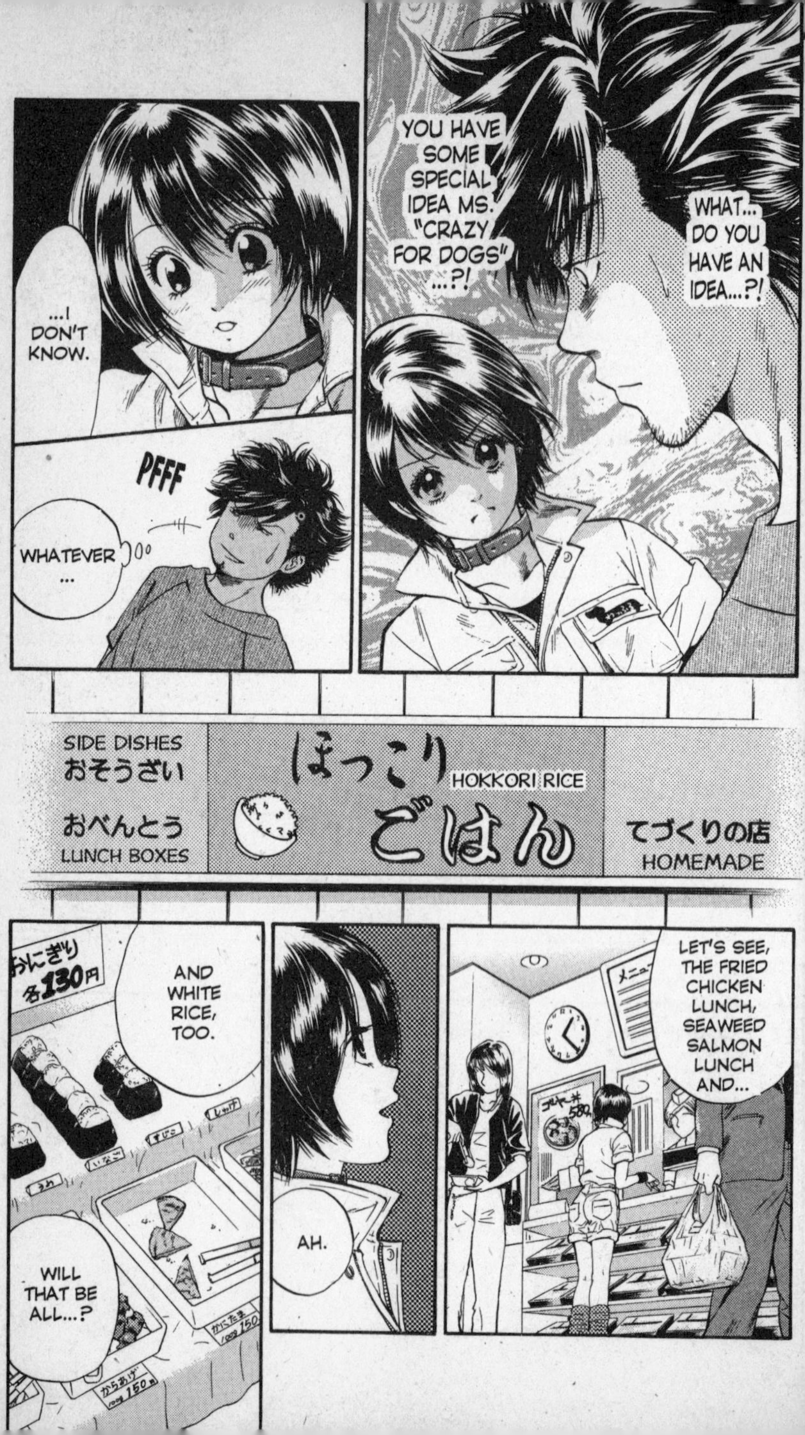
WHAT... DO YOU HAVE AN IDEA...?!
YOU HAVE SOME SPECIAL IDEA MS. "CRAZY FOR DOGS" ...?!
...I DON'T KNOW.
PFFF
WHATEVER ...
てづくりの店
HOMEMADE
ほっこり ごはん
HOKKORI RICE
SIDE DISHES
おそうざい
おべんとう
LUNCH BOXES
LET'S SEE, THE FRIED CHICKEN LUNCH, SEAWEED SALMON LUNCH AND...
AH.
おにぎり 各130円
AND WHITE RICE, TOO.
WILL THAT BE ALL...?

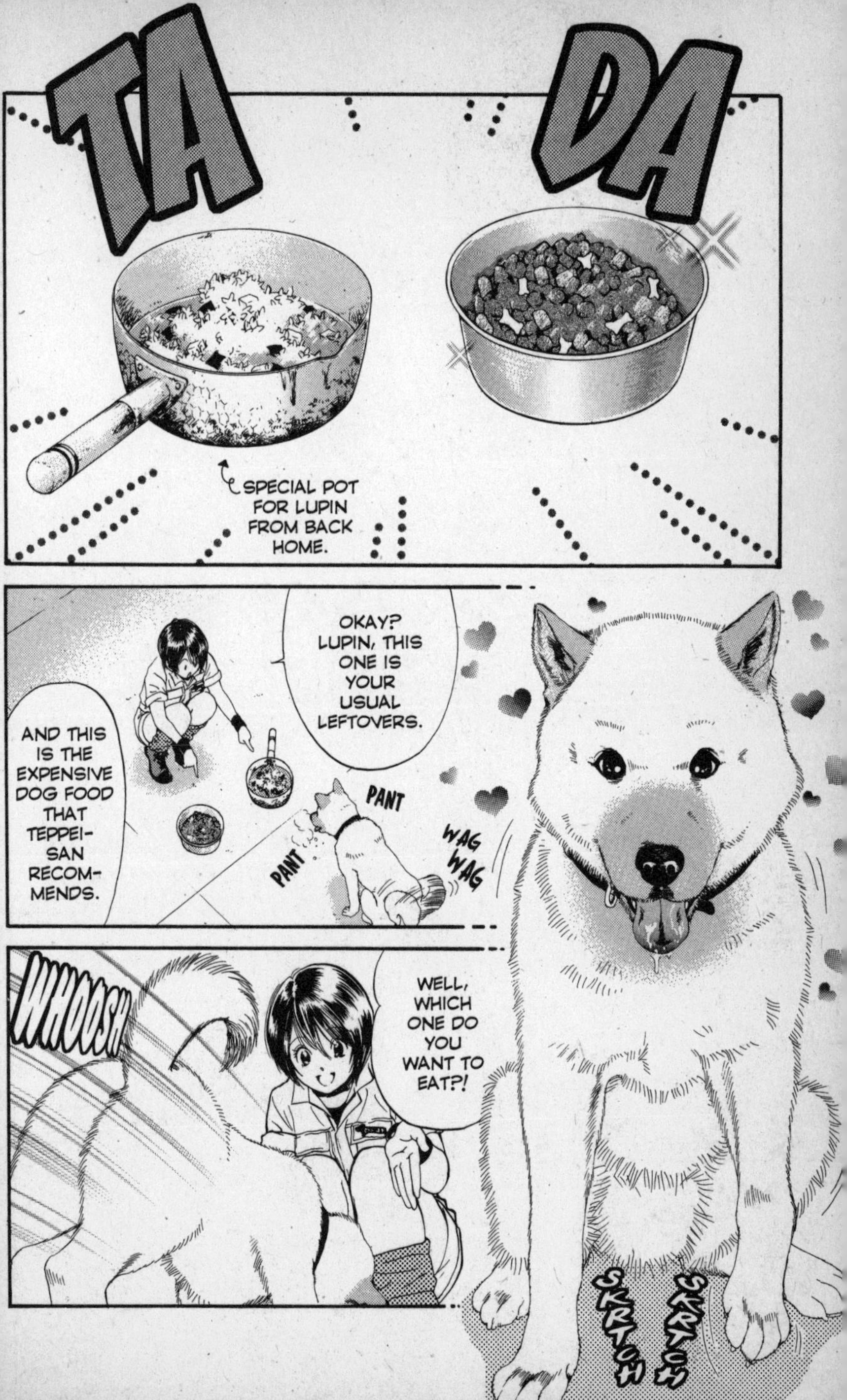
TA DA
SPECIAL POT FOR LUPIN FROM BACK HOME.
SKRTCH SKRTCH
OKAY? LUPIN, THIS ONE IS YOUR USUAL LEFTOVERS.
PANT
WAG WAG
PANT
AND THIS IS THE EXPENSIVE DOG FOOD THAT TEPPEI-SAN RECOMMENDS.
WELL, WHICH ONE DO YOU WANT TO EAT?!
WHOOSH

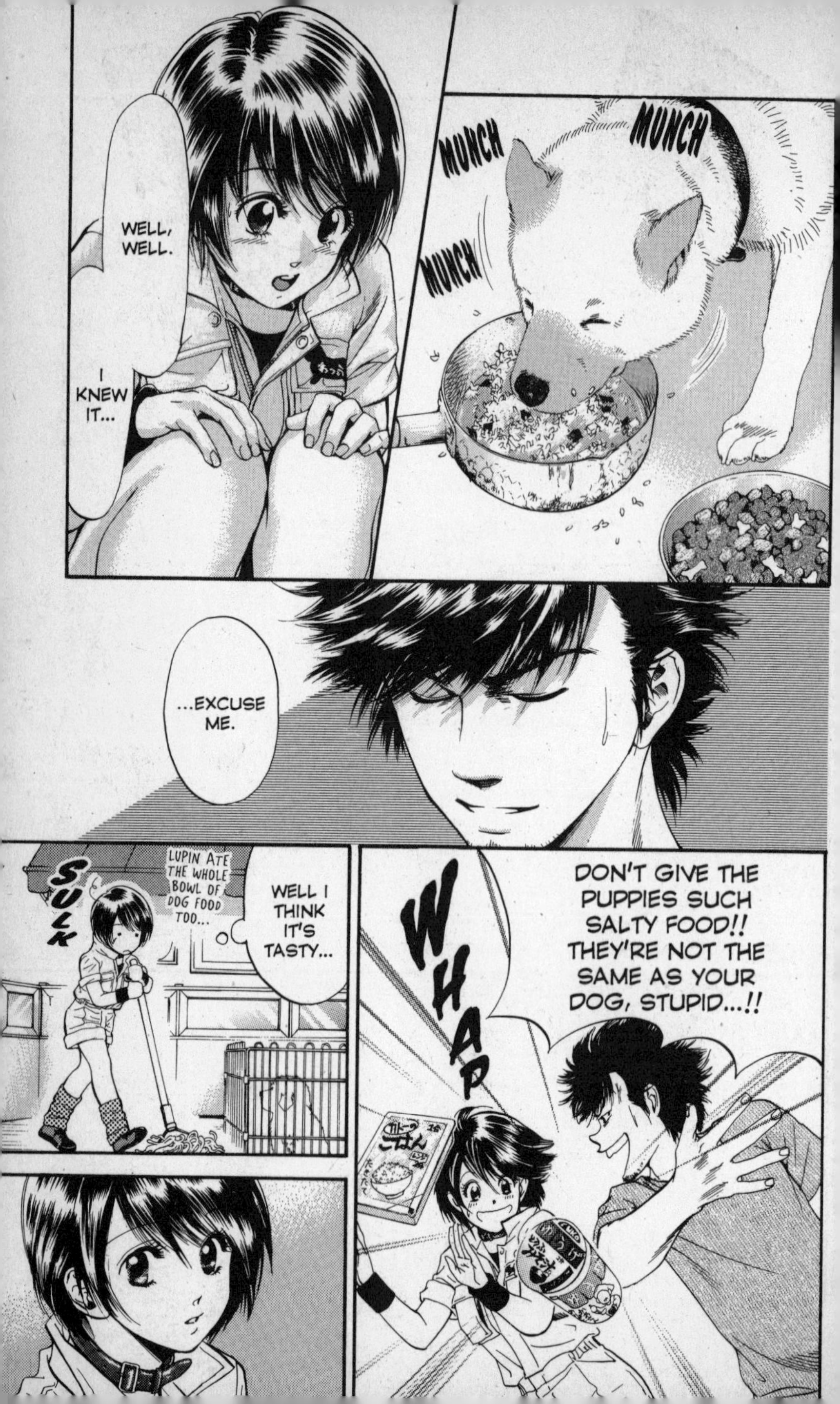
MUNCH
MUNCH
MUNCH
WELL, WELL.
I KNEW IT...
...EXCUSE ME.
DON'T GIVE THE PUPPIES SUCH SALTY FOOD!! THEY'RE NOT THE SAME AS YOUR DOG, STUPID...!!
WHAP
WELL I THINK IT'S TASTY...
LUPIN ATE THE WHOLE BOWL OF DOG FOOD TOO...
SULK

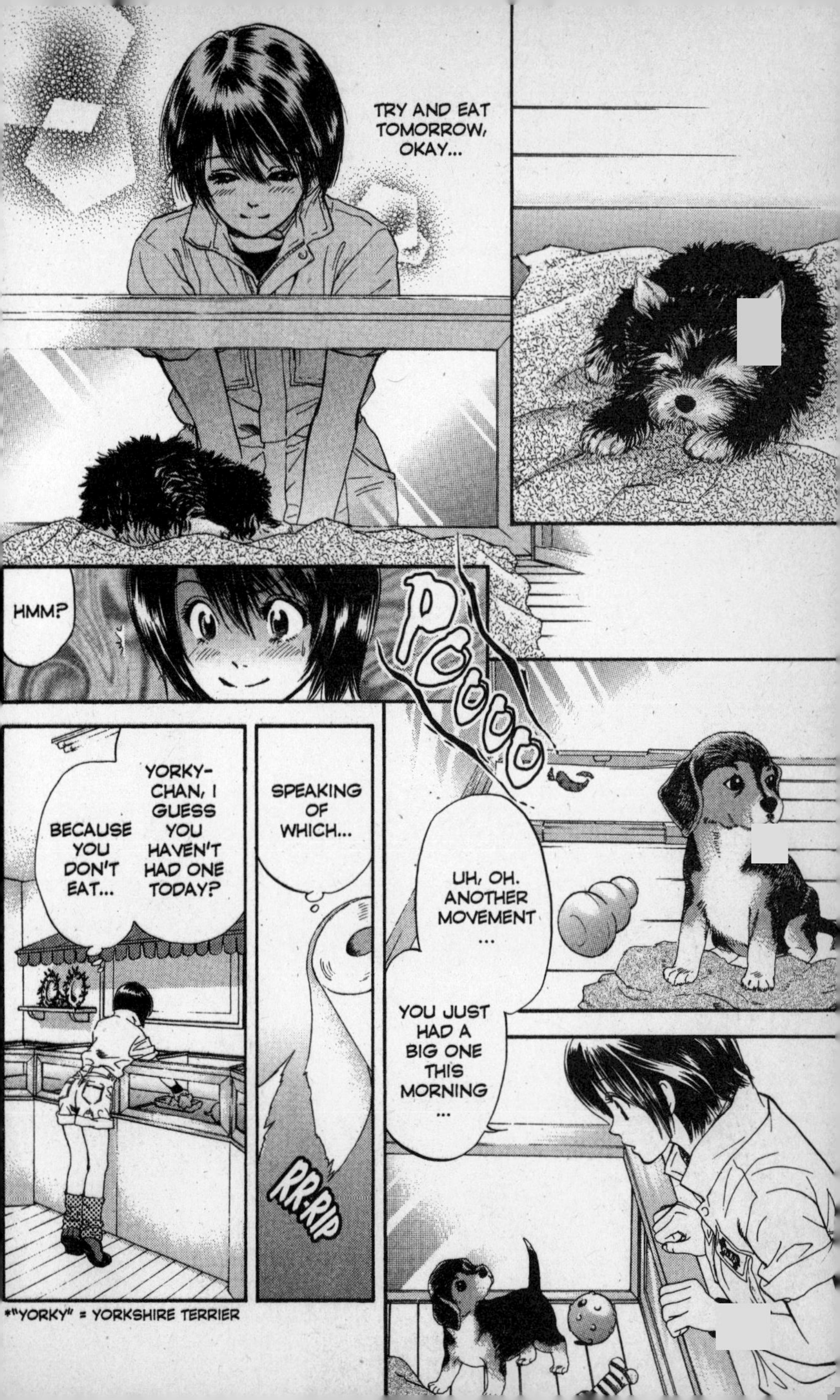
TRY AND EAT TOMORROW, OKAY...
HMM?
POOOO
UH, OH. ANOTHER MOVEMENT...
YOU JUST HAD A BIG ONE THIS MORNING...
SPEAKING OF WHICH...
RR-RIP
YORKY-CHAN, I GUESS YOU HAVEN'T HAD ONE TODAY?
BECAUSE YOU DON'T EAT...
*"YORKY" = YORKSHIRE TERRIER

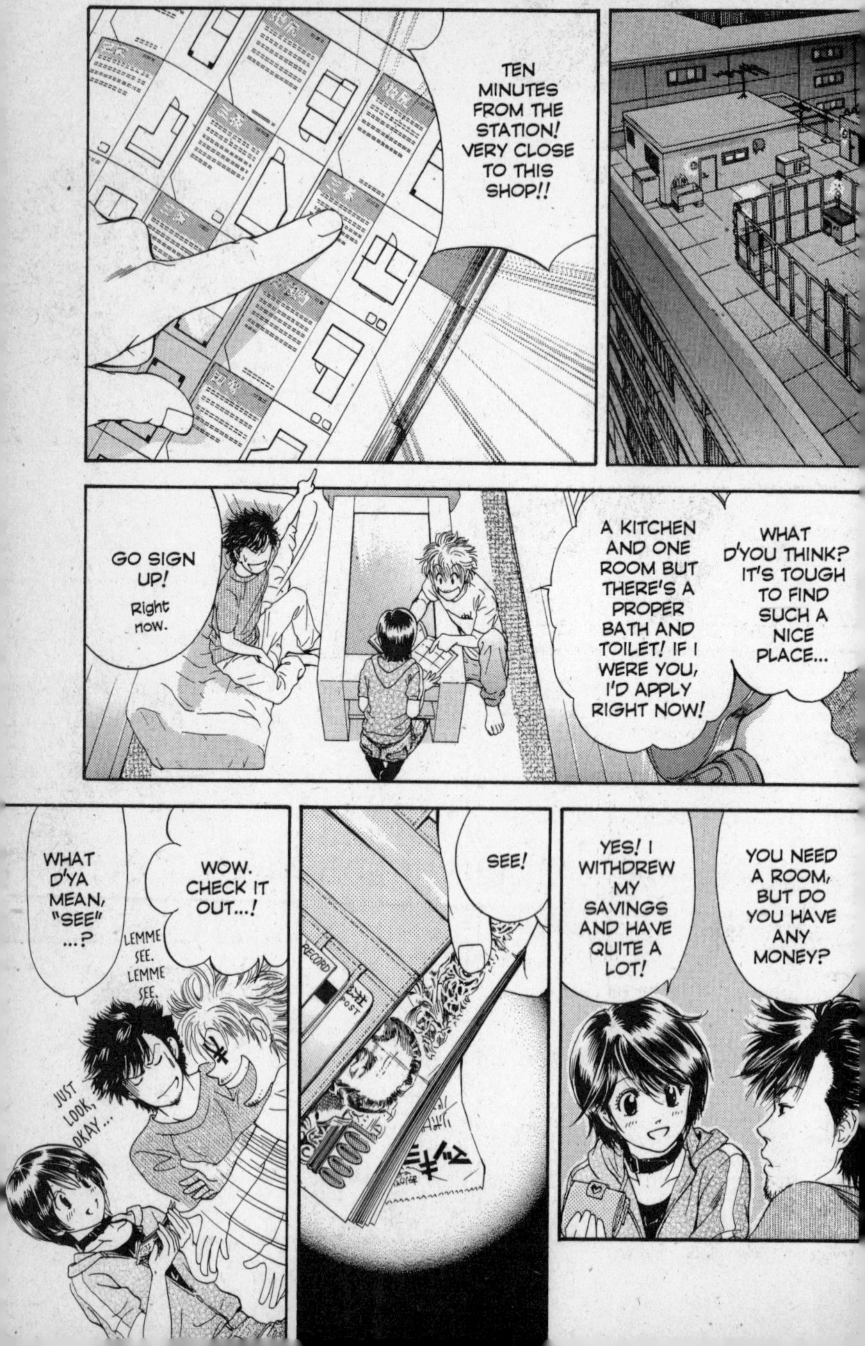
TEN MINUTES FROM THE STATION! VERY CLOSE TO THIS SHOP!!
WHAT D'YOU THINK? IT'S TOUGH TO FIND SUCH A NICE PLACE...
A KITCHEN AND ONE ROOM BUT THERE'S A PROPER BATH AND TOILET! IF I WERE YOU, I'D APPLY RIGHT NOW!
GO SIGN UP!
Right now.
YOU NEED A ROOM, BUT DO YOU HAVE ANY MONEY?
YES! I WITHDREW MY SAVINGS AND HAVE QUITE A LOT!
SEE!
RECORD
POST
WOW. CHECK IT OUT...!
WHAT D'YA MEAN, "SEE" ...?
LEMME SEE. LEMME SEE.
JUST LOOK, OKAY...

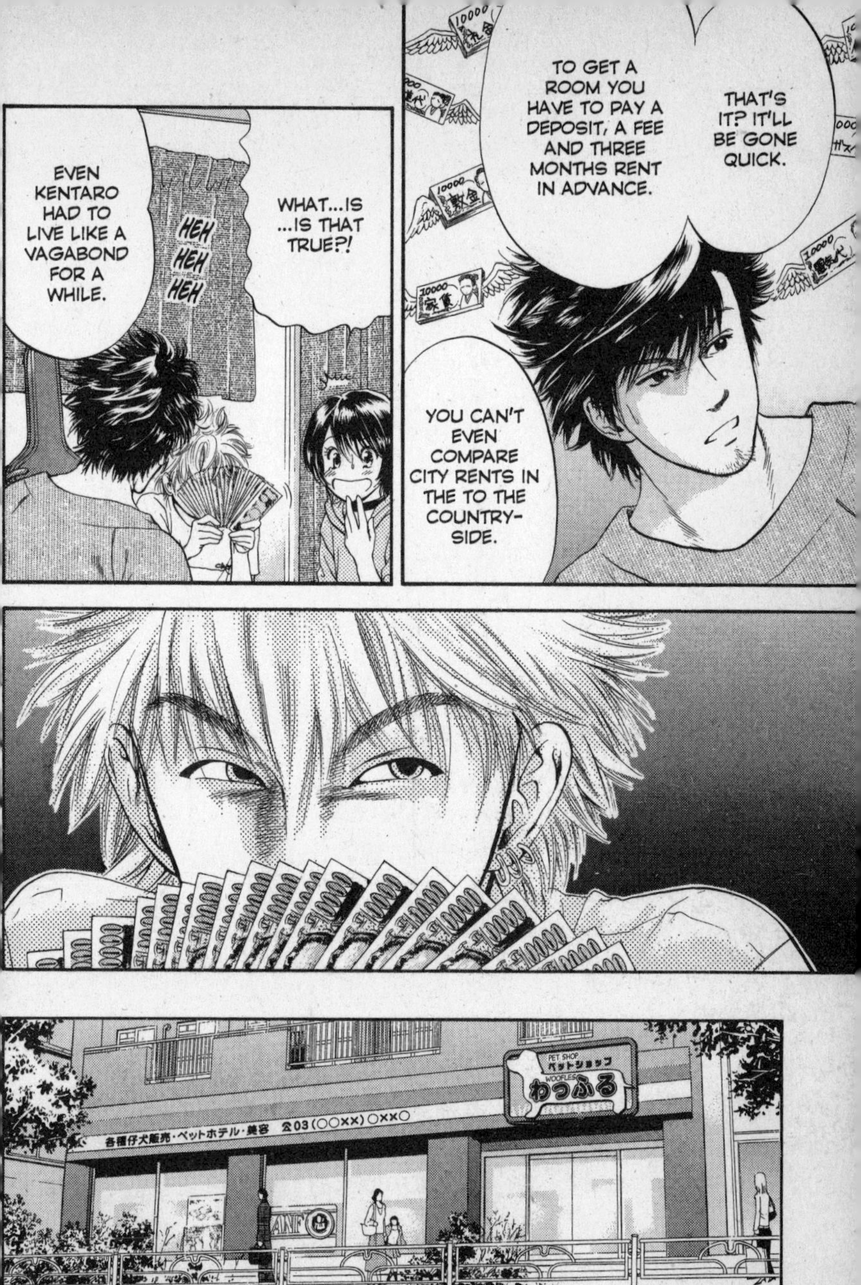
THAT'S IT? IT'LL BE GONE QUICK.
TO GET A ROOM YOU HAVE TO PAY A DEPOSIT, A FEE AND THREE MONTHS RENT IN ADVANCE.
YOU CAN'T EVEN COMPARE CITY RENTS IN THE TO THE COUNTRY-SIDE.
WHAT...IS ...IS THAT TRUE?!
HEH HEH HEH
EVEN KENTARO HAD TO LIVE LIKE A VAGABOND FOR A WHILE.
PET SHOP
ペットショップ
WOOFLES
わっふる
各種仔犬販売・ペットホテル・美容 ☎03(○○××)○××○

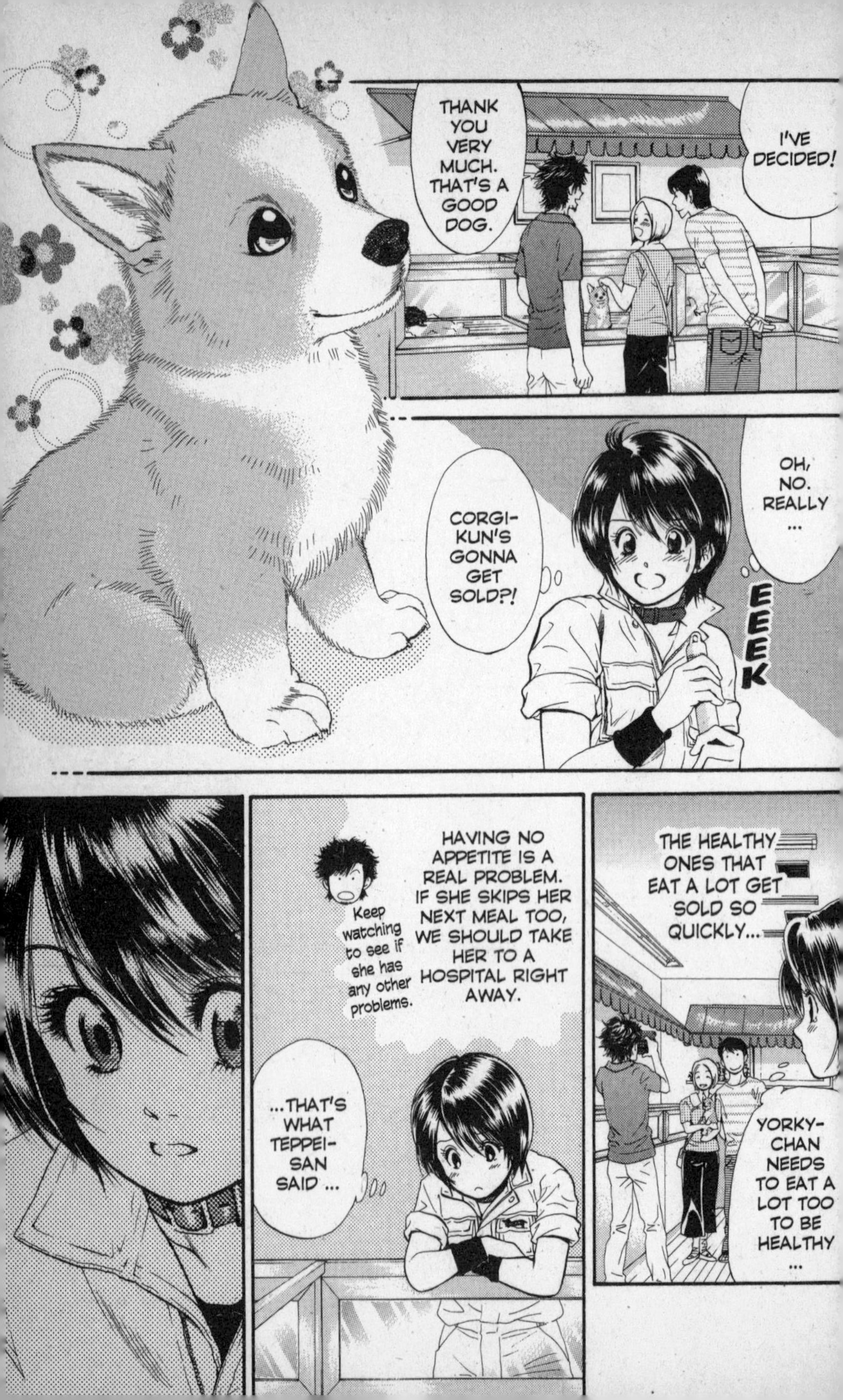
I'VE DECIDED!
THANK YOU VERY MUCH. THAT'S A GOOD DOG.
OH, NO. REALLY ...
EEEK
CORGI-KUN'S GONNA GET SOLD?!
THE HEALTHY ONES THAT EAT A LOT GET SOLD SO QUICKLY...
YORKY-CHAN NEEDS TO EAT A LOT TOO TO BE HEALTHY ...
HAVING NO APPETITE IS A REAL PROBLEM. IF SHE SKIPS HER NEXT MEAL TOO, WE SHOULD TAKE HER TO A HOSPITAL RIGHT AWAY.
Keep watching to see if she has any other problems.
...THAT'S WHAT TEPPEI-SAN SAID ...

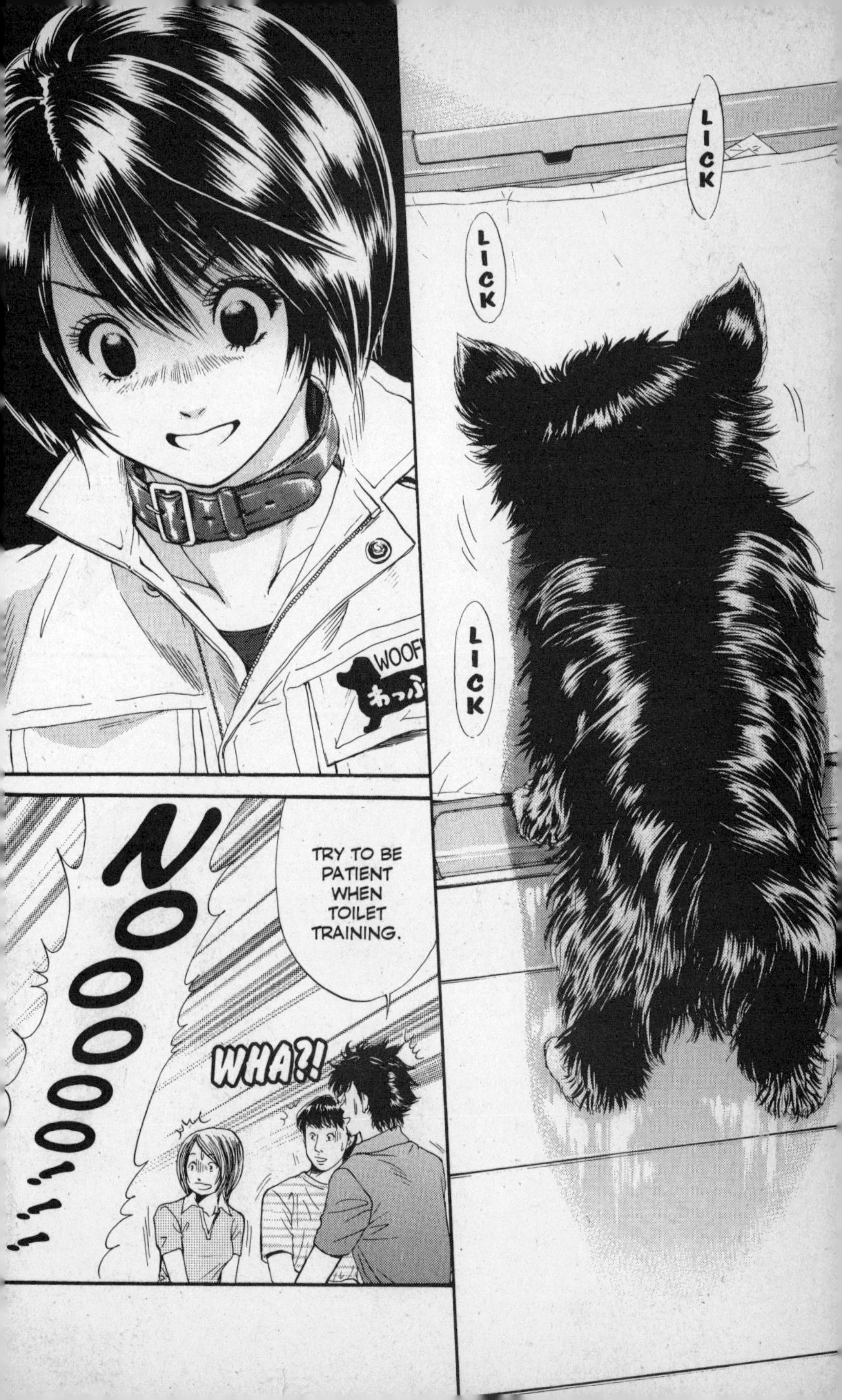
LICK
LICK
LICK
WOOF
わっふ
TRY TO BE PATIENT WHEN TOILET TRAINING.
NOOOOO!!!!
WHA?!

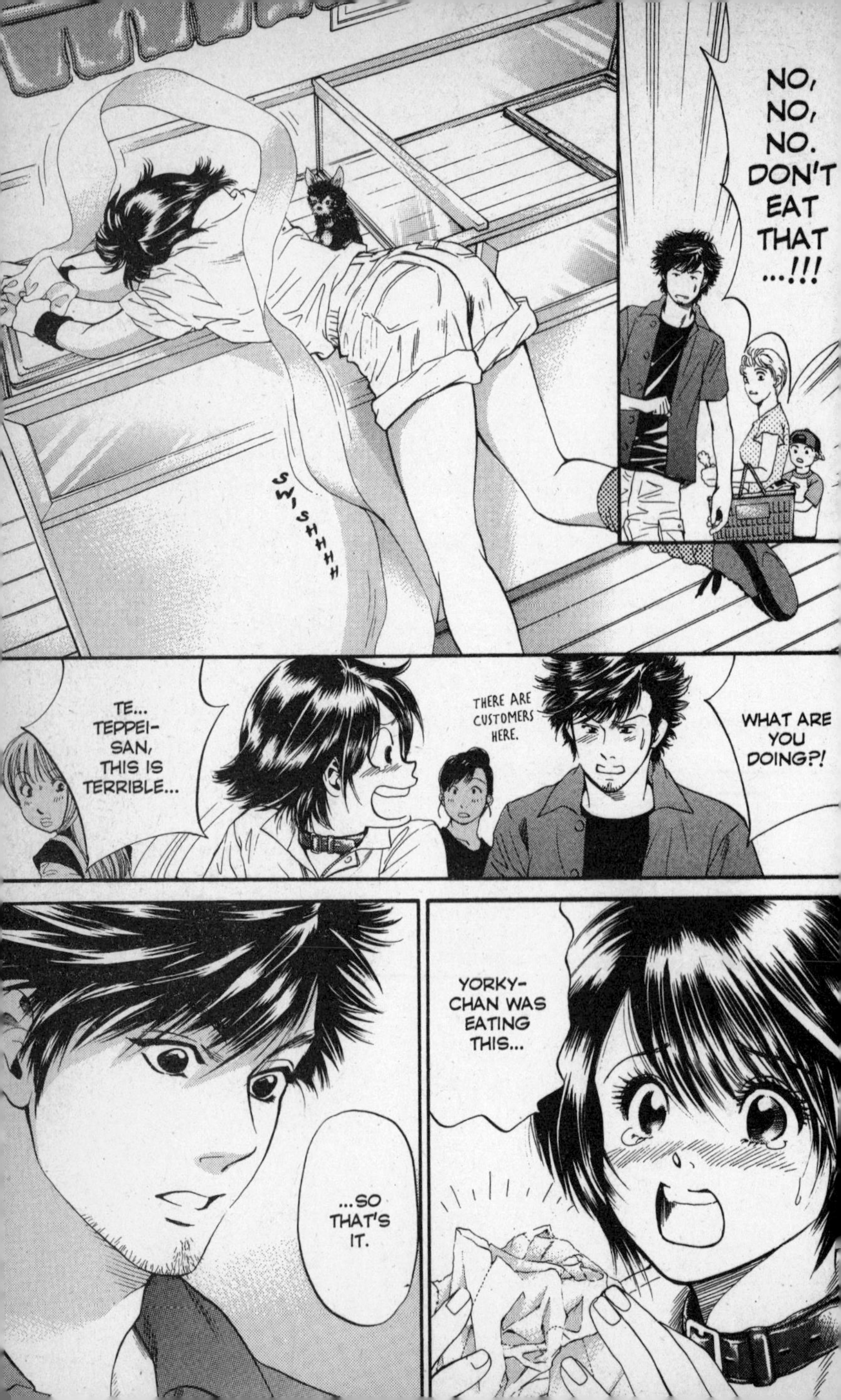
NO, NO, NO. DON'T EAT THAT ...!!!
SWISHHHH
WHAT ARE YOU DOING?!
THERE ARE CUSTOMERS HERE.
TE... TEPPEI-SAN, THIS IS TERRIBLE...
YORKY-CHAN WAS EATING THIS...
...SO THAT'S IT.

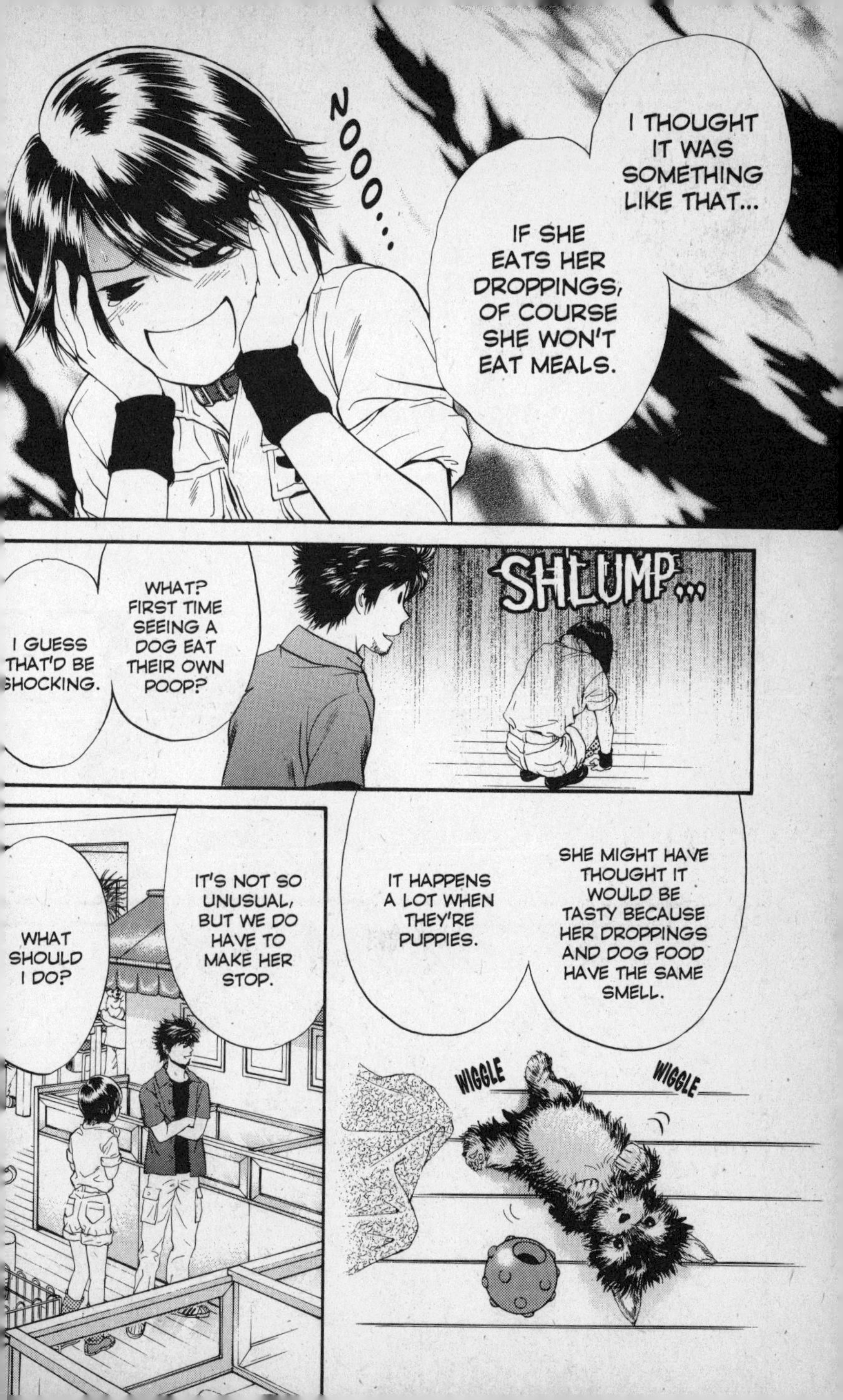
I THOUGHT IT WAS SOMETHING LIKE THAT...
IF SHE EATS HER DROPPINGS, OF COURSE SHE WON'T EAT MEALS.
NOOO...
SHLUMP...
WHAT? FIRST TIME SEEING A DOG EAT THEIR OWN POOP?
I GUESS THAT'D BE SHOCKING.
SHE MIGHT HAVE THOUGHT IT WOULD BE TASTY BECAUSE HER DROPPINGS AND DOG FOOD HAVE THE SAME SMELL.
IT HAPPENS A LOT WHEN THEY'RE PUPPIES.
IT'S NOT SO UNUSUAL, BUT WE DO HAVE TO MAKE HER STOP.
WHAT SHOULD I DO?
WIGGLE
WIGGLE

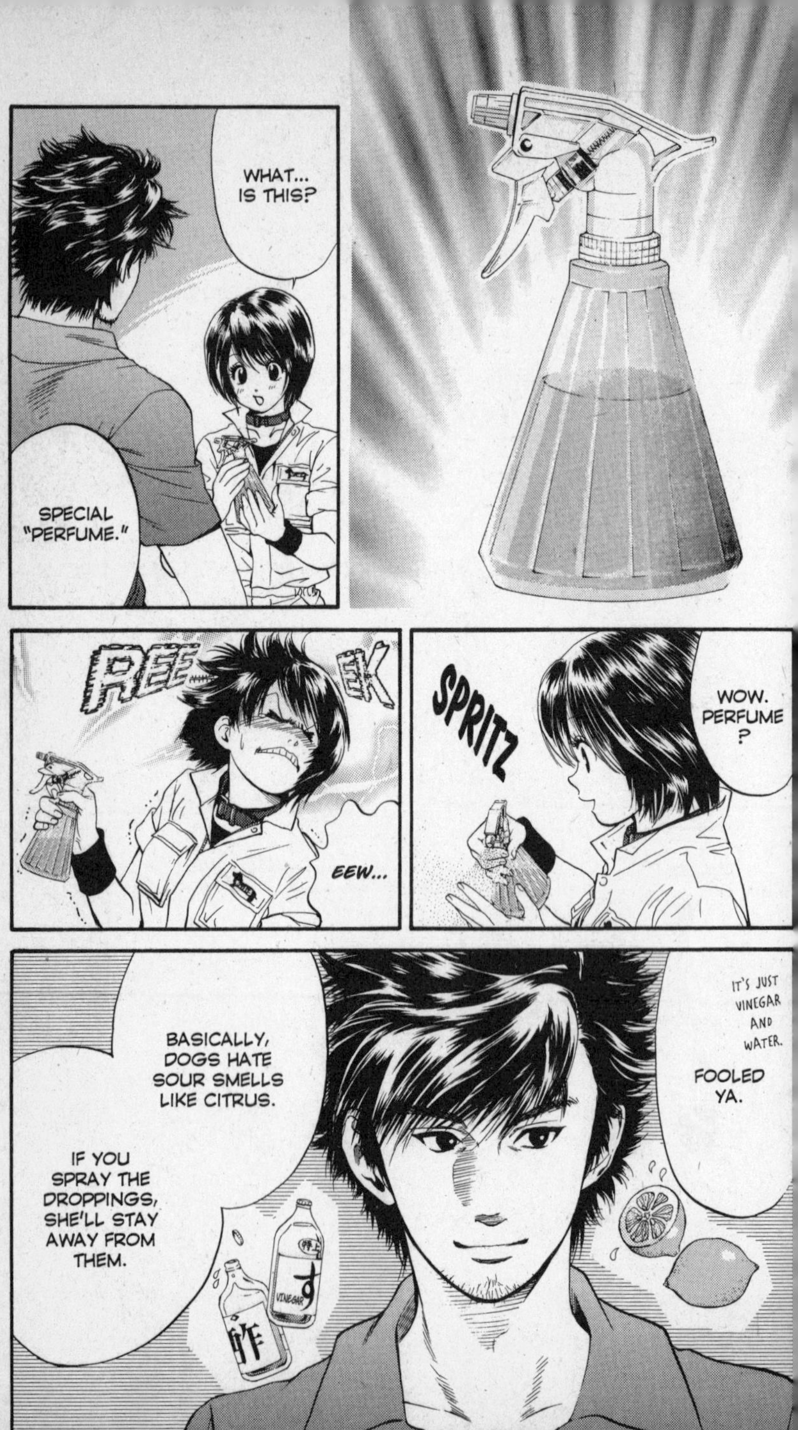
WHAT... IS THIS?
SPECIAL "PERFUME."
WOW. PERFUME?
SPRITZ
REE EK
EEW...
FOOLED YA.
IT'S JUST VINEGAR AND WATER.
BASICALLY, DOGS HATE SOUR SMELLS LIKE CITRUS.
IF YOU SPRAY THE DROPPINGS, SHE'LL STAY AWAY FROM THEM.
VINEGAR

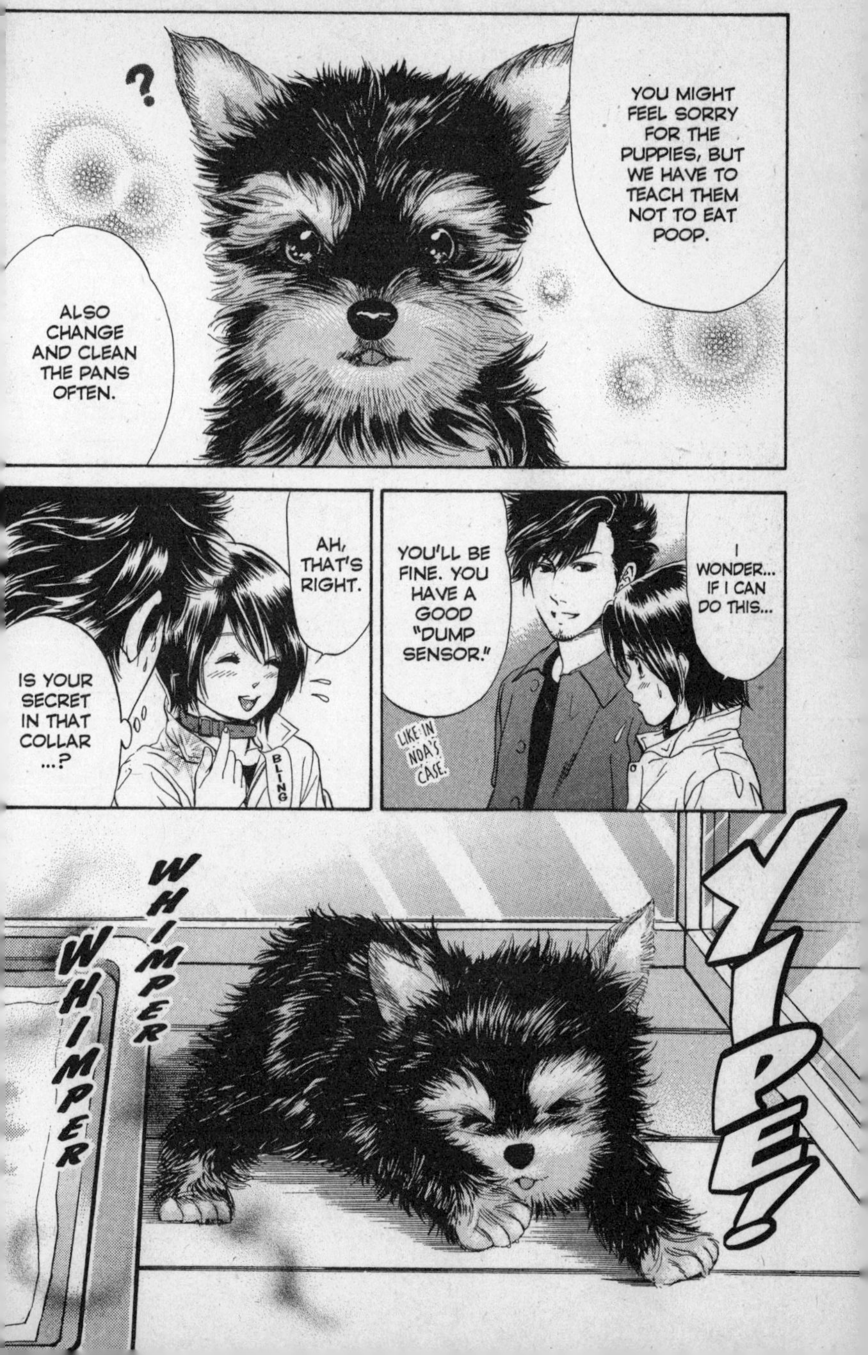
YOU MIGHT FEEL SORRY FOR THE PUPPIES, BUT WE HAVE TO TEACH THEM NOT TO EAT POOP.
?
ALSO CHANGE AND CLEAN THE PANS OFTEN.
I WONDER... IF I CAN DO THIS...
YOU'LL BE FINE. YOU HAVE A GOOD "DUMP SENSOR."
LIKE IN NOA'S CASE.
AH, THAT'S RIGHT.
IS YOUR SECRET IN THAT COLLAR ...?
BLING
YIPE!
WHIMPER
WHIMPER

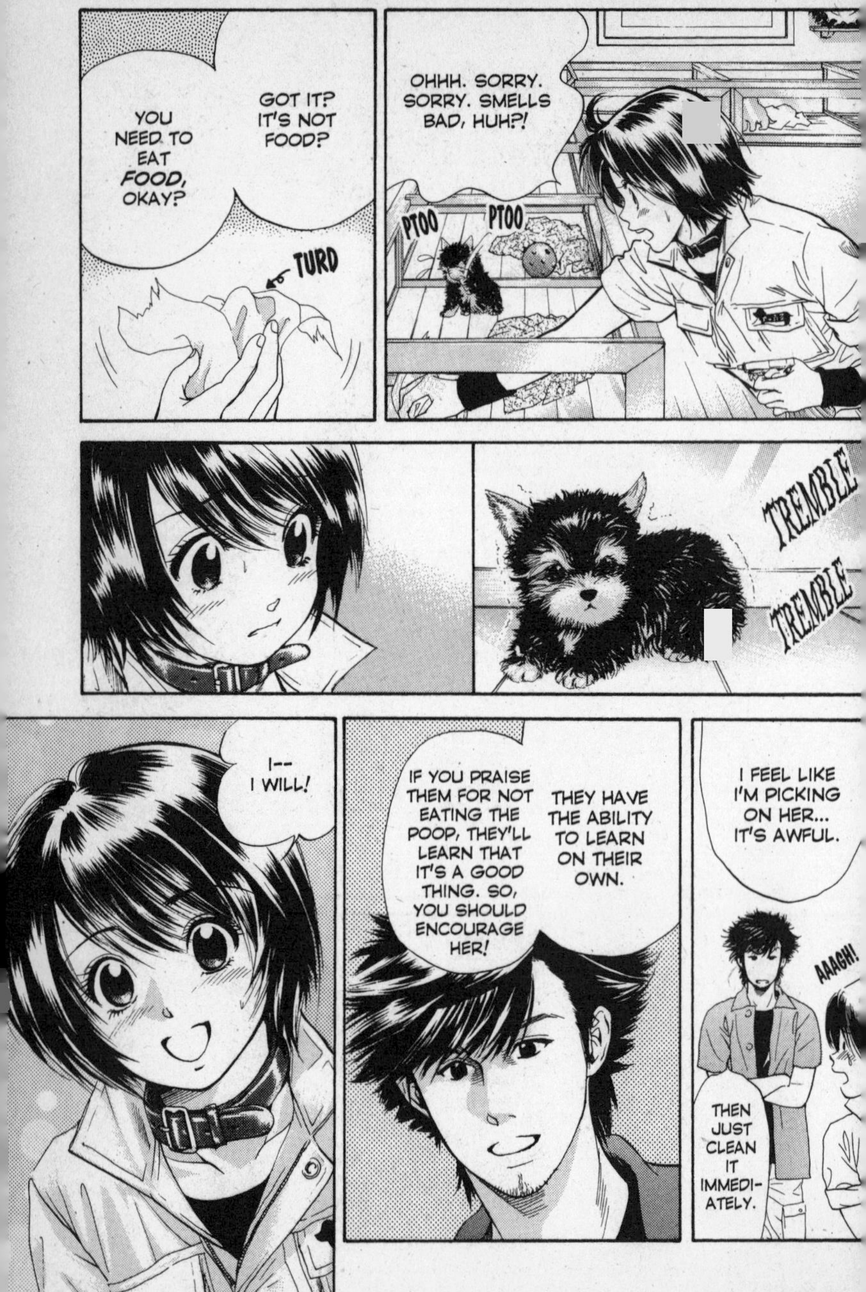
OHHH. SORRY. SORRY. SMELLS BAD, HUH?!
PTOO
PTOO
GOT IT? IT'S NOT FOOD?
YOU NEED TO EAT *FOOD*, OKAY?
TURD
TREMBLE
TREMBLE
I FEEL LIKE I'M PICKING ON HER... IT'S AWFUL.
AAAGH!
THEN JUST CLEAN IT IMMEDI-ATELY.
THEY HAVE THE ABILITY TO LEARN ON THEIR OWN.
IF YOU PRAISE THEM FOR NOT EATING THE POOP, THEY'LL LEARN THAT IT'S A GOOD THING. SO, YOU SHOULD ENCOURAGE HER!
I-- I WILL!

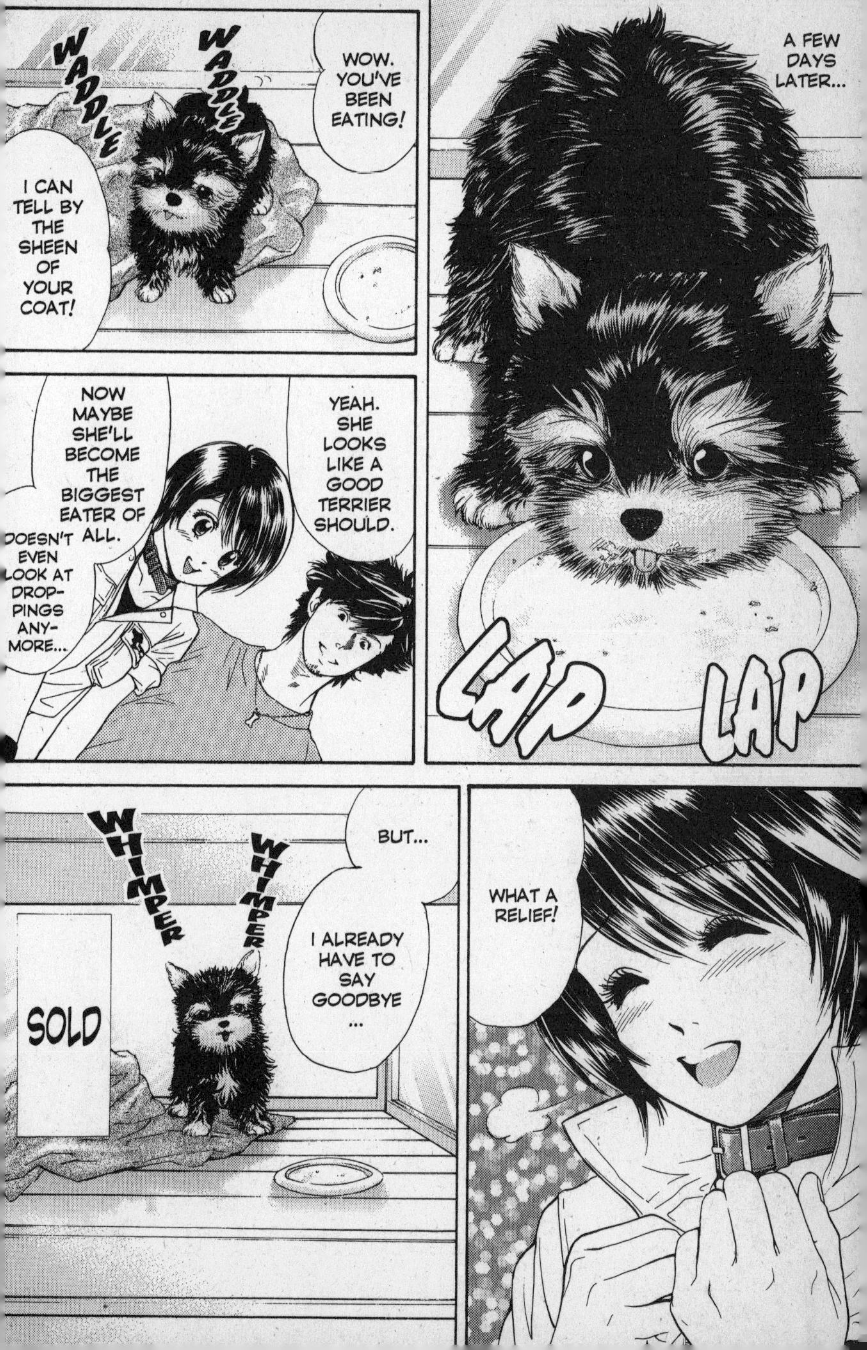
A FEW DAYS LATER...
LAP LAP
WADDLE WADDLE
WOW. YOU'VE BEEN EATING!
I CAN TELL BY THE SHEEN OF YOUR COAT!
YEAH. SHE LOOKS LIKE A GOOD TERRIER SHOULD.
NOW MAYBE SHE'LL BECOME THE BIGGEST EATER OF ALL.
DOESN'T EVEN LOOK AT DROPPINGS ANYMORE...
WHAT A RELIEF!
BUT...
I ALREADY HAVE TO SAY GOODBYE ...
WHIMPER WHIMPER
SOLD

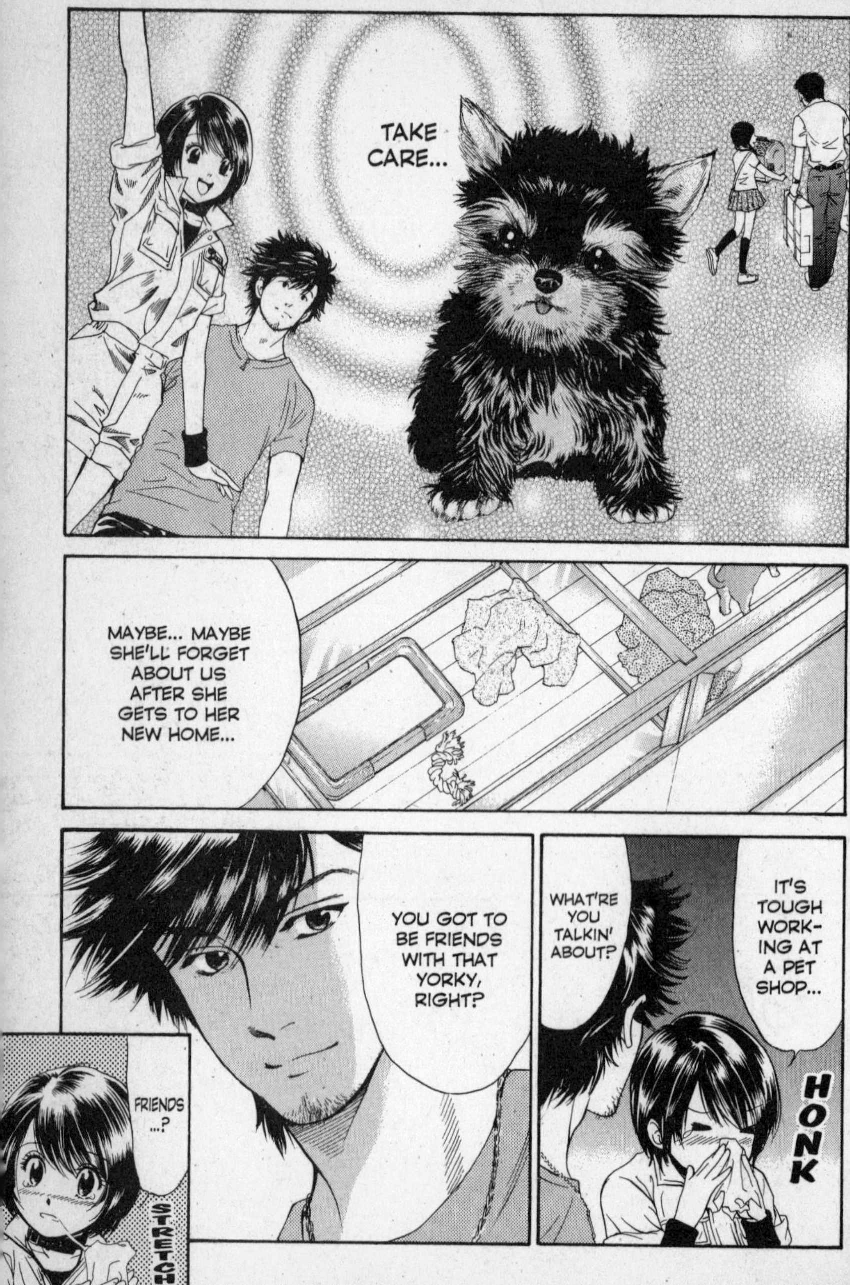
TAKE CARE...
MAYBE... MAYBE SHE'LL FORGET ABOUT US AFTER SHE GETS TO HER NEW HOME...
IT'S TOUGH WORK-ING AT A PET SHOP...
WHAT'RE YOU TALKIN' ABOUT?
HONK
YOU GOT TO BE FRIENDS WITH THAT YORKY, RIGHT?
FRIENDS ...?
STRETCH

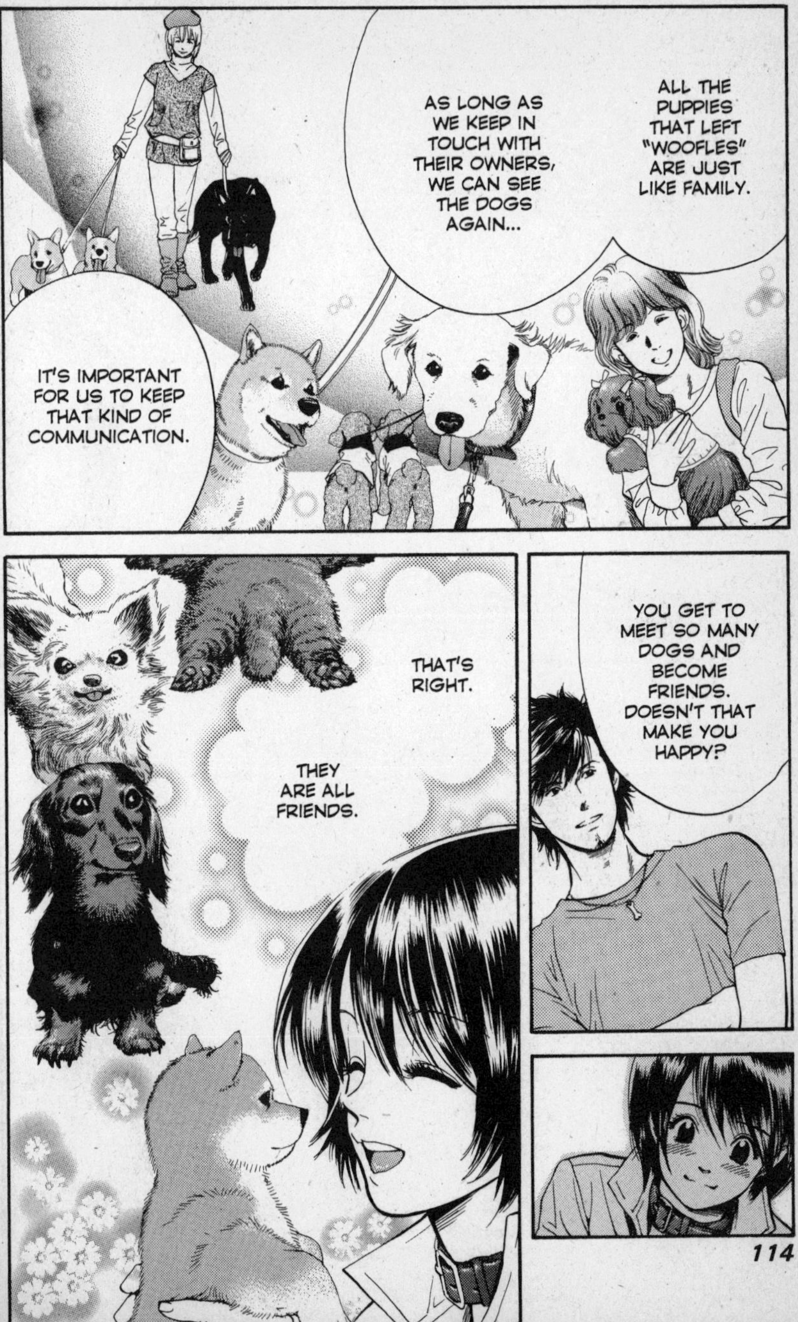
ALL THE PUPPIES THAT LEFT "WOOFLES" ARE JUST LIKE FAMILY.
AS LONG AS WE KEEP IN TOUCH WITH THEIR OWNERS, WE CAN SEE THE DOGS AGAIN...
IT'S IMPORTANT FOR US TO KEEP THAT KIND OF COMMUNICATION.
YOU GET TO MEET SO MANY DOGS AND BECOME FRIENDS. DOESN'T THAT MAKE YOU HAPPY?
THAT'S RIGHT.
THEY ARE ALL FRIENDS.

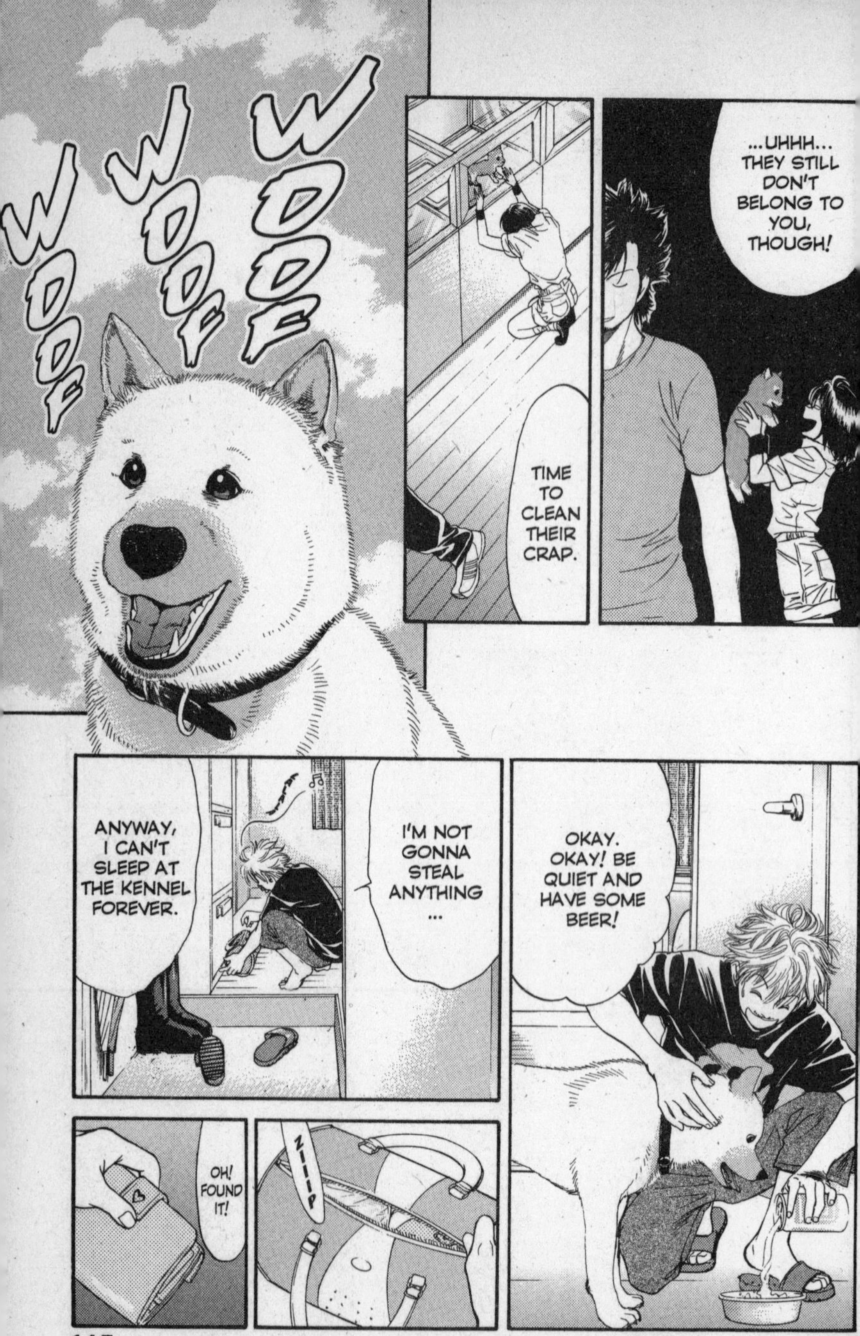
...UHHH... THEY STILL DON'T BELONG TO YOU, THOUGH!
TIME TO CLEAN THEIR CRAP.
WOOF
WOOF
WOOF
OKAY. OKAY! BE QUIET AND HAVE SOME BEER!
I'M NOT GONNA STEAL ANYTHING ...
ANYWAY, I CAN'T SLEEP AT THE KENNEL FOREVER.
ZIIIP
OH! FOUND IT!

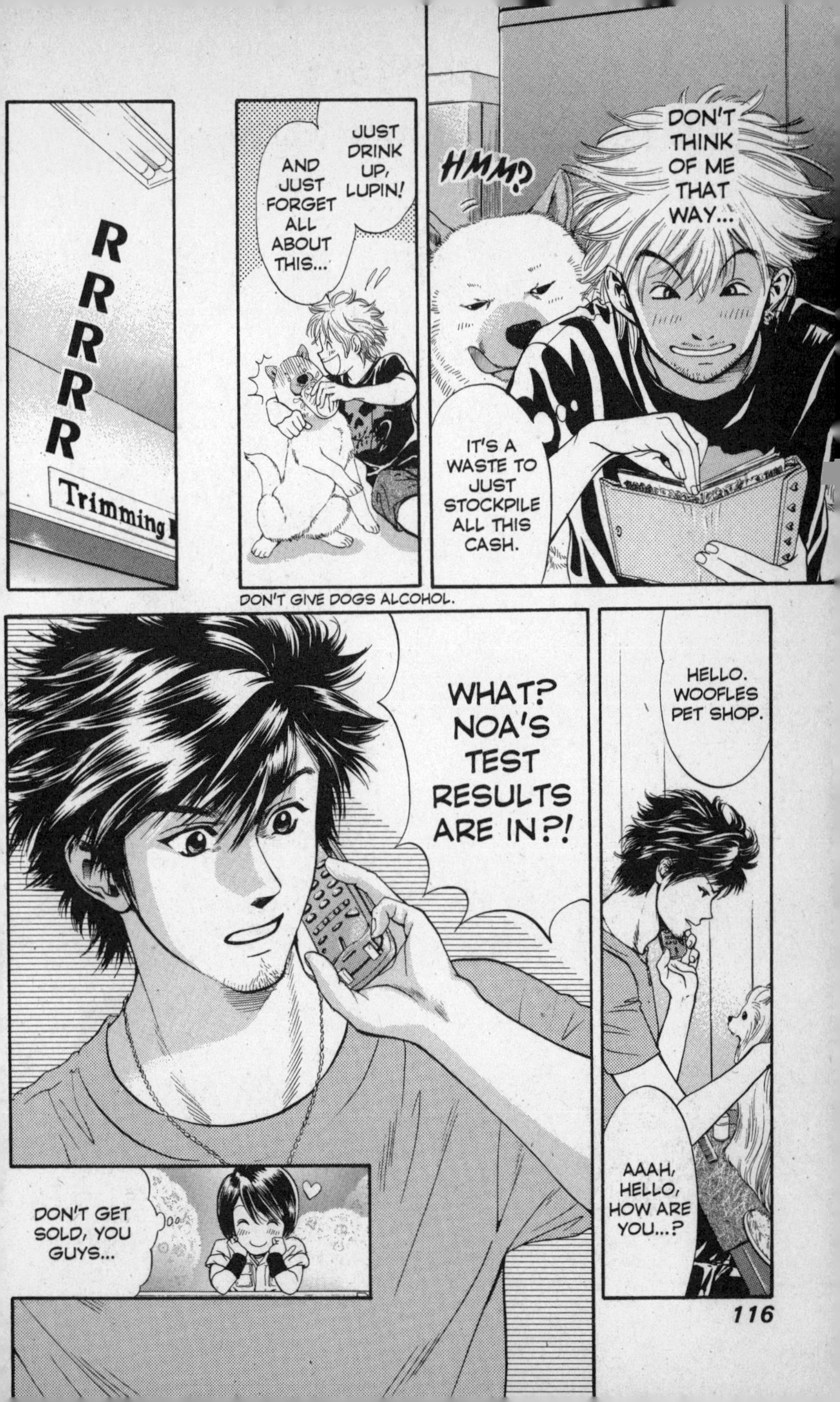
DON'T THINK OF ME THAT WAY...
HMM?
IT'S A WASTE TO JUST STOCKPILE ALL THIS CASH.
JUST DRINK UP, LUPIN!
AND JUST FORGET ALL ABOUT THIS...
RRRRR
Trimming
DON'T GIVE DOGS ALCOHOL.
HELLO. WOOFLES PET SHOP.
AAAH, HELLO, HOW ARE YOU...?
WHAT? NOA'S TEST RESULTS ARE IN?!
DON'T GET SOLD, YOU GUYS...

Chapter 4
To Save That Puppy...

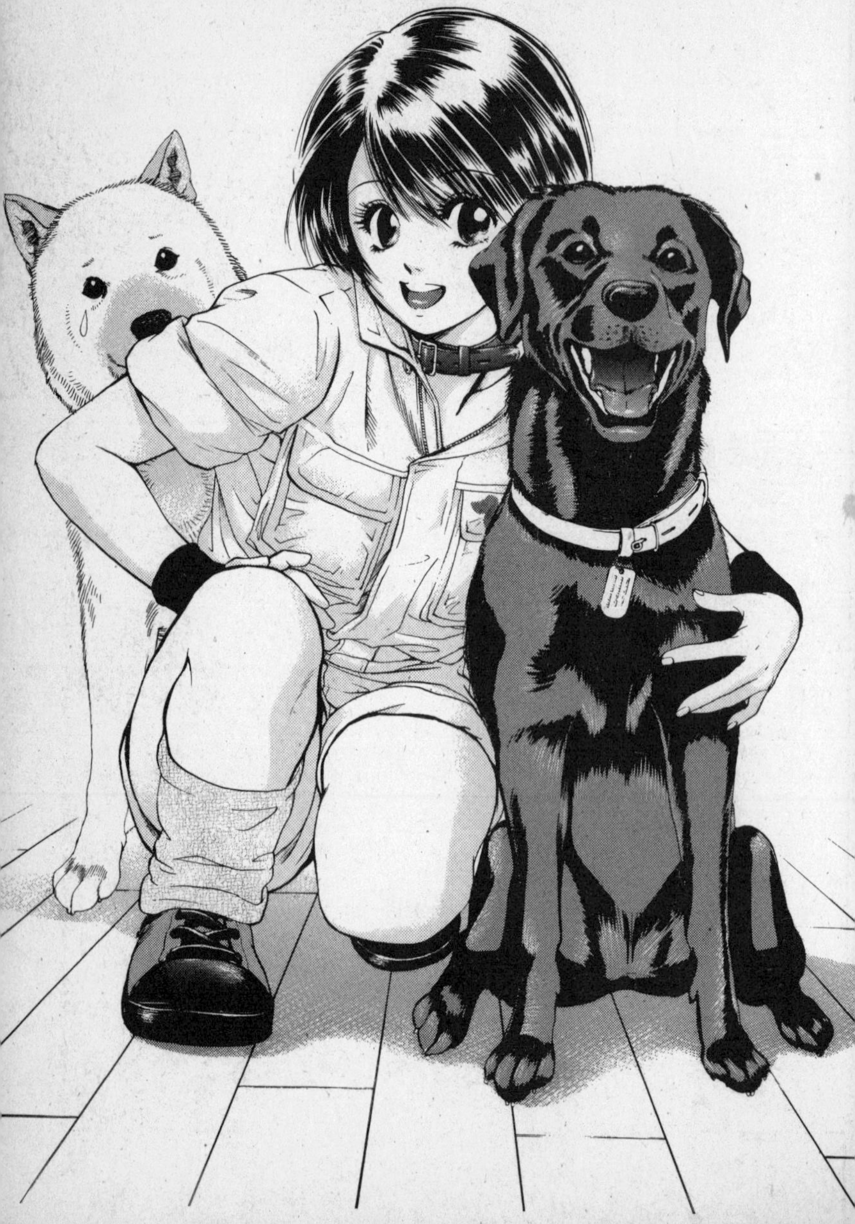

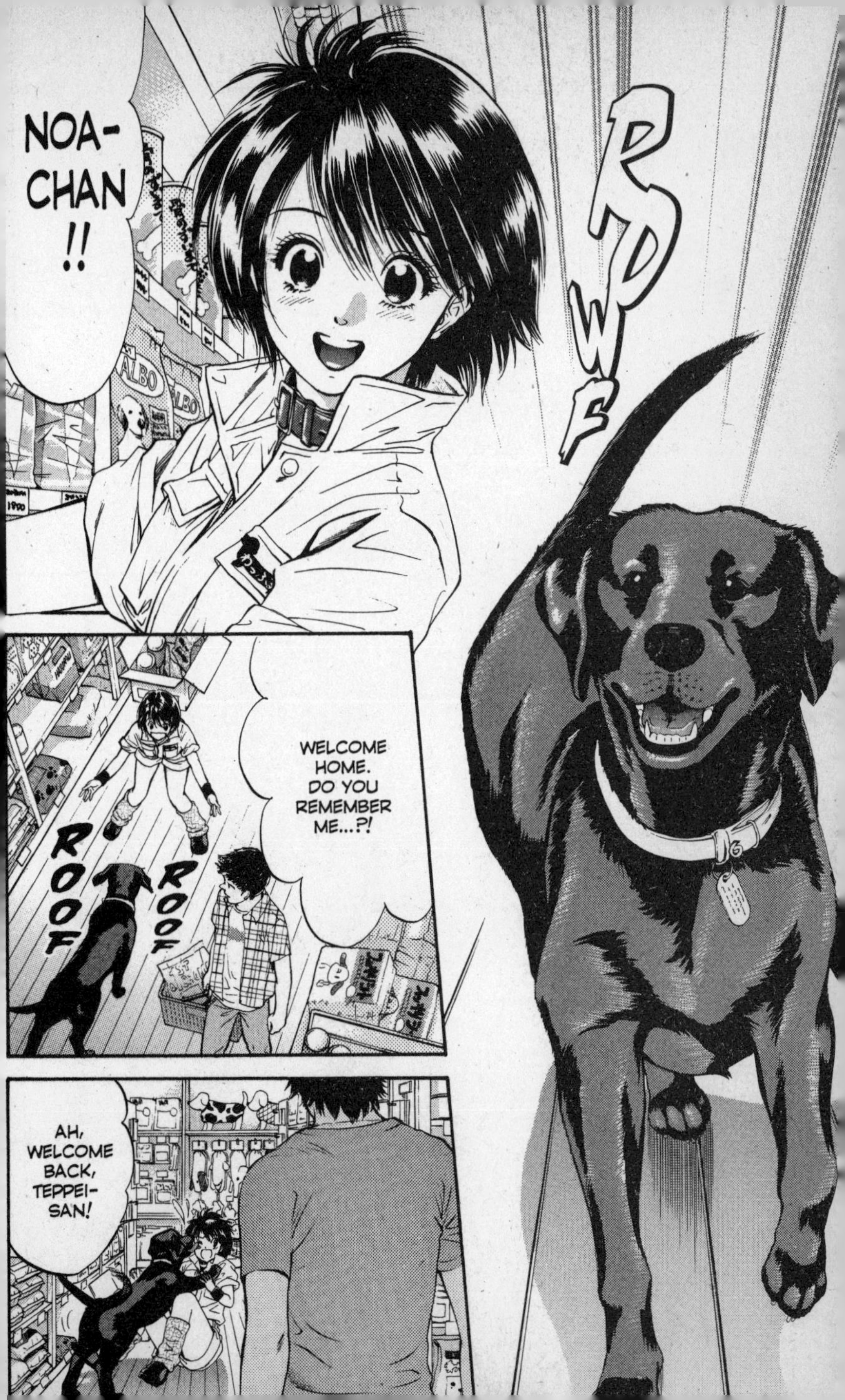
RUWF
NOA-CHAN!!
WELCOME HOME. DO YOU REMEMBER ME...?!
ROOF
ROOF
AH, WELCOME BACK, TEPPEI-SAN!

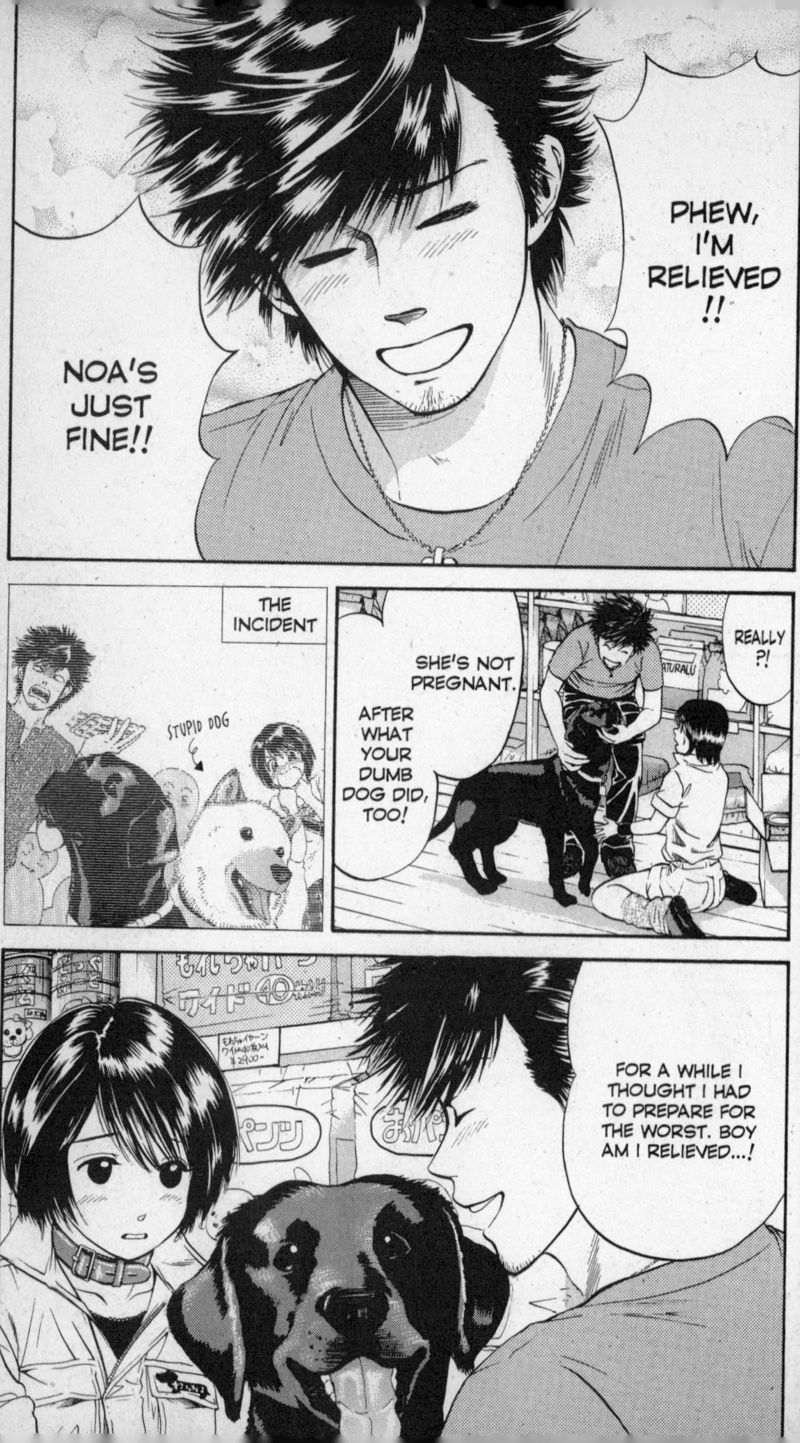
PHEW, I'M RELIEVED!!
NOA'S JUST FINE!!
REALLY?!
SHE'S NOT PREGNANT.
AFTER WHAT YOUR DUMB DOG DID, TOO!
THE INCIDENT
STUPID DOG
FOR A WHILE I THOUGHT I HAD TO PREPARE FOR THE WORST. BOY AM I RELIEVED...!

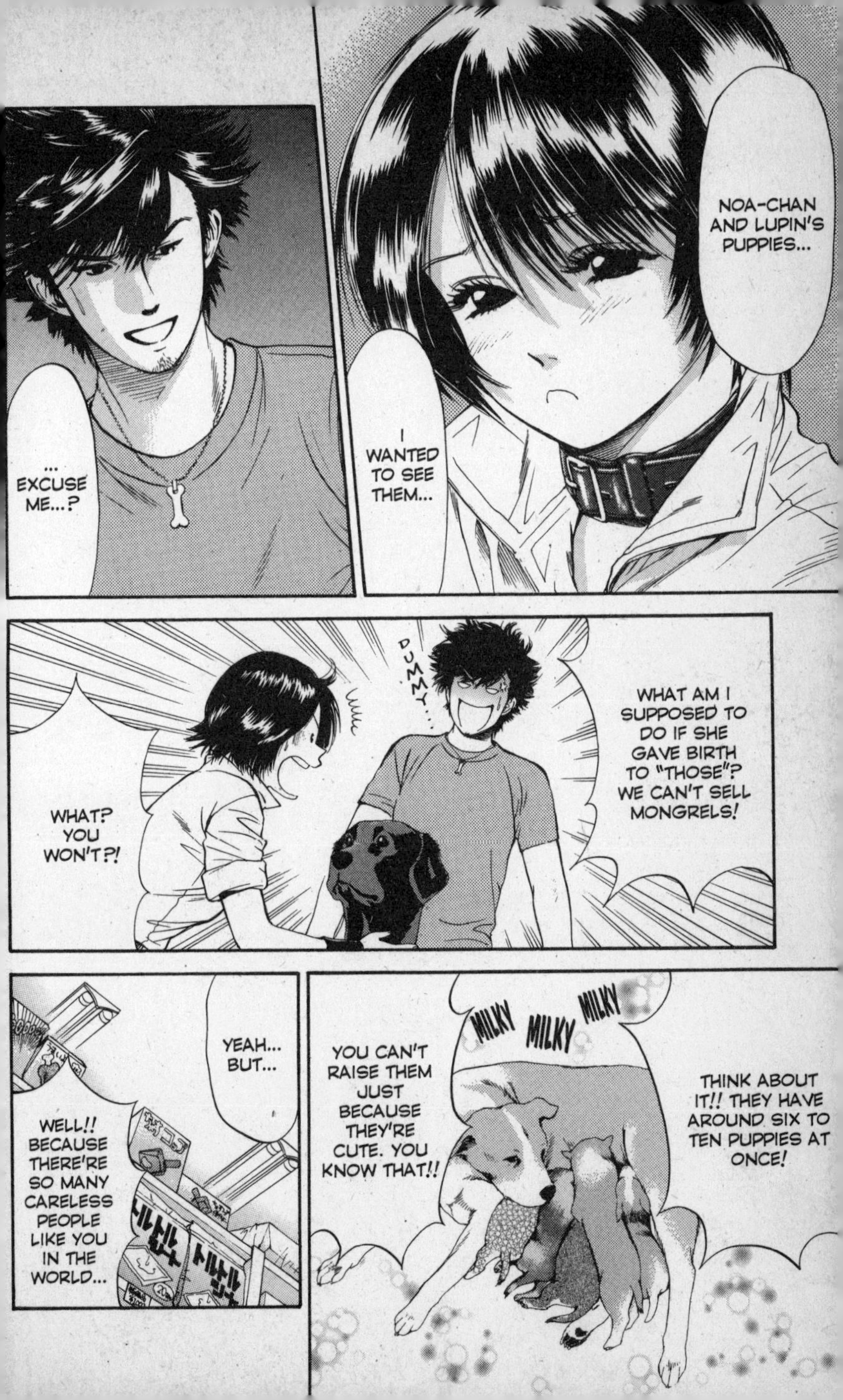
NOA-CHAN AND LUPIN'S PUPPIES...
I WANTED TO SEE THEM...
... EXCUSE ME...?
WHAT AM I SUPPOSED TO DO IF SHE GAVE BIRTH TO "THOSE"? WE CAN'T SELL MONGRELS!
DUMMY...
WHAT? YOU WON'T?!
MILKY MILKY MILKY
THINK ABOUT IT!! THEY HAVE AROUND SIX TO TEN PUPPIES AT ONCE!
YOU CAN'T RAISE THEM JUST BECAUSE THEY'RE CUTE. YOU KNOW THAT!!
YEAH... BUT...
WELL!! BECAUSE THERE'RE SO MANY CARELESS PEOPLE LIKE YOU IN THE WORLD...

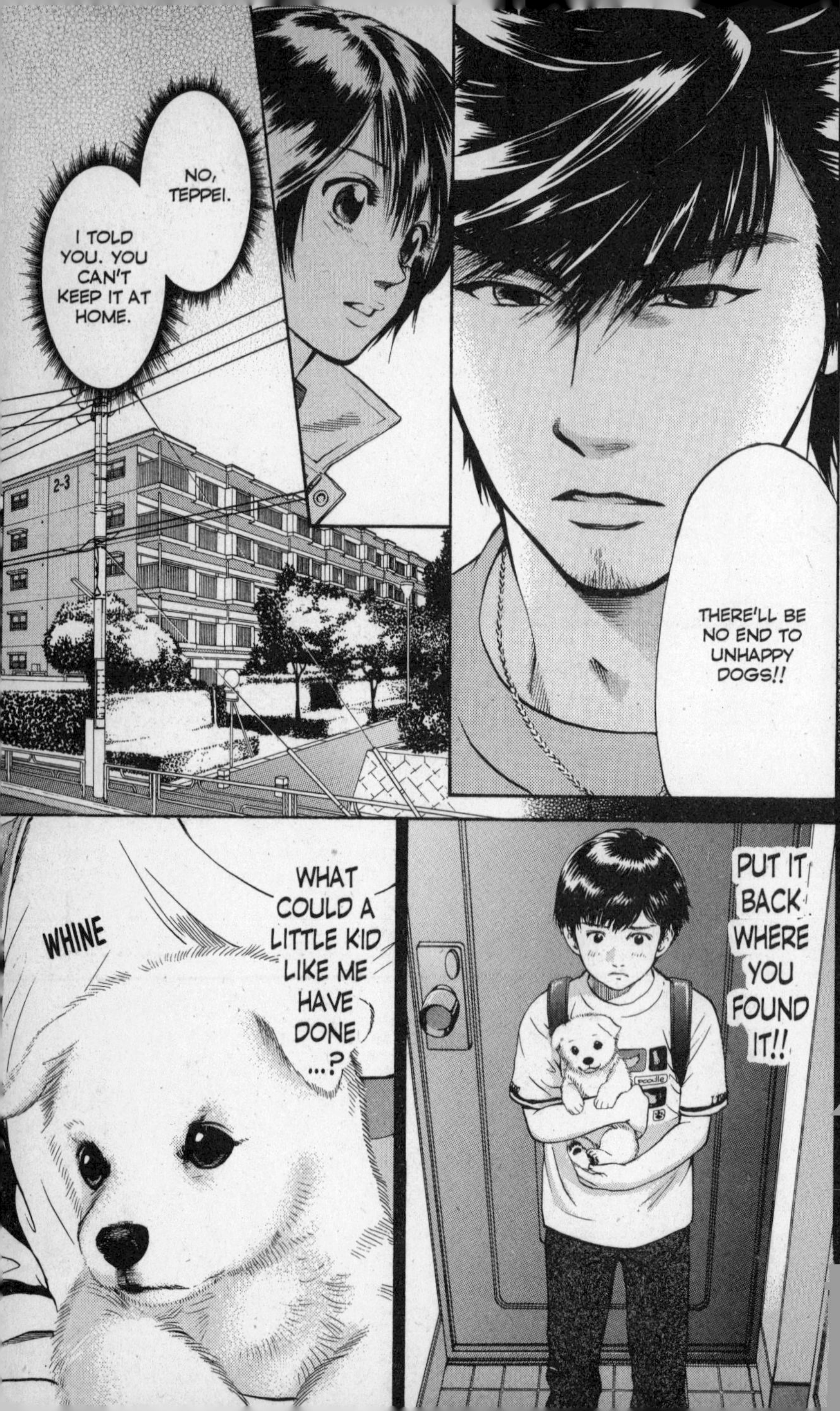
THERE'LL BE NO END TO UNHAPPY DOGS!!
NO, TEPPEI.
I TOLD YOU. YOU CAN'T KEEP IT AT HOME.
PUT IT BACK WHERE YOU FOUND IT!!
WHAT COULD A LITTLE KID LIKE ME HAVE DONE ...?
WHINE

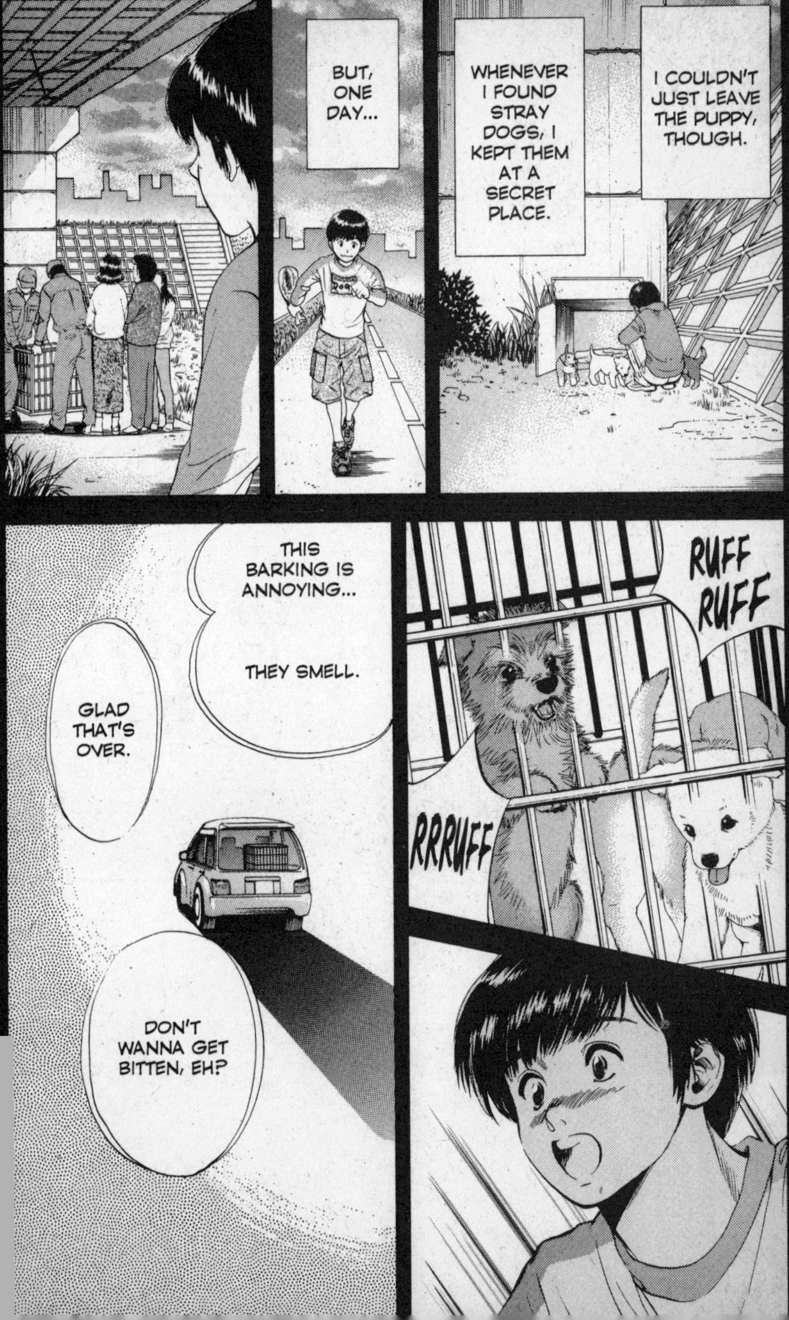
I COULDN'T JUST LEAVE THE PUPPY, THOUGH.
WHENEVER I FOUND STRAY DOGS, I KEPT THEM AT A SECRET PLACE.
BUT, ONE DAY...
RUFF RUFF
RRRUFF
THIS BARKING IS ANNOYING...
THEY SMELL.
GLAD THAT'S OVER.
DON'T WANNA GET BITTEN, EH?

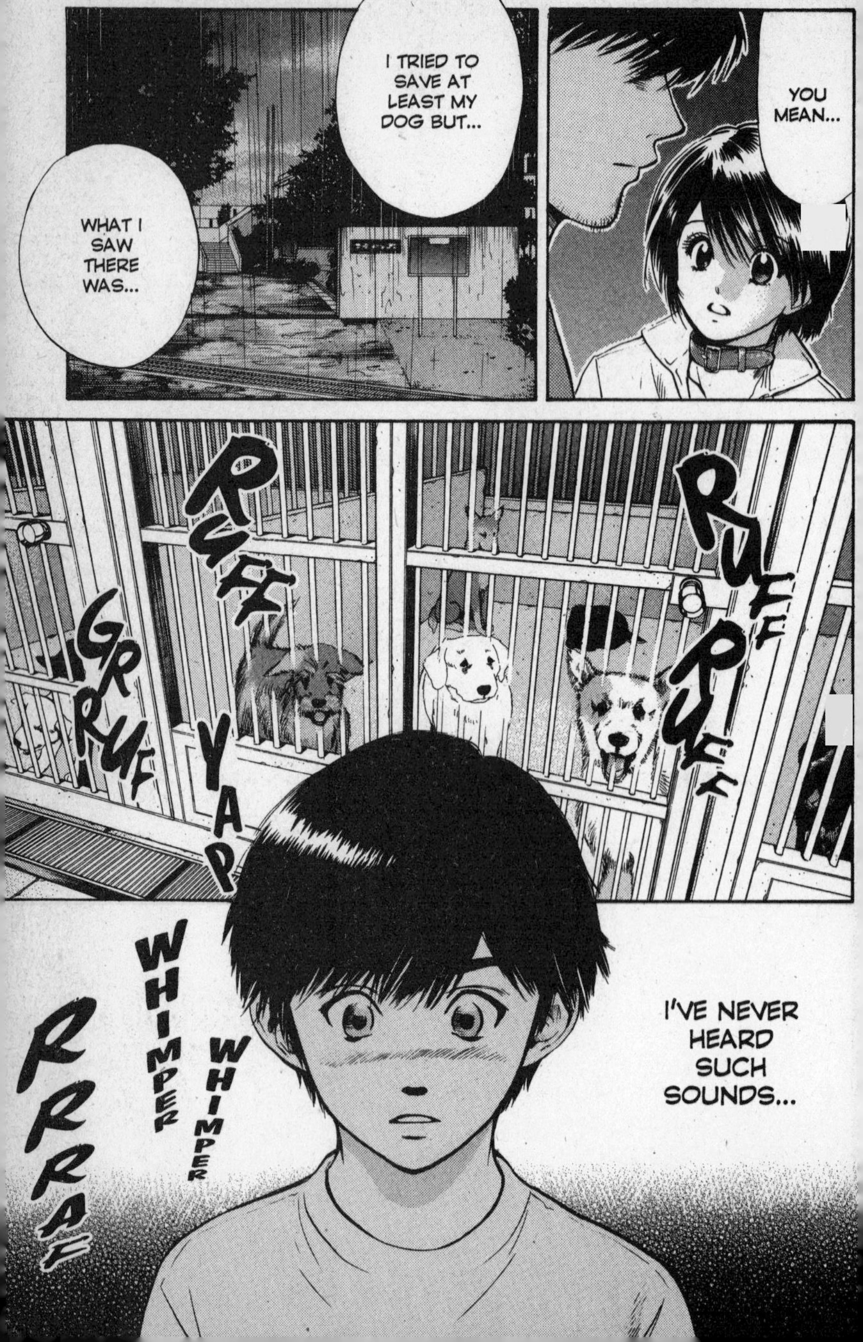
YOU MEAN...
I TRIED TO SAVE AT LEAST MY DOG BUT...
WHAT I SAW THERE WAS...
RUFF
RUFF
RUFF
GRRUF
YAP
I'VE NEVER HEARD SUCH SOUNDS...
WHIMPER
WHIMPER
RRRAF

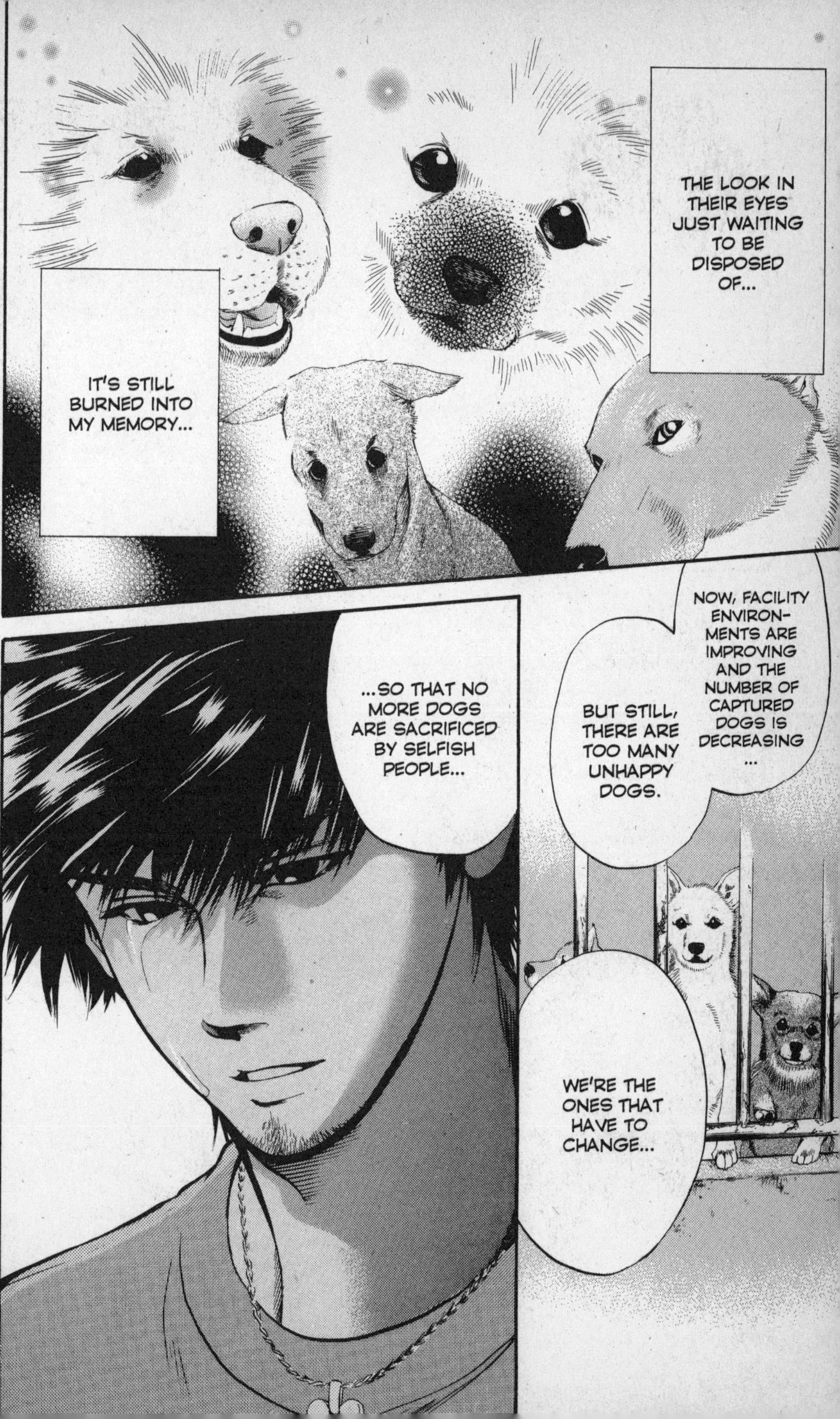

THE LOOK IN THEIR EYES JUST WAITING TO BE DISPOSED OF...
IT'S STILL BURNED INTO MY MEMORY...
NOW, FACILITY ENVIRON-MENTS ARE IMPROVING AND THE NUMBER OF CAPTURED DOGS IS DECREASING ...
BUT STILL, THERE ARE TOO MANY UNHAPPY DOGS.
WE'RE THE ONES THAT HAVE TO CHANGE...
...SO THAT NO MORE DOGS ARE SACRIFICED BY SELFISH PEOPLE...

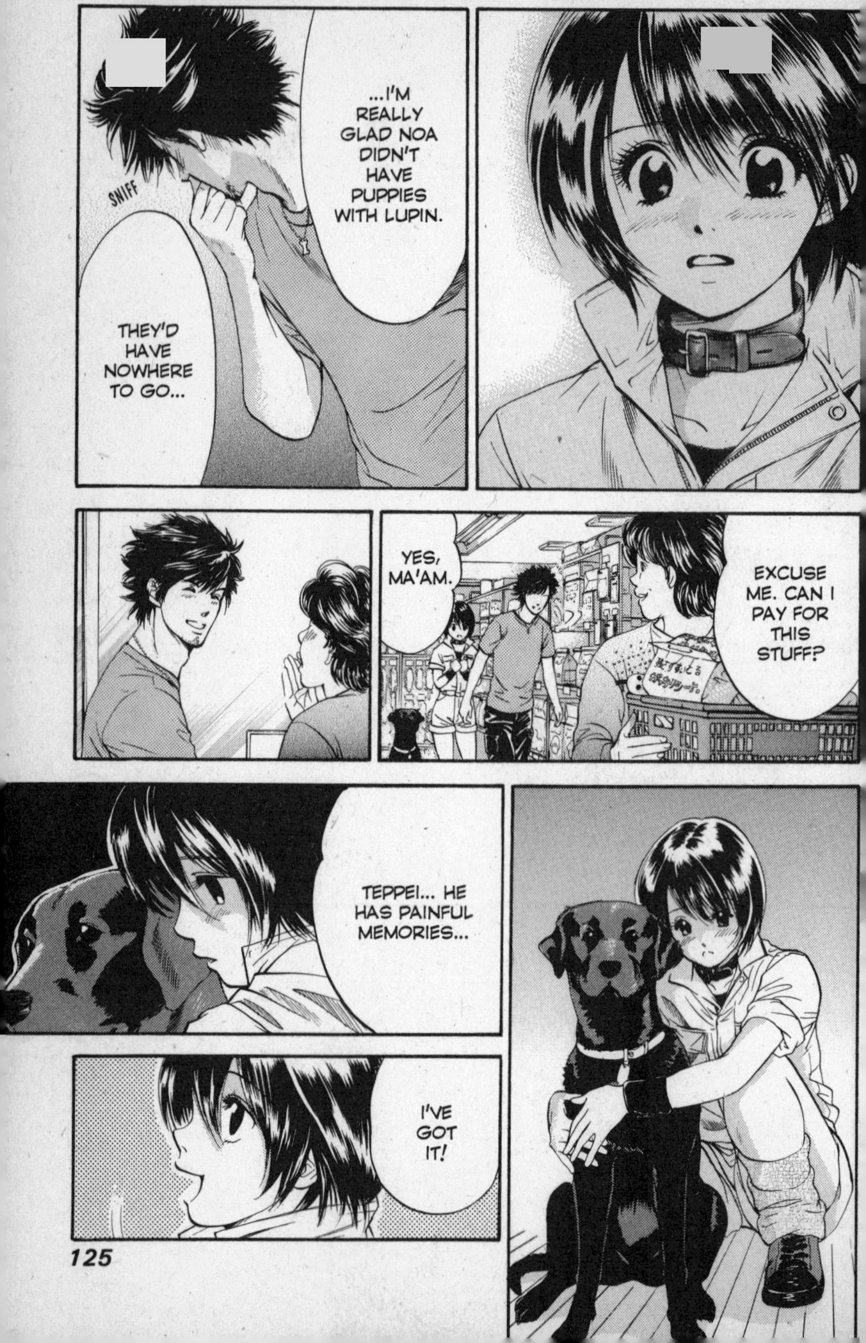
...I'M REALLY GLAD NOA DIDN'T HAVE PUPPIES WITH LUPIN.
SNIFF
THEY'D HAVE NOWHERE TO GO...
EXCUSE ME. CAN I PAY FOR THIS STUFF?
YES, MA'AM.
TEPPEI... HE HAS PAINFUL MEMORIES...
I'VE GOT IT!

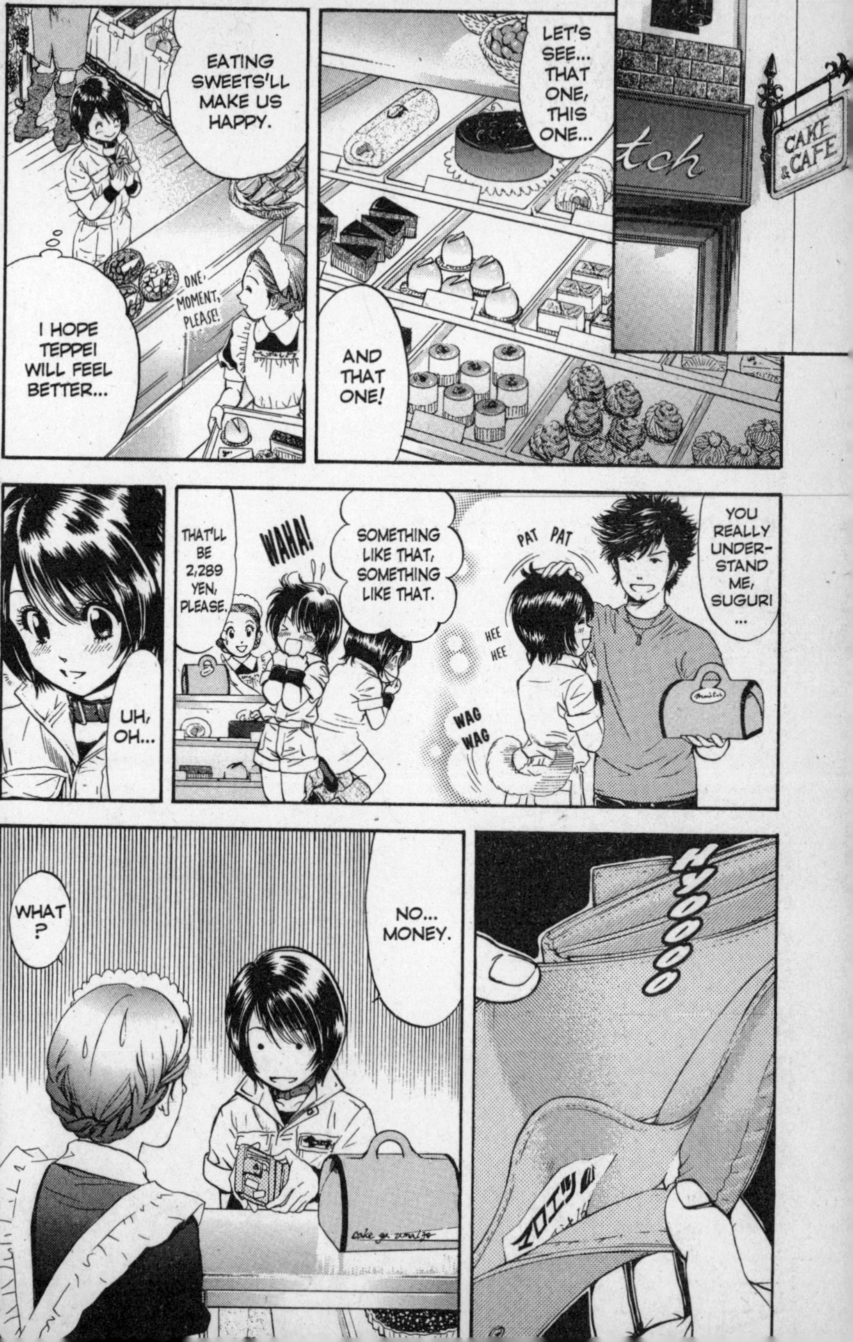
CAKE & CAFE
LET'S SEE... THAT ONE, THIS ONE...
AND THAT ONE!
EATING SWEETS'LL MAKE US HAPPY.
ONE MOMENT, PLEASE!
I HOPE TEPPEI WILL FEEL BETTER...
YOU REALLY UNDER-STAND ME, SUGURI...
PAT PAT
HEE HEE
WAG WAG
SOMETHING LIKE THAT, SOMETHING LIKE THAT.
WAHA!
THAT'LL BE 2,289 YEN, PLEASE.
UH, OH...
HYOOOOO
NO... MONEY.
WHAT?

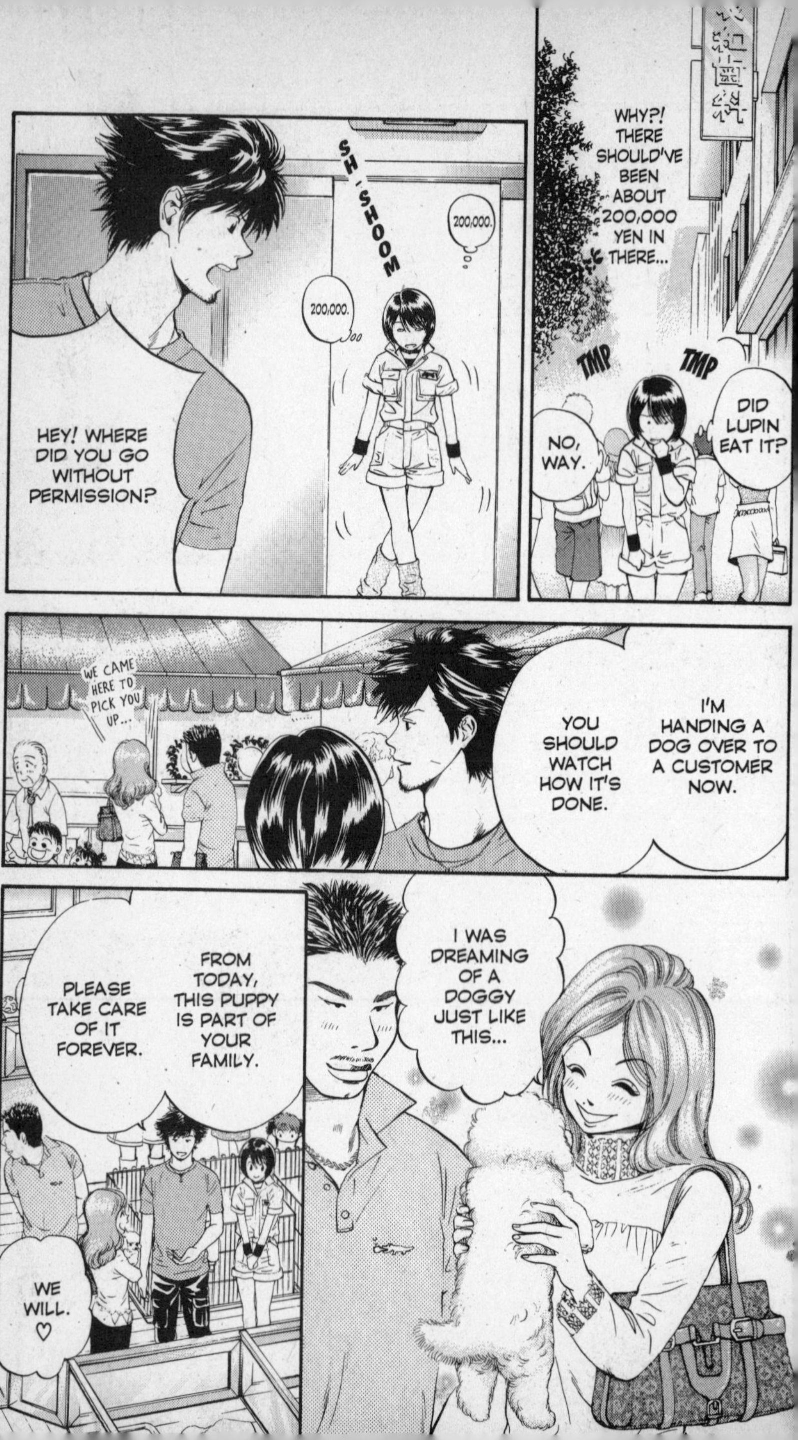
WHY?! THERE SHOULD'VE BEEN ABOUT 200,000 YEN IN THERE...
TMP
TMP
DID LUPIN EAT IT?
NO, WAY.
SH SHOOM
200,000.
200,000.
HEY! WHERE DID YOU GO WITHOUT PERMISSION?
I'M HANDING A DOG OVER TO A CUSTOMER NOW.
YOU SHOULD WATCH HOW IT'S DONE.
WE CAME HERE TO PICK YOU UP...
I WAS DREAMING OF A DOGGY JUST LIKE THIS...
FROM TODAY, THIS PUPPY IS PART OF YOUR FAMILY.
PLEASE TAKE CARE OF IT FOREVER.
WE WILL. ♡

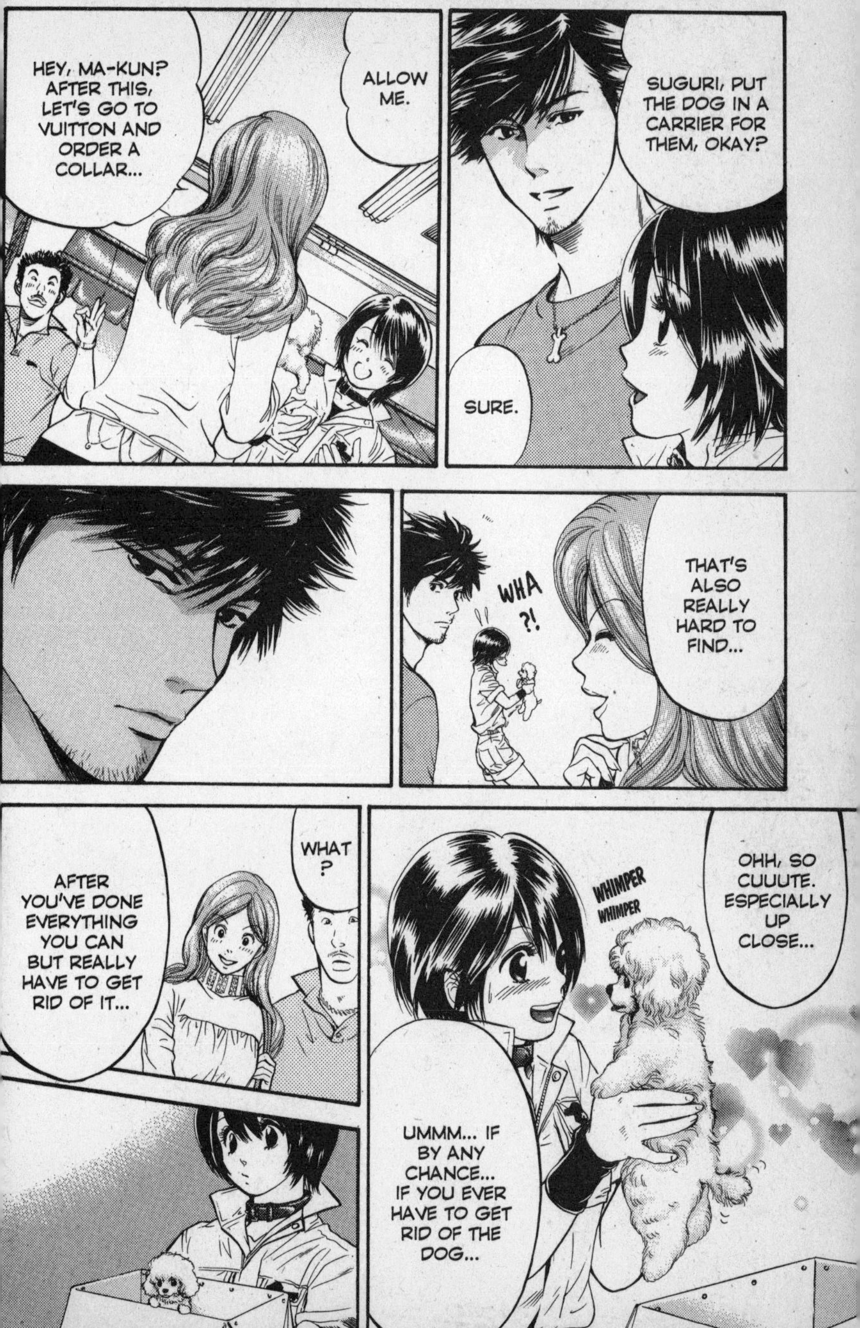
SUGURI, PUT THE DOG IN A CARRIER FOR THEM, OKAY?
SURE.
ALLOW ME.
HEY, MA-KUN? AFTER THIS, LET'S GO TO VUITTON AND ORDER A COLLAR...
THAT'S ALSO REALLY HARD TO FIND...
WHA ?!
OHH, SO CUUUTE. ESPECIALLY UP CLOSE...
WHIMPER WHIMPER
UMMM... IF BY ANY CHANCE... IF YOU EVER HAVE TO GET RID OF THE DOG...
WHAT ?
AFTER YOU'VE DONE EVERYTHING YOU CAN BUT REALLY HAVE TO GET RID OF IT...

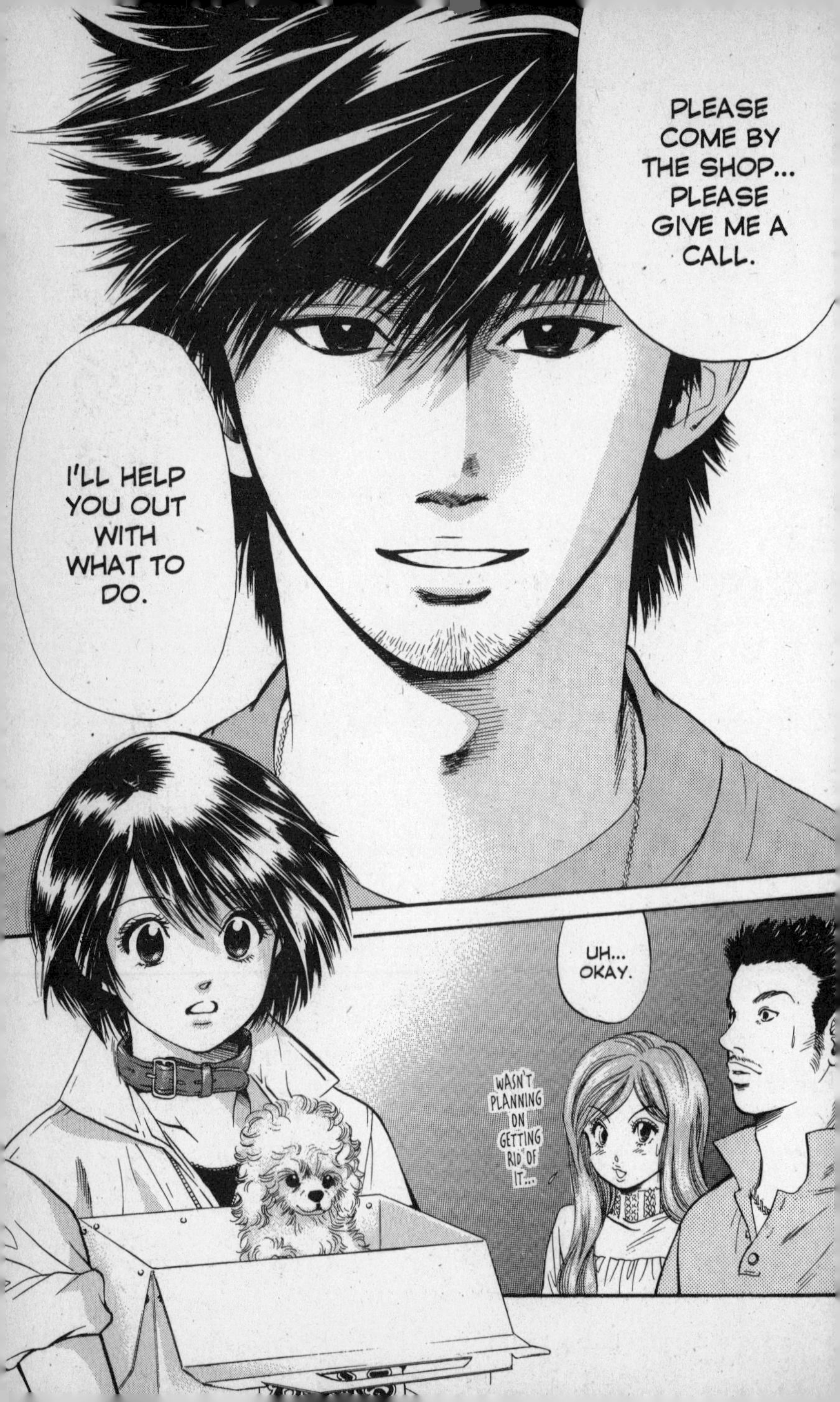
PLEASE COME BY THE SHOP... PLEASE GIVE ME A CALL.
I'LL HELP YOU OUT WITH WHAT TO DO.
UH... OKAY.
WASN'T PLANNING ON GETTING RID OF IT...

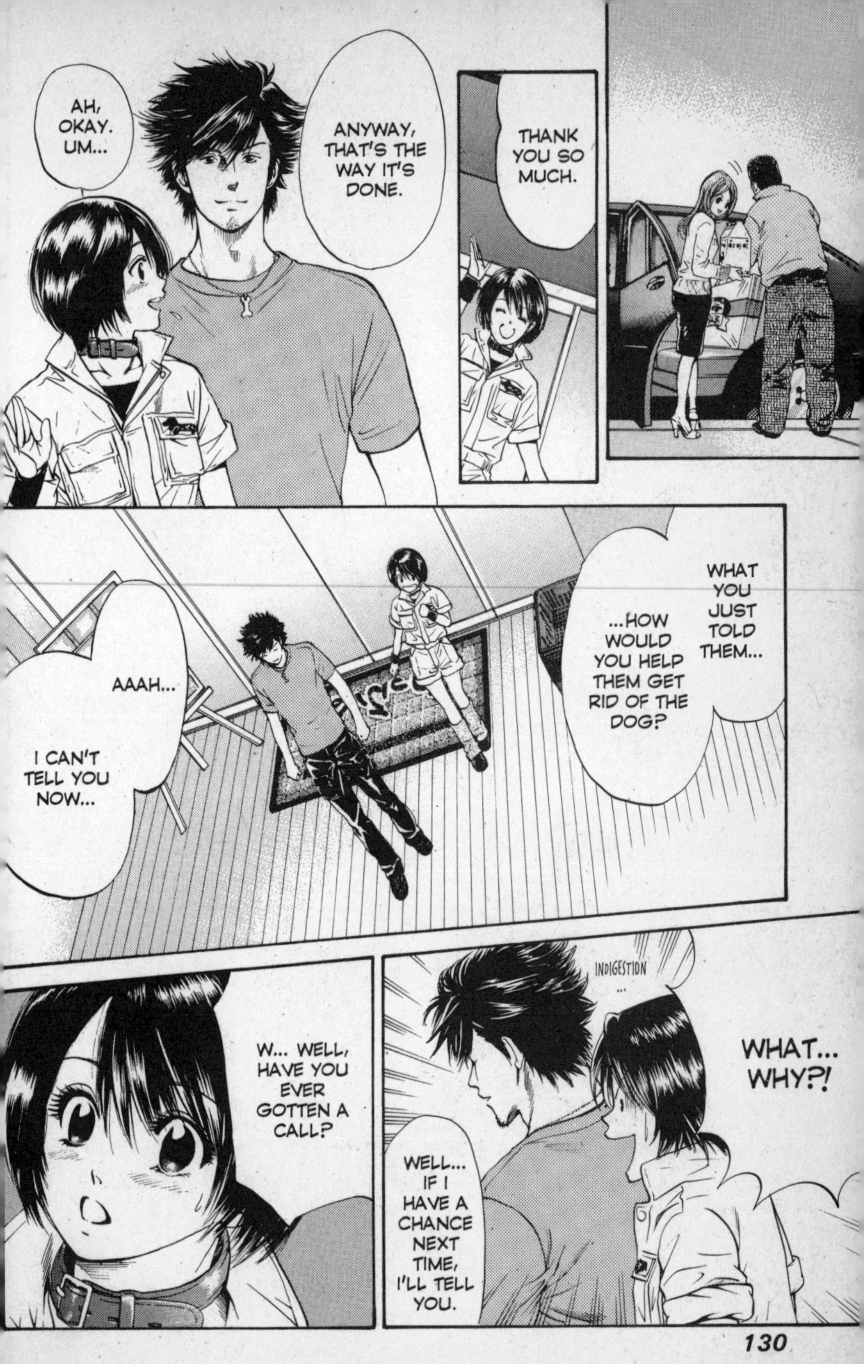
THANK YOU SO MUCH.
ANYWAY, THAT'S THE WAY IT'S DONE.
AH, OKAY. UM...
WHAT YOU JUST TOLD THEM...
...HOW WOULD YOU HELP THEM GET RID OF THE DOG?
AAAH...
I CAN'T TELL YOU NOW...
WHAT... WHY?!
INDIGESTION ...
WELL... IF I HAVE A CHANCE NEXT TIME, I'LL TELL YOU.
W... WELL, HAVE YOU EVER GOTTEN A CALL?

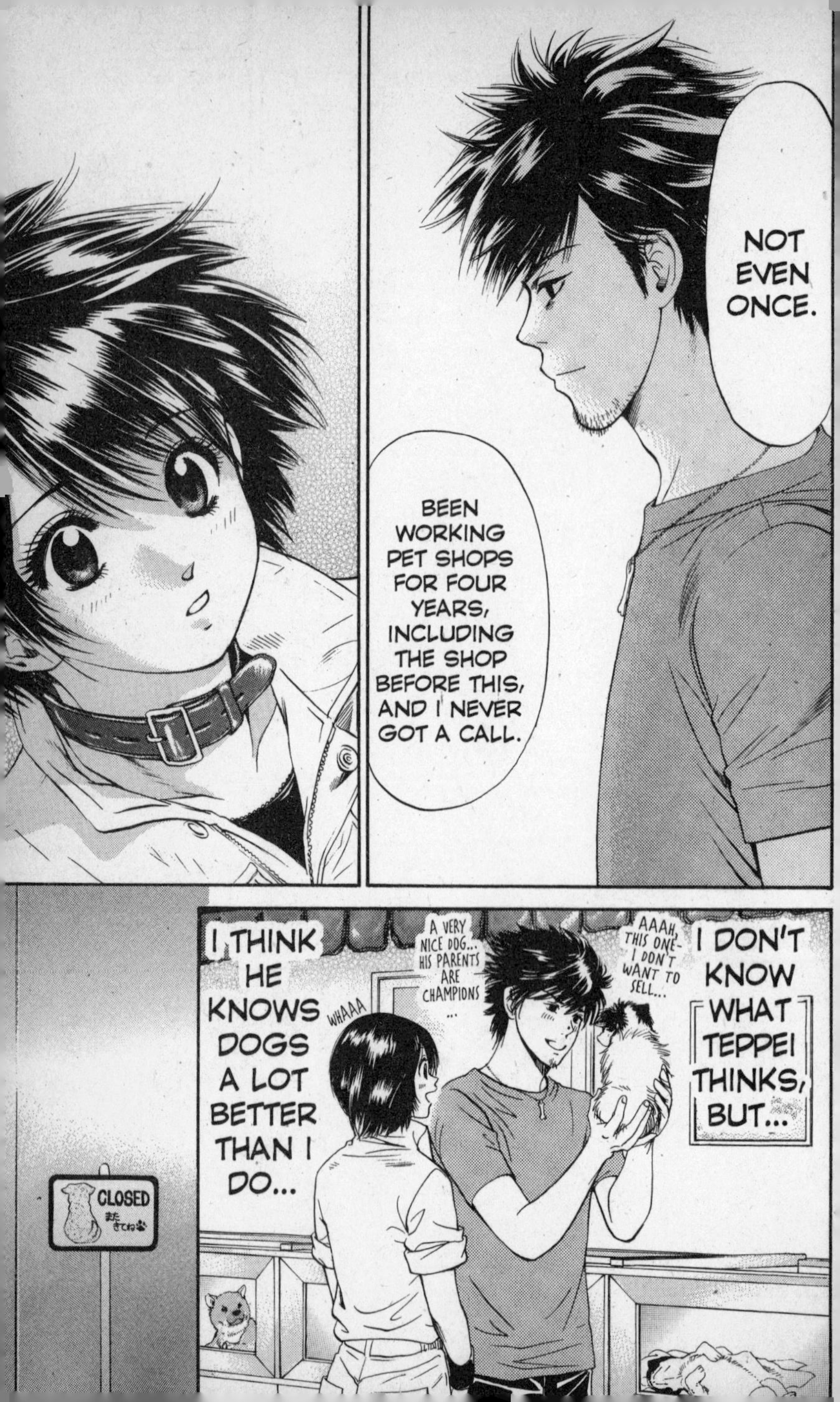
NOT EVEN ONCE.
BEEN WORKING PET SHOPS FOR FOUR YEARS, INCLUDING THE SHOP BEFORE THIS, AND I NEVER GOT A CALL.
I DON'T KNOW WHAT TEPPEI THINKS, BUT...
AAAH, THIS ONE- I DON'T WANT TO SELL...
A VERY NICE DOG... HIS PARENTS ARE CHAMPIONS ...
WHAAA
I THINK HE KNOWS DOGS A LOT BETTER THAN I DO...
CLOSED
またきてね

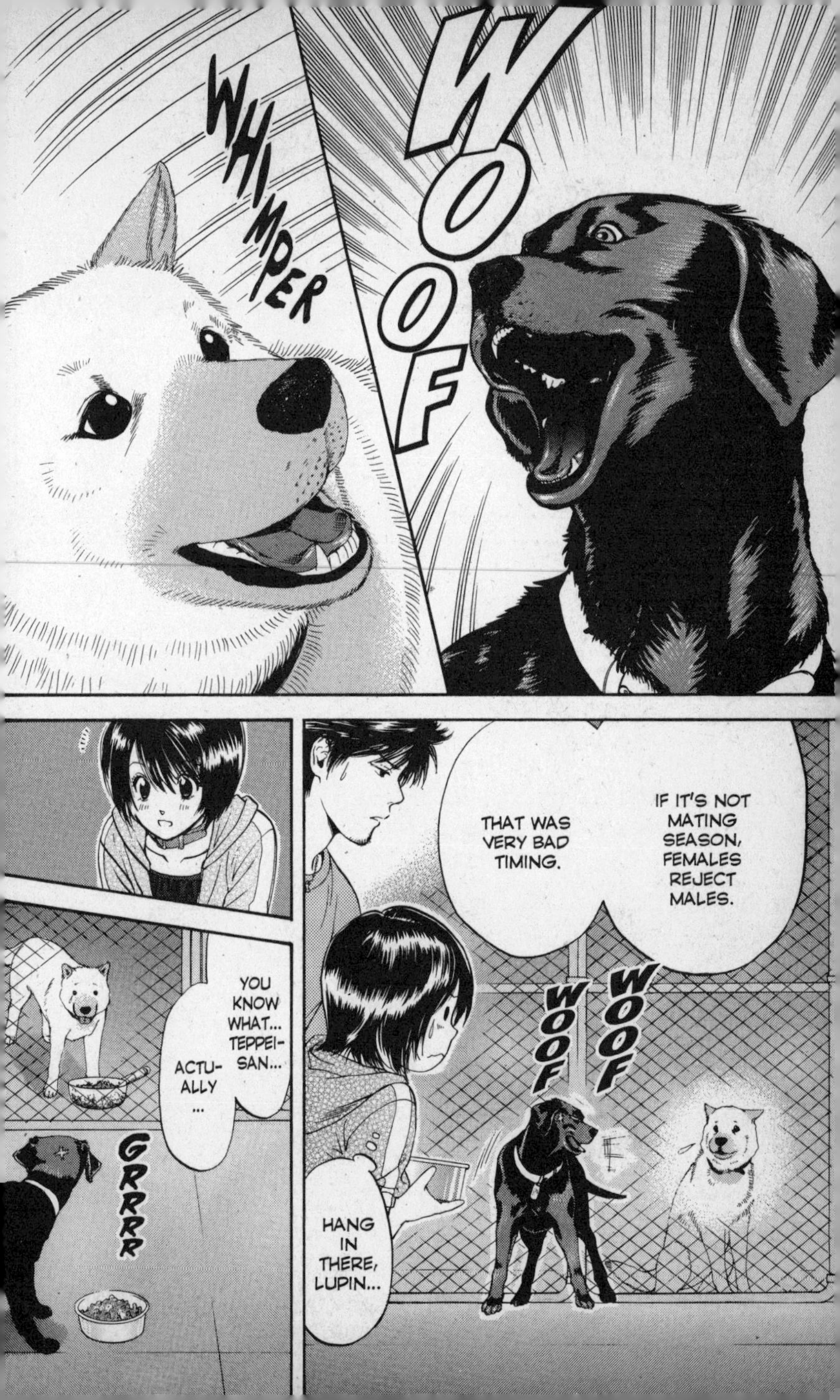
WOOF
WHIMPER
IF IT'S NOT MATING SEASON, FEMALES REJECT MALES.
THAT WAS VERY BAD TIMING.
WOOF
WOOF
HANG IN THERE, LUPIN...
YOU KNOW WHAT... TEPPEI-SAN...
ACTU-ALLY...
GRRRR

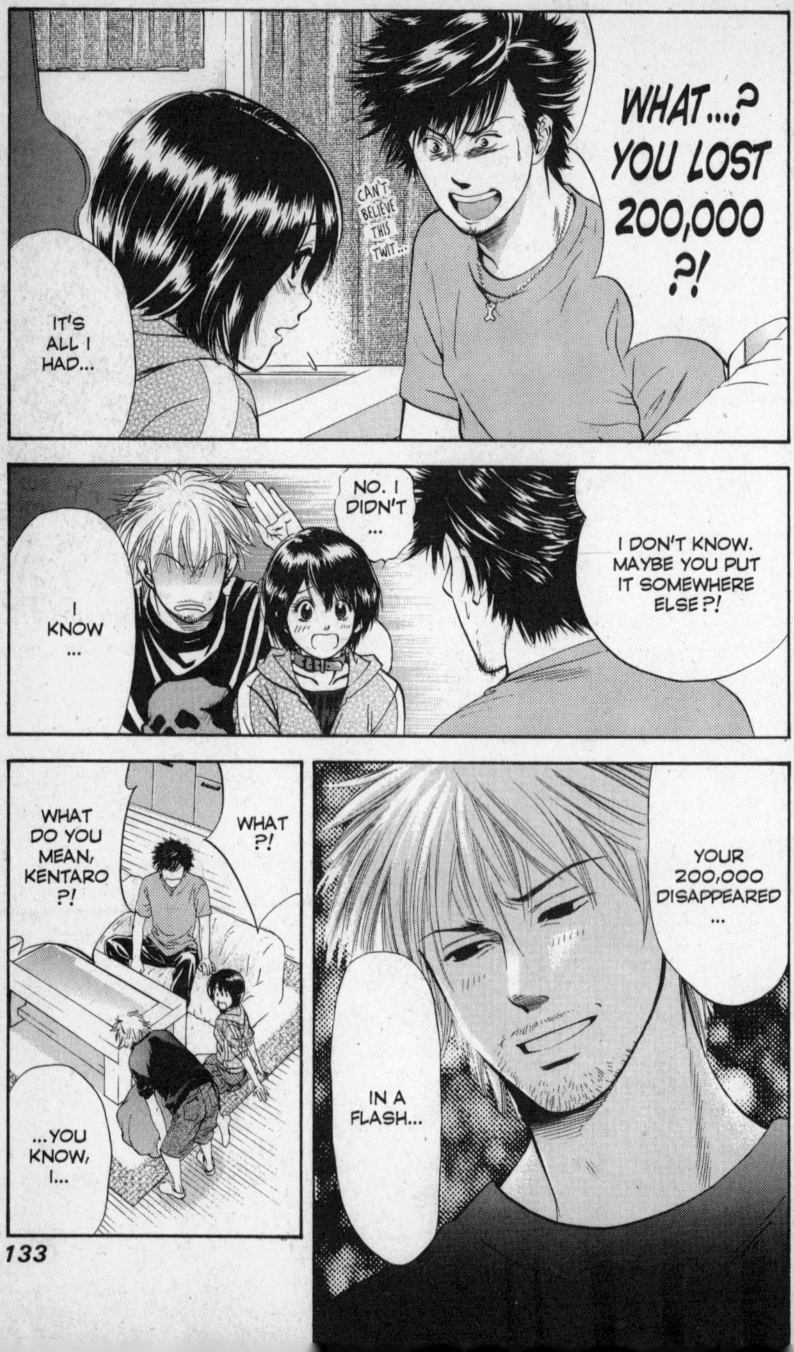
WHAT...? YOU LOST 200,000 ?!
CAN'T BELIEVE THIS TWIT...
IT'S ALL I HAD...
I DON'T KNOW. MAYBE YOU PUT IT SOMEWHERE ELSE?!
NO. I DIDN'T ...
I KNOW ...
YOUR 200,000 DISAPPEARED ...
IN A FLASH...
WHAT ?!
WHAT DO YOU MEAN, KENTARO ?!
...YOU KNOW, I...

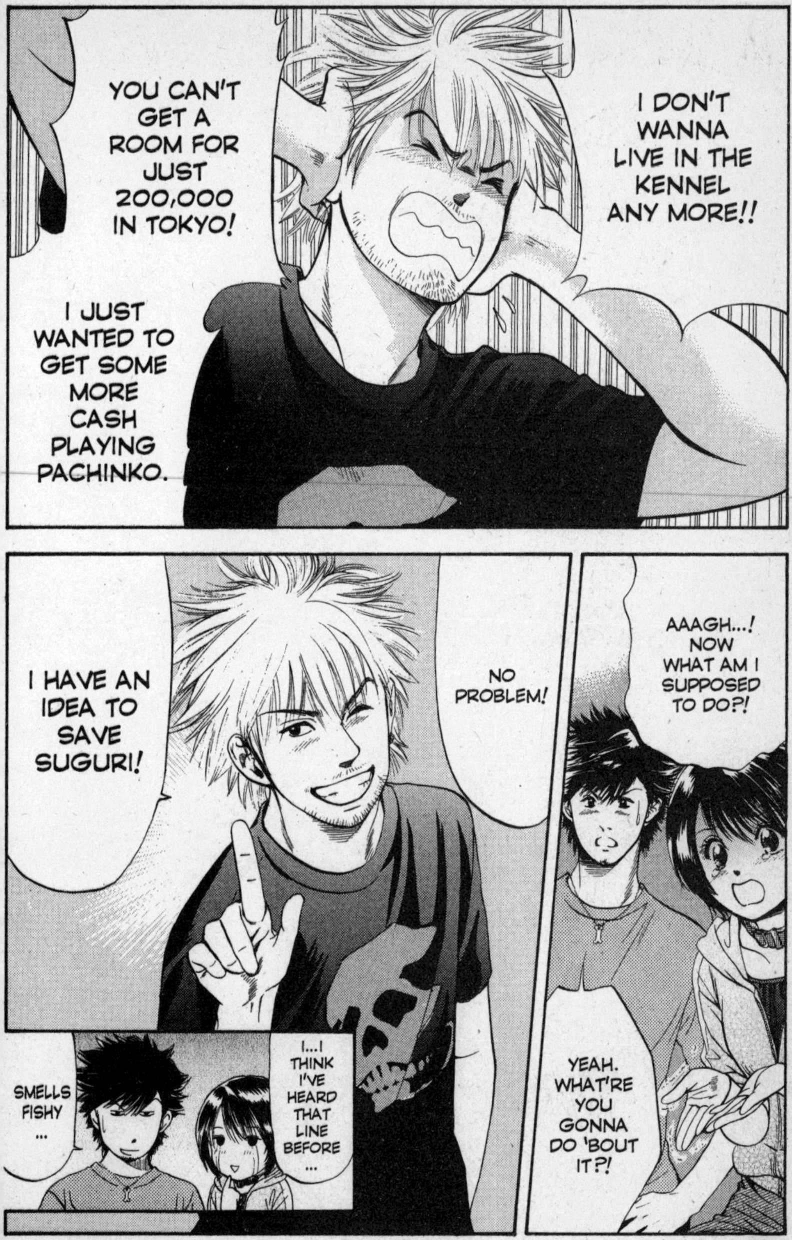
I DON'T WANNA LIVE IN THE KENNEL ANY MORE!!
YOU CAN'T GET A ROOM FOR JUST 200,000 IN TOKYO!
I JUST WANTED TO GET SOME MORE CASH PLAYING PACHINKO.
AAAGH...! NOW WHAT AM I SUPPOSED TO DO?!
YEAH. WHAT'RE YOU GONNA DO 'BOUT IT?!
NO PROBLEM!
I HAVE AN IDEA TO SAVE SUGURI!
I...I THINK I'VE HEARD THAT LINE BEFORE ...
SMELLS FISHY ...

CHAPTER 5
A DOG COMES CALLING ALL BY ITSELF?

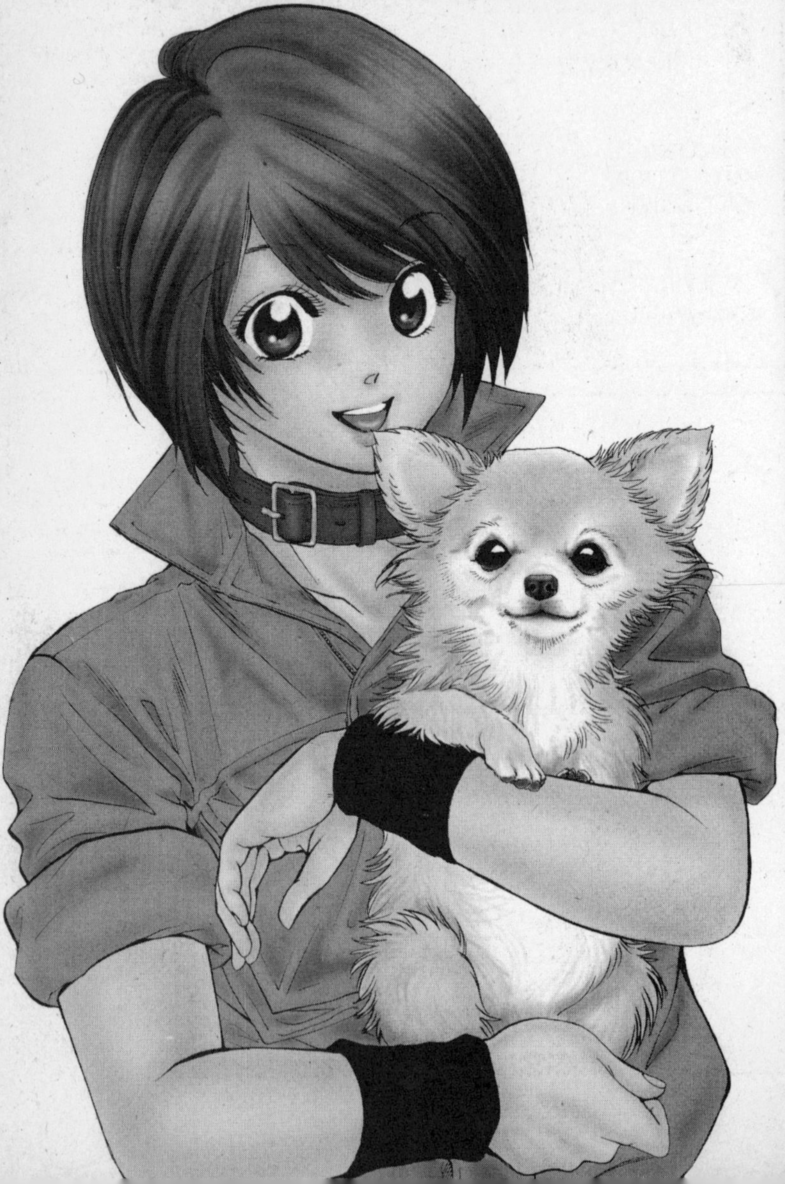

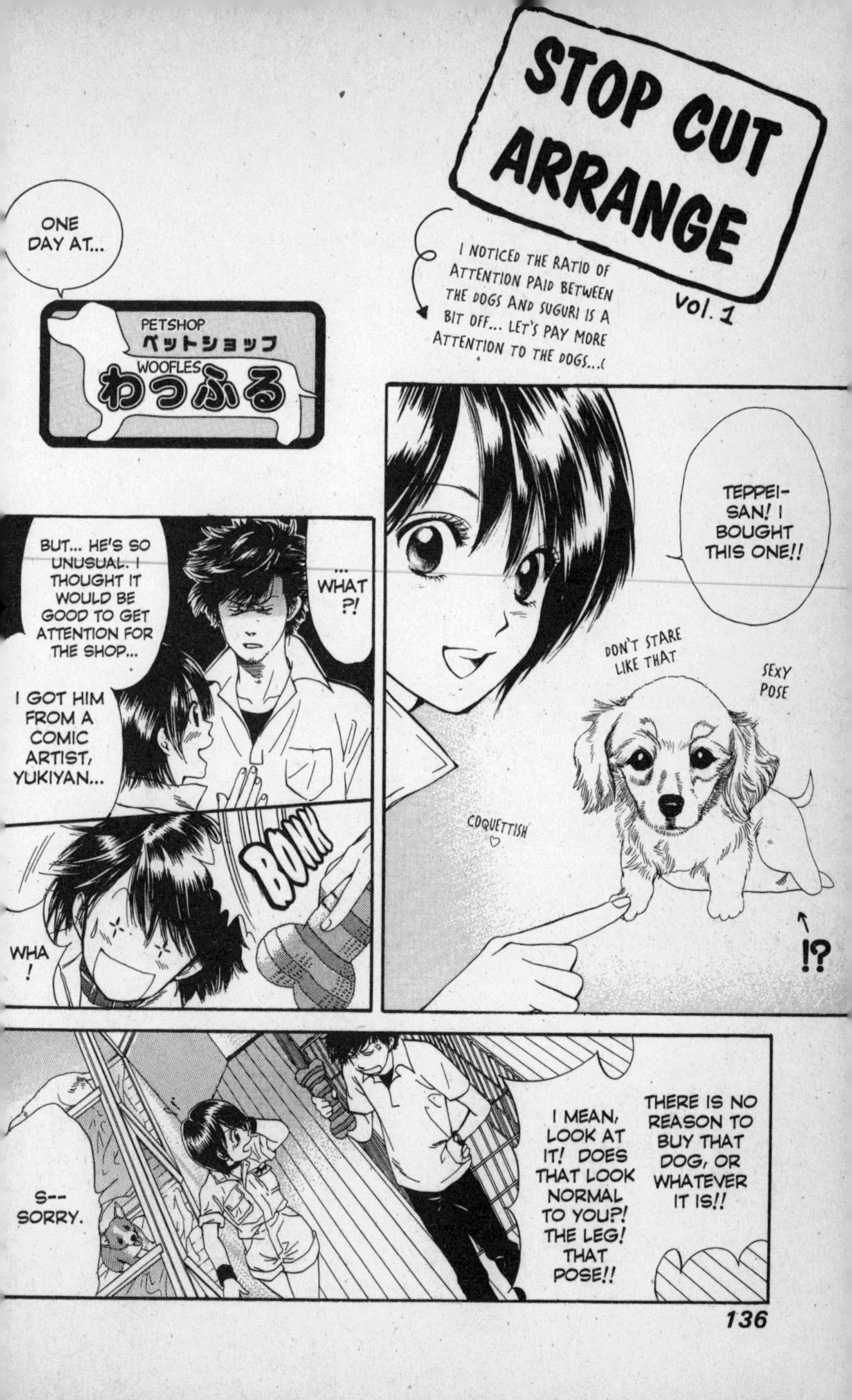
STOP CUT ARRANGE
vol. 1
I NOTICED THE RATIO OF ATTENTION PAID BETWEEN THE DOGS AND SUGURI IS A BIT OFF... LET'S PAY MORE ATTENTION TO THE DOGS...(
ONE DAY AT...
PETSHOP
ペットショップ
WOOFLES
わつふる
TEPPEI-SAN! I BOUGHT THIS ONE!!
SEXY POSE
DON'T STARE LIKE THAT
COQUETTISH ♡
!?
...WHAT?!
BUT... HE'S SO UNUSUAL. I THOUGHT IT WOULD BE GOOD TO GET ATTENTION FOR THE SHOP...
I GOT HIM FROM A COMIC ARTIST, YUKIYAN...
BONK
WHA!
THERE IS NO REASON TO BUY THAT DOG, OR WHATEVER IT IS!!
I MEAN, LOOK AT IT! DOES THAT LOOK NORMAL TO YOU?! THE LEG! THAT POSE!!
S-- SORRY.

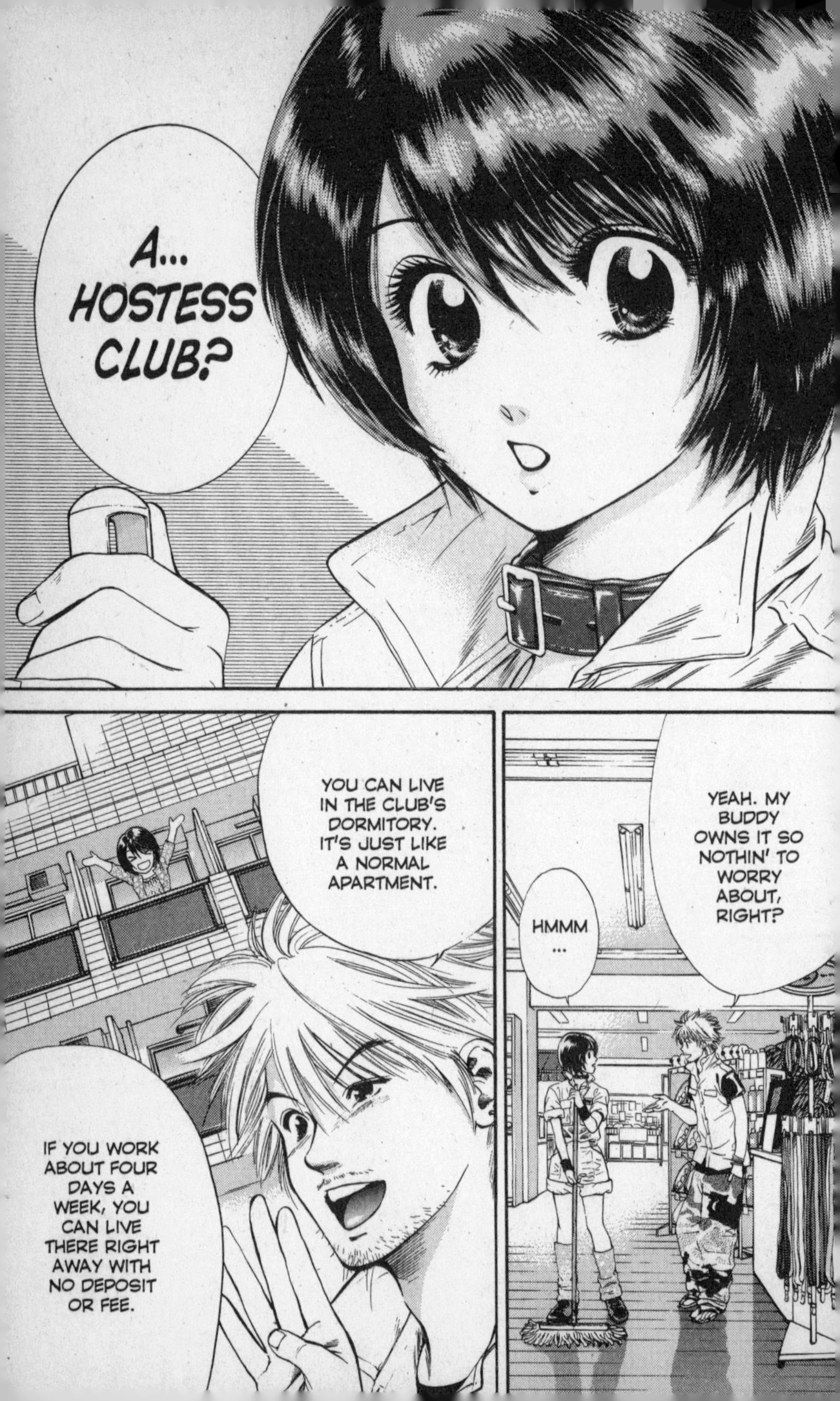
A... HOSTESS CLUB?
YEAH. MY BUDDY OWNS IT SO NOTHIN' TO WORRY ABOUT, RIGHT?
HMMM...
YOU CAN LIVE IN THE CLUB'S DORMITORY. IT'S JUST LIKE A NORMAL APARTMENT.
IF YOU WORK ABOUT FOUR DAYS A WEEK, YOU CAN LIVE THERE RIGHT AWAY WITH NO DEPOSIT OR FEE.

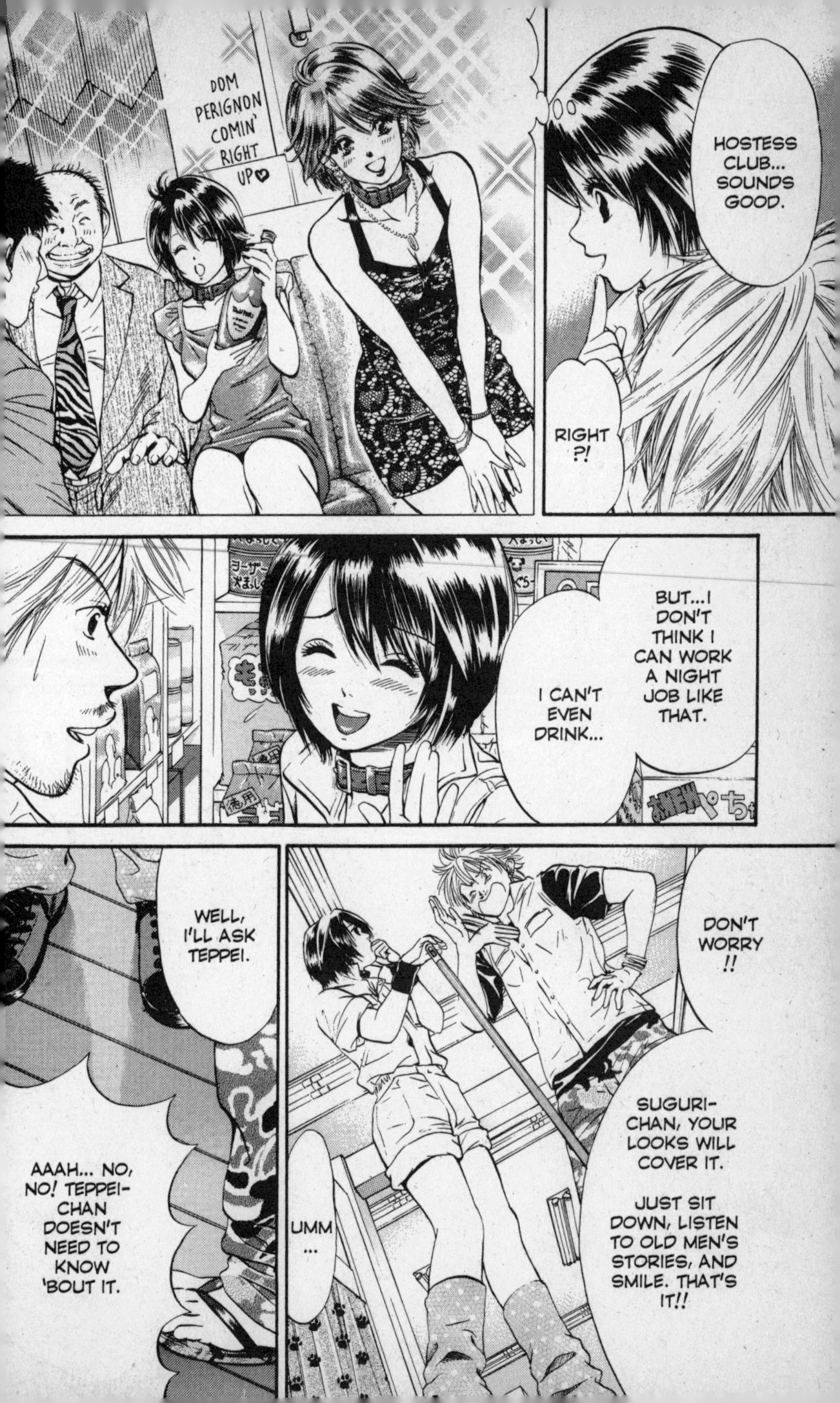
HOSTESS CLUB... SOUNDS GOOD.
RIGHT ?!
DOM PERIGNON COMIN' RIGHT UP♥
BUT...I DON'T THINK I CAN WORK A NIGHT JOB LIKE THAT.
I CAN'T EVEN DRINK...
DON'T WORRY !!
SUGURI-CHAN, YOUR LOOKS WILL COVER IT.
JUST SIT DOWN, LISTEN TO OLD MEN'S STORIES, AND SMILE. THAT'S IT!!
UMM ...
WELL, I'LL ASK TEPPEI.
AAAH... NO, NO! TEPPEI-CHAN DOESN'T NEED TO KNOW 'BOUT IT.

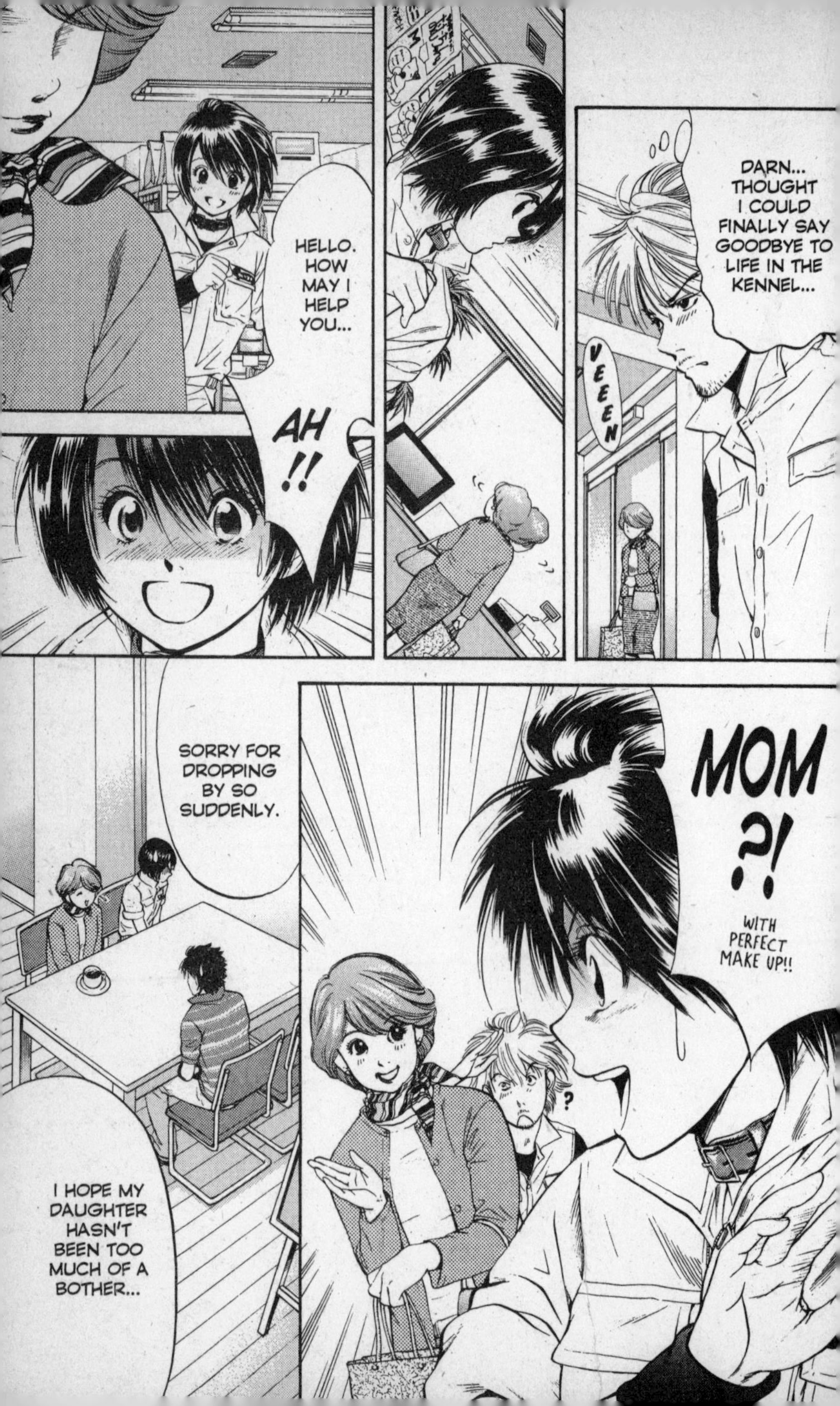

DARN... THOUGHT I COULD FINALLY SAY GOODBYE TO LIFE IN THE KENNEL...
VEEEEN
HELLO. HOW MAY I HELP YOU...
AH!!
MOM?!
WITH PERFECT MAKE UP!!
SORRY FOR DROPPING BY SO SUDDENLY.
I HOPE MY DAUGHTER HASN'T BEEN TOO MUCH OF A BOTHER...

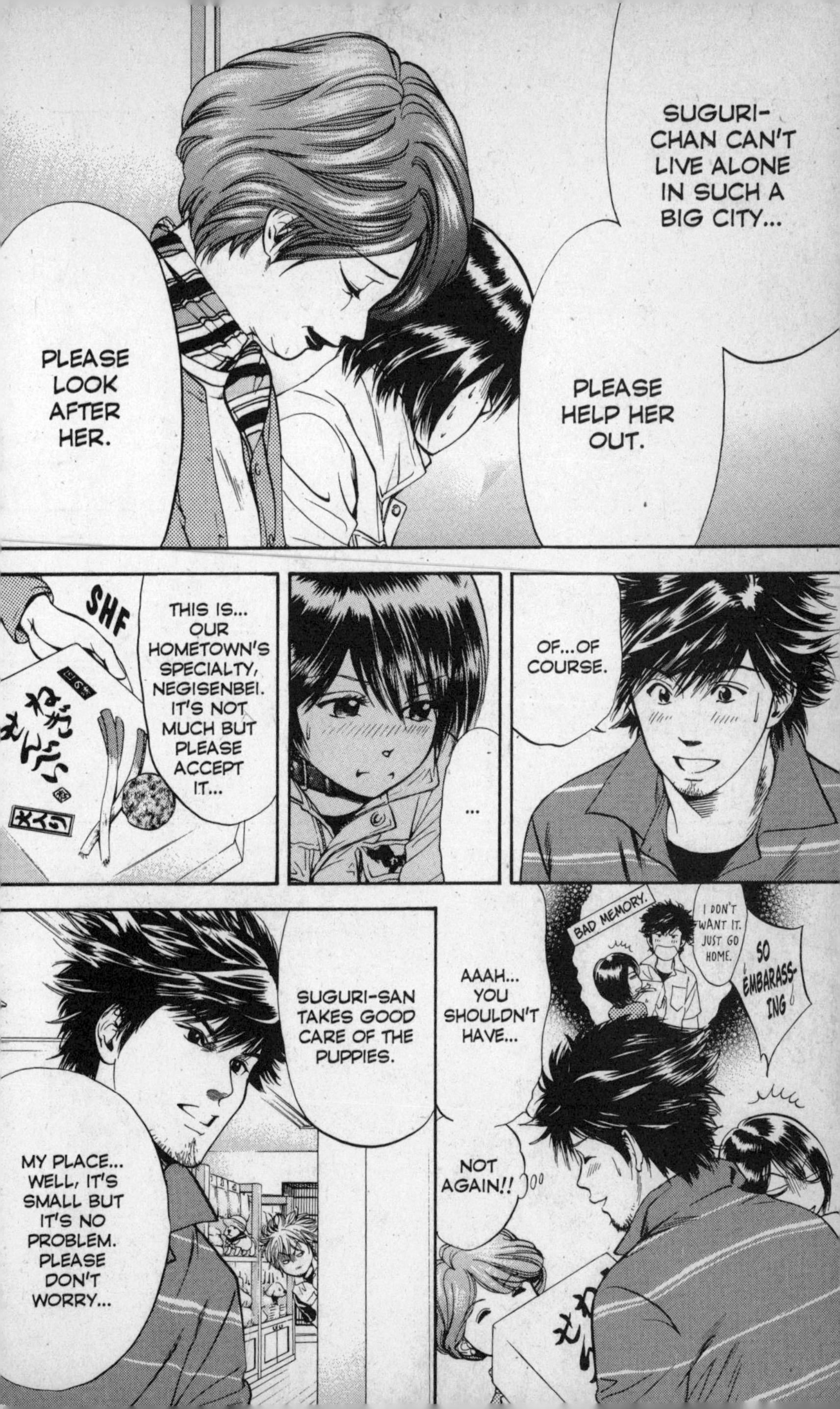
SUGURI-CHAN CAN'T LIVE ALONE IN SUCH A BIG CITY...
PLEASE HELP HER OUT.
PLEASE LOOK AFTER HER.
OF...OF COURSE.
...
SHF
THIS IS... OUR HOMETOWN'S SPECIALTY, NEGISENBEI. IT'S NOT MUCH BUT PLEASE ACCEPT IT...
SO EMBARASS-ING
I DON'T WANT IT. JUST GO HOME.
BAD MEMORY.
AAAH... YOU SHOULDN'T HAVE...
NOT AGAIN!!
SUGURI-SAN TAKES GOOD CARE OF THE PUPPIES.
MY PLACE... WELL, IT'S SMALL BUT IT'S NO PROBLEM. PLEASE DON'T WORRY...

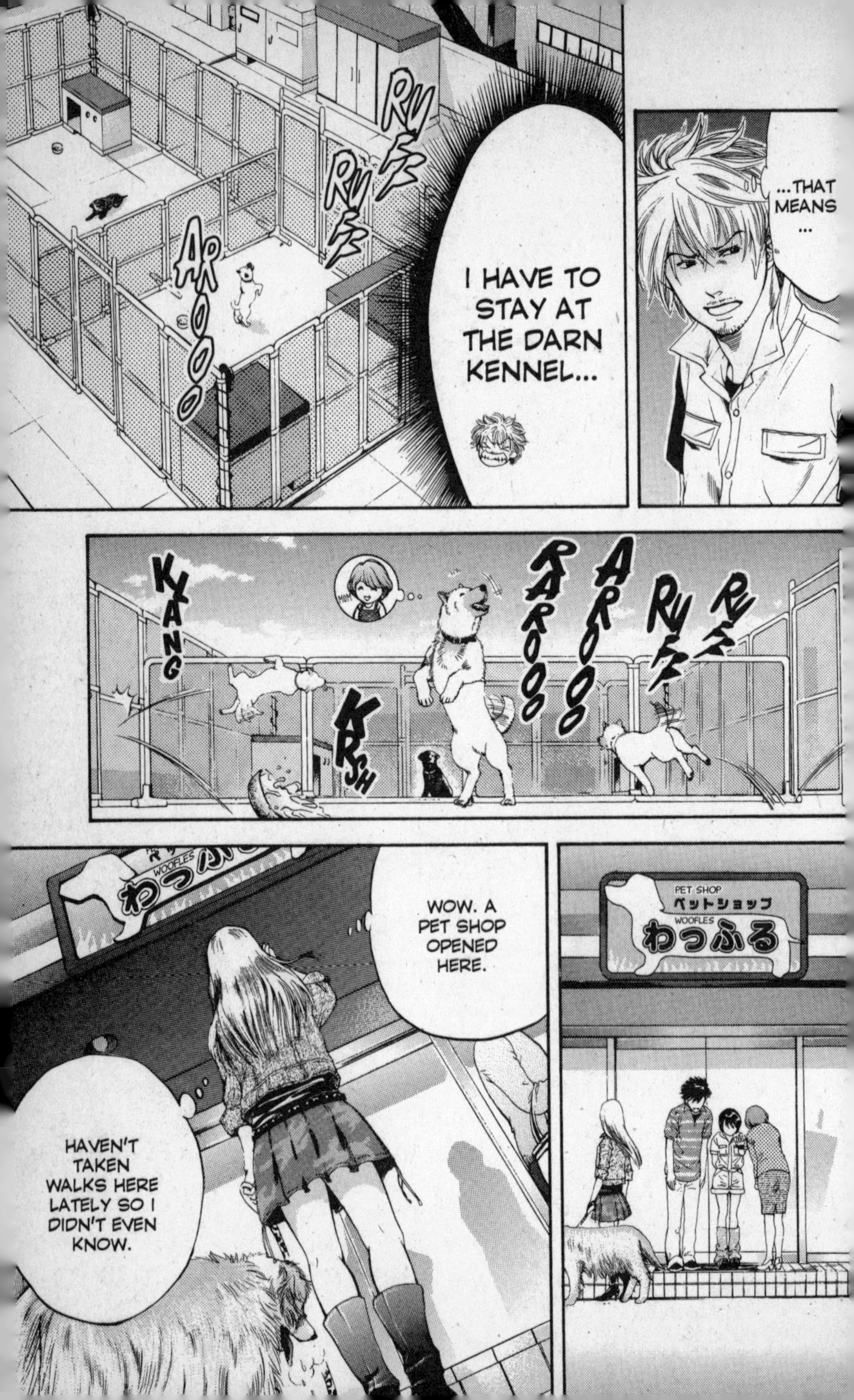
...THAT MEANS ...
RUFF
RUFF
AROOOO
I HAVE TO STAY AT THE DARN KENNEL...
RUFF
RUFF
AROOOO
RAROOOO
MOM
KYANG
KRSH
PET SHOP
ペットショップ
WOOFLES
わっふる
WOOFLES
WOW. A PET SHOP OPENED HERE.
HAVEN'T TAKEN WALKS HERE LATELY SO I DIDN'T EVEN KNOW.

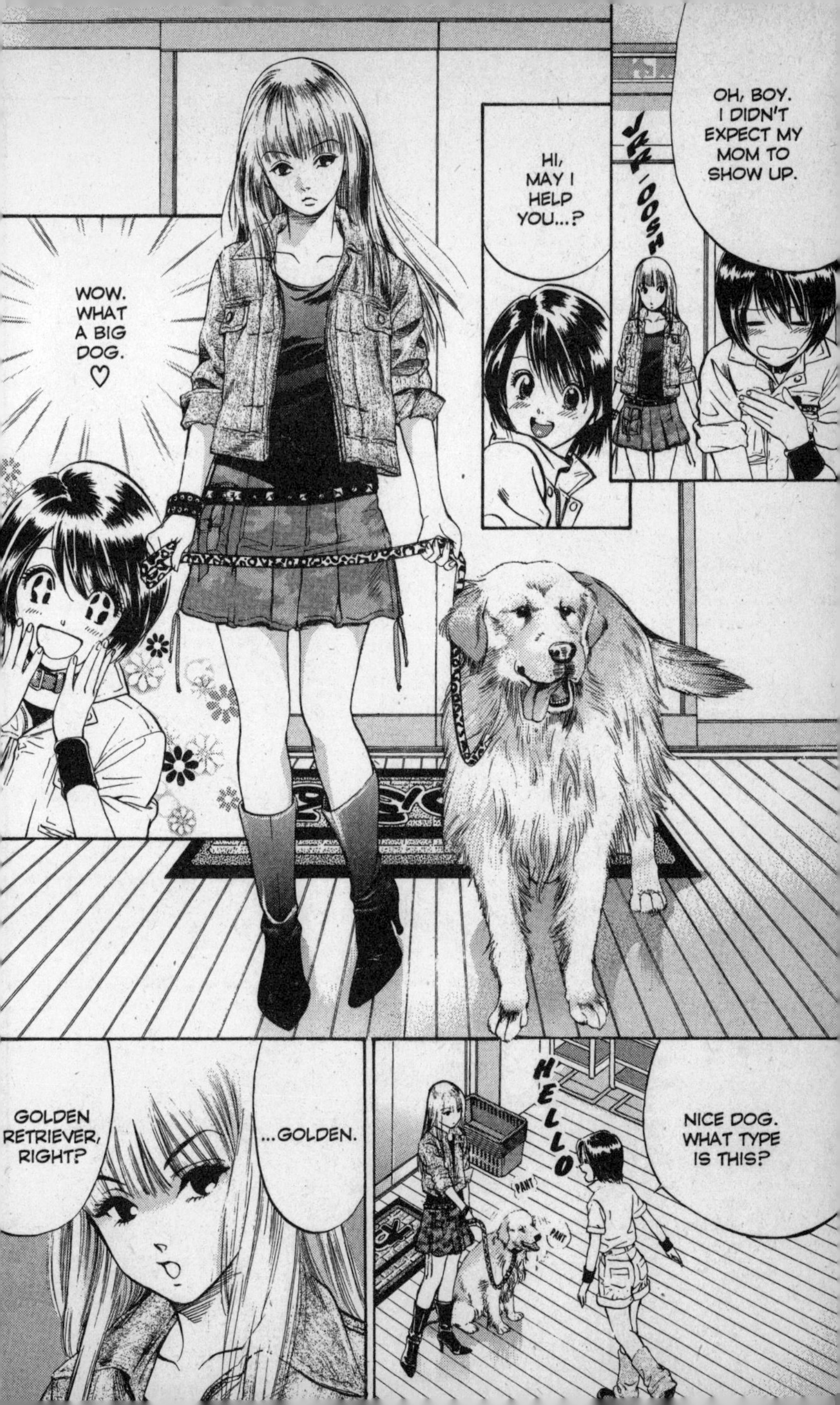
OH, BOY. I DIDN'T EXPECT MY MOM TO SHOW UP.
JRR-OOSH
HI, MAY I HELP YOU...?
WOW. WHAT A BIG DOG. ♡
NICE DOG. WHAT TYPE IS THIS?
HELLO
PANT
PANT
...GOLDEN.
GOLDEN RETRIEVER, RIGHT?

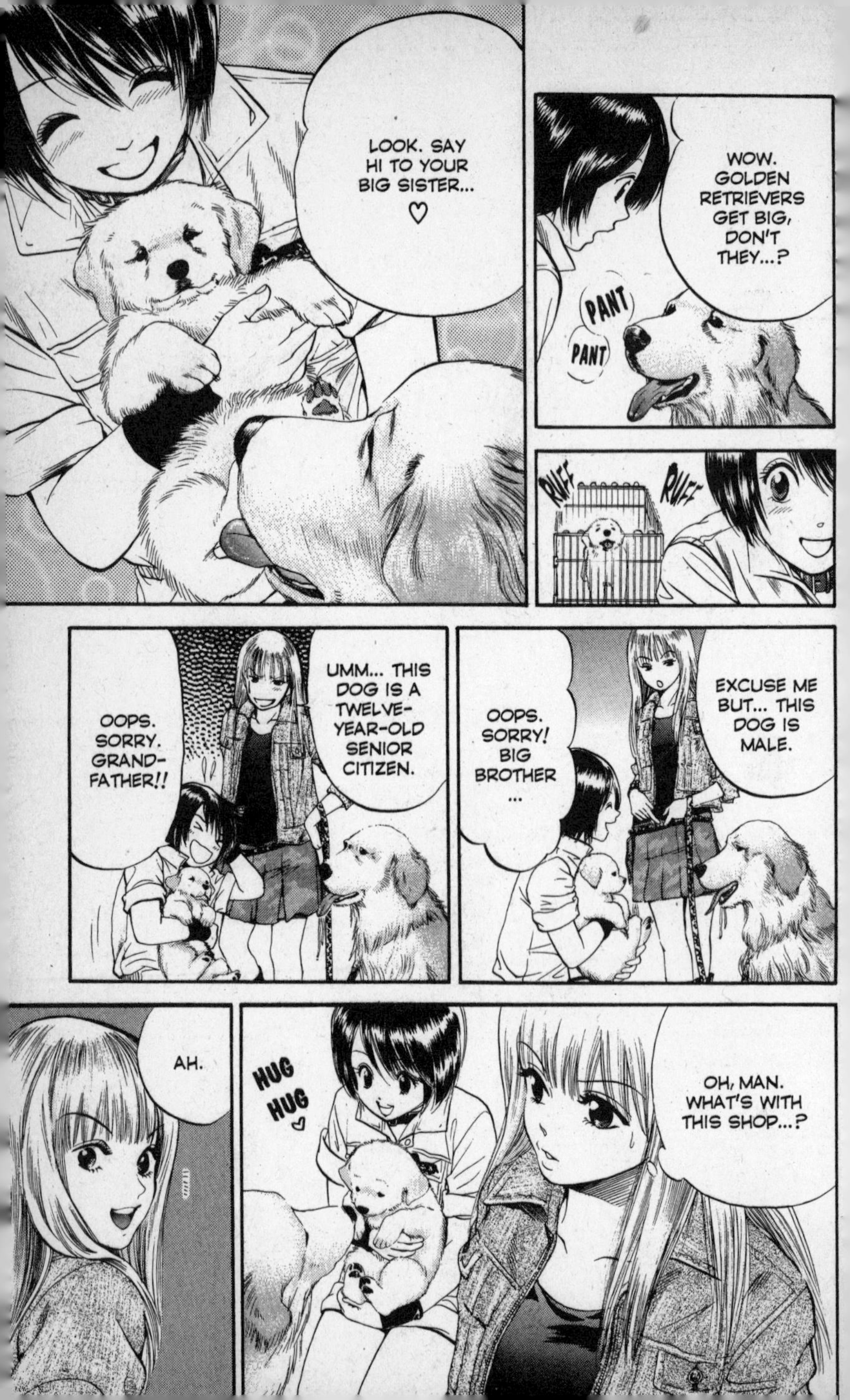
WOW. GOLDEN RETRIEVERS GET BIG, DON'T THEY...?
PANT
PANT
RUFF
RUFF
LOOK. SAY HI TO YOUR BIG SISTER... ♡
EXCUSE ME BUT... THIS DOG IS MALE.
OOPS. SORRY! BIG BROTHER ...
UMM... THIS DOG IS A TWELVE-YEAR-OLD SENIOR CITIZEN.
OOPS. SORRY. GRAND-FATHER!!
OH, MAN. WHAT'S WITH THIS SHOP...?
HUG HUG ♡
AH.

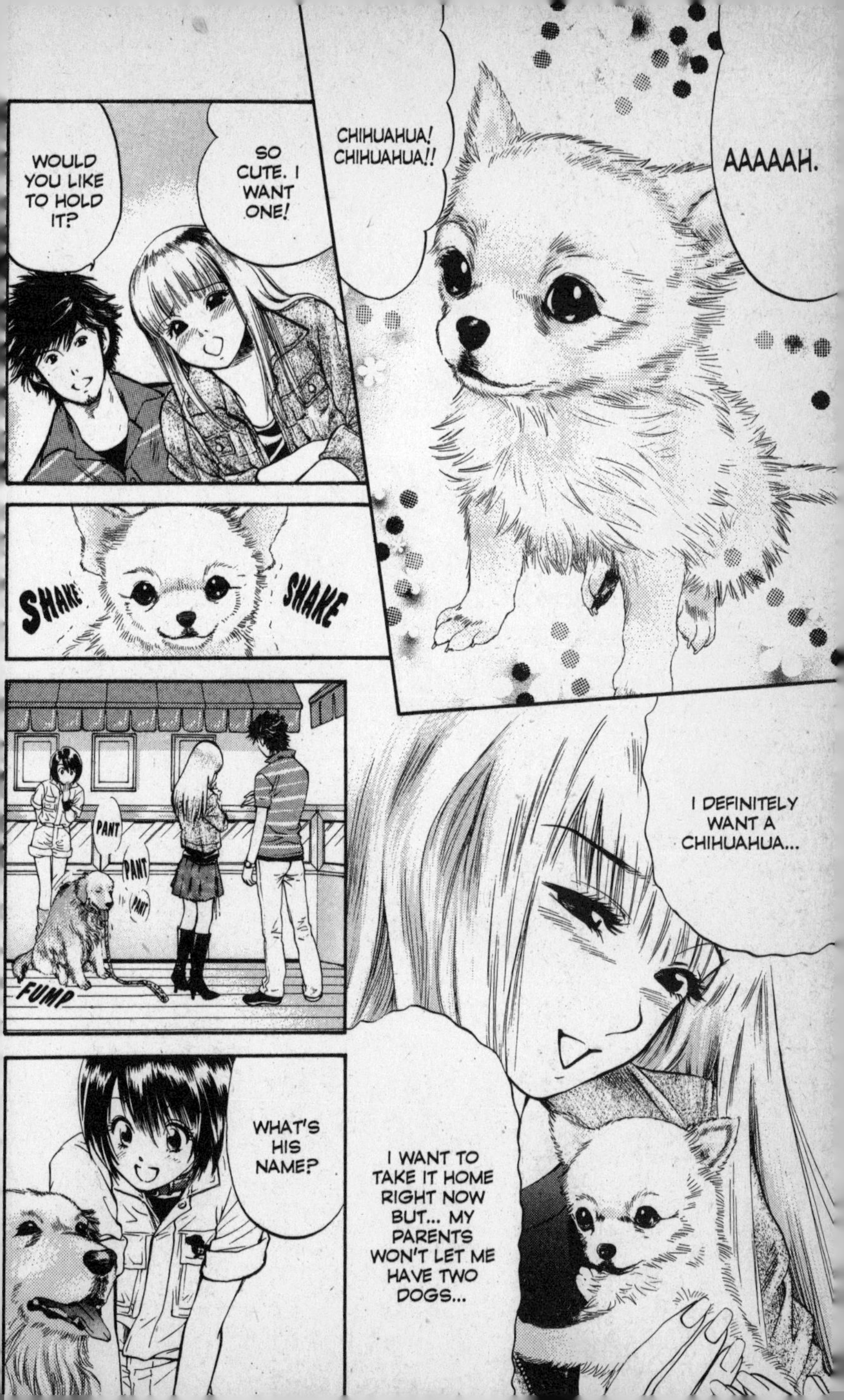
AAAAAH.
CHIHUAHUA! CHIHUAHUA!!
SO CUTE. I WANT ONE!
WOULD YOU LIKE TO HOLD IT?
SHAKE
SHAKE
I DEFINITELY WANT A CHIHUAHUA...
I WANT TO TAKE IT HOME RIGHT NOW BUT... MY PARENTS WON'T LET ME HAVE TWO DOGS...
PANT
PANT
PANT
FUMP
WHAT'S HIS NAME?

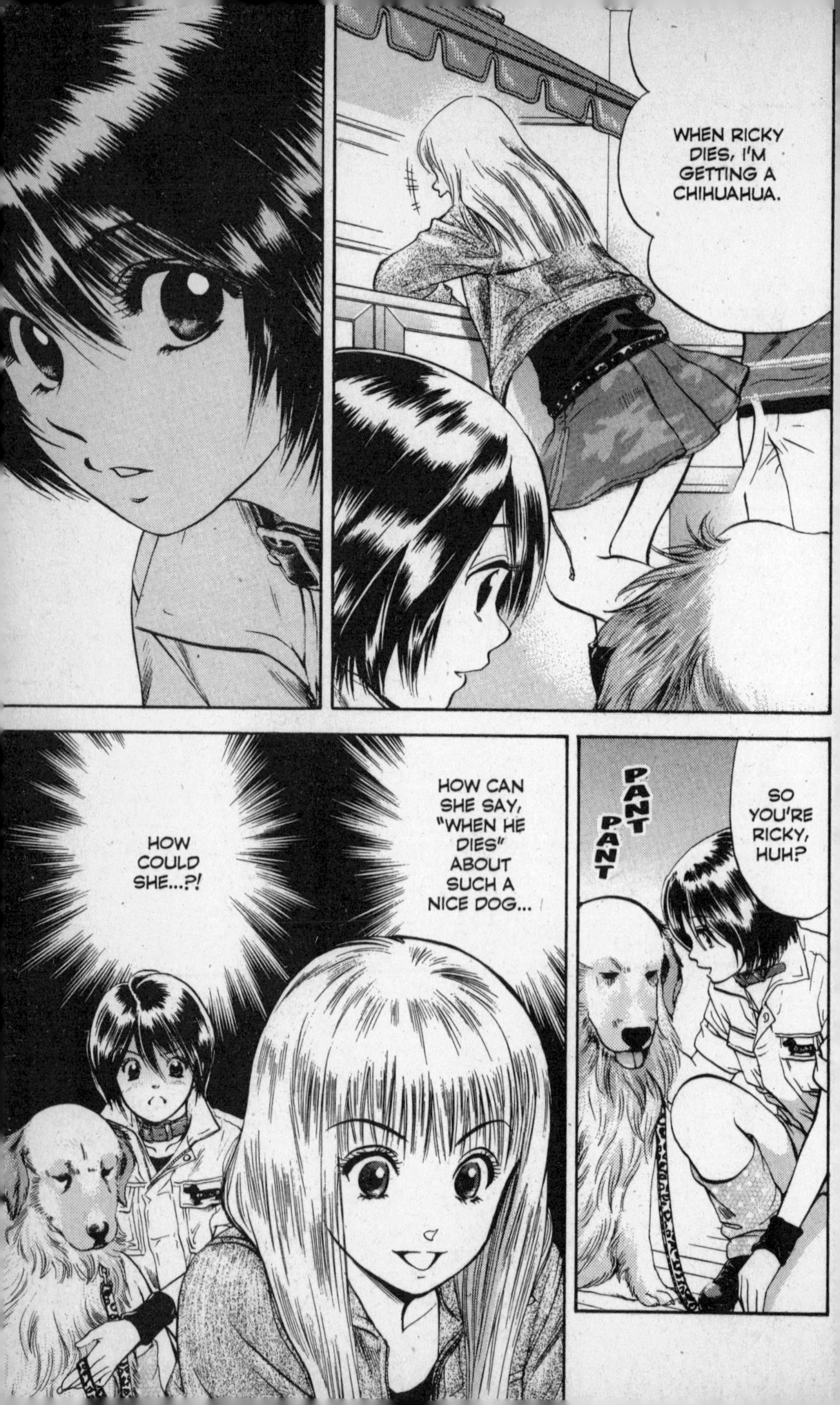
WHEN RICKY DIES, I'M GETTING A CHIHUAHUA.
SO YOU'RE RICKY, HUH?
PANT
PANT
HOW CAN SHE SAY, "WHEN HE DIES" ABOUT SUCH A NICE DOG...
HOW COULD SHE...?!

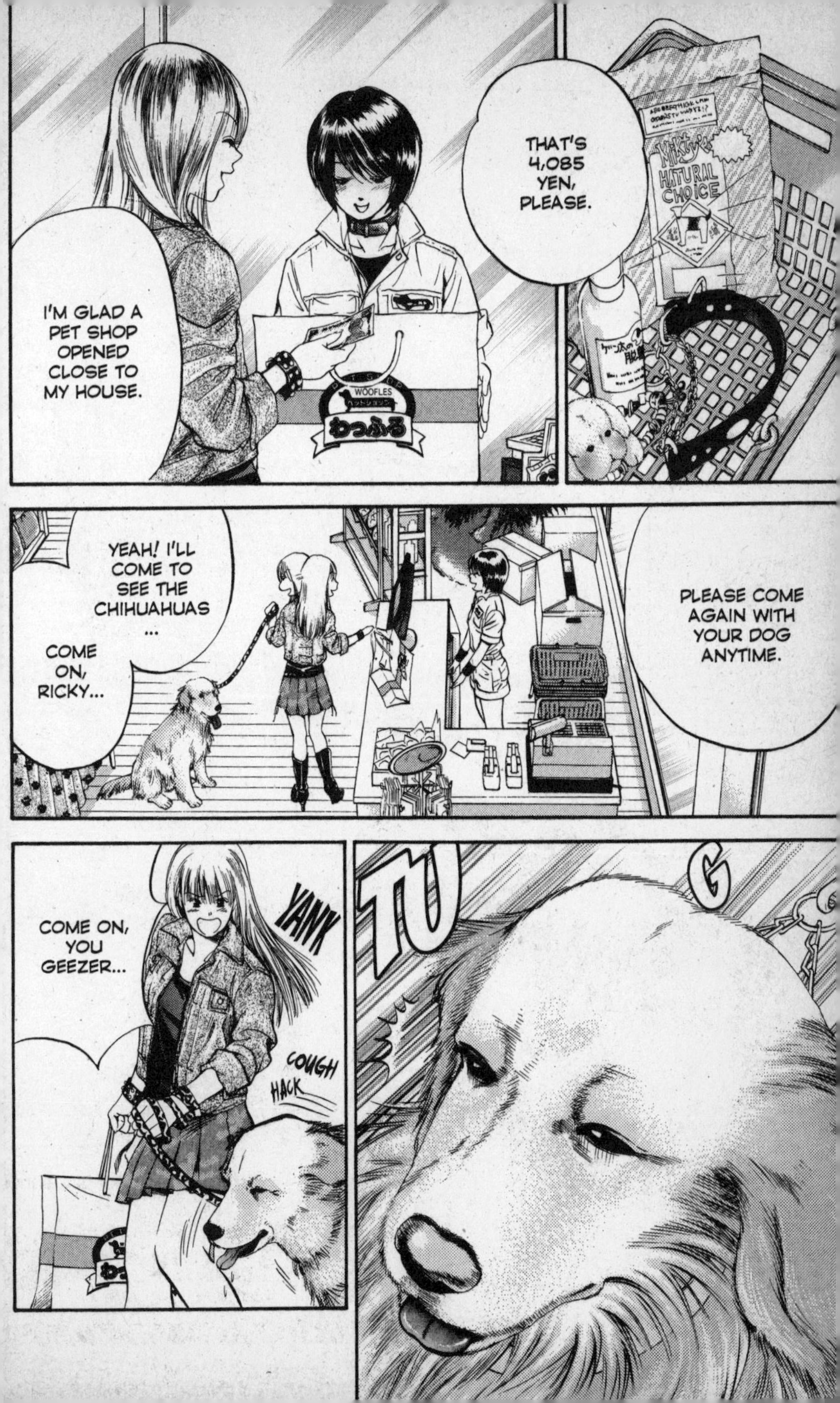
THAT'S 4,085 YEN, PLEASE.
I'M GLAD A PET SHOP OPENED CLOSE TO MY HOUSE.
WOOFLES
PLEASE COME AGAIN WITH YOUR DOG ANYTIME.
YEAH! I'LL COME TO SEE THE CHIHUAHUAS ...
COME ON, RICKY...
TUG
YANK
COME ON, YOU GEEZER...
COUGH
HACK

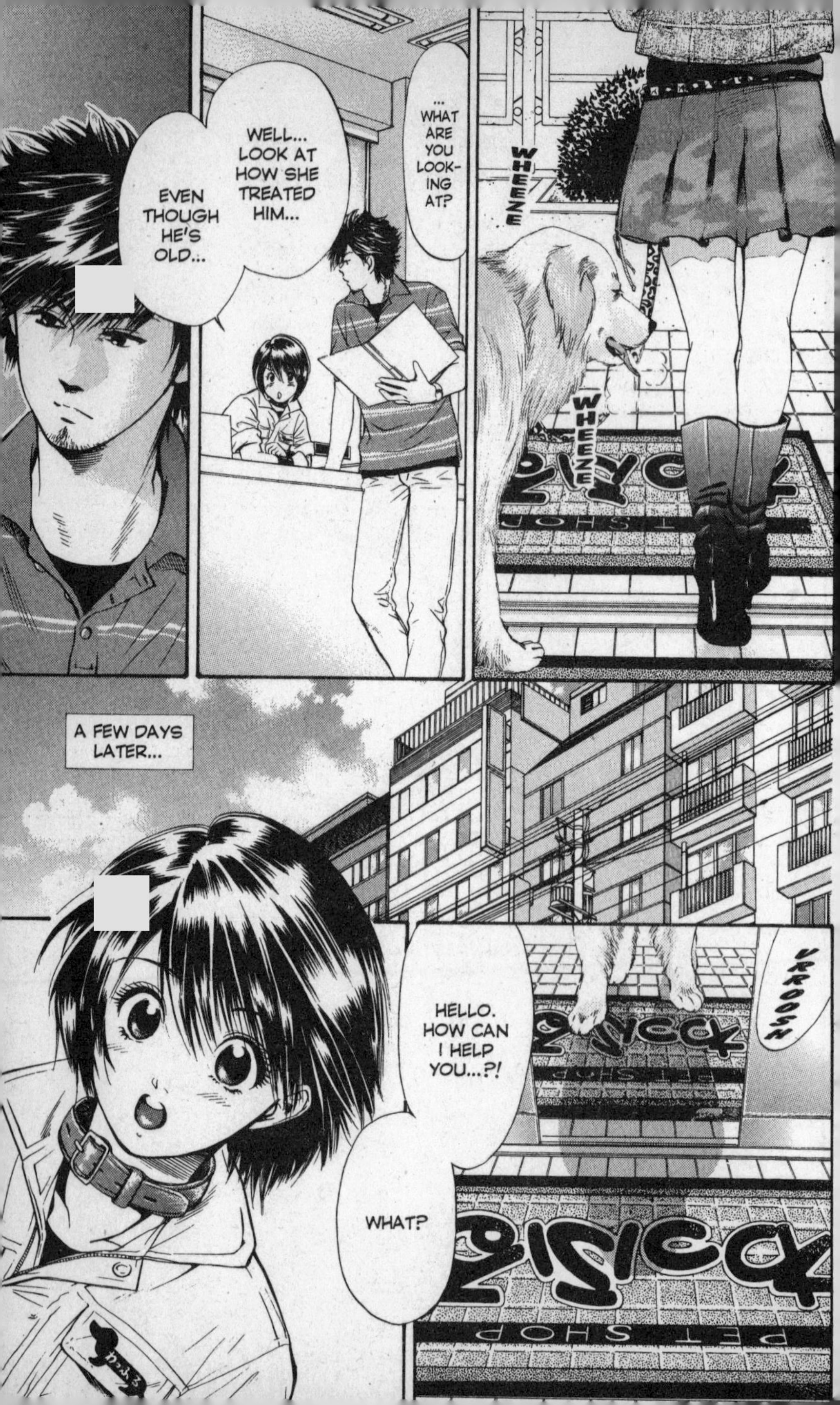
WHEEZE
WHEEZE
PET SHOP
... WHAT ARE YOU LOOK-ING AT?
WELL... LOOK AT HOW SHE TREATED HIM...
EVEN THOUGH HE'S OLD...
A FEW DAYS LATER...
URROOSH
HELLO. HOW CAN I HELP YOU...?!
PET SHOP
WHAT?

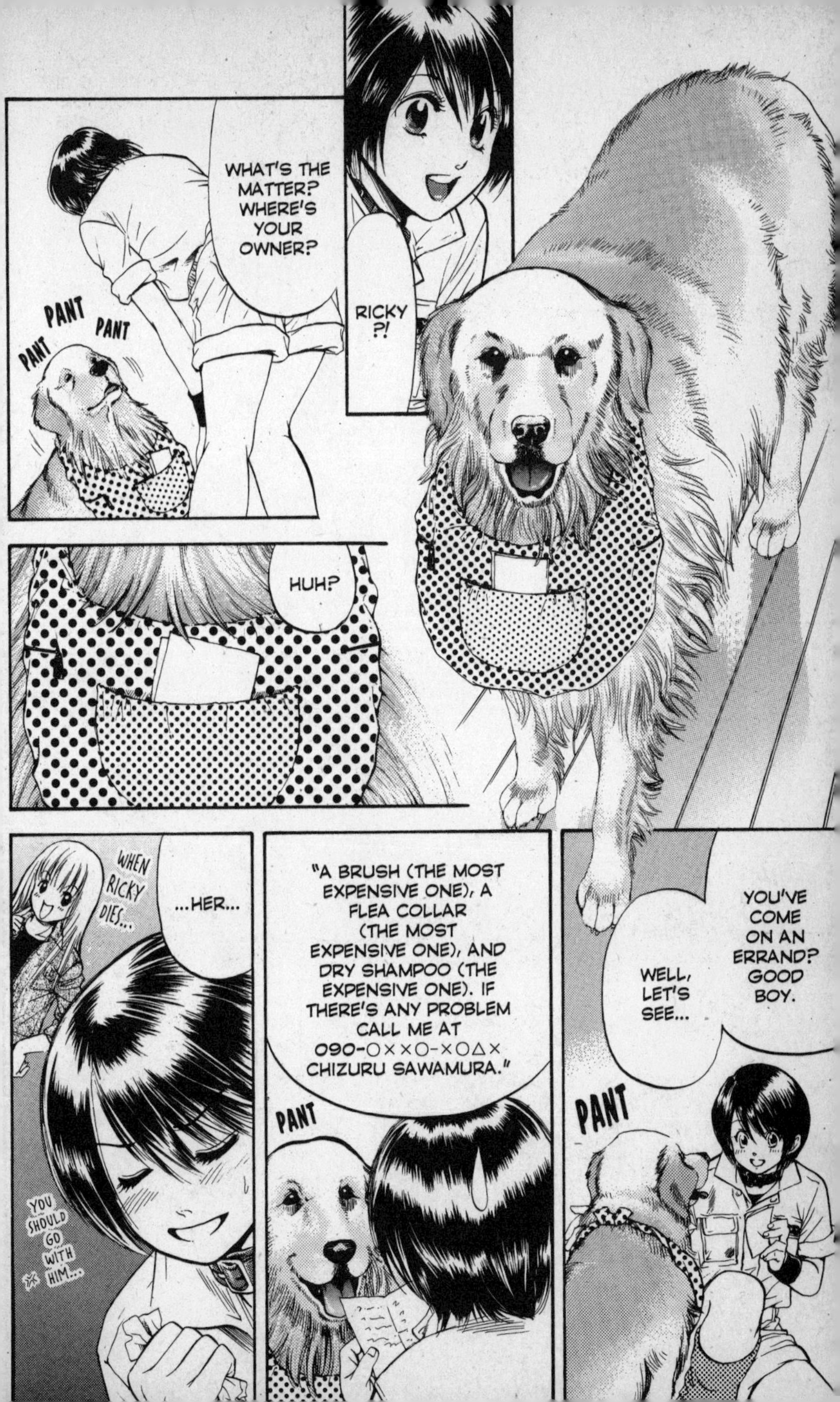
RICKY ?!
WHAT'S THE MATTER? WHERE'S YOUR OWNER?
PANT
PANT
PANT
HUH?
YOU'VE COME ON AN ERRAND? GOOD BOY.
WELL, LET'S SEE...
PANT
"A BRUSH (THE MOST EXPENSIVE ONE), A FLEA COLLAR (THE MOST EXPENSIVE ONE), AND DRY SHAMPOO (THE EXPENSIVE ONE). IF THERE'S ANY PROBLEM CALL ME AT 090-○××○-×○△× CHIZURU SAWAMURA."
PANT
...HER...
WHEN RICKY DIES...
YOU SHOULD GO WITH HIM...

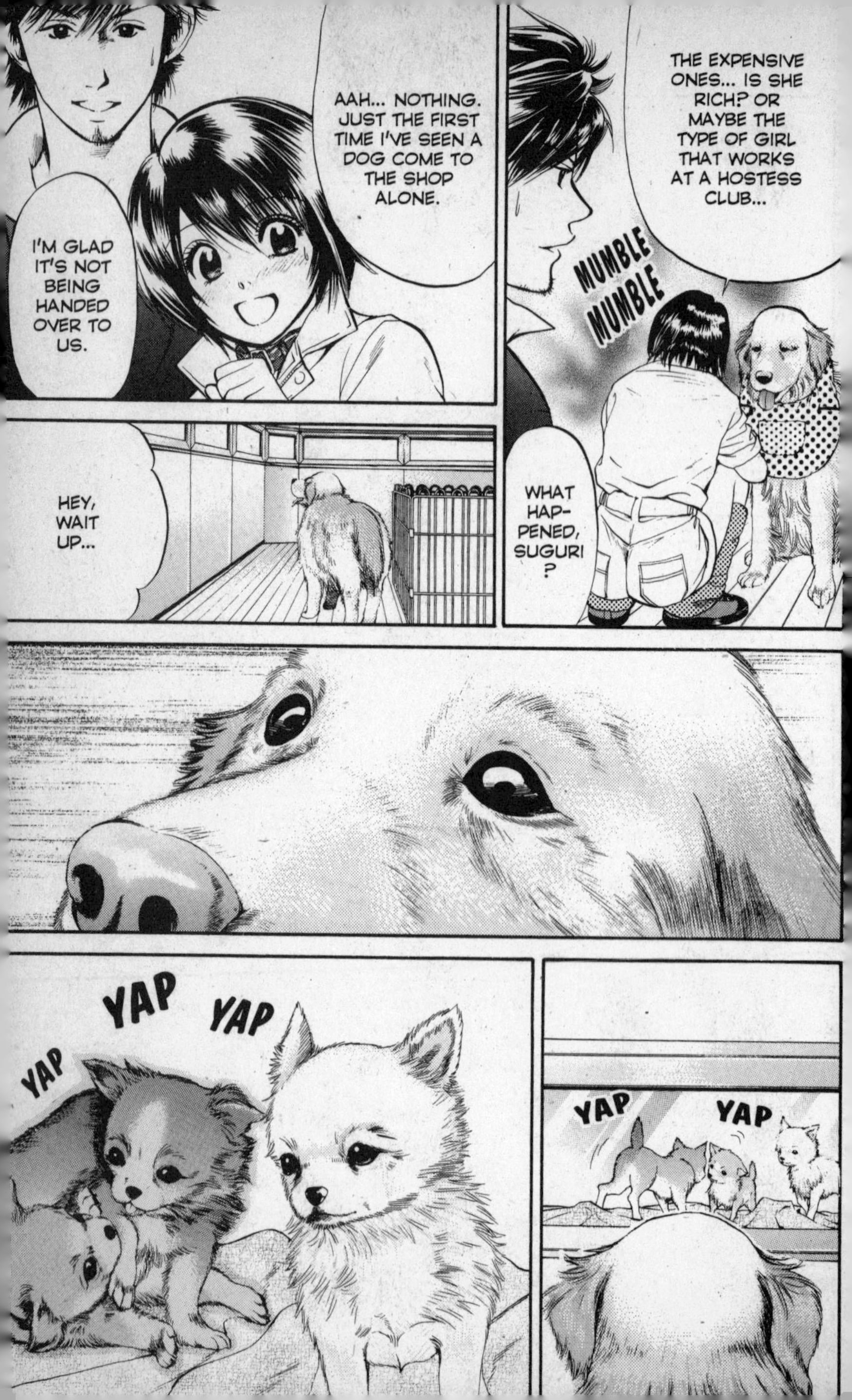
THE EXPENSIVE ONES... IS SHE RICH? OR MAYBE THE TYPE OF GIRL THAT WORKS AT A HOSTESS CLUB...
MUMBLE MUMBLE
WHAT HAP-PENED, SUGURI?
AAH... NOTHING. JUST THE FIRST TIME I'VE SEEN A DOG COME TO THE SHOP ALONE.
I'M GLAD IT'S NOT BEING HANDED OVER TO US.
HEY, WAIT UP...
YAP
YAP
YAP
YAP
YAP

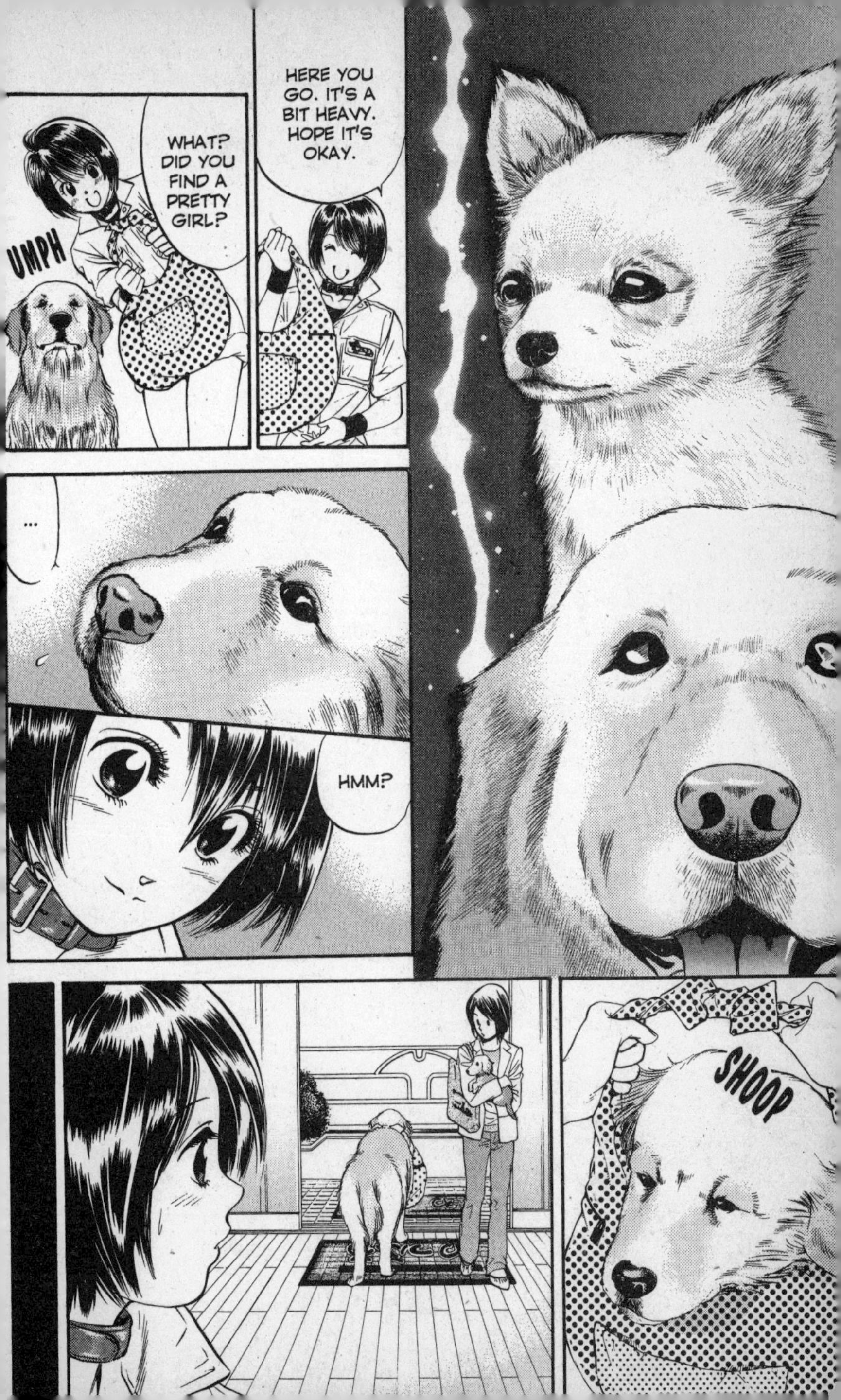
HERE YOU GO. IT'S A BIT HEAVY. HOPE IT'S OKAY.
WHAT? DID YOU FIND A PRETTY GIRL?
UMPH
...
HMM?
SHOOP

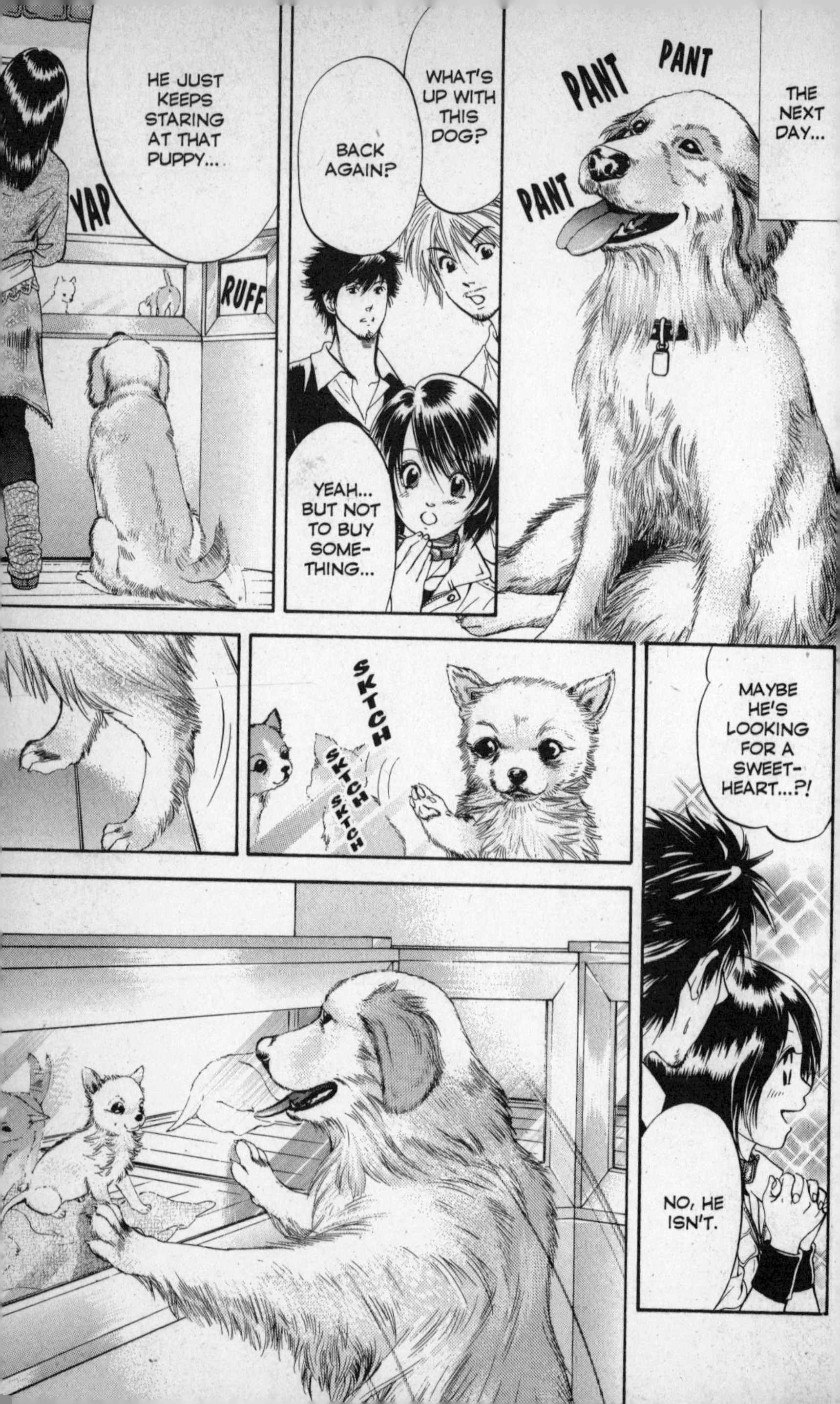
THE NEXT DAY...
PANT
PANT
PANT
WHAT'S UP WITH THIS DOG?
BACK AGAIN?
YEAH... BUT NOT TO BUY SOME-THING...
HE JUST KEEPS STARING AT THAT PUPPY...
YAP
RUFF
MAYBE HE'S LOOKING FOR A SWEET-HEART...?!
NO, HE ISN'T.
SKTCH
SKTCH
SKTCH

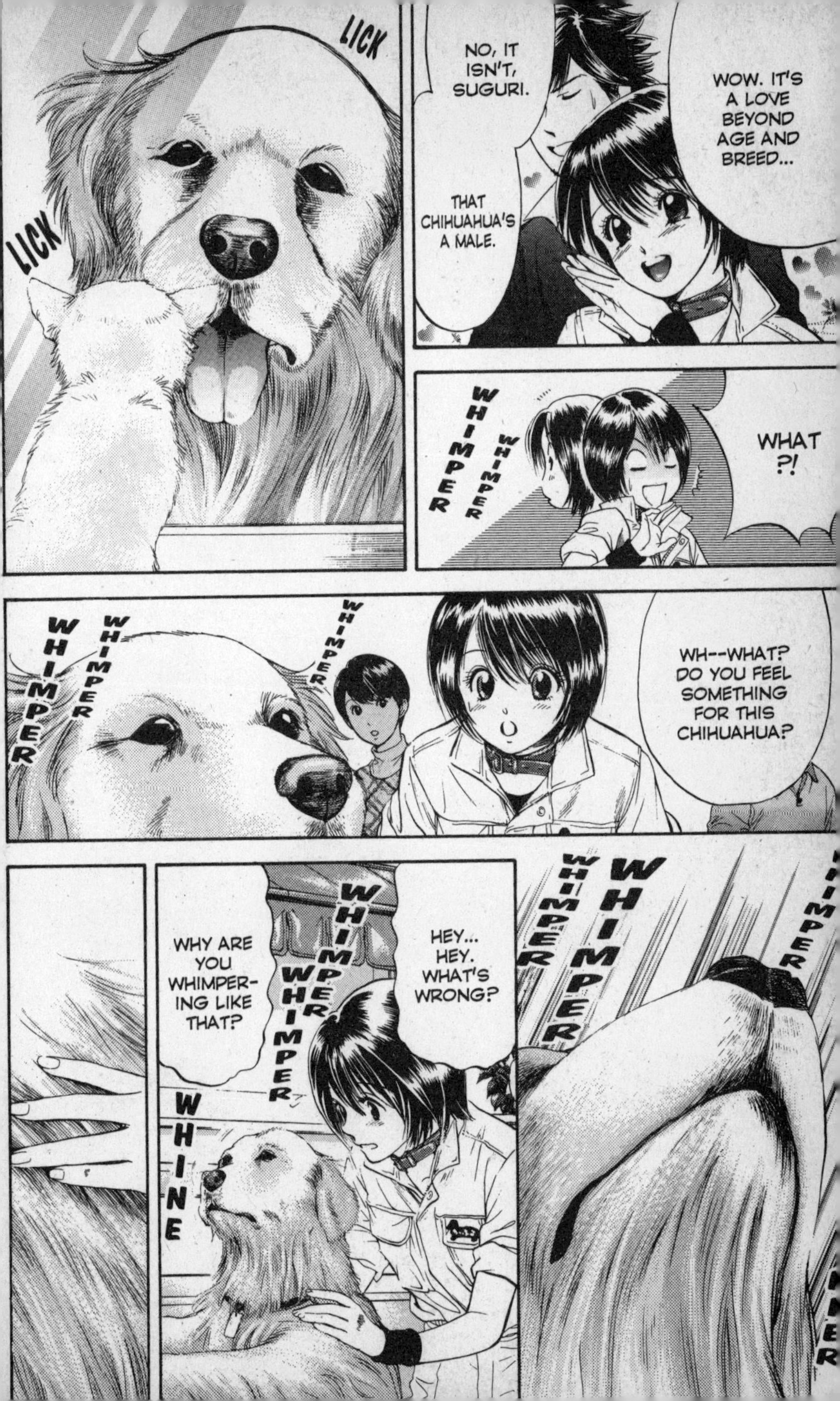
WOW. IT'S A LOVE BEYOND AGE AND BREED...
NO, IT ISN'T, SUGURI.
THAT CHIHUAHUA'S A MALE.
WHAT ?!
WHIMPER
WHIMPER
LICK
LICK
WH--WHAT? DO YOU FEEL SOMETHING FOR THIS CHIHUAHUA?
WHIMPER
WHIMPER
WHIMPER
WHIMPER
WHIMPER
WHIMPER
HEY... HEY. WHAT'S WRONG?
WHIMPER
WHIMPER
WHY ARE YOU WHIMPERING LIKE THAT?
WHINE

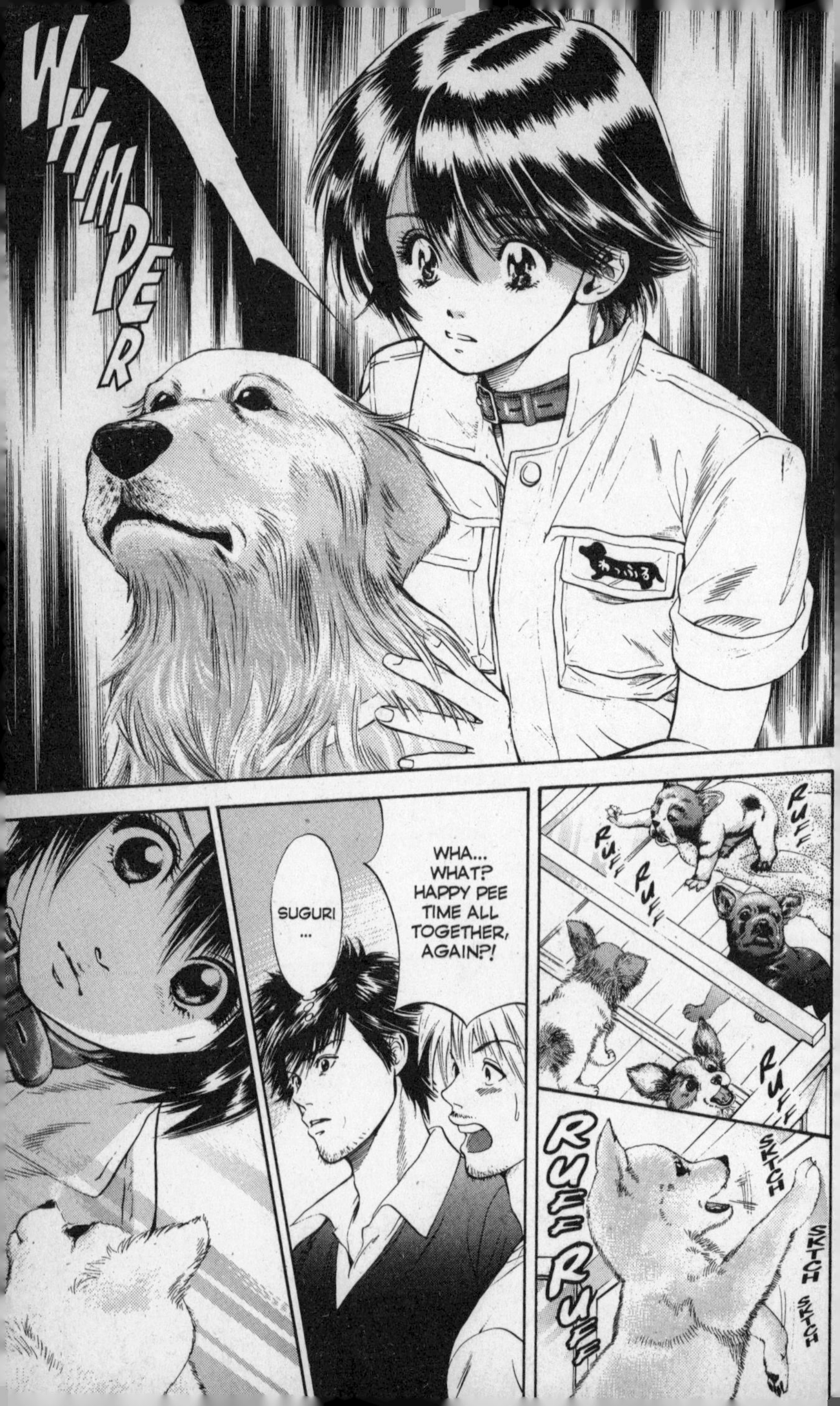
WHIMPER
RUFF
RUFF
RUFF
RUFF
RUFF RUFF
SKTCH
SKTCH SKTCH
WHA... WHAT? HAPPY PEE TIME ALL TOGETHER, AGAIN?!
SUGURI ...

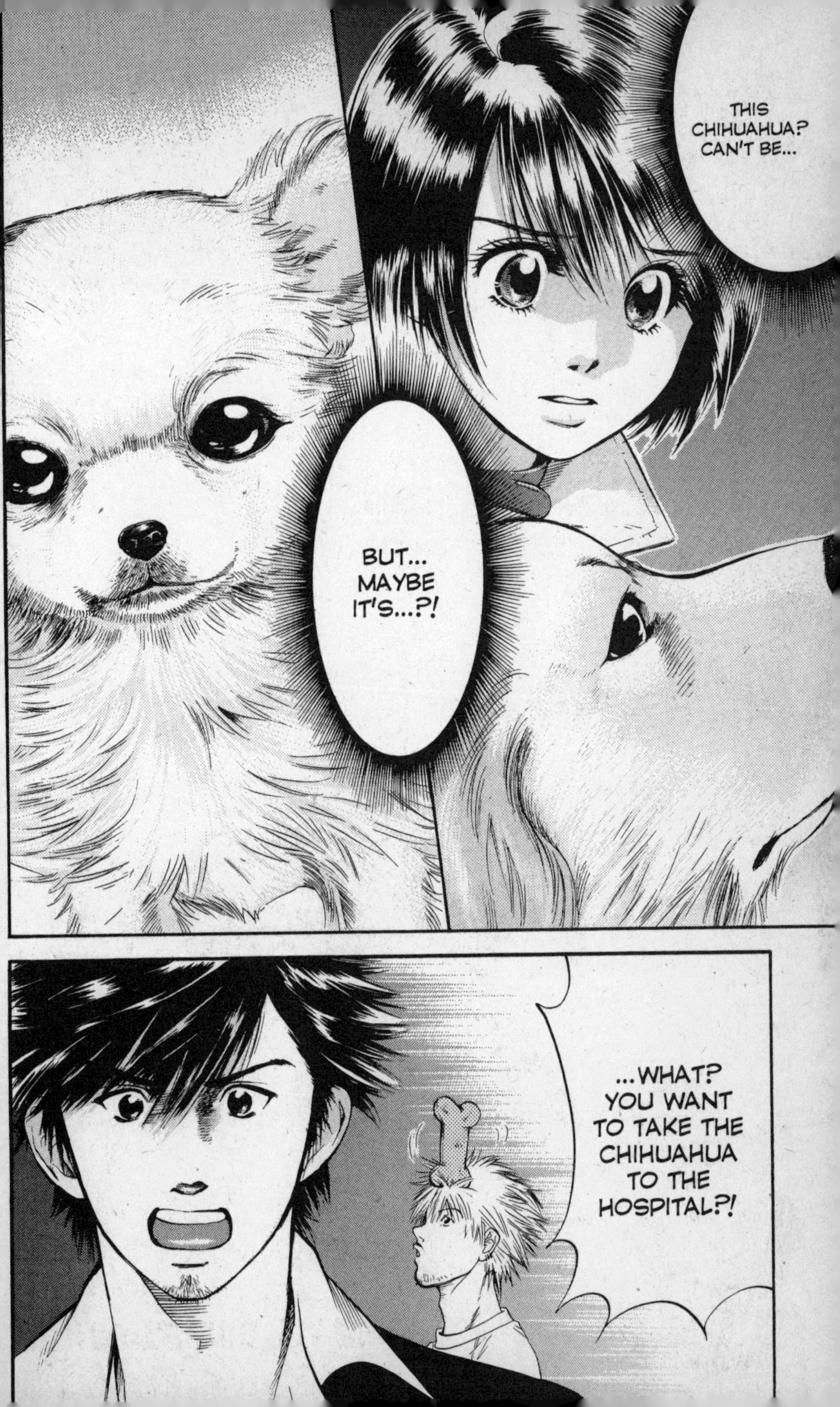
THIS CHIHUAHUA? CAN'T BE...
BUT... MAYBE IT'S...?!
...WHAT? YOU WANT TO TAKE THE CHIHUAHUA TO THE HOSPITAL?!

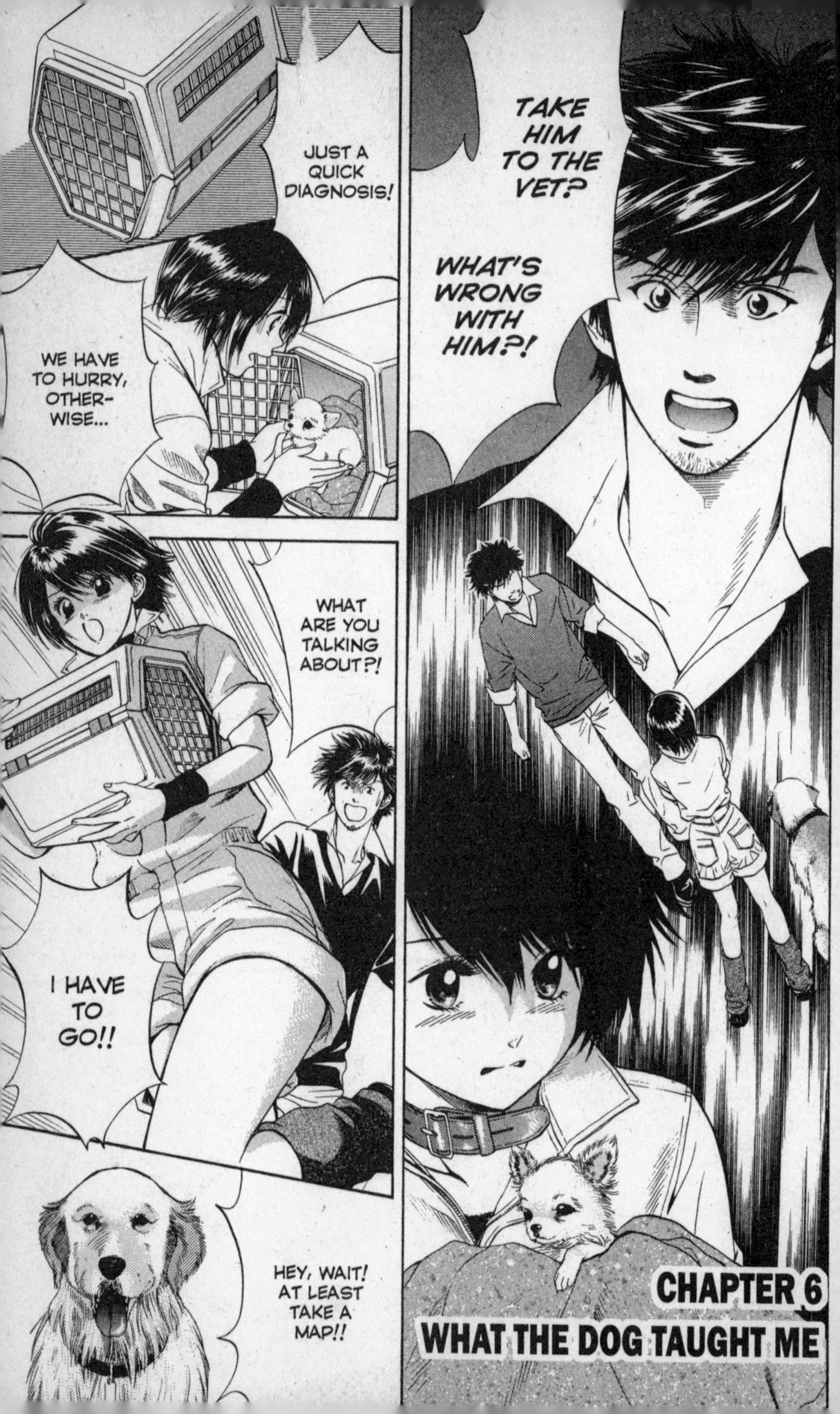
TAKE HIM TO THE VET?
WHAT'S WRONG WITH HIM?!
CHAPTER 6
WHAT THE DOG TAUGHT ME
JUST A QUICK DIAGNOSIS!
WE HAVE TO HURRY, OTHER-WISE...
WHAT ARE YOU TALKING ABOUT?!
I HAVE TO GO!!
HEY, WAIT! AT LEAST TAKE A MAP!!

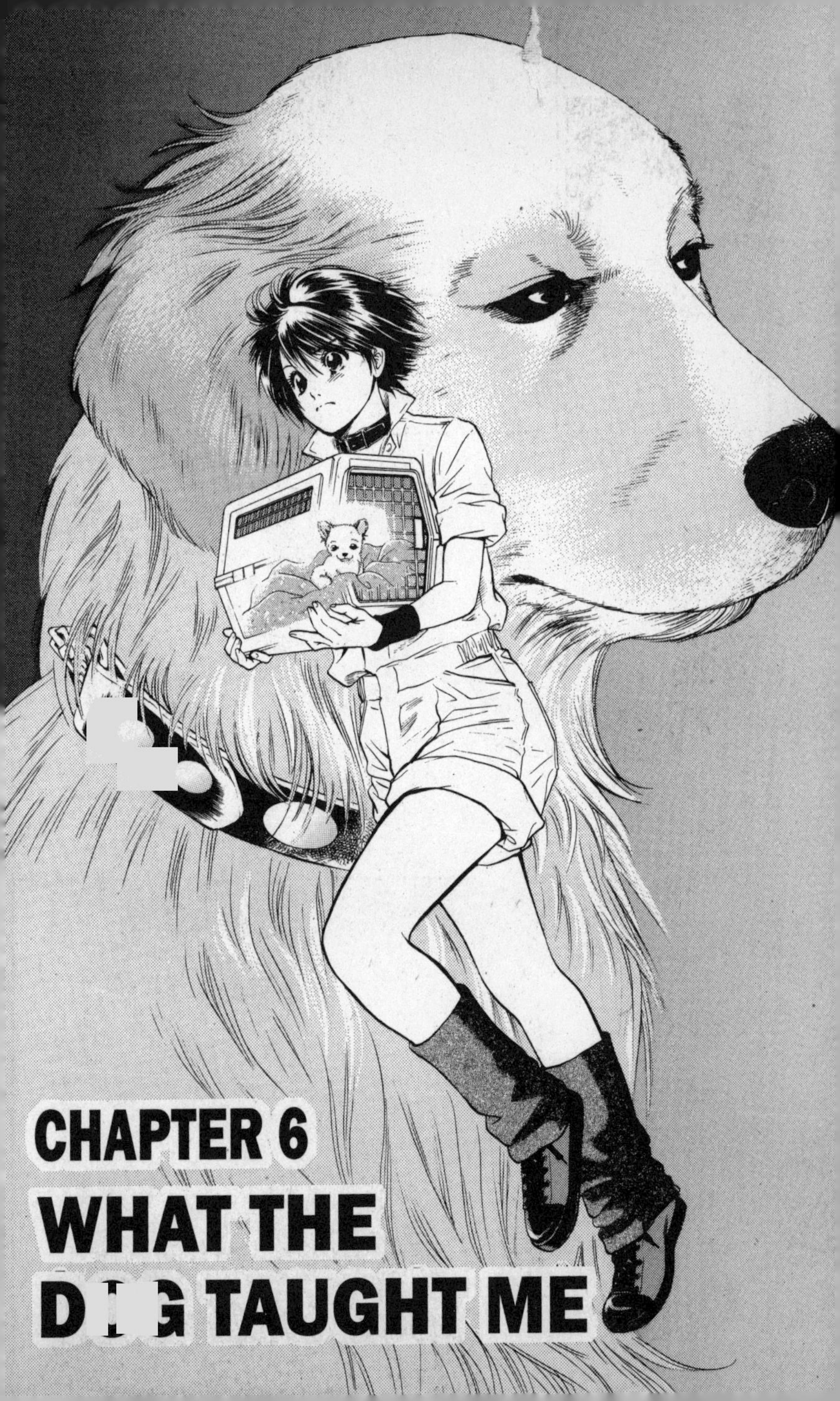
CHAPTER 6
WHAT THE
D G TAUGHT ME

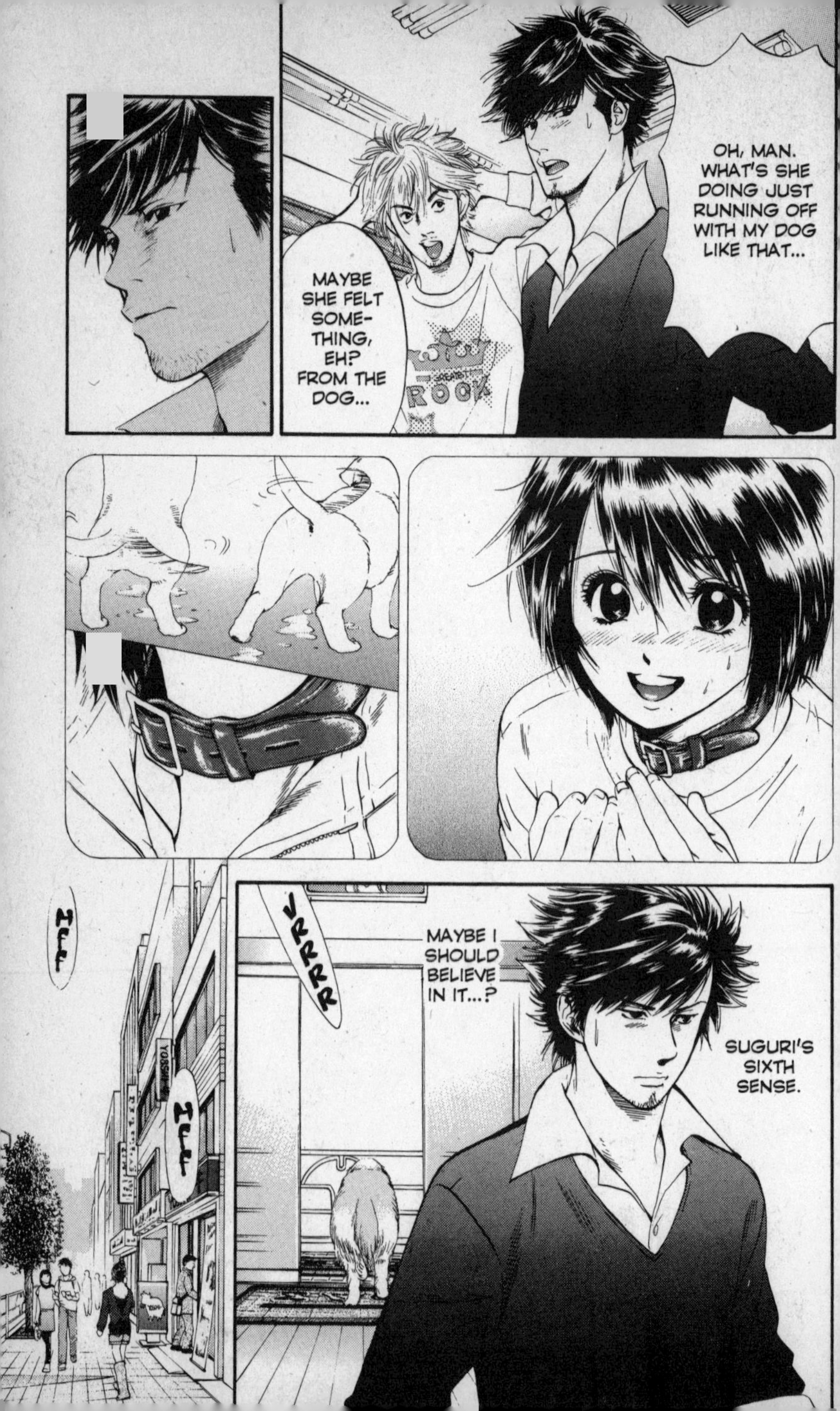
OH, MAN. WHAT'S SHE DOING JUST RUNNING OFF WITH MY DOG LIKE THAT...
MAYBE SHE FELT SOMETHING, EH? FROM THE DOG...
VRRRR
SUGURI'S SIXTH SENSE.
MAYBE I SHOULD BELIEVE IN IT...?
HFF
HFF

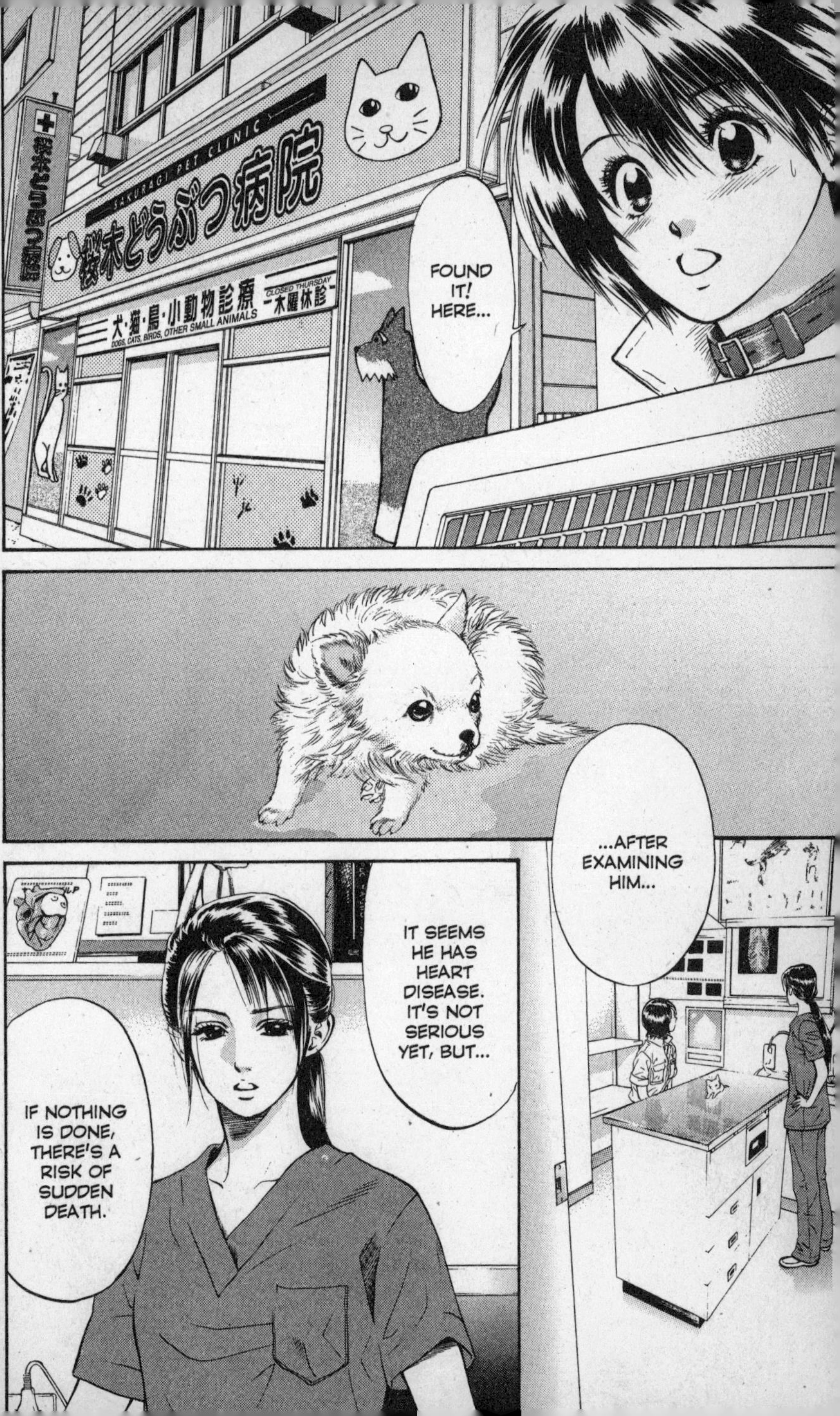
SAKURAGI PET CLINIC
桜木どうぶつ病院
犬·猫·鳥·小動物診療
DOGS, CATS, BIRDS, OTHER SMALL ANIMALS
CLOSED THURSDAY
木曜休診
FOUND IT! HERE...
...AFTER EXAMINING HIM...
IT SEEMS HE HAS HEART DISEASE. IT'S NOT SERIOUS YET, BUT...
IF NOTHING IS DONE, THERE'S A RISK OF SUDDEN DEATH.

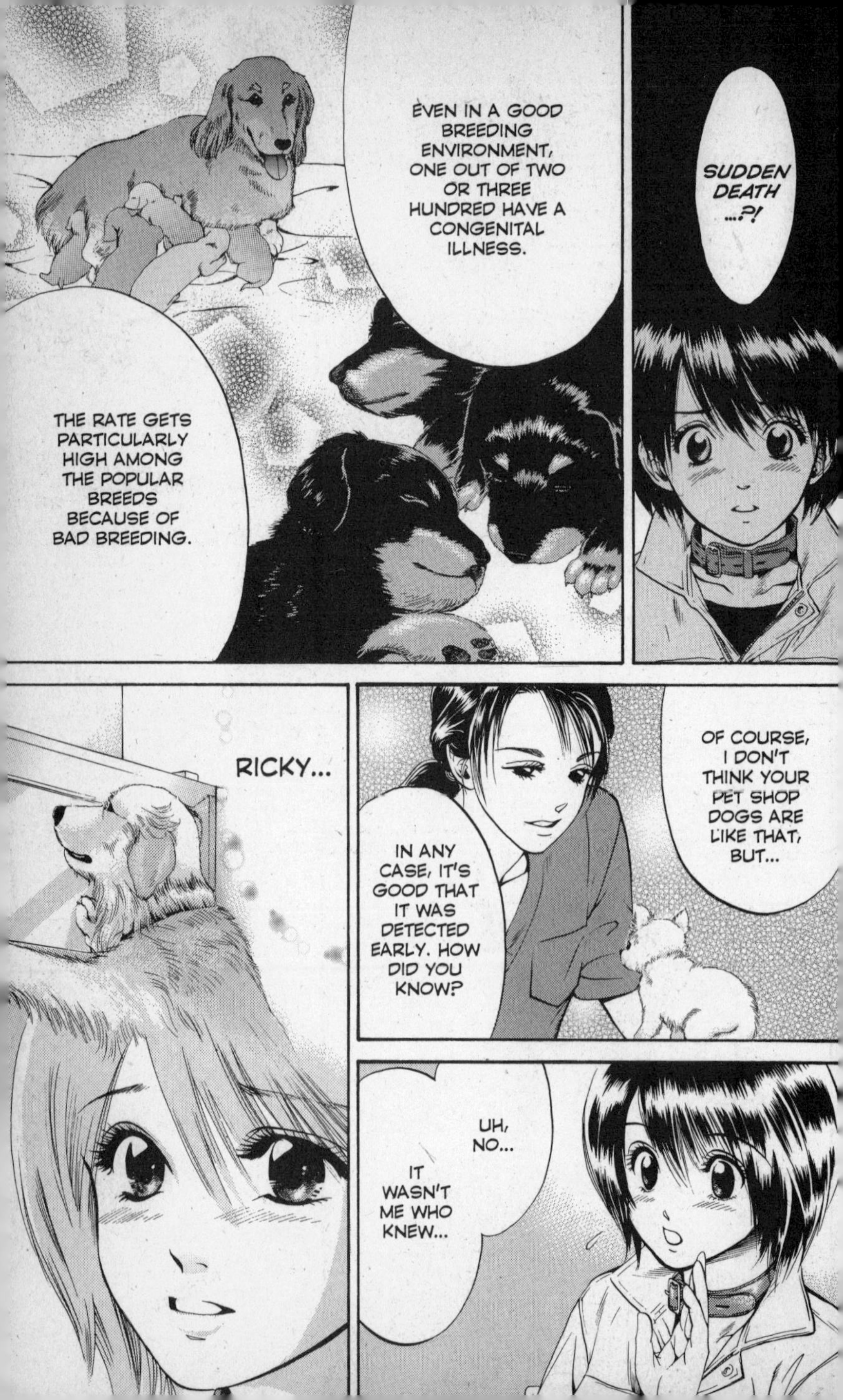
SUDDEN DEATH ...?!
EVEN IN A GOOD BREEDING ENVIRONMENT, ONE OUT OF TWO OR THREE HUNDRED HAVE A CONGENITAL ILLNESS.
THE RATE GETS PARTICULARLY HIGH AMONG THE POPULAR BREEDS BECAUSE OF BAD BREEDING.
OF COURSE, I DON'T THINK YOUR PET SHOP DOGS ARE LIKE THAT, BUT...
IN ANY CASE, IT'S GOOD THAT IT WAS DETECTED EARLY. HOW DID YOU KNOW?
UH, NO...
IT WASN'T ME WHO KNEW...
RICKY...

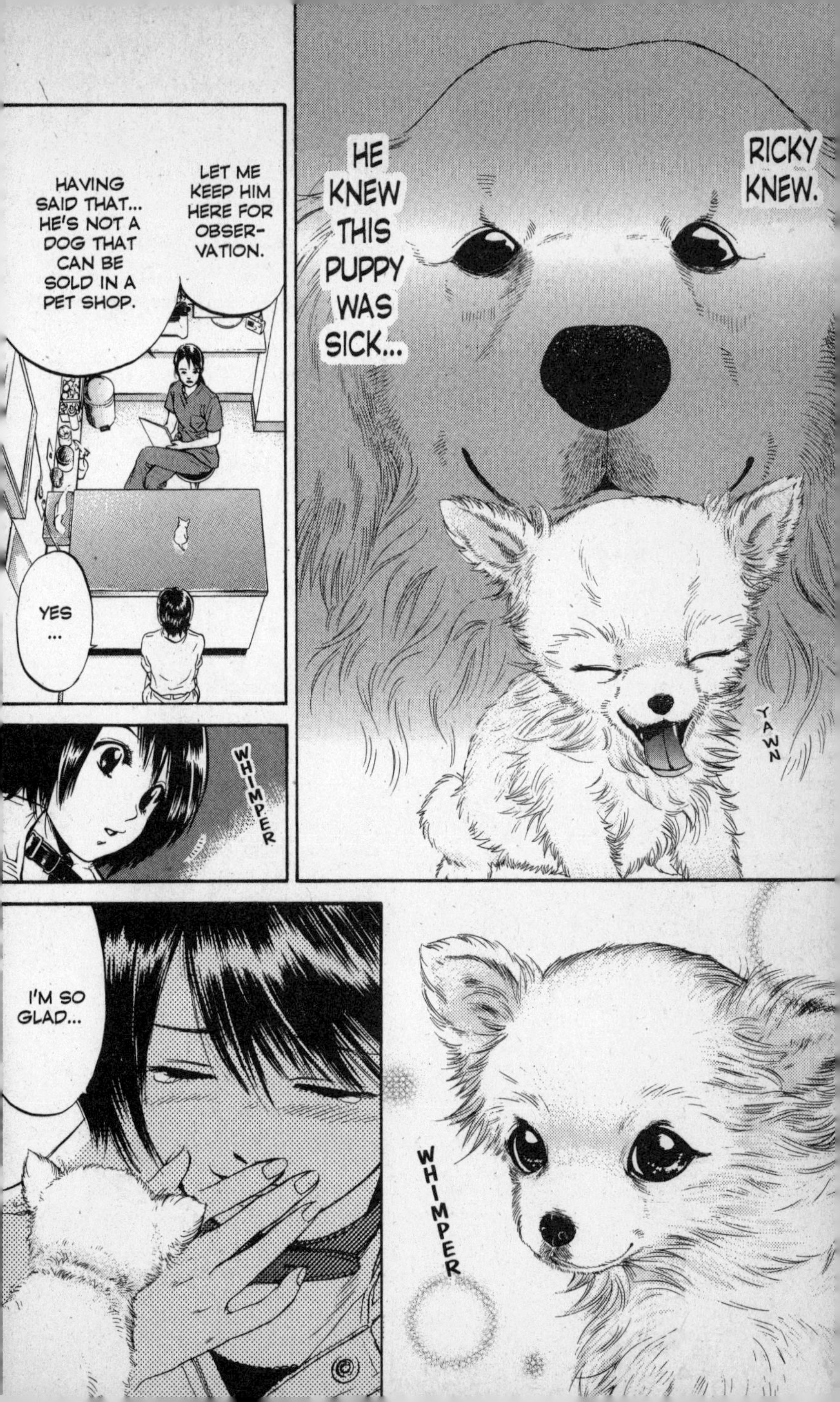

RICKY KNEW.
HE KNEW THIS PUPPY WAS SICK...
YAWN
LET ME KEEP HIM HERE FOR OBSERVATION.
HAVING SAID THAT... HE'S NOT A DOG THAT CAN BE SOLD IN A PET SHOP.
YES ...
WHIMPER
WHIMPER
I'M SO GLAD...

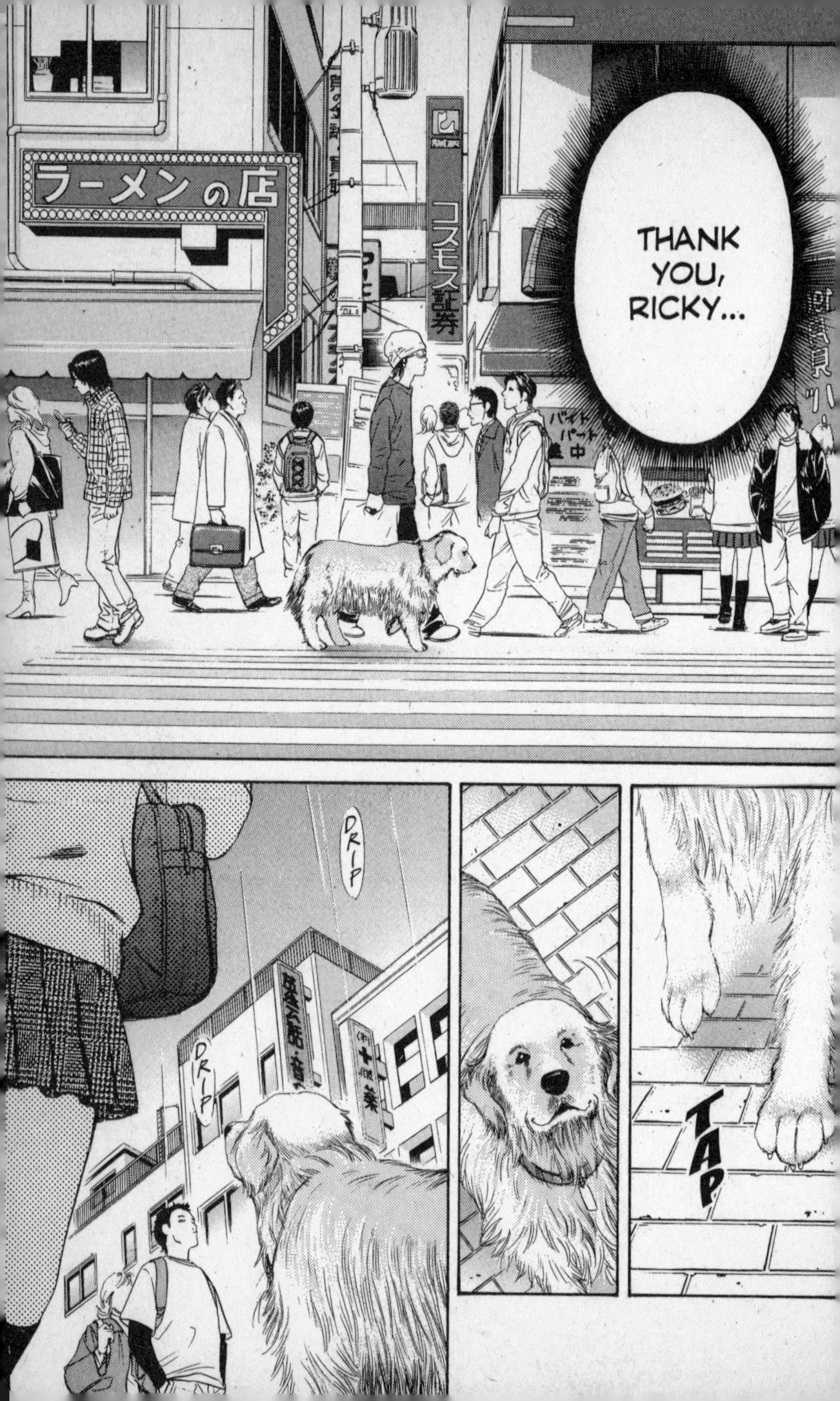
ラーメンの店
コスモス証券
THANK YOU, RICKY...
TAP
DRIP
DRIP

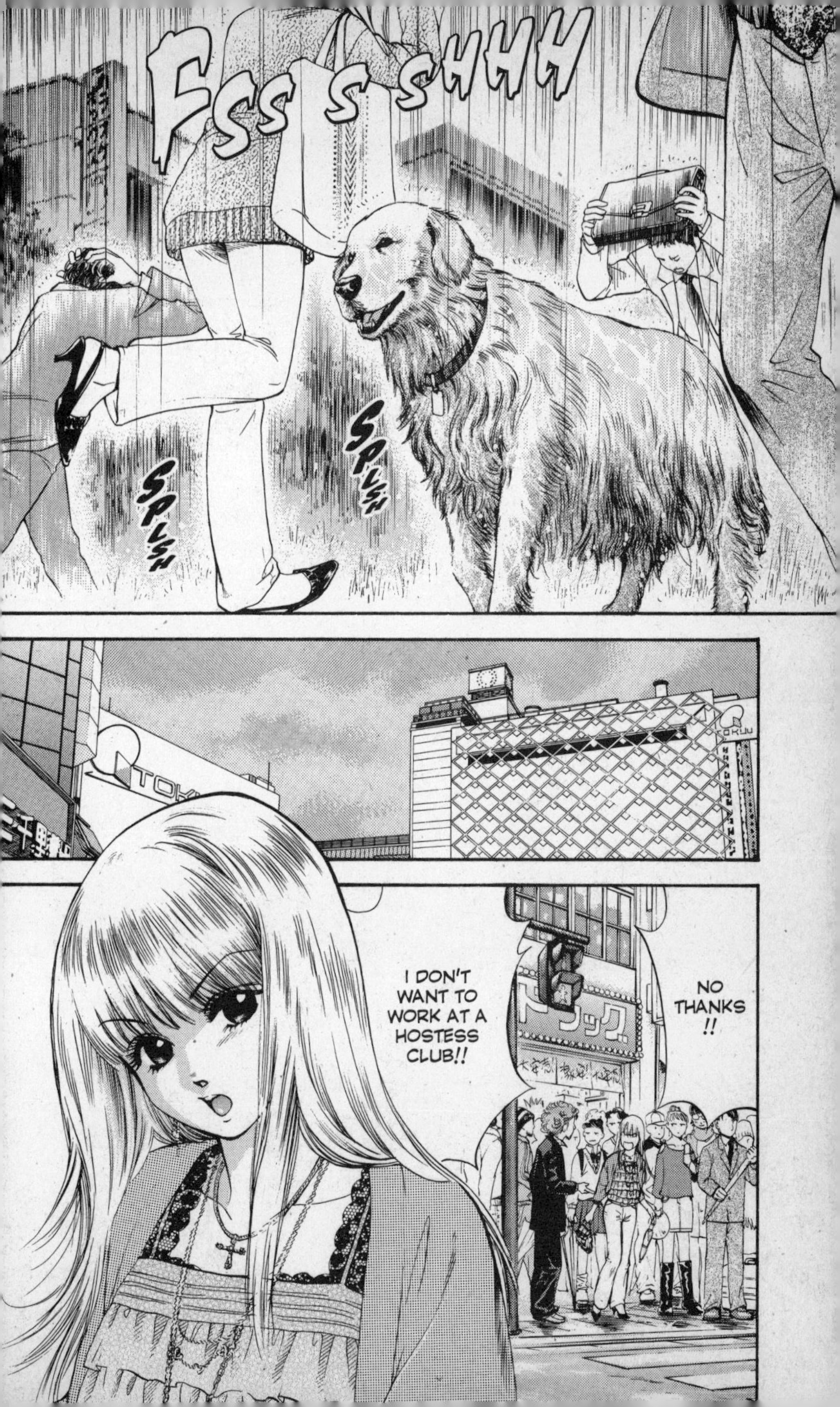
FSSSSHHH
SPLSH
SPLSH
NO THANKS!!
I DON'T WANT TO WORK AT A HOSTESS CLUB!!

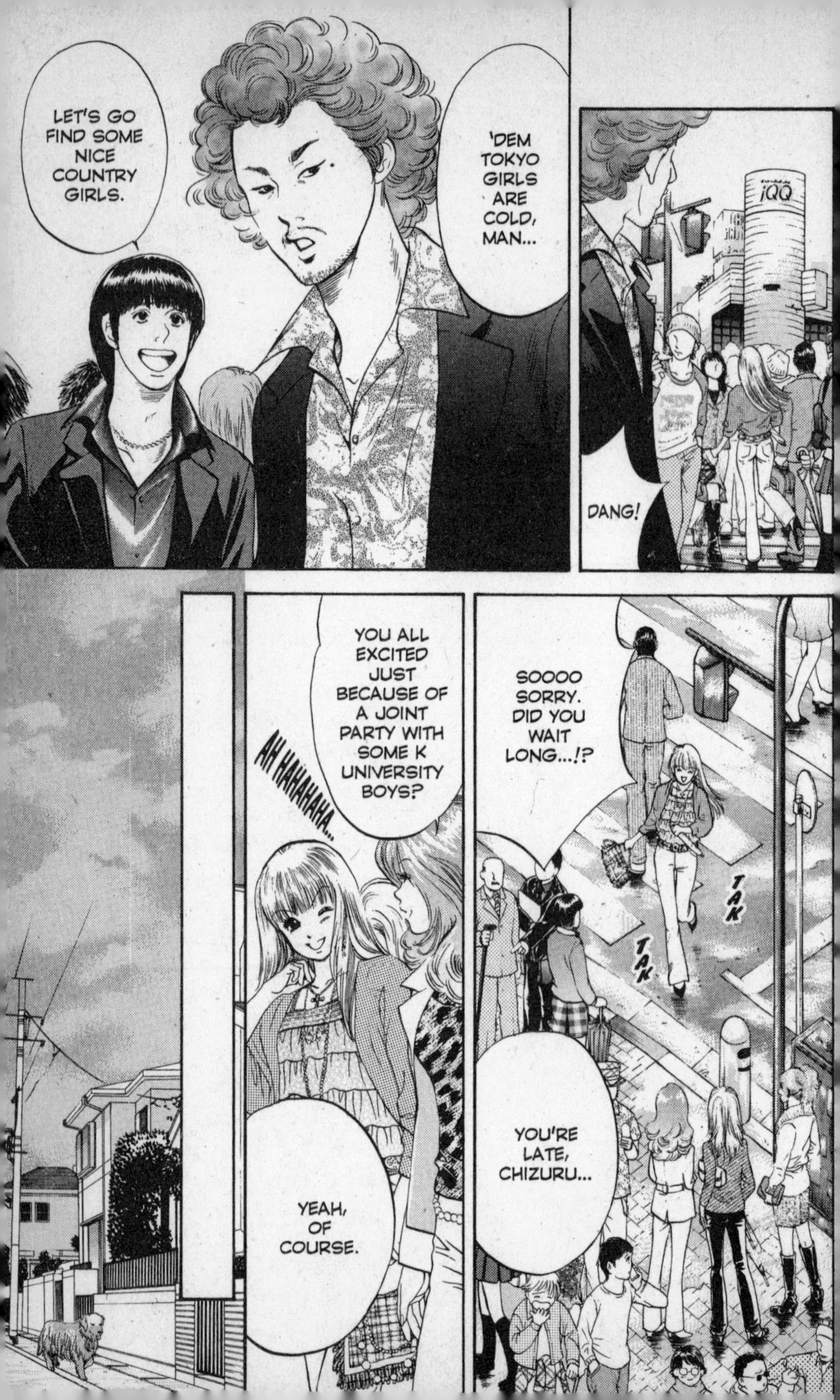
DANG!
'DEM TOKYO GIRLS ARE COLD, MAN...
LET'S GO FIND SOME NICE COUNTRY GIRLS.
SOOOO SORRY. DID YOU WAIT LONG...!?
TAK
TAK
YOU'RE LATE, CHIZURU...
YOU ALL EXCITED JUST BECAUSE OF A JOINT PARTY WITH SOME K UNIVERSITY BOYS?
AH HAHAHAHA...
YEAH, OF COURSE.

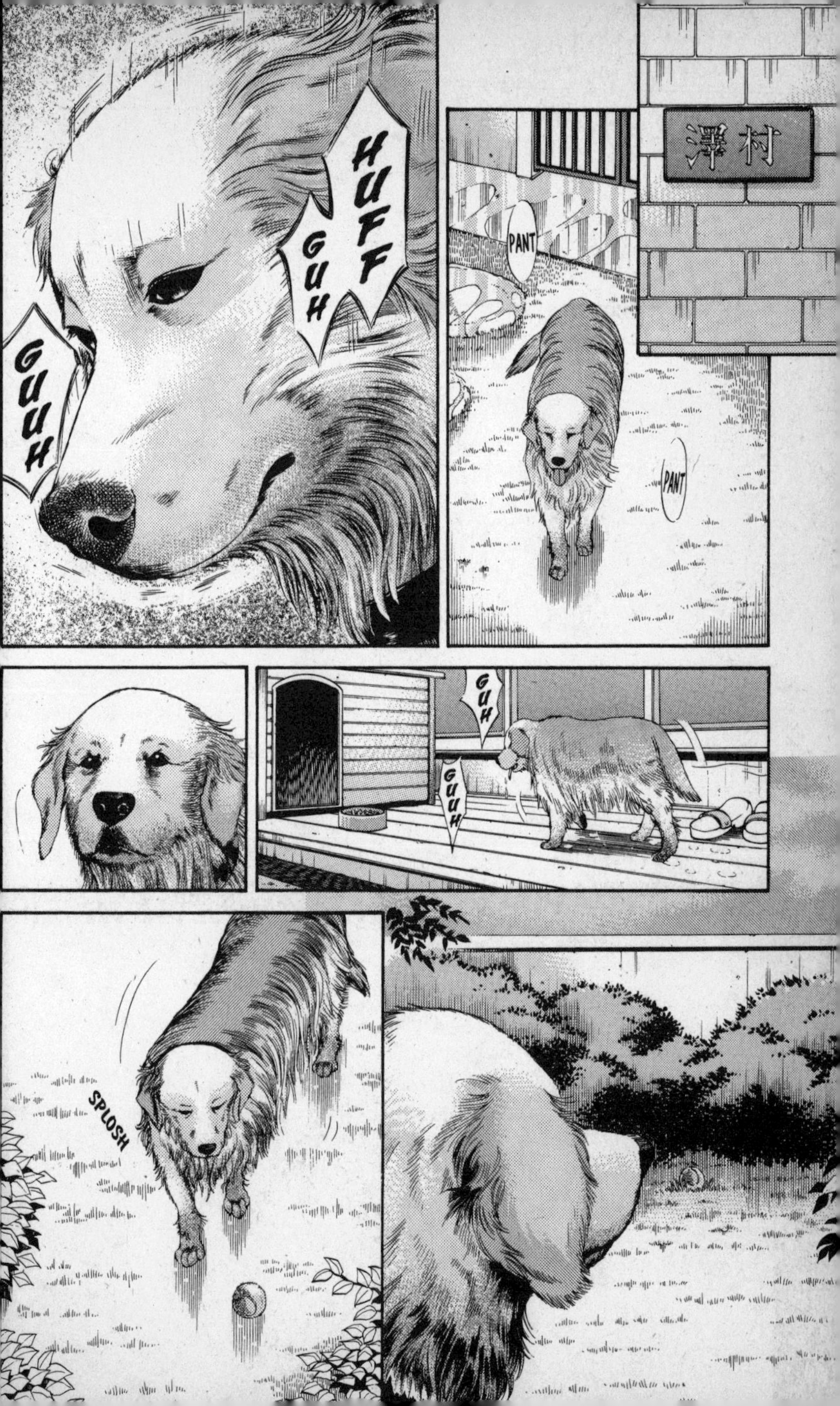

澤村
PANT
PANT
HUFF
GUH
GUUH
GUH
GUUH
SPLOSH

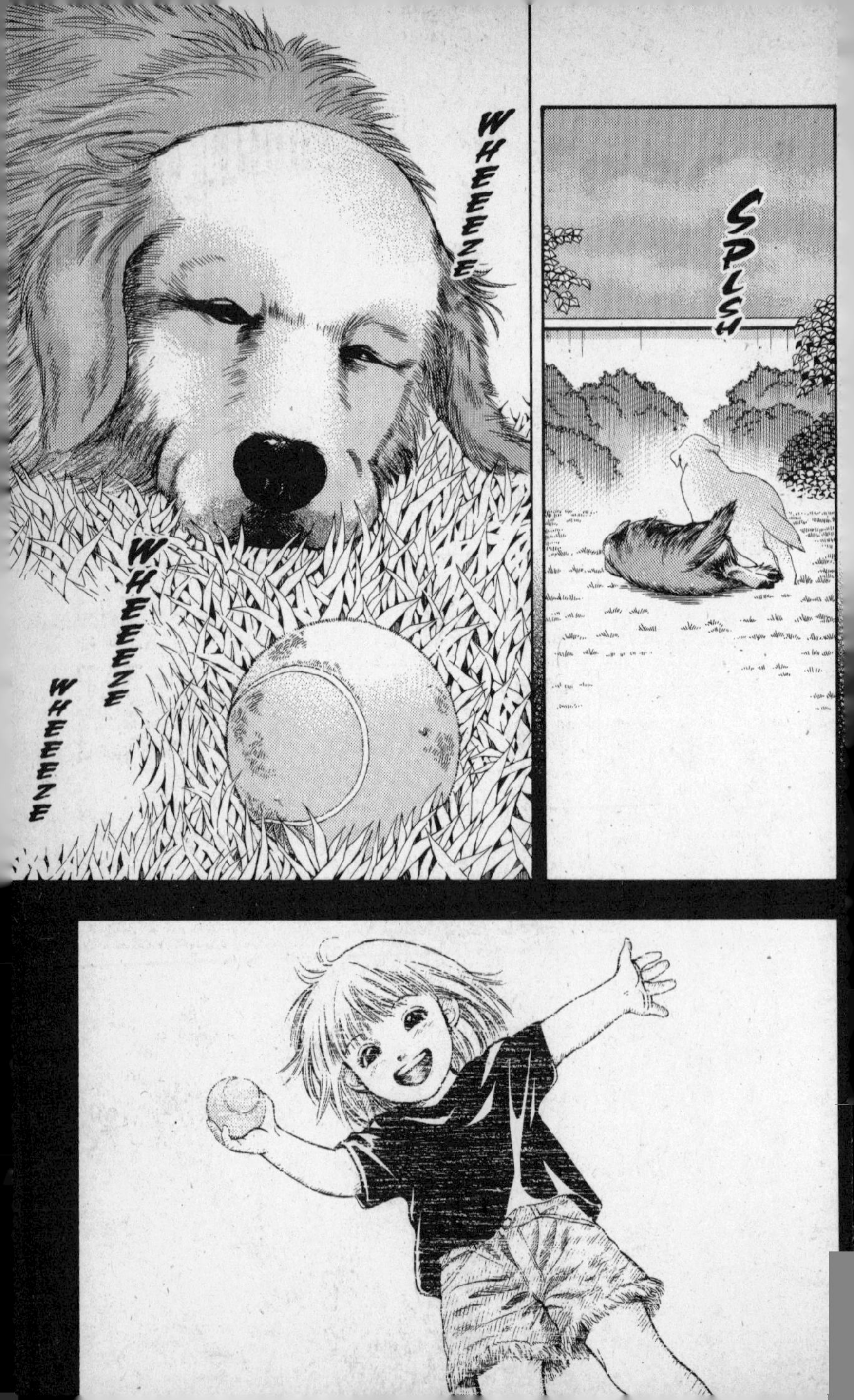
SPLSH
WHEEEZE
WHEEEZE
WHEEEZE

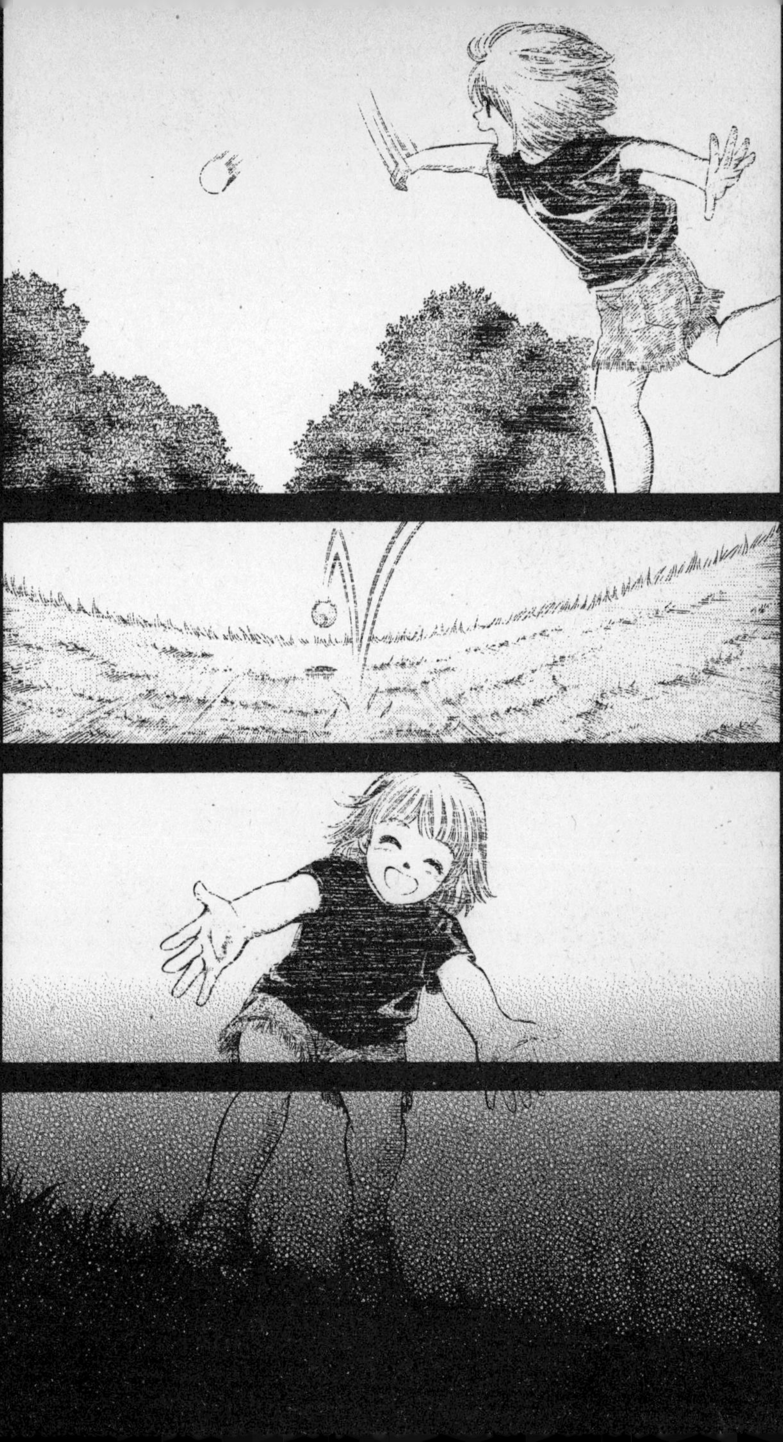

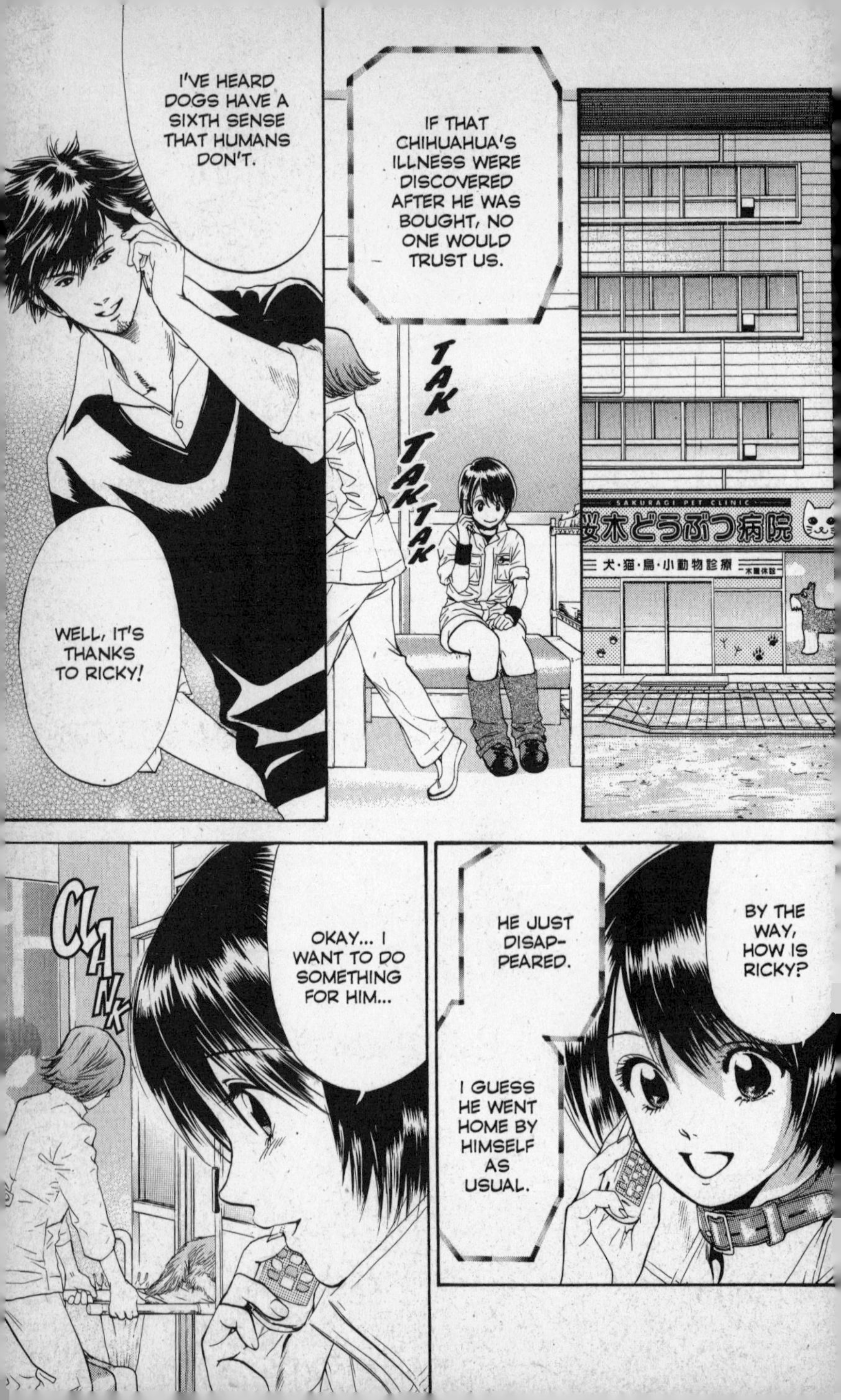
SAKURAGI PET CLINIC
桜木どうぶつ病院
犬・猫・鳥・小動物診療
木曜休診
IF THAT CHIHUAHUA'S ILLNESS WERE DISCOVERED AFTER HE WAS BOUGHT, NO ONE WOULD TRUST US.
TAK TAK TAK TAK
I'VE HEARD DOGS HAVE A SIXTH SENSE THAT HUMANS DON'T.
WELL, IT'S THANKS TO RICKY!
BY THE WAY, HOW IS RICKY?
HE JUST DISAPPEARED.
I GUESS HE WENT HOME BY HIMSELF AS USUAL.
OKAY... I WANT TO DO SOMETHING FOR HIM...
CLANK

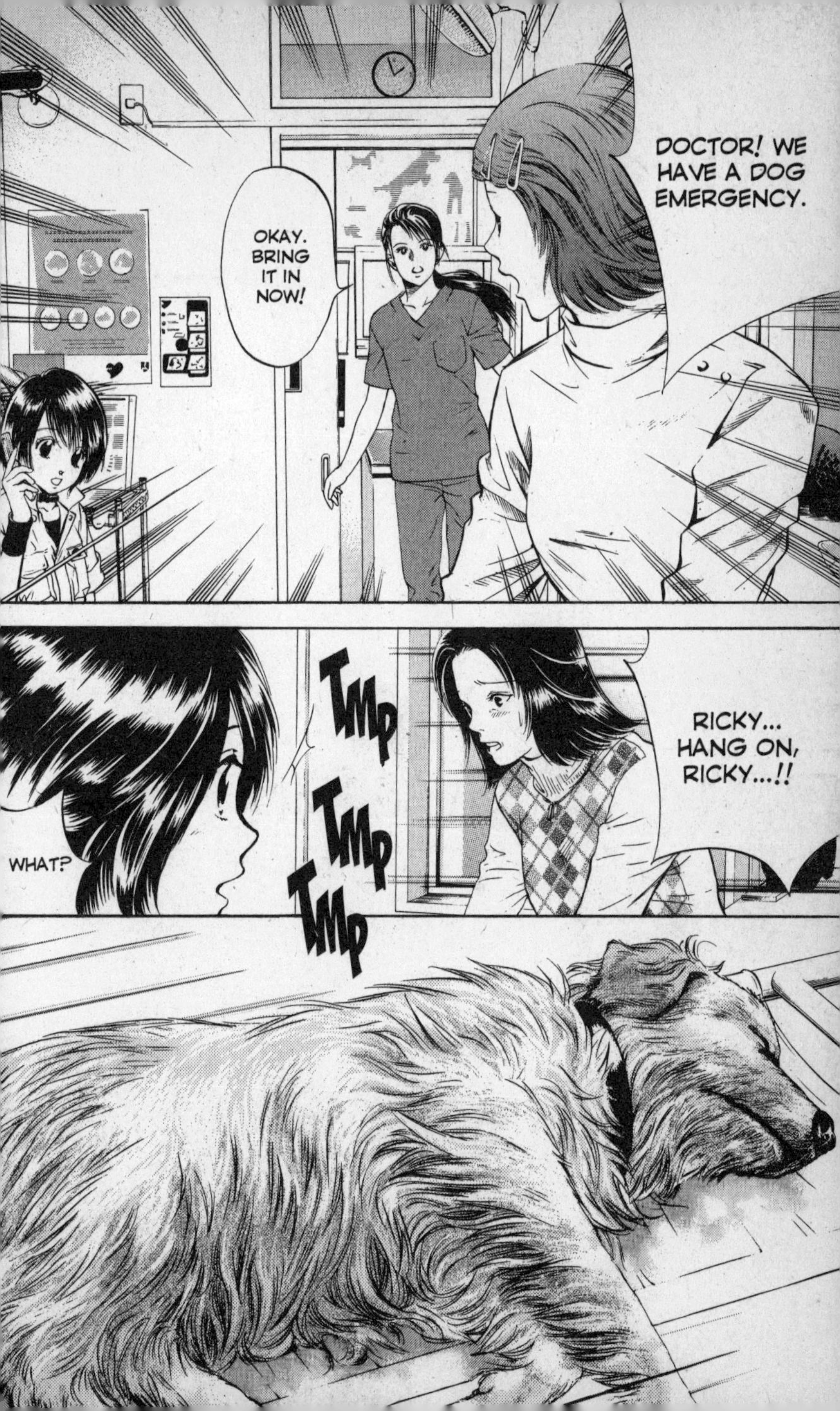
DOCTOR! WE HAVE A DOG EMERGENCY.
OKAY. BRING IT IN NOW!
RICKY... HANG ON, RICKY...!!
TMP TMP TMP
WHAT?

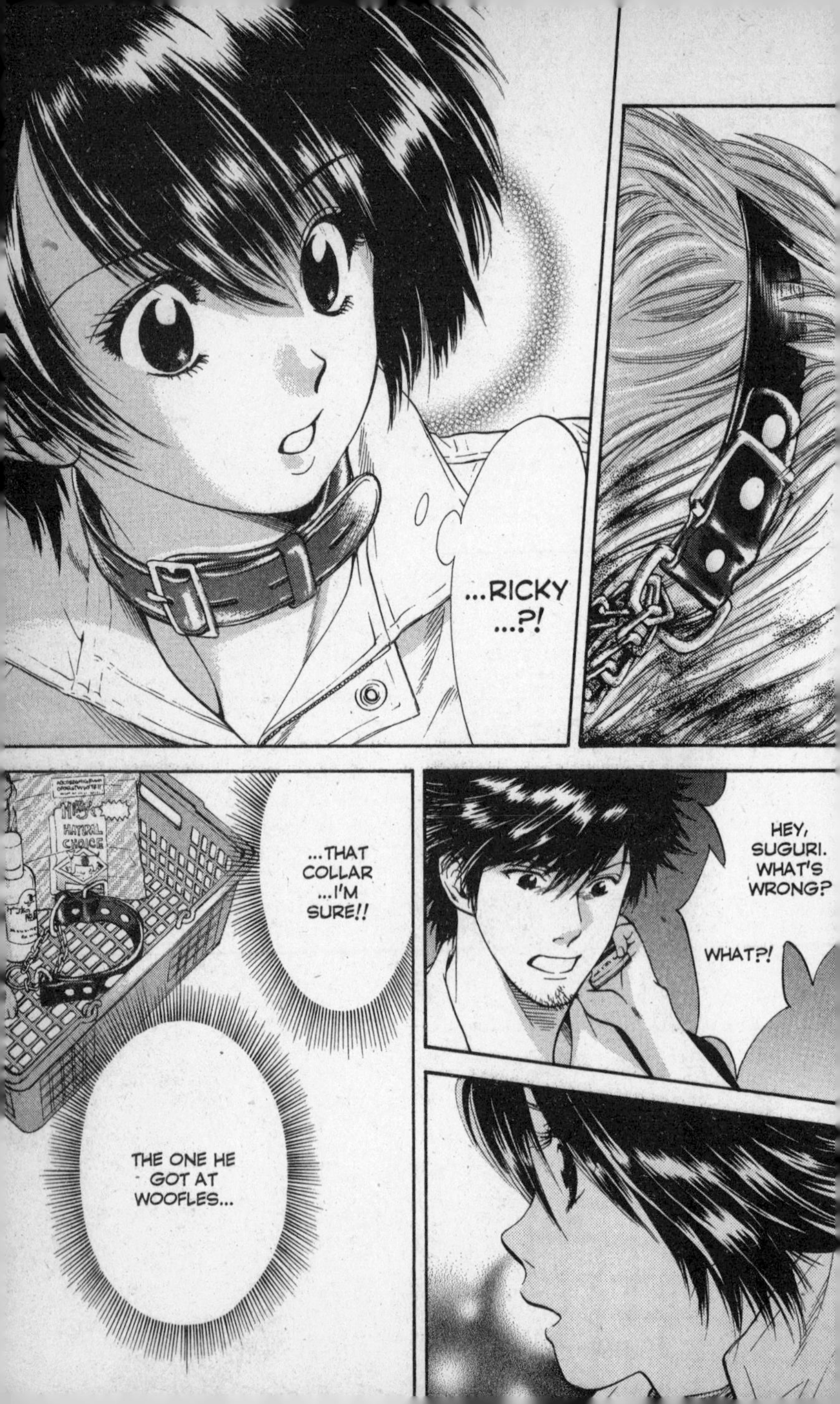
...RICKY ...?!
HEY, SUGURI. WHAT'S WRONG?
WHAT?!
...THAT COLLAR ...I'M SURE!!
THE ONE HE GOT AT WOOFLES...

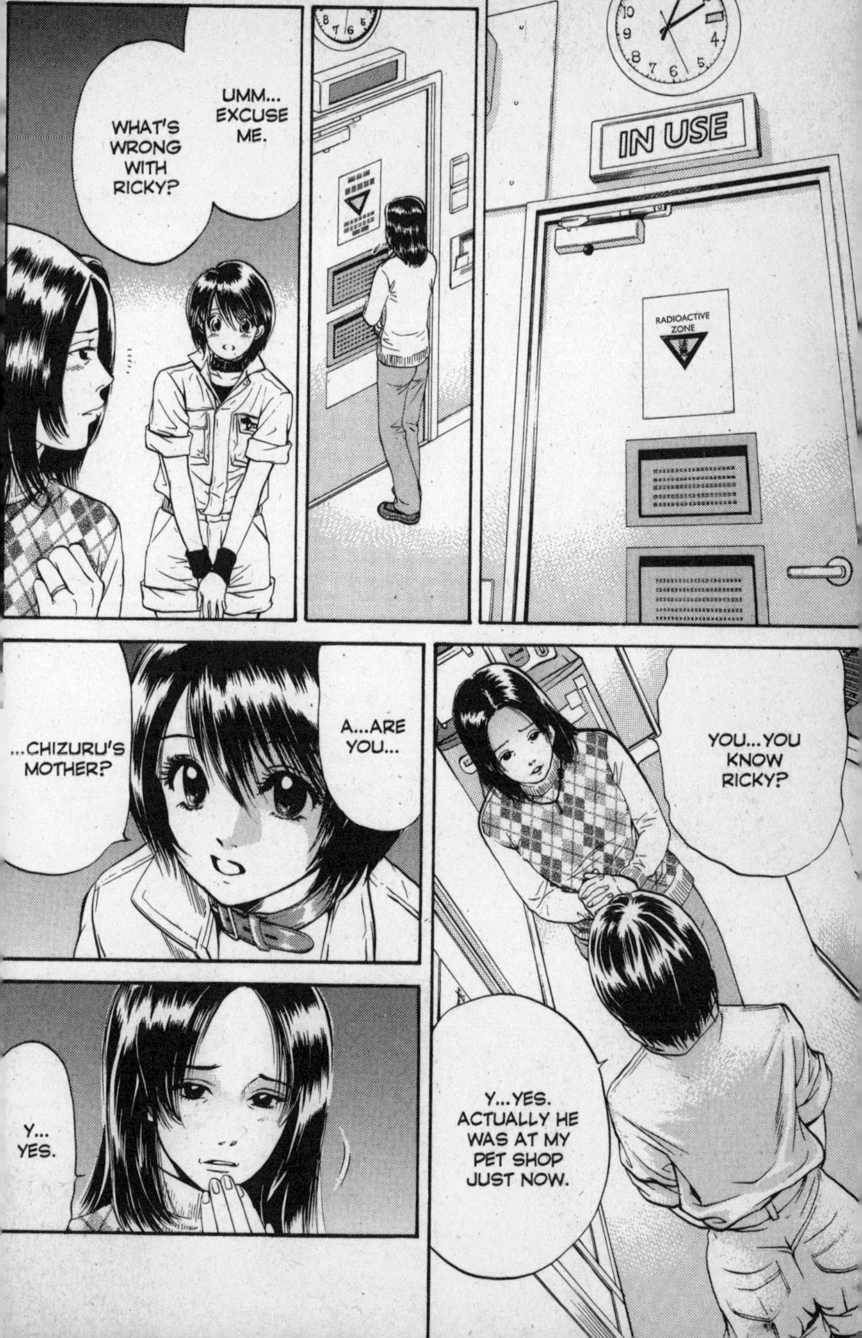
IN USE
RADIOACTIVE ZONE
UMM... EXCUSE ME.
WHAT'S WRONG WITH RICKY?
YOU...YOU KNOW RICKY?
Y...YES. ACTUALLY HE WAS AT MY PET SHOP JUST NOW.
A...ARE YOU...
...CHIZURU'S MOTHER?
Y... YES.

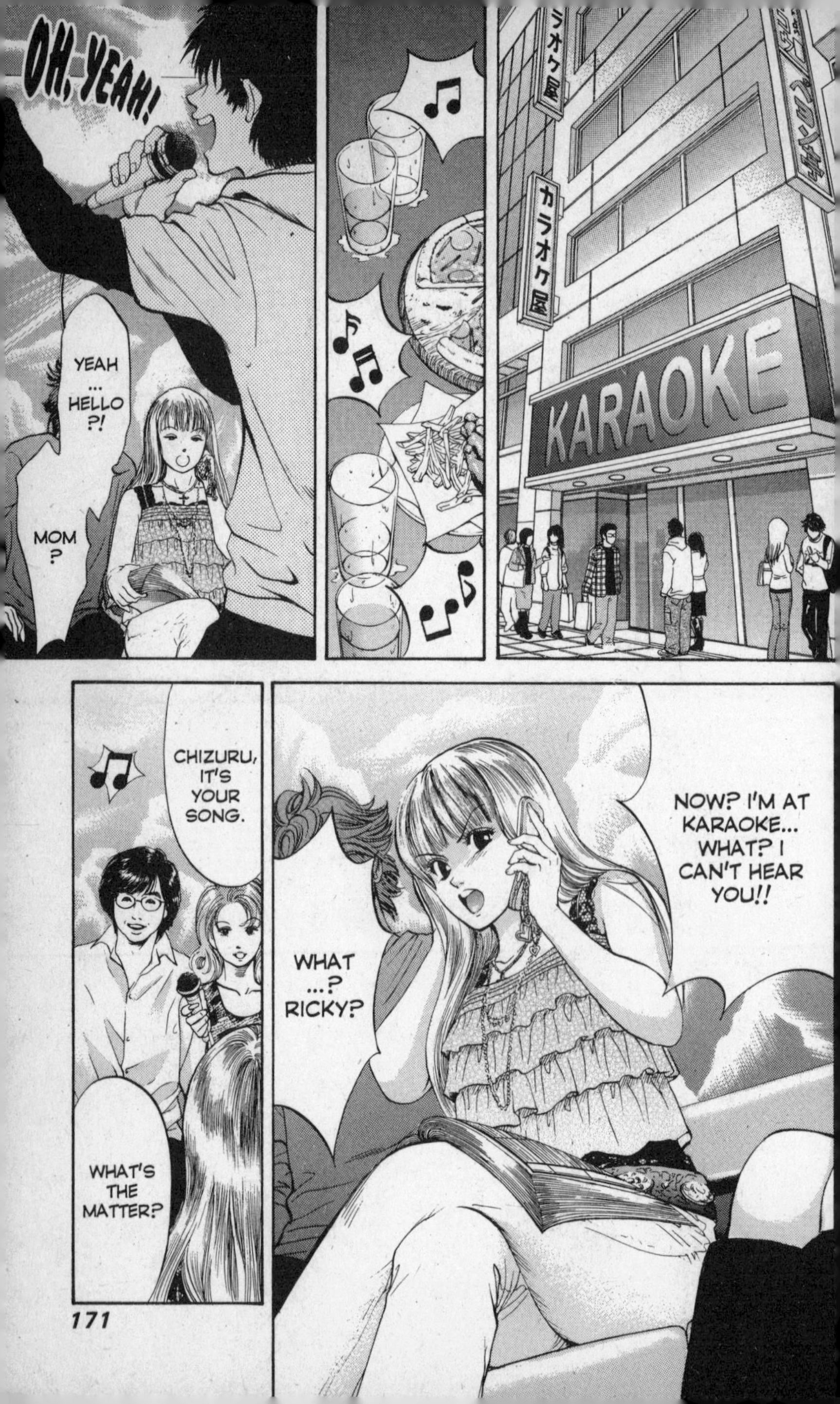
ラオケ屋
カラオケ屋
KARAOKE
OH, YEAH!
YEAH ... HELLO ?!
MOM ?
NOW? I'M AT KARAOKE... WHAT? I CAN'T HEAR YOU!!
WHAT ...? RICKY?
CHIZURU, IT'S YOUR SONG.
WHAT'S THE MATTER?

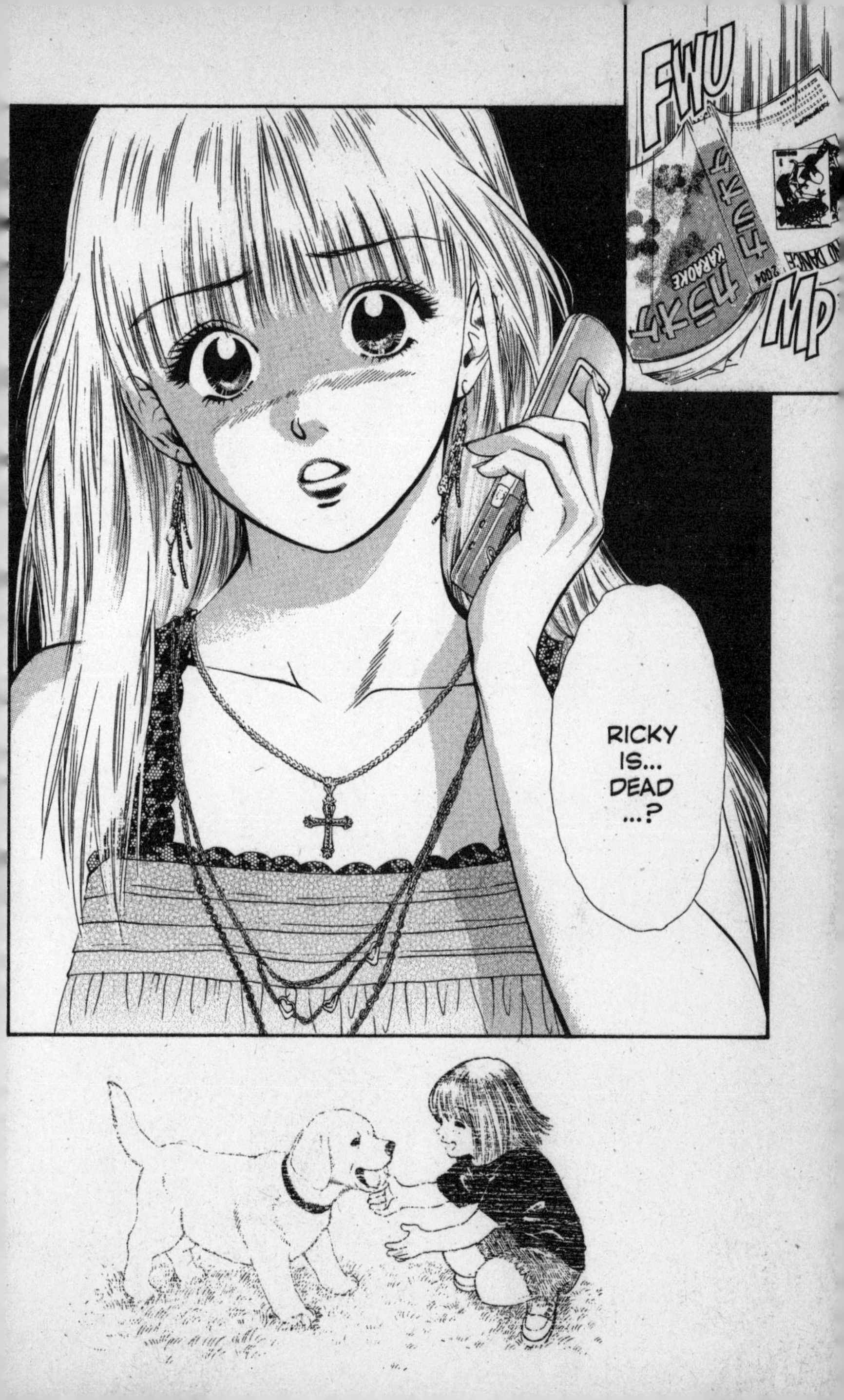
FWU
MP
RICKY IS... DEAD ...?

CHAPTER 7
FOR THIS LITTLE LIFE...

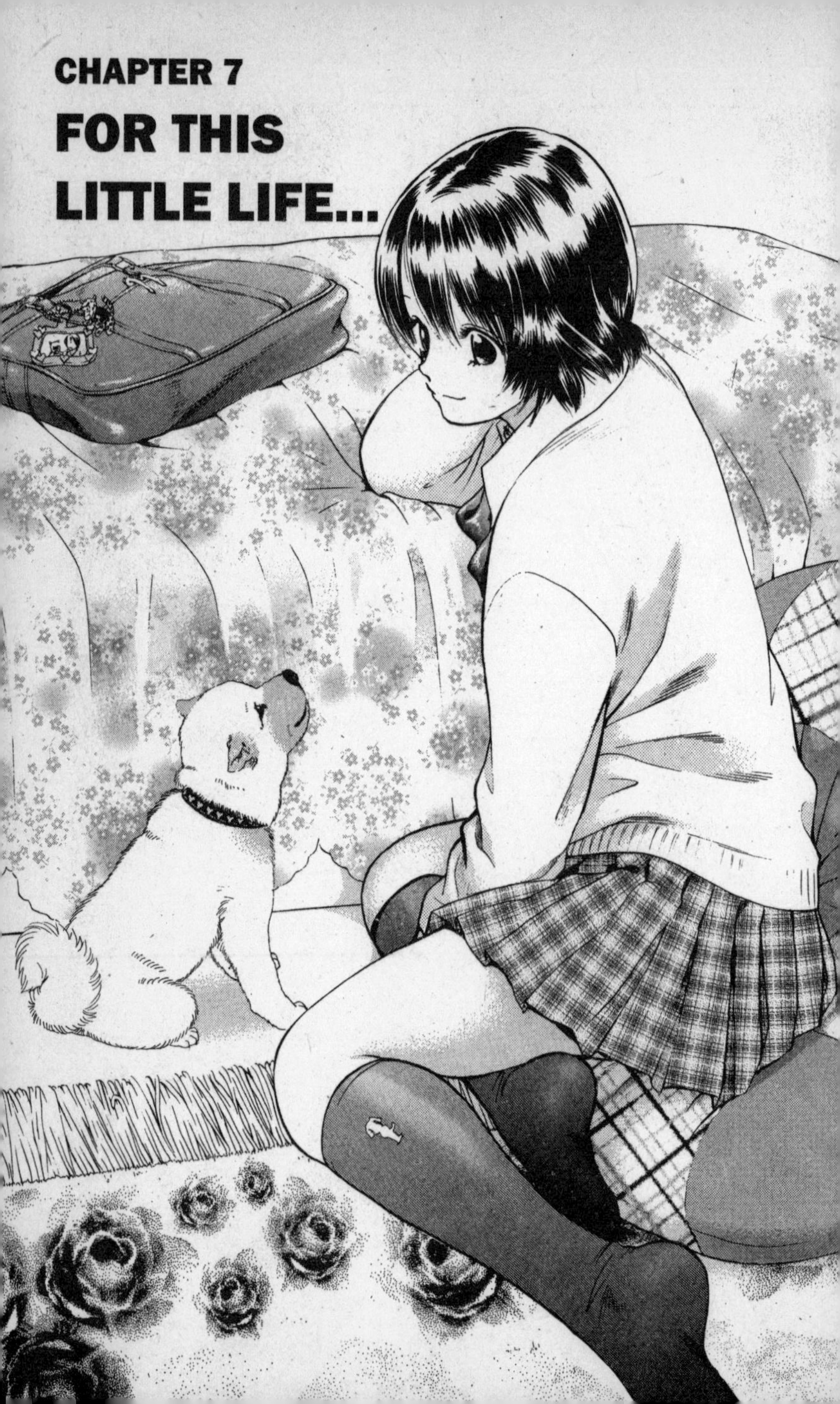

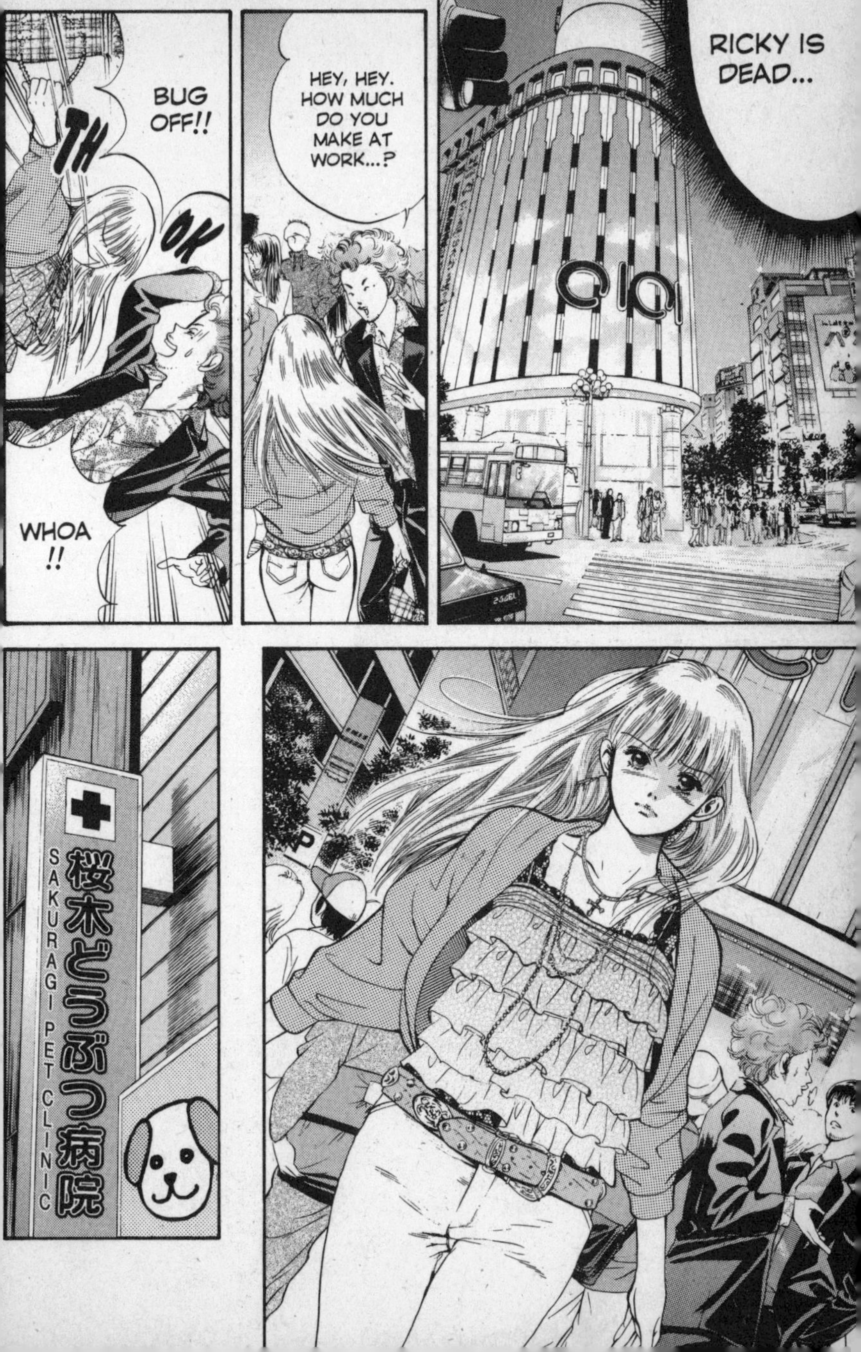
RICKY IS DEAD...
HEY, HEY. HOW MUCH DO YOU MAKE AT WORK...?
BUG OFF!!
TH
OK
WHOA !!
桜木どうぶつ病院
SAKURAGI PET CLINIC

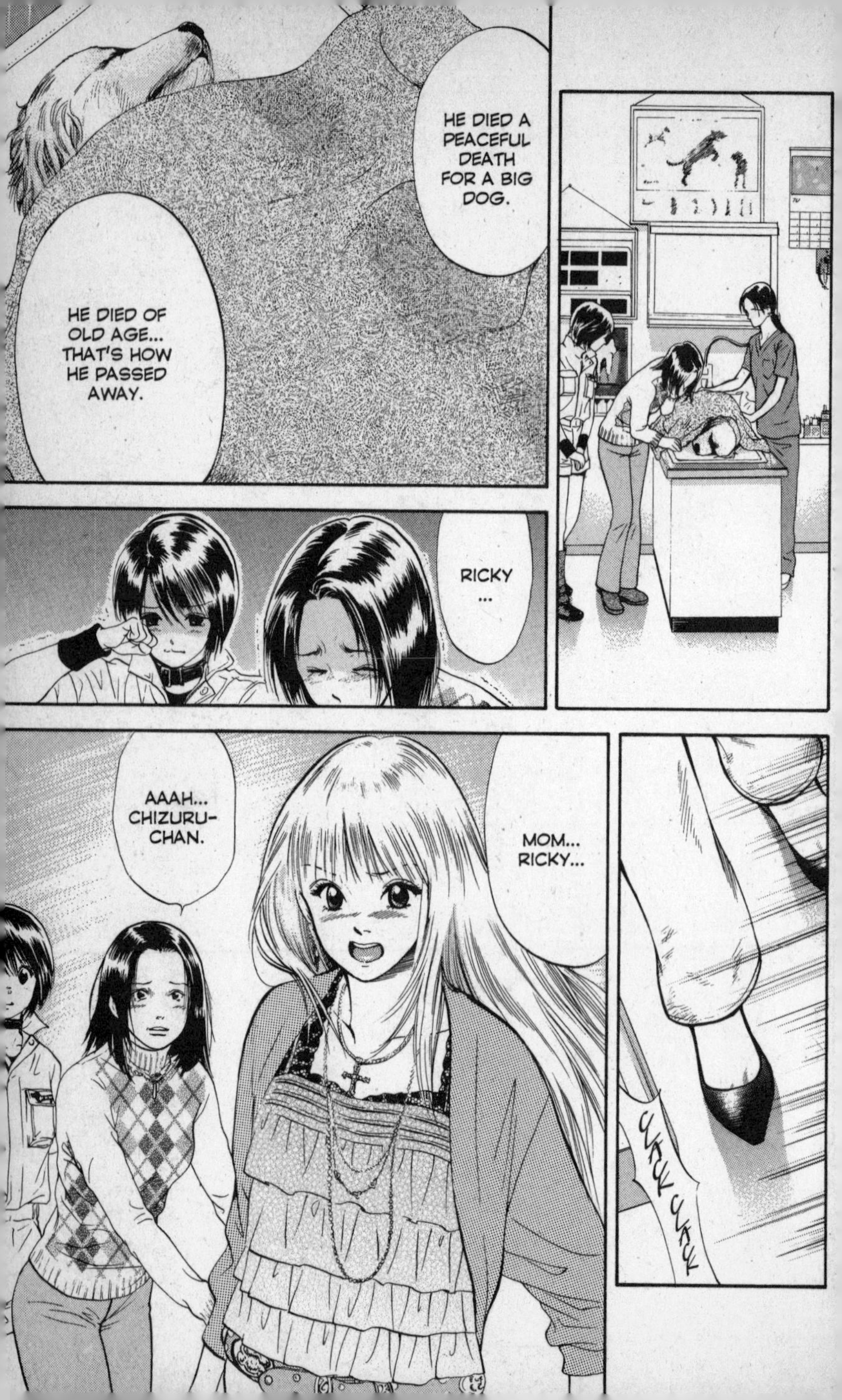

HE DIED A PEACEFUL DEATH FOR A BIG DOG.
HE DIED OF OLD AGE... THAT'S HOW HE PASSED AWAY.
RICKY ...
CLACK CLACK
MOM... RICKY...
AAAH... CHIZURU-CHAN.

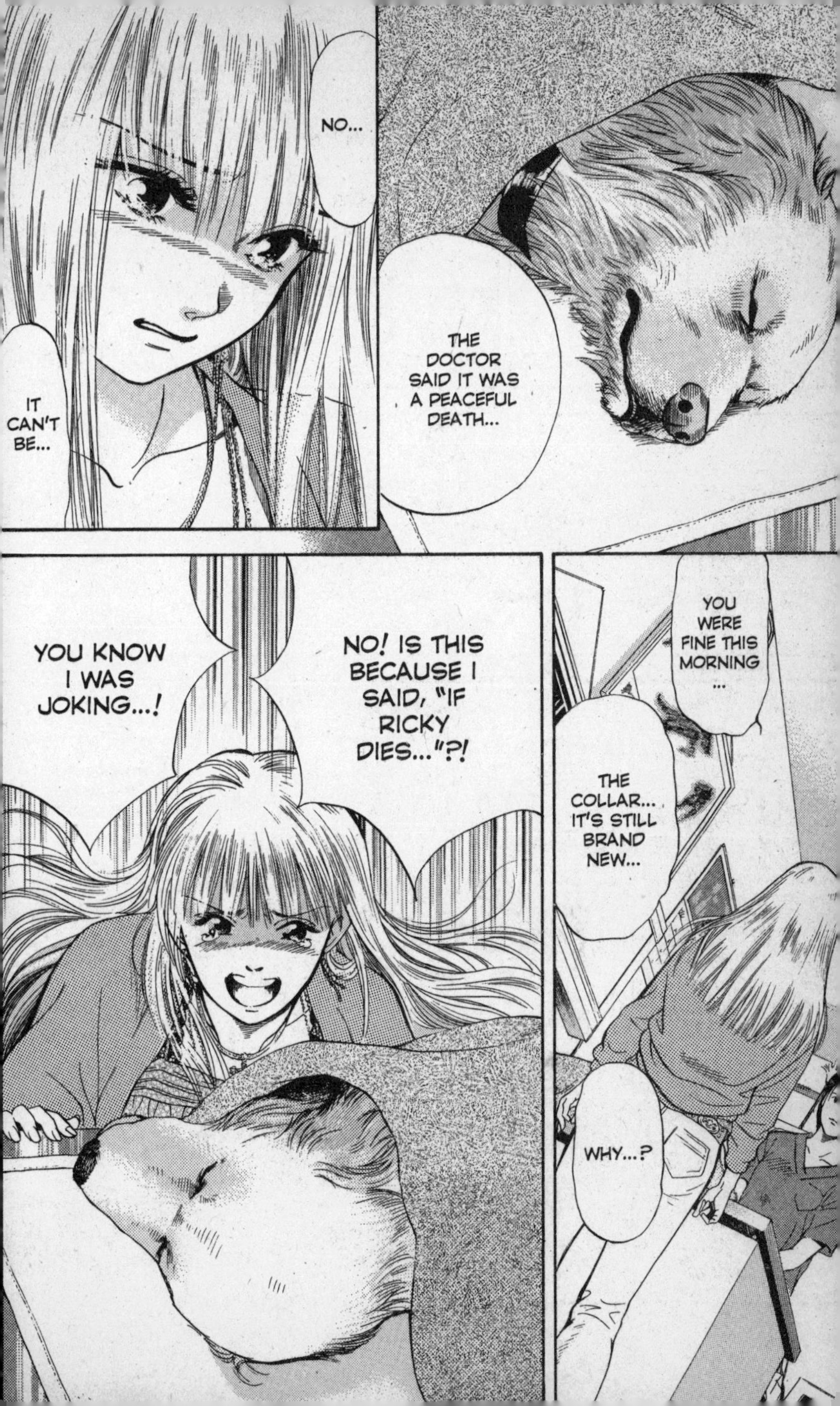
THE DOCTOR SAID IT WAS A PEACEFUL DEATH...
NO...
IT CAN'T BE...
YOU WERE FINE THIS MORNING ...
THE COLLAR... IT'S STILL BRAND NEW...
WHY...?
NO! IS THIS BECAUSE I SAID, "IF RICKY DIES..."?!
YOU KNOW I WAS JOKING...!

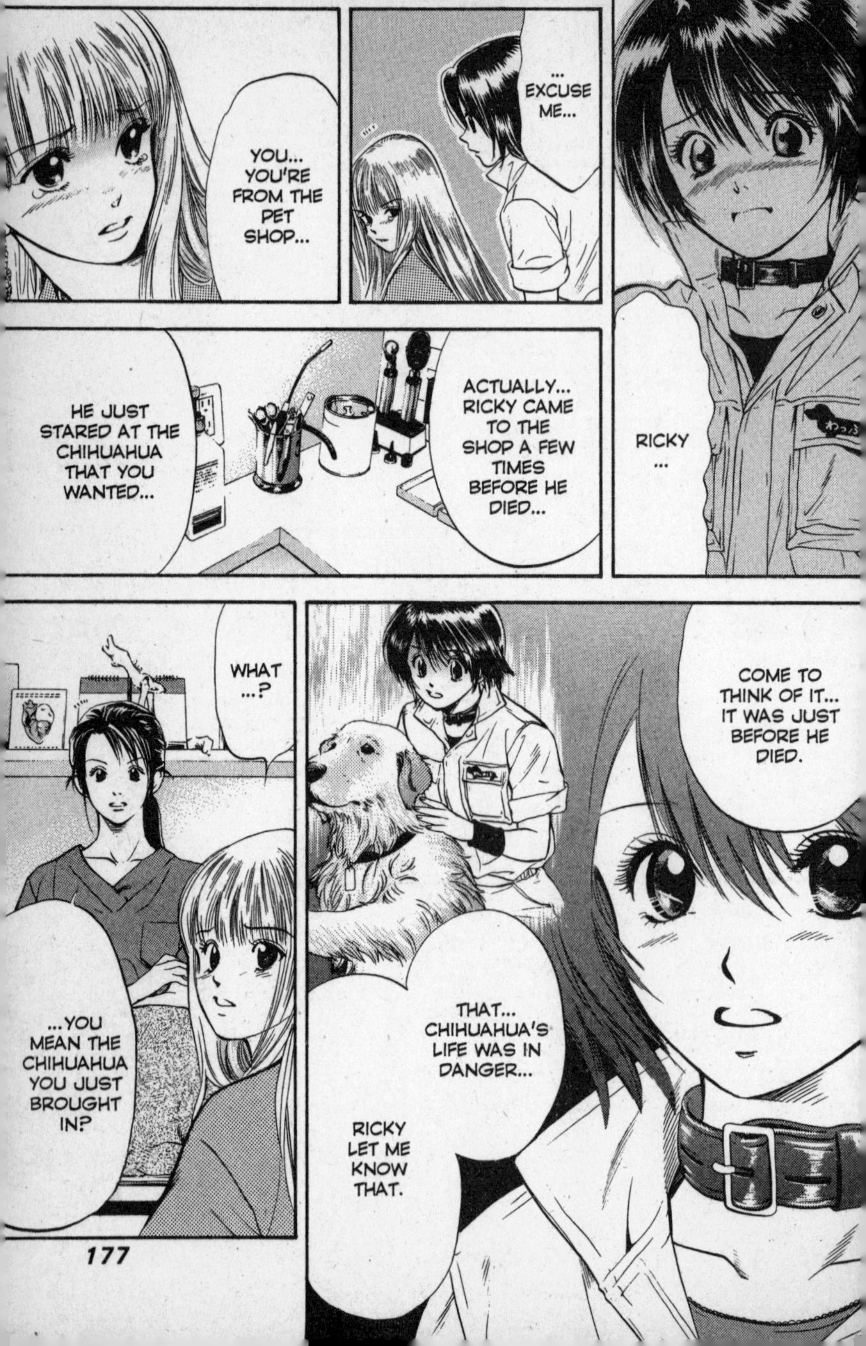
RICKY ...
... EXCUSE ME...
YOU... YOU'RE FROM THE PET SHOP...
ACTUALLY... RICKY CAME TO THE SHOP A FEW TIMES BEFORE HE DIED...
HE JUST STARED AT THE CHIHUAHUA THAT YOU WANTED...
COME TO THINK OF IT... IT WAS JUST BEFORE HE DIED.
THAT... CHIHUAHUA'S LIFE WAS IN DANGER...
RICKY LET ME KNOW THAT.
WHAT ...?
...YOU MEAN THE CHIHUAHUA YOU JUST BROUGHT IN?

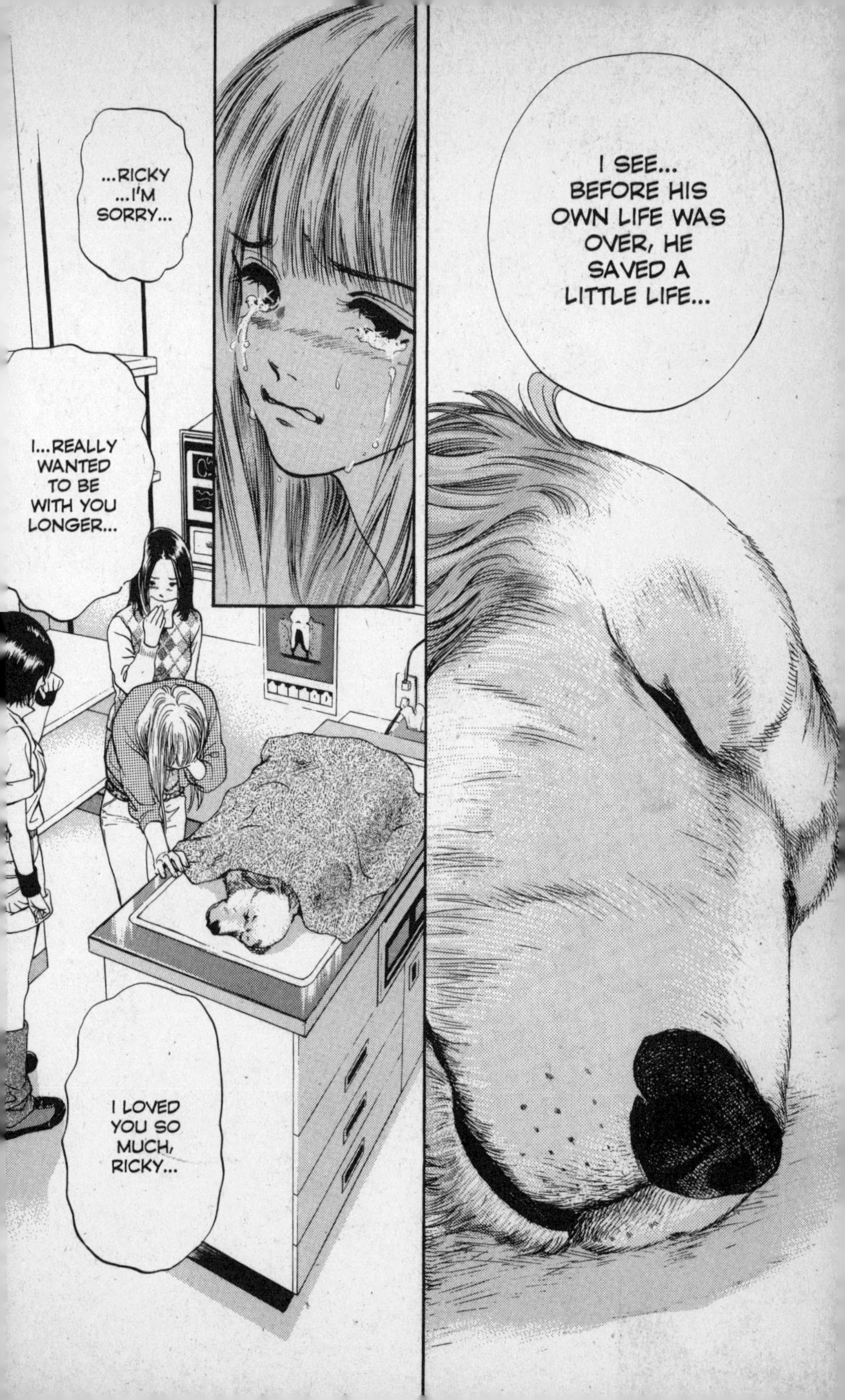
I SEE... BEFORE HIS OWN LIFE WAS OVER, HE SAVED A LITTLE LIFE...
...RICKY ...I'M SORRY...
I...REALLY WANTED TO BE WITH YOU LONGER...
I LOVED YOU SO MUCH, RICKY...

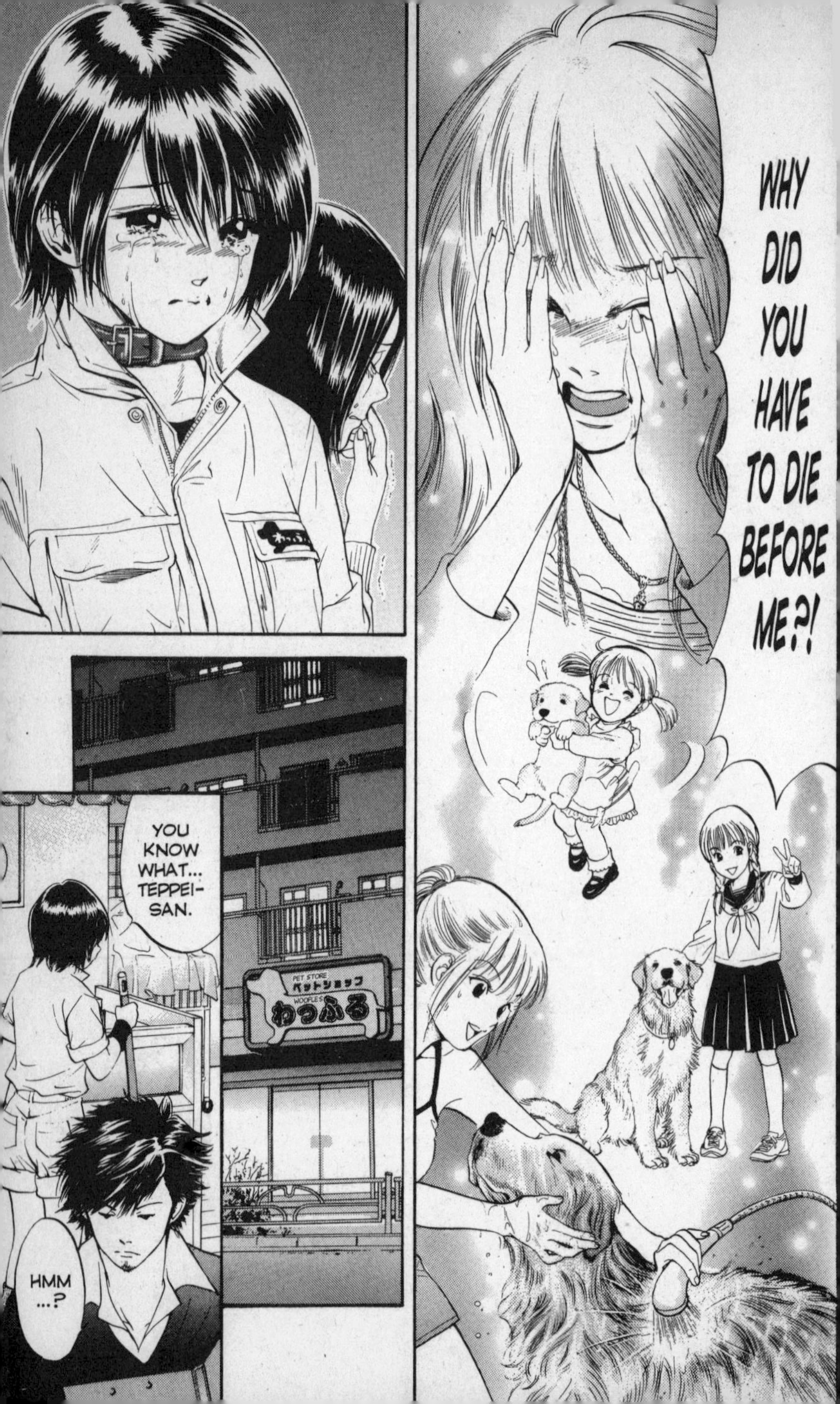
WHY DID YOU HAVE TO DIE BEFORE ME?!
PET STORE
ペットショップ
WOOFLES
わつふる
YOU KNOW WHAT... TEPPEI-SAN.
HMM ...?

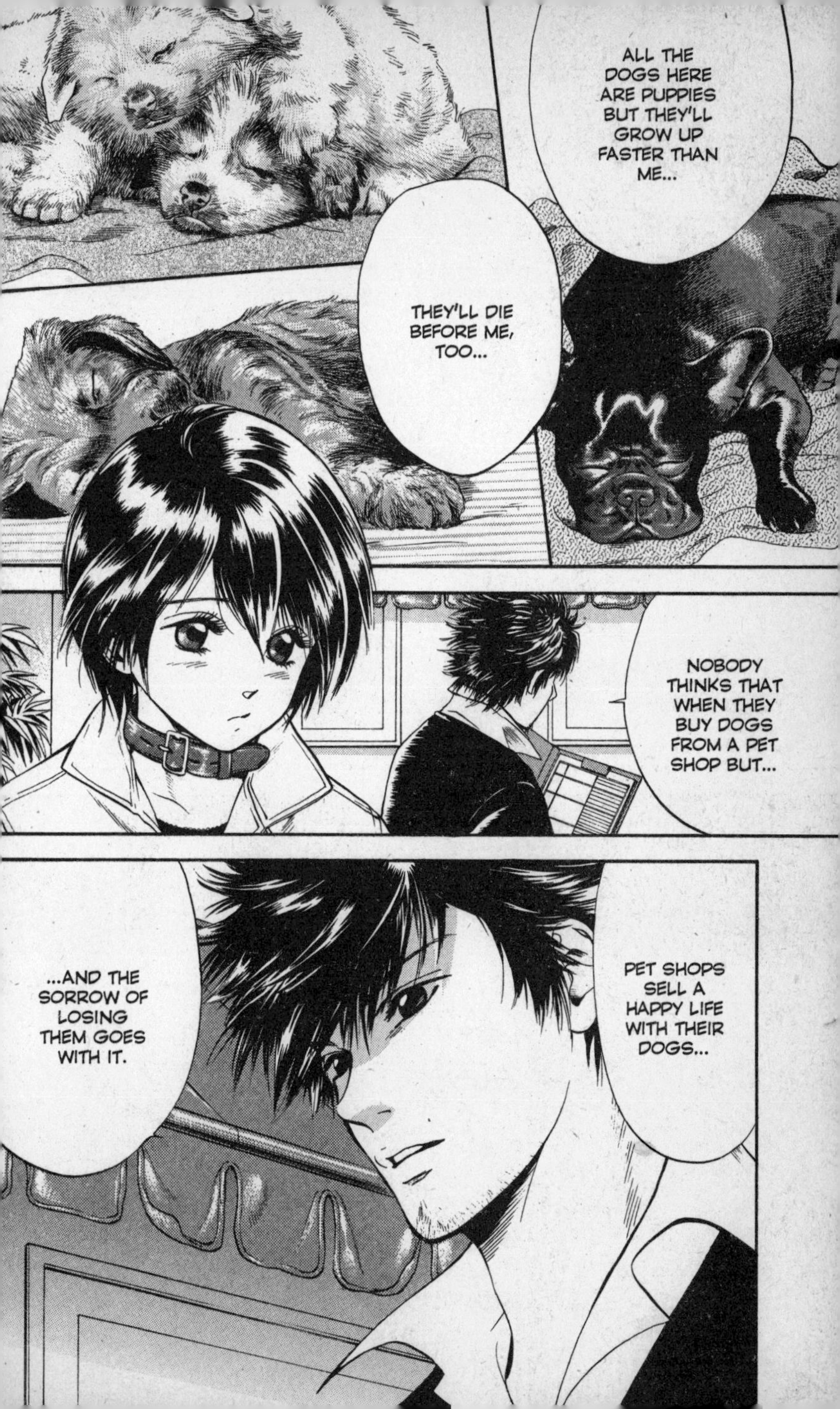
ALL THE DOGS HERE ARE PUPPIES BUT THEY'LL GROW UP FASTER THAN ME...
THEY'LL DIE BEFORE ME, TOO...
NOBODY THINKS THAT WHEN THEY BUY DOGS FROM A PET SHOP BUT...
PET SHOPS SELL A HAPPY LIFE WITH THEIR DOGS...
...AND THE SORROW OF LOSING THEM GOES WITH IT.

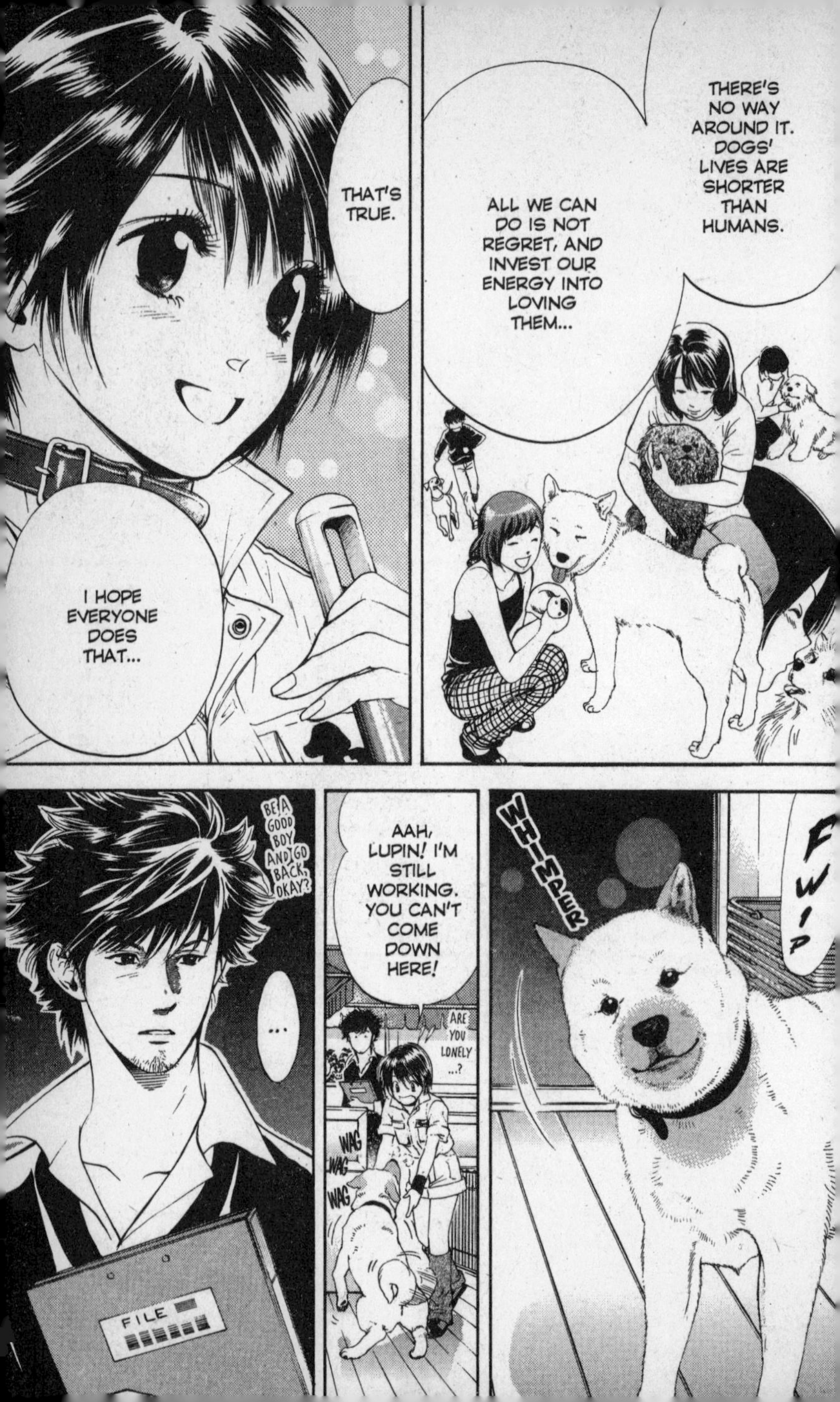
THERE'S NO WAY AROUND IT. DOGS' LIVES ARE SHORTER THAN HUMANS.
ALL WE CAN DO IS NOT REGRET, AND INVEST OUR ENERGY INTO LOVING THEM...
THAT'S TRUE.
I HOPE EVERYONE DOES THAT...
WHIMPER
FWIP
AAH, LUPIN! I'M STILL WORKING. YOU CAN'T COME DOWN HERE!
ARE YOU LONELY ...?
WAG
WAG
WAG
BE A GOOD BOY AND GO BACK, OKAY?
...
FILE

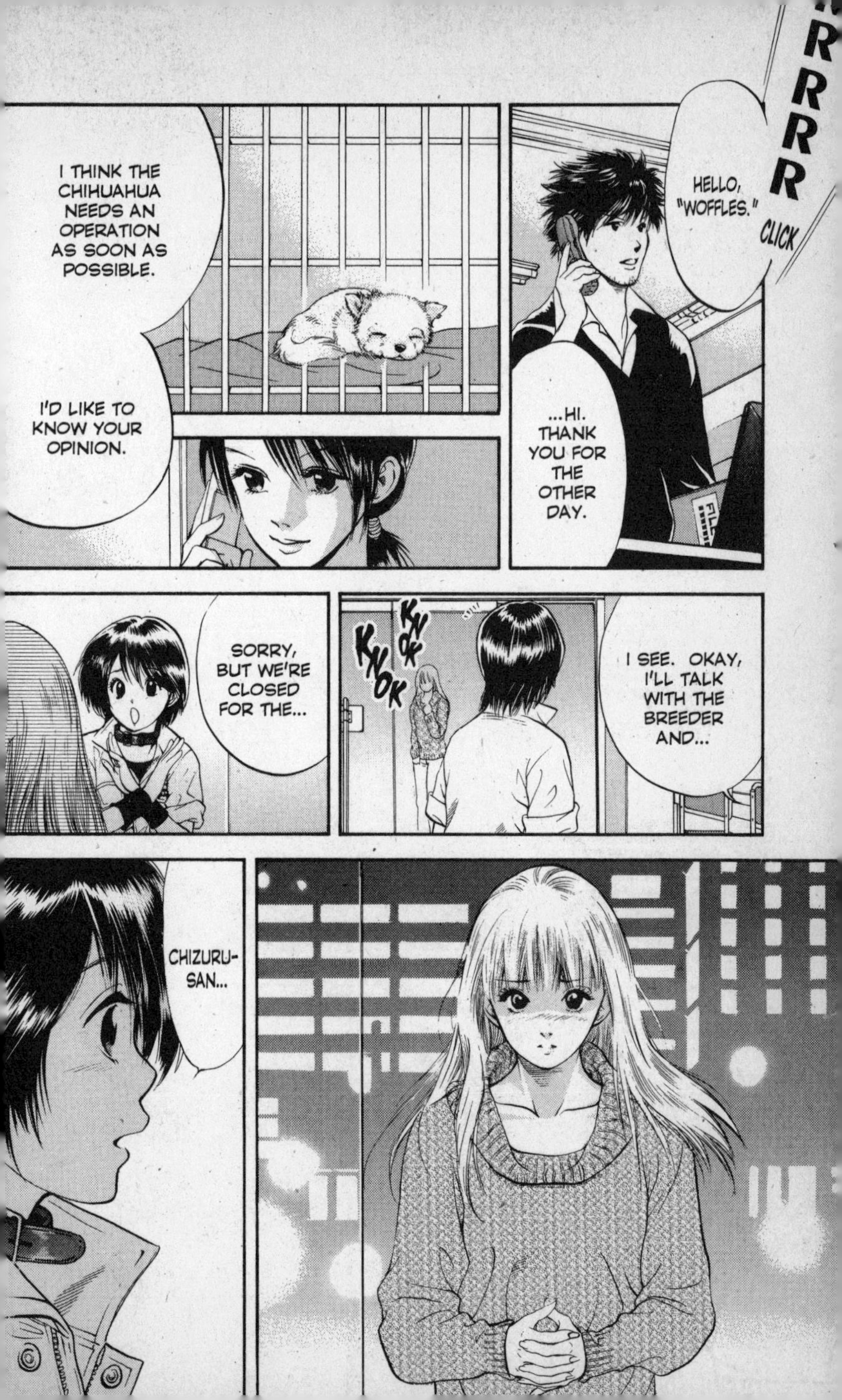
RRRR
CLICK
HELLO, "WOFFLES."
...HI. THANK YOU FOR THE OTHER DAY.
I THINK THE CHIHUAHUA NEEDS AN OPERATION AS SOON AS POSSIBLE.
I'D LIKE TO KNOW YOUR OPINION.
I SEE. OKAY, I'LL TALK WITH THE BREEDER AND...
KNOK
KNOK
SORRY, BUT WE'RE CLOSED FOR THE...
CHIZURU-SAN...

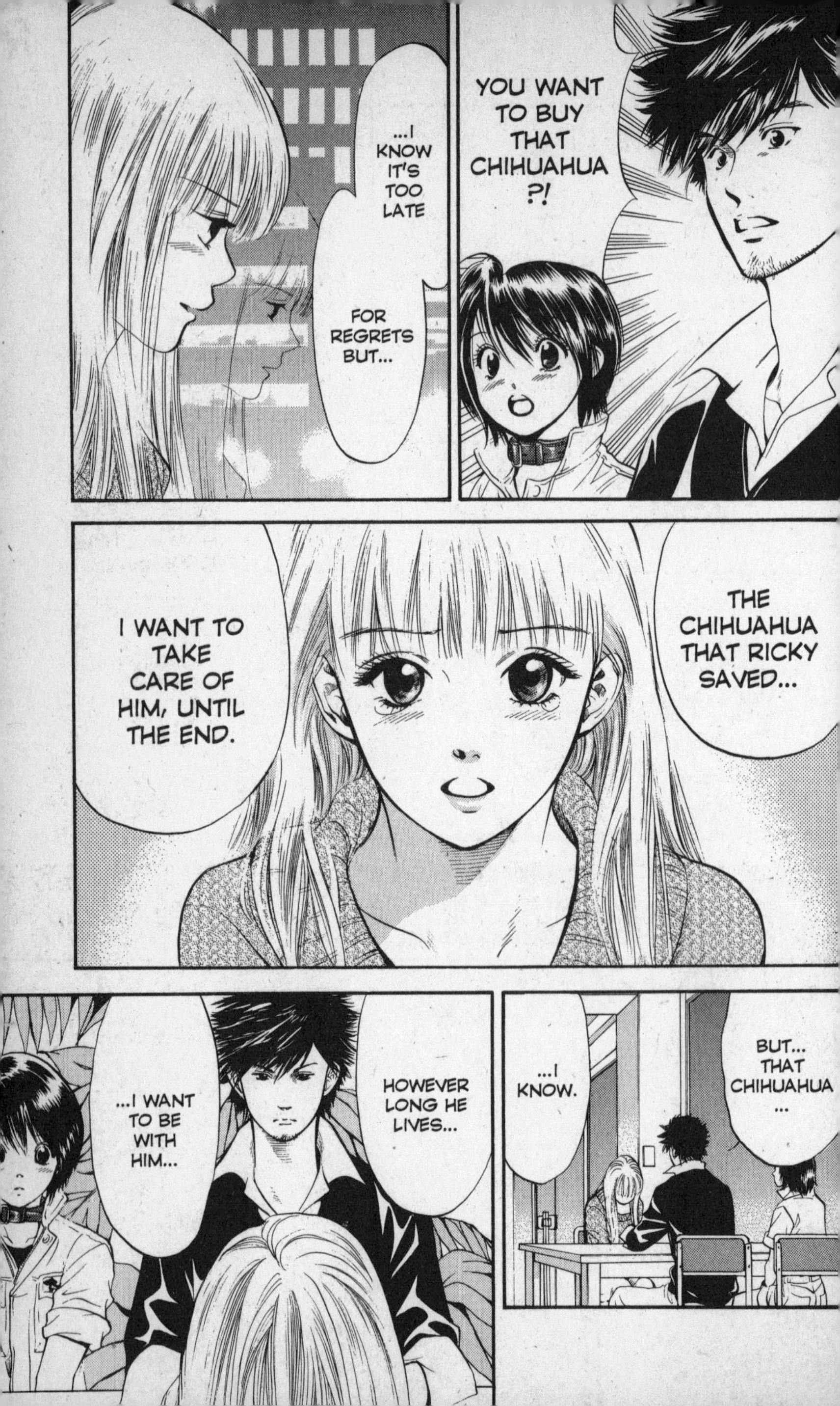
YOU WANT TO BUY THAT CHIHUAHUA ?!
...I KNOW IT'S TOO LATE
FOR REGRETS BUT...
THE CHIHUAHUA THAT RICKY SAVED...
I WANT TO TAKE CARE OF HIM, UNTIL THE END.
BUT... THAT CHIHUAHUA ...
...I KNOW.
HOWEVER LONG HE LIVES...
...I WANT TO BE WITH HIM...

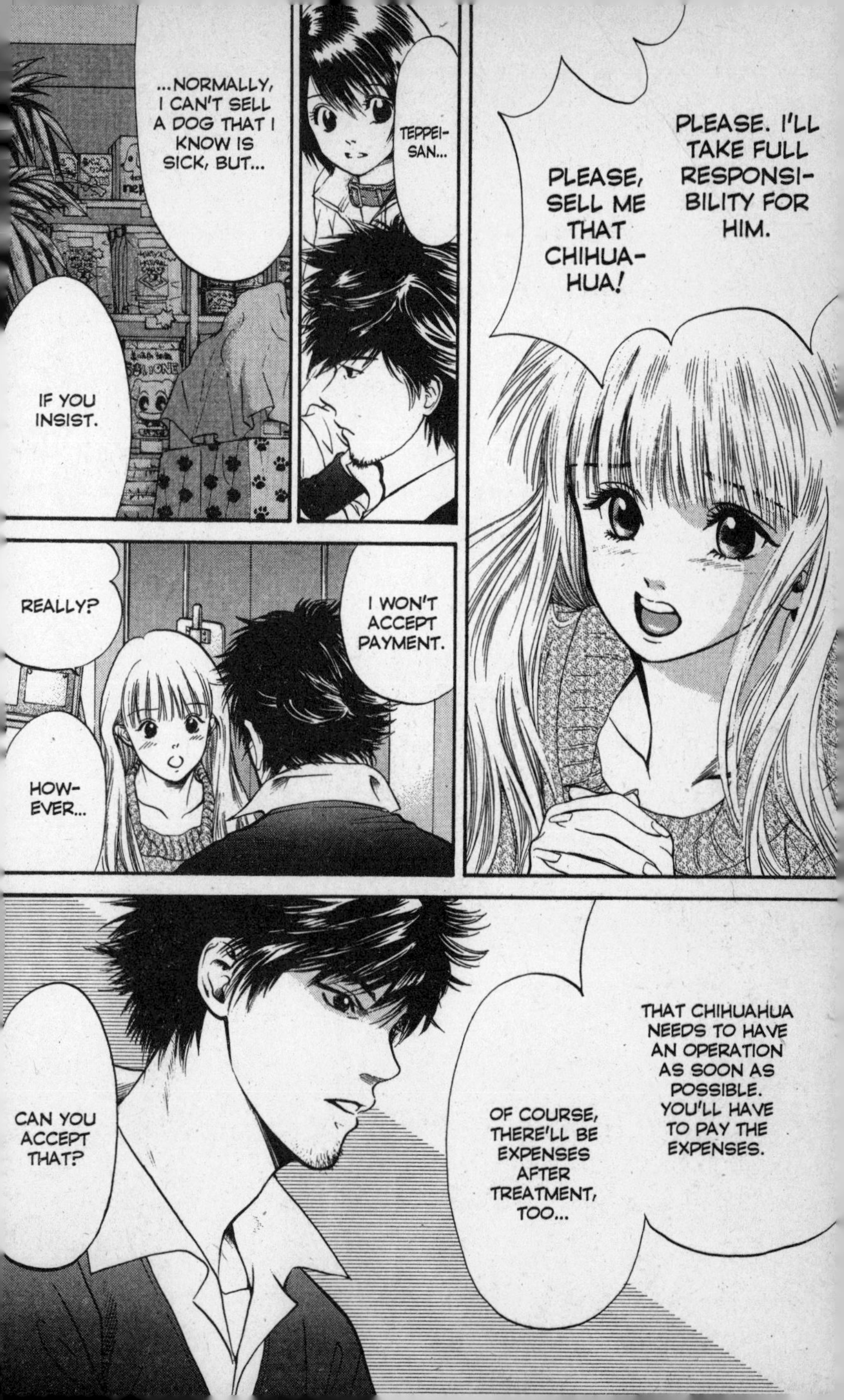
PLEASE. I'LL TAKE FULL RESPONSI-BILITY FOR HIM.
PLEASE, SELL ME THAT CHIHUA-HUA!
TEPPEI-SAN...
...NORMALLY, I CAN'T SELL A DOG THAT I KNOW IS SICK, BUT...
IF YOU INSIST.
I WON'T ACCEPT PAYMENT.
REALLY?
HOW-EVER...
THAT CHIHUAHUA NEEDS TO HAVE AN OPERATION AS SOON AS POSSIBLE. YOU'LL HAVE TO PAY THE EXPENSES.
OF COURSE, THERE'LL BE EXPENSES AFTER TREATMENT, TOO...
CAN YOU ACCEPT THAT?

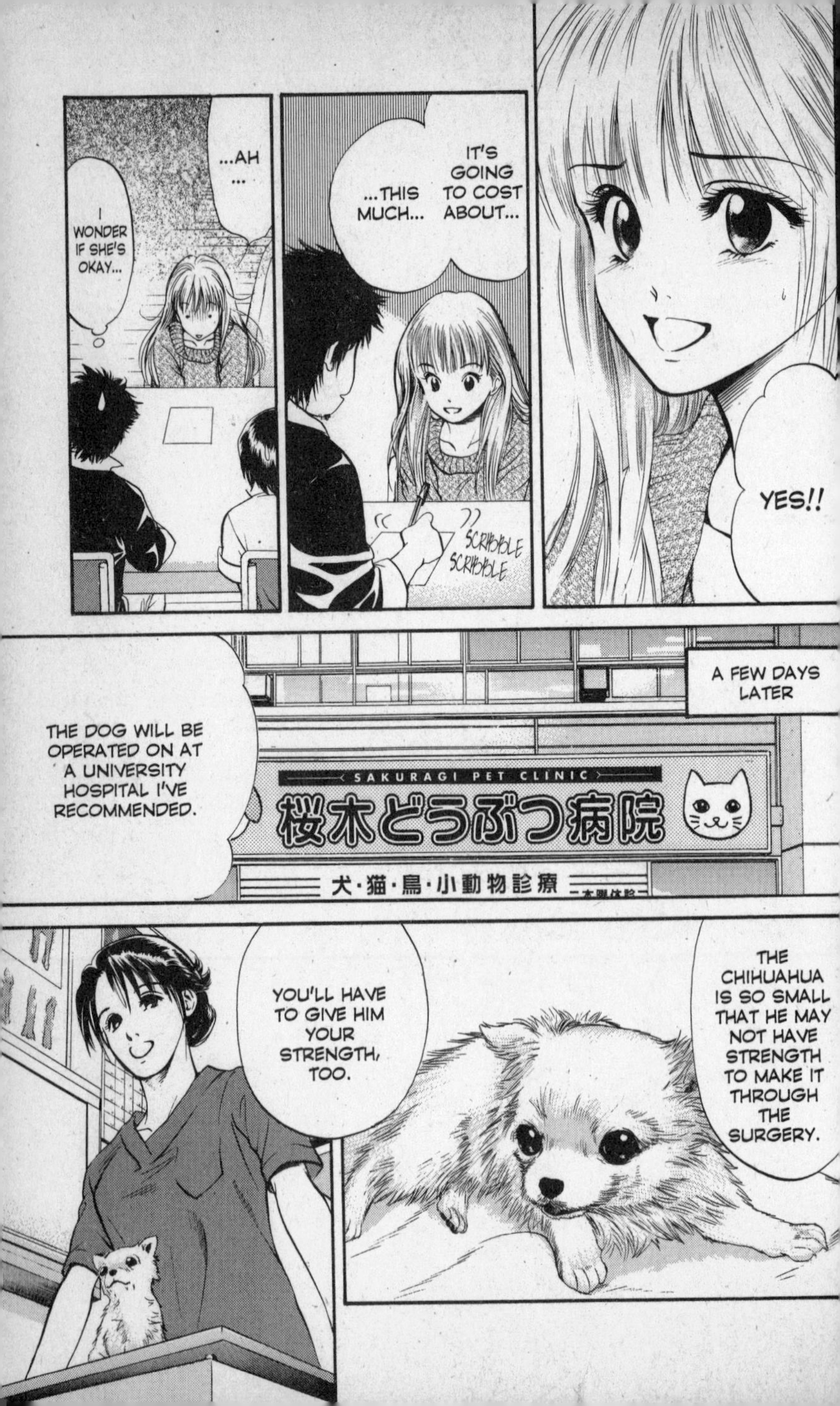
YES!!
IT'S GOING TO COST ABOUT...
...THIS MUCH...
SCRIBBLE SCRIBBLE
...AH ...
I WONDER IF SHE'S OKAY...
A FEW DAYS LATER
SAKURAGI PET CLINIC
桜木どうぶつ病院
犬・猫・鳥・小動物診療
THE DOG WILL BE OPERATED ON AT A UNIVERSITY HOSPITAL I'VE RECOMMENDED.
THE CHIHUAHUA IS SO SMALL THAT HE MAY NOT HAVE STRENGTH TO MAKE IT THROUGH THE SURGERY.
YOU'LL HAVE TO GIVE HIM YOUR STRENGTH, TOO.

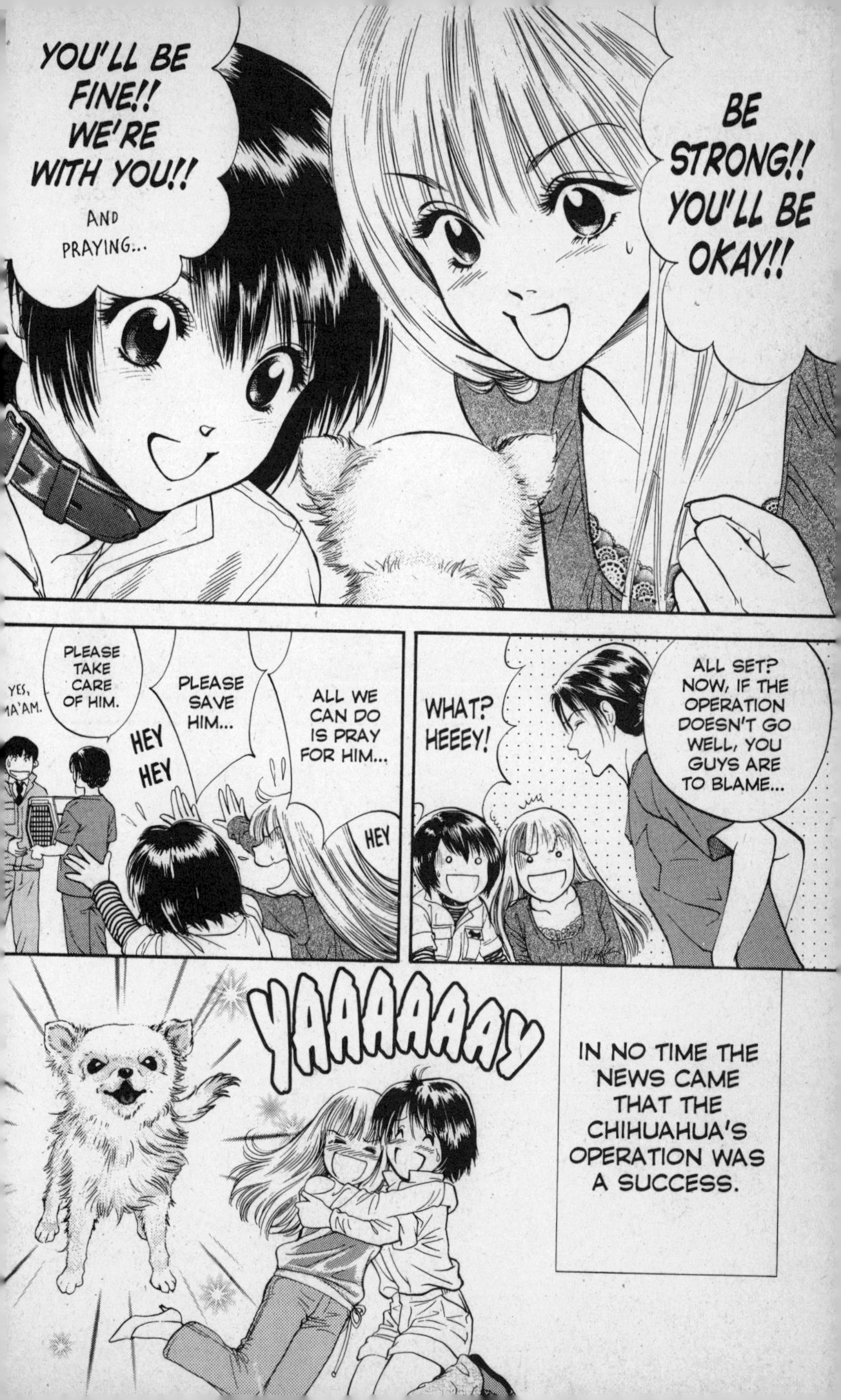
BE STRONG!! YOU'LL BE OKAY!!
YOU'LL BE FINE!! WE'RE WITH YOU!!
AND PRAYING...
ALL SET? NOW, IF THE OPERATION DOESN'T GO WELL, YOU GUYS ARE TO BLAME...
WHAT? HEEEY!
ALL WE CAN DO IS PRAY FOR HIM...
HEY
PLEASE SAVE HIM...
HEY HEY
PLEASE TAKE CARE OF HIM.
YES, MA'AM.
IN NO TIME THE NEWS CAME THAT THE CHIHUAHUA'S OPERATION WAS A SUCCESS.
YAAAAAAAY

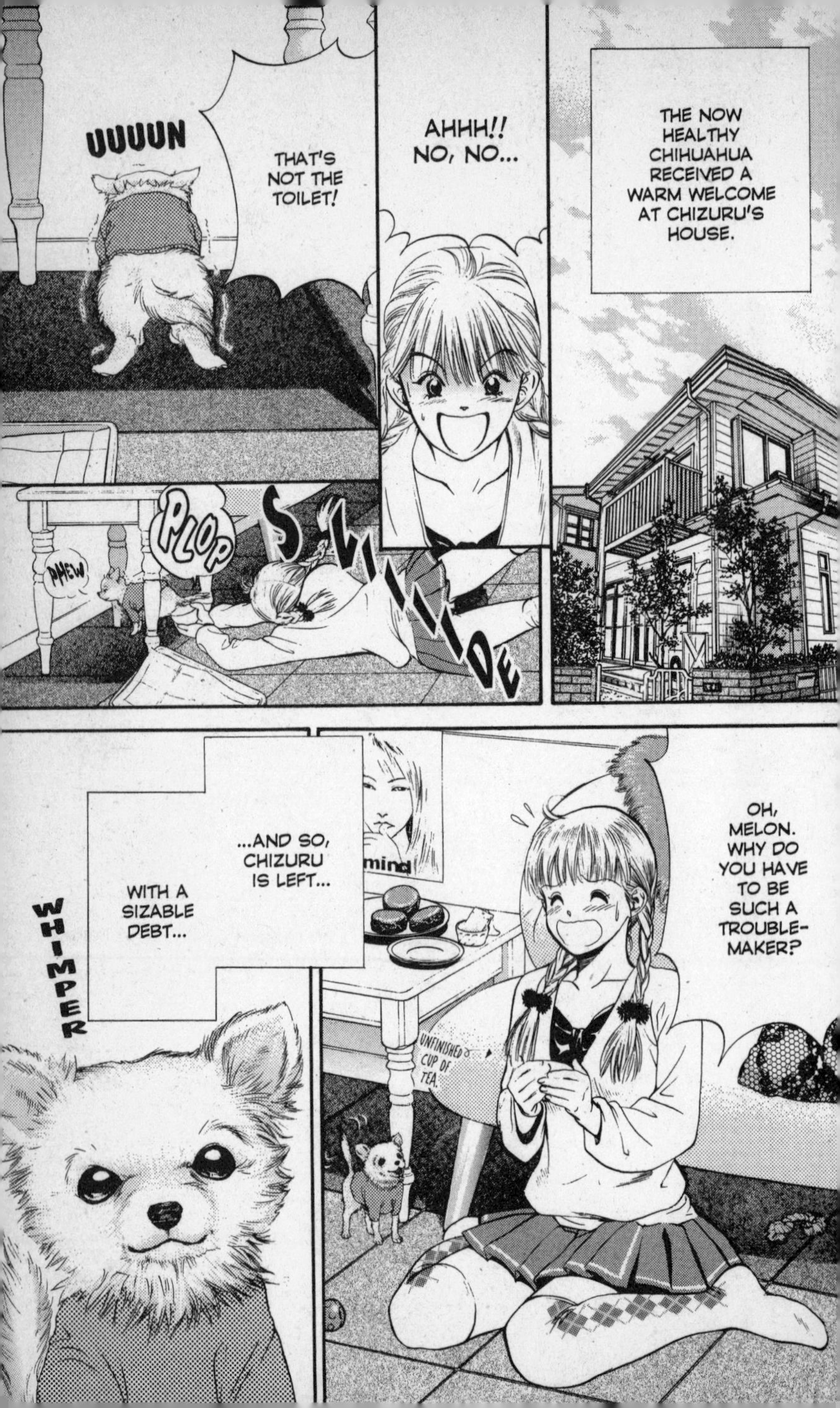
THE NOW HEALTHY CHIHUAHUA RECEIVED A WARM WELCOME AT CHIZURU'S HOUSE.
AHHH!! NO, NO...
THAT'S NOT THE TOILET!
UUUUN
SWIIIIDE
PLOP
PHEW
OH, MELON. WHY DO YOU HAVE TO BE SUCH A TROUBLE-MAKER?
mind
UNFINISHED CUP OF TEA.
...AND SO, CHIZURU IS LEFT...
WITH A SIZABLE DEBT...
WHIMPER

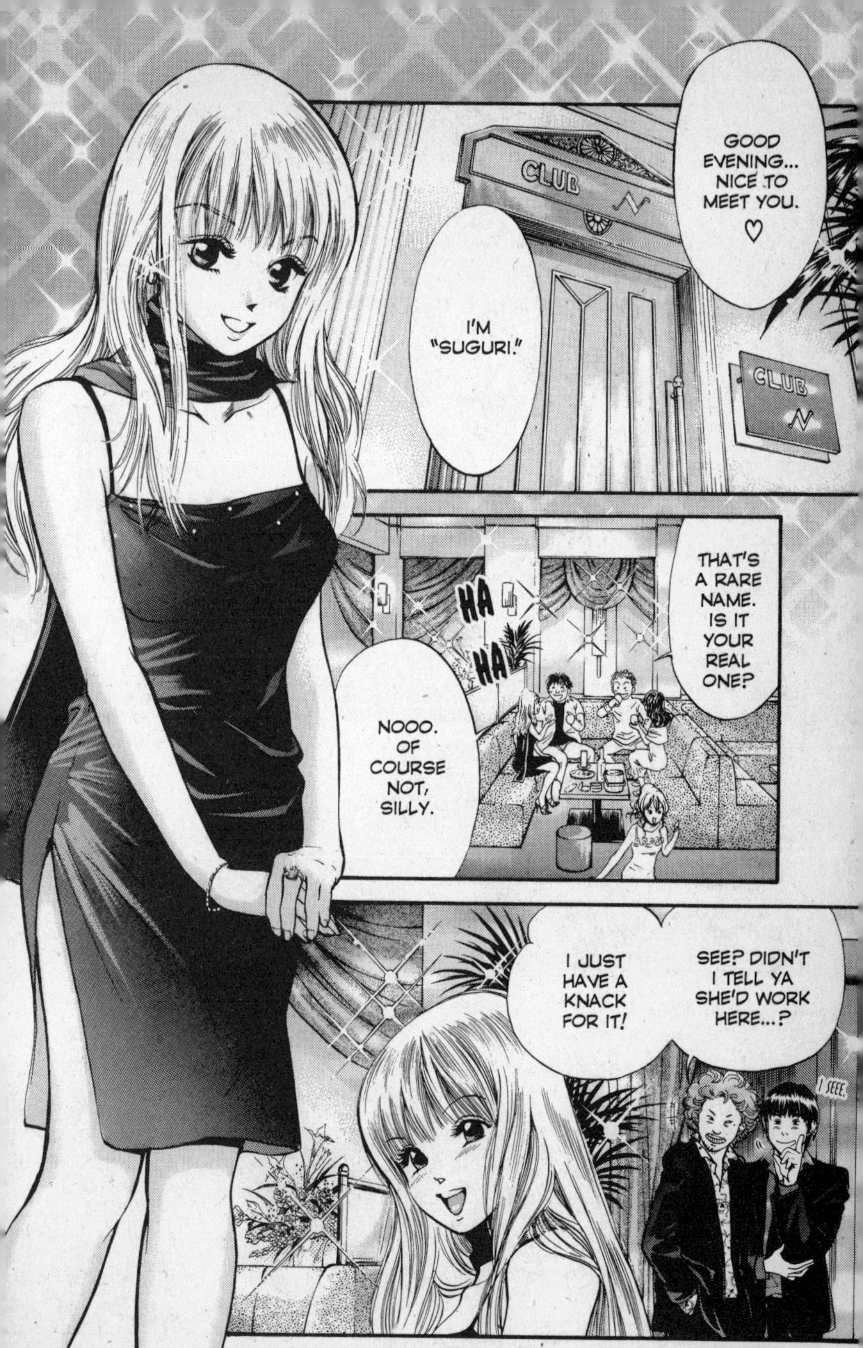
GOOD EVENING... NICE TO MEET YOU. ♡
I'M "SUGURI."
THAT'S A RARE NAME. IS IT YOUR REAL ONE?
HA HA
NOOO. OF COURSE NOT, SILLY.
SEE? DIDN'T I TELL YA SHE'D WORK HERE...?
I SEE.
I JUST HAVE A KNACK FOR IT!

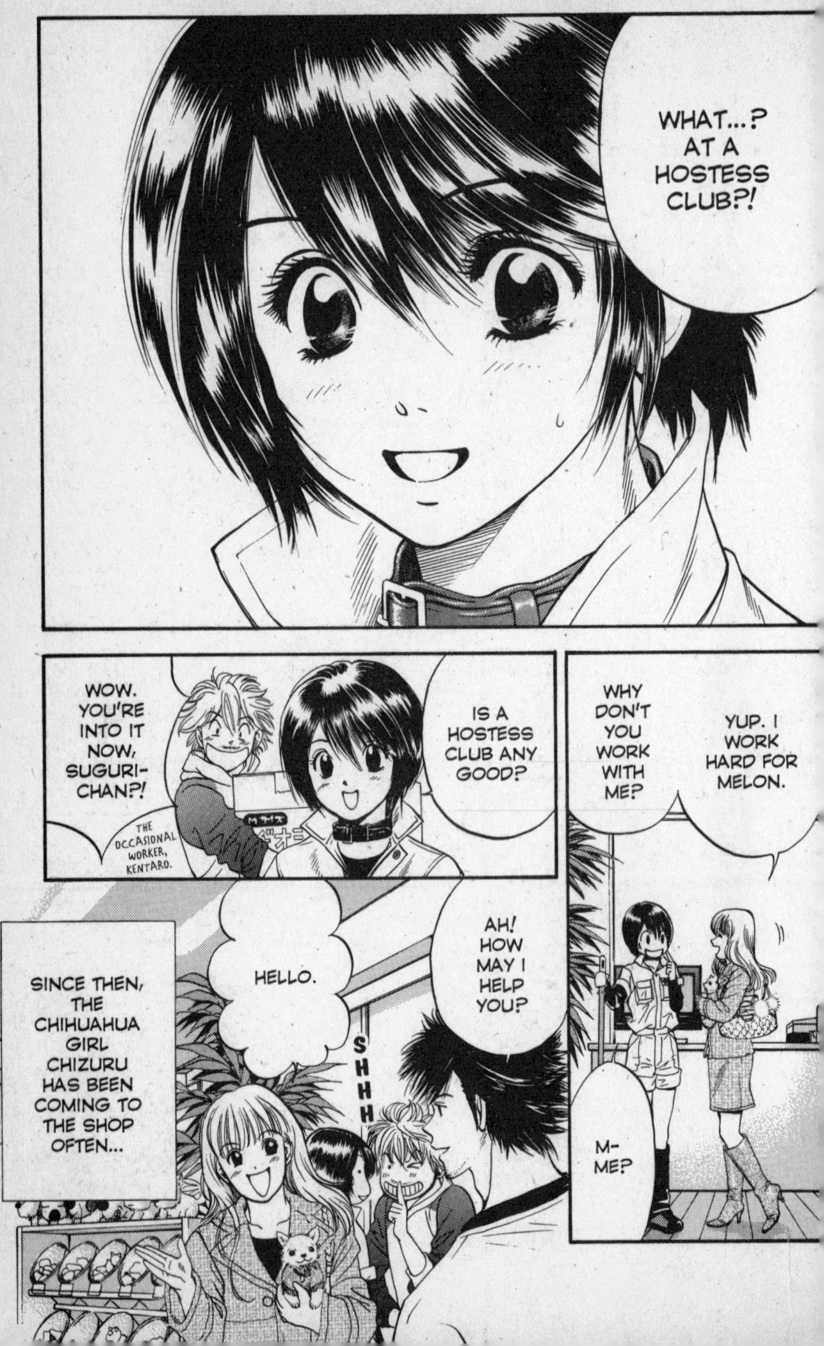
WHAT...? AT A HOSTESS CLUB?!
YUP. I WORK HARD FOR MELON.
WHY DON'T YOU WORK WITH ME?
M-ME?
IS A HOSTESS CLUB ANY GOOD?
WOW. YOU'RE INTO IT NOW, SUGURI-CHAN?!
THE OCCASIONAL WORKER, KENTARO.
AH! HOW MAY I HELP YOU?
HELLO.
SHHH
SINCE THEN, THE CHIHUAHUA GIRL CHIZURU HAS BEEN COMING TO THE SHOP OFTEN...

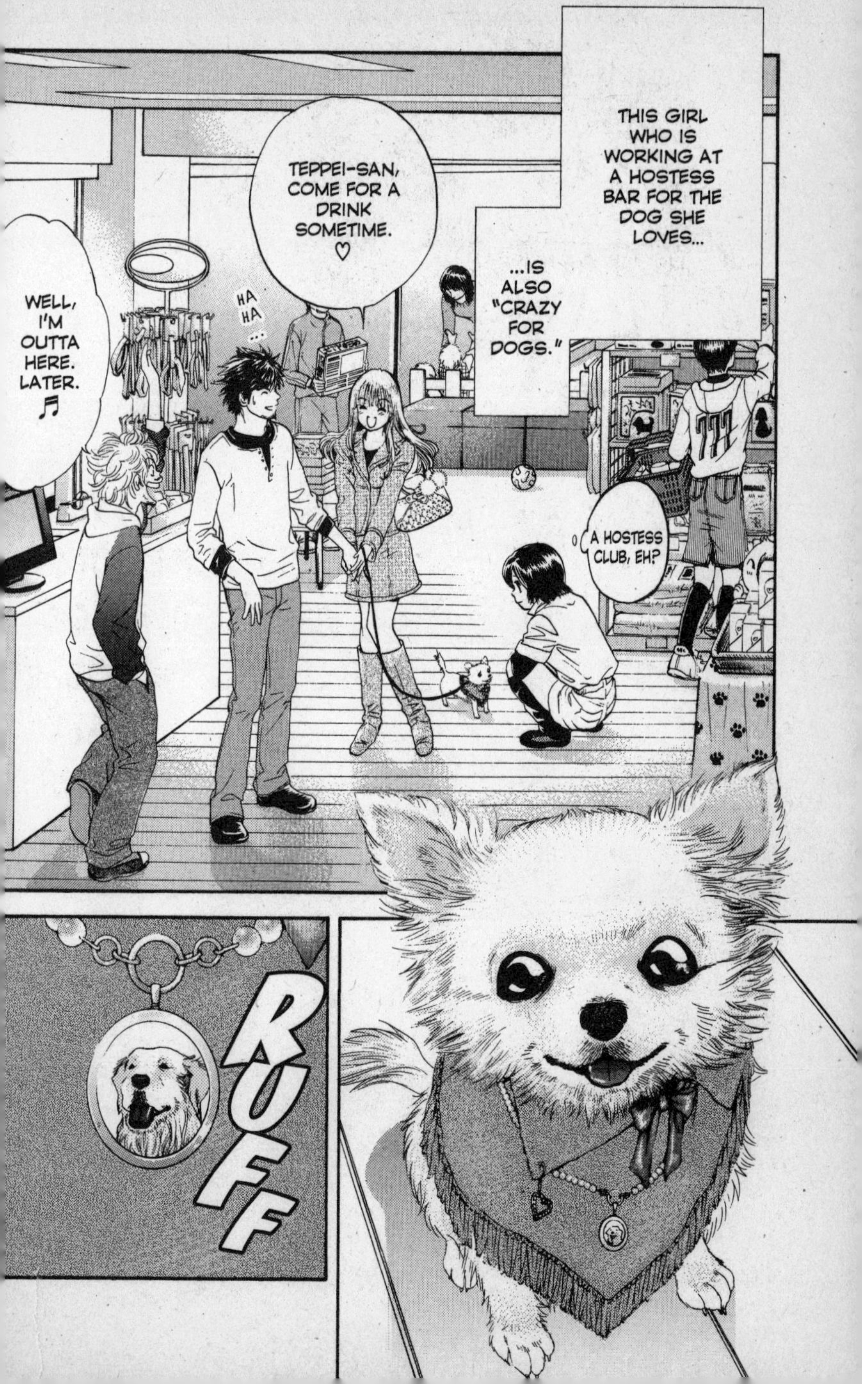
THIS GIRL WHO IS WORKING AT A HOSTESS BAR FOR THE DOG SHE LOVES...
...IS ALSO "CRAZY FOR DOGS."
TEPPEI-SAN, COME FOR A DRINK SOMETIME. ♡
HA HA ...
A HOSTESS CLUB, EH?
WELL, I'M OUTTA HERE. LATER. ♬
RUFF

CHAPTER 8
THE MYSTERIOUS POWER OF THE DOG-CRAZY GIRL!

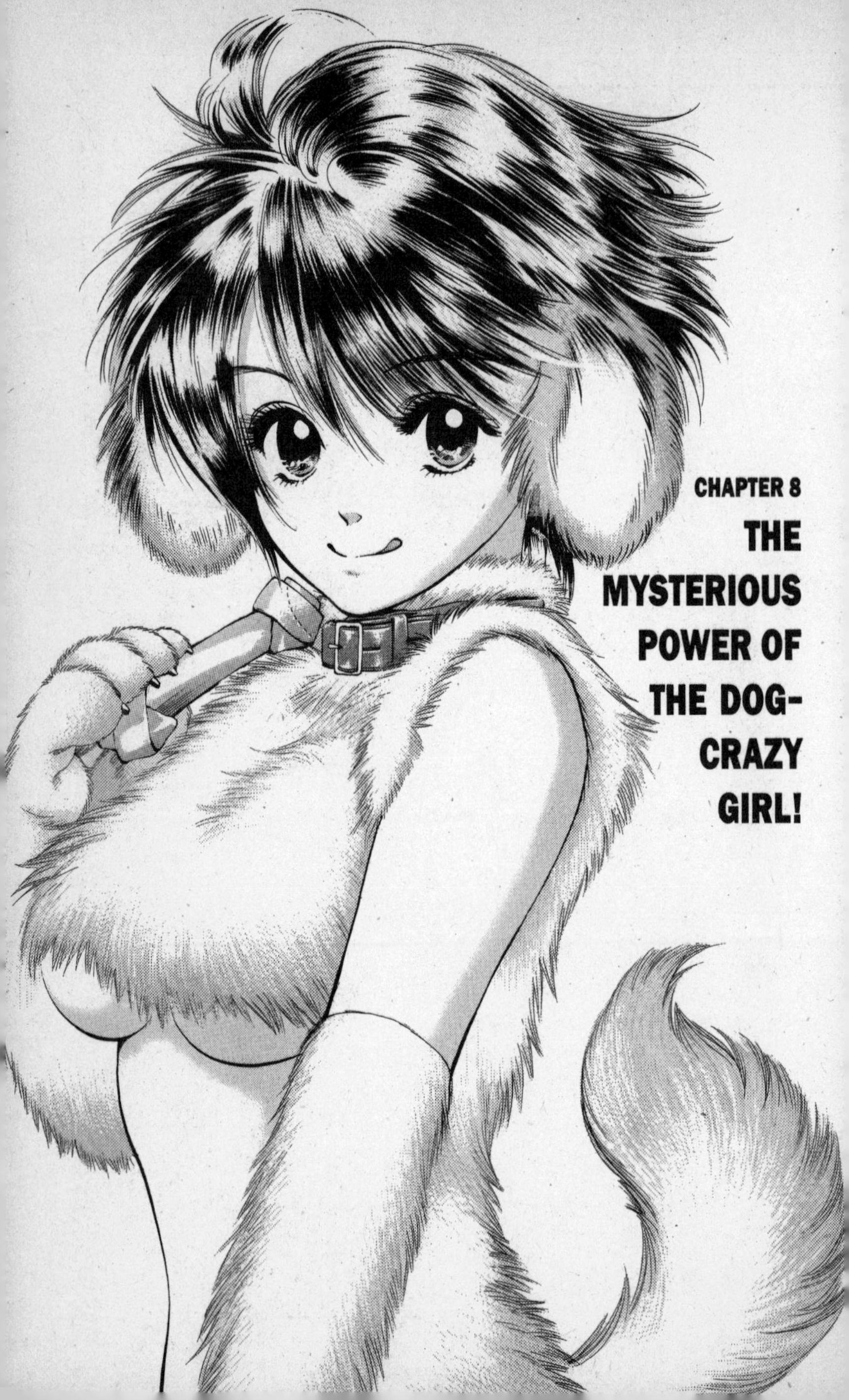

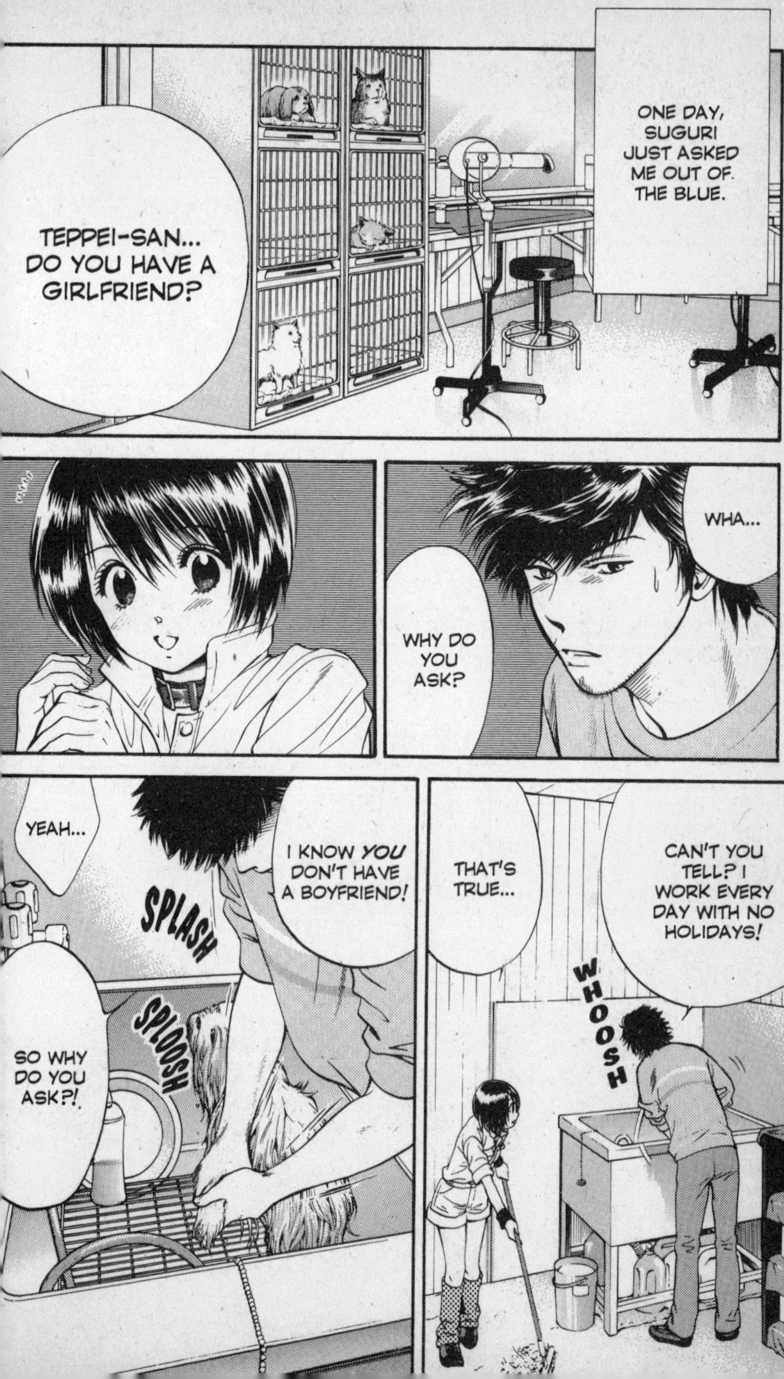
ONE DAY, SUGURI JUST ASKED ME OUT OF THE BLUE.
TEPPEI-SAN... DO YOU HAVE A GIRLFRIEND?
WHA...
WHY DO YOU ASK?
CAN'T YOU TELL? I WORK EVERY DAY WITH NO HOLIDAYS!
WHOOSH
THAT'S TRUE...
I KNOW *YOU* DON'T HAVE A BOYFRIEND!
YEAH...
SPLASH
SPLOOSH
SO WHY DO YOU ASK?!

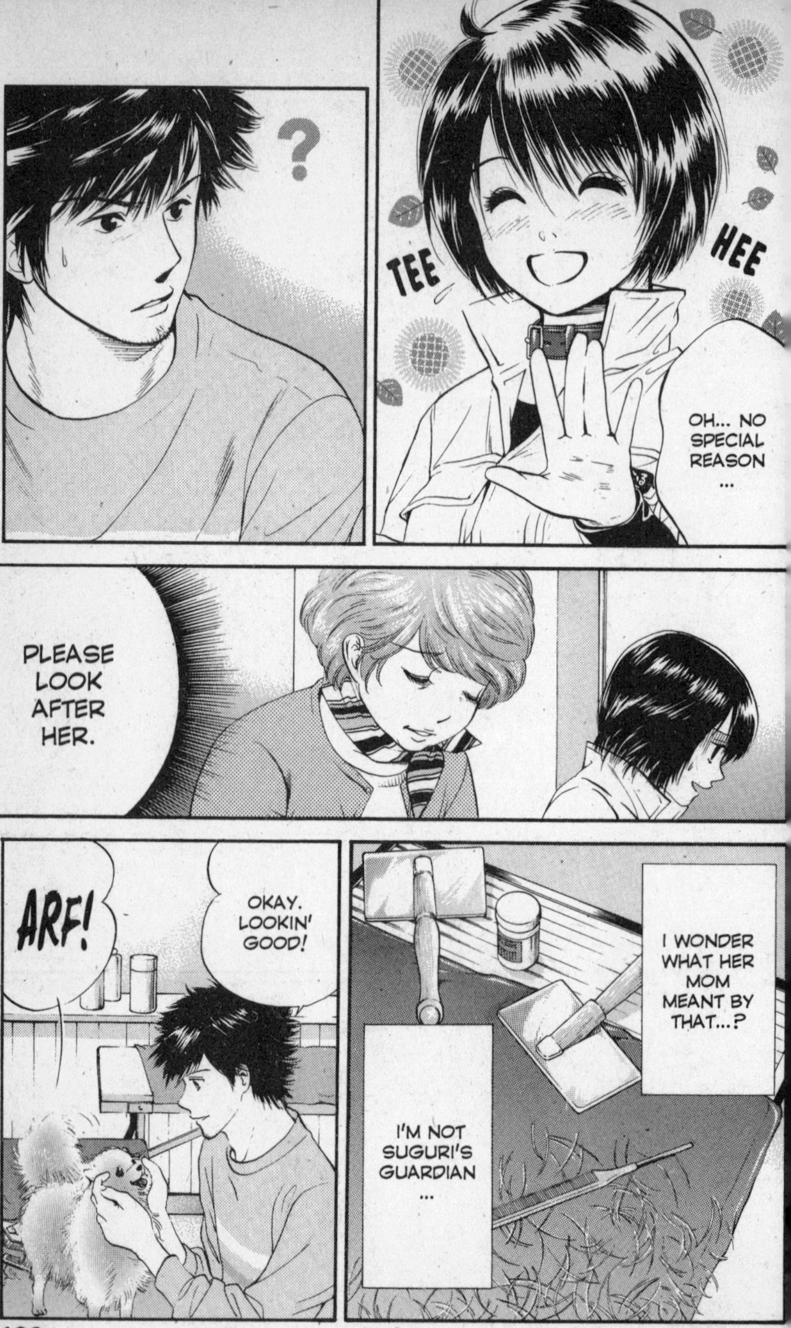
TEE
HEE
OH... NO SPECIAL REASON ...
?
PLEASE LOOK AFTER HER.
I WONDER WHAT HER MOM MEANT BY THAT...?
I'M NOT SUGURI'S GUARDIAN ...
OKAY. LOOKIN' GOOD!
ARF!

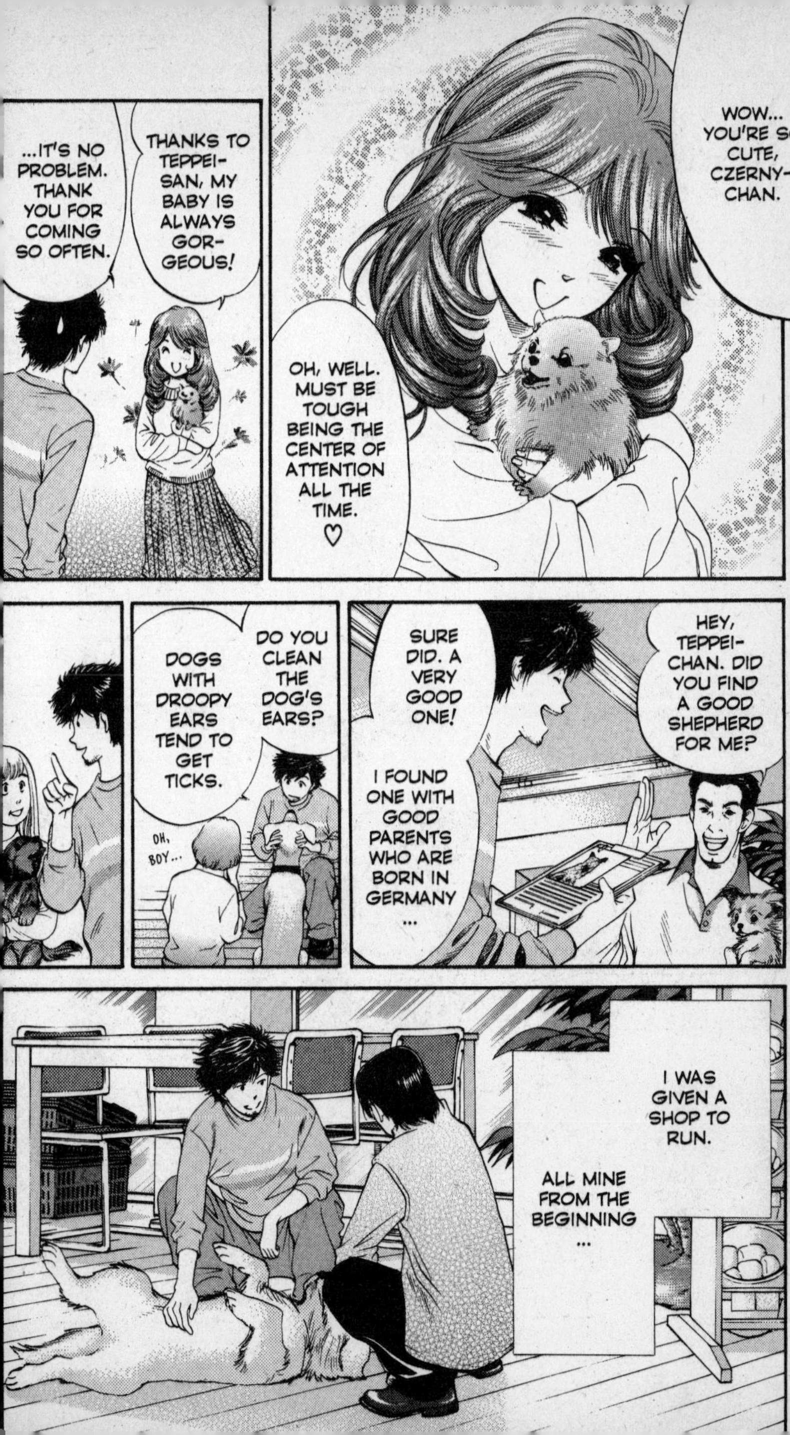
WOW... YOU'RE SO CUTE, CZERNY-CHAN.
OH, WELL. MUST BE TOUGH BEING THE CENTER OF ATTENTION ALL THE TIME. ♡
THANKS TO TEPPEI-SAN, MY BABY IS ALWAYS GORGEOUS!
...IT'S NO PROBLEM. THANK YOU FOR COMING SO OFTEN.
HEY, TEPPEI-CHAN. DID YOU FIND A GOOD SHEPHERD FOR ME?
SURE DID. A VERY GOOD ONE!
I FOUND ONE WITH GOOD PARENTS WHO ARE BORN IN GERMANY ...
DO YOU CLEAN THE DOG'S EARS?
DOGS WITH DROOPY EARS TEND TO GET TICKS.
OH, BOY...
I WAS GIVEN A SHOP TO RUN.
ALL MINE FROM THE BEGINNING ...

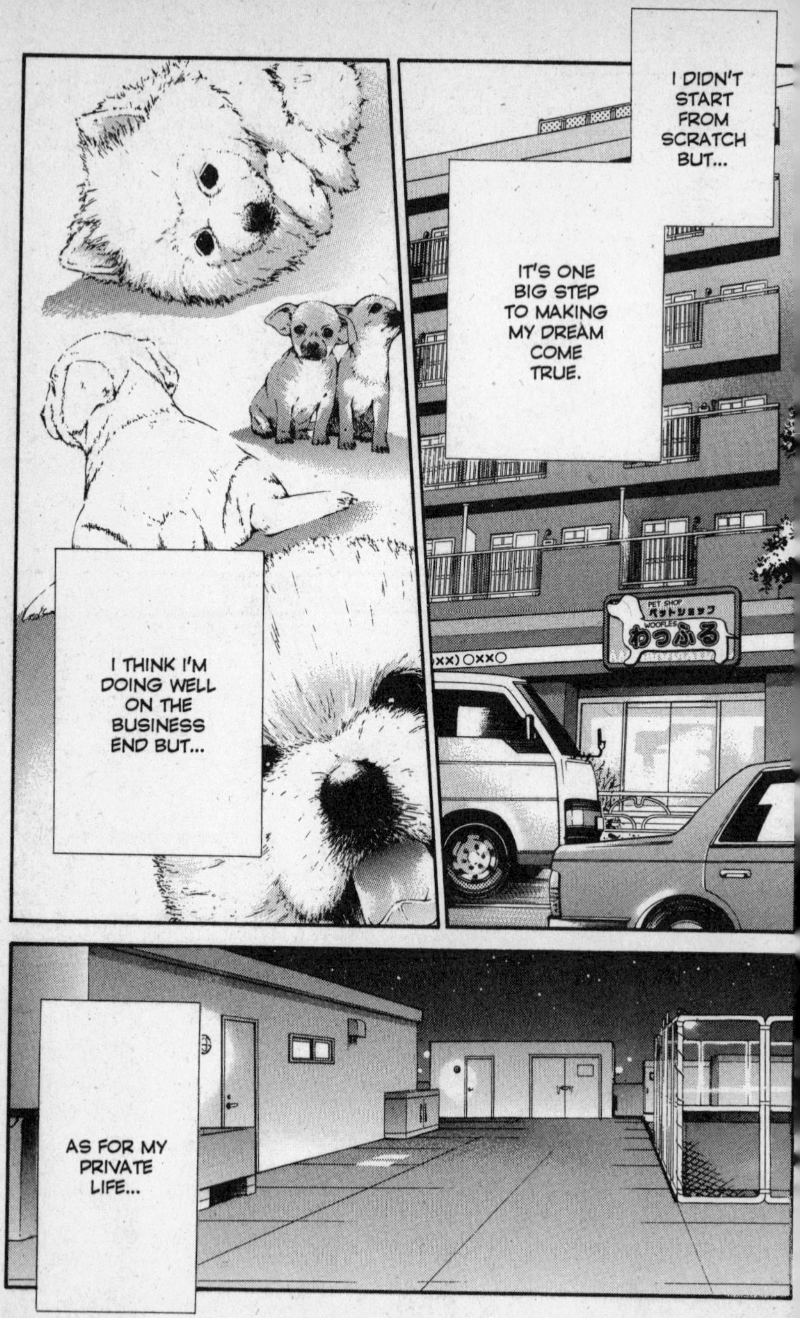
I DIDN'T START FROM SCRATCH BUT...
IT'S ONE BIG STEP TO MAKING MY DREAM COME TRUE.
PET SHOP
ペットショップ
WOOFLES
わっふる
I THINK I'M DOING WELL ON THE BUSINESS END BUT...
AS FOR MY PRIVATE LIFE...

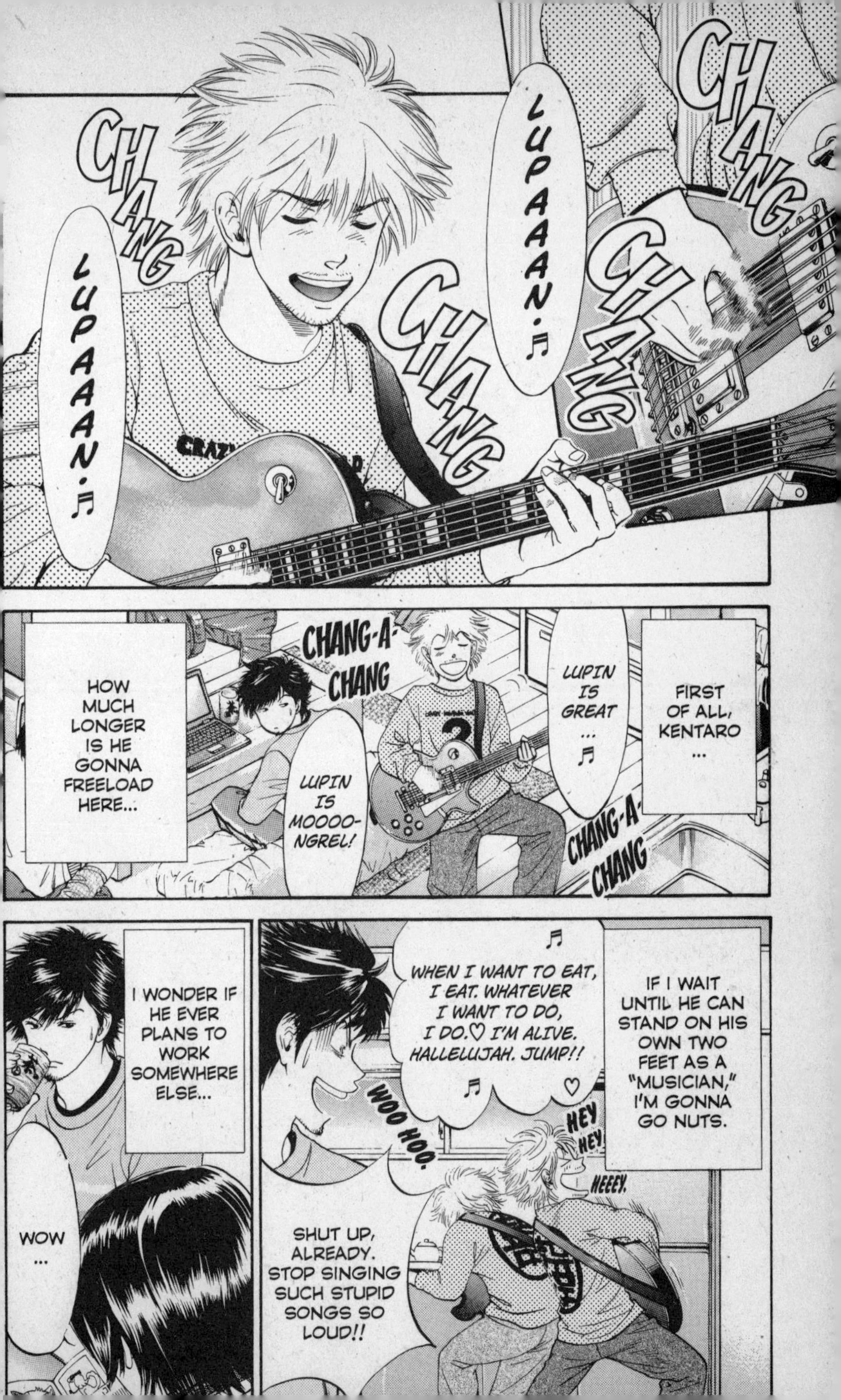
CHANG
CHANG
LUPAAAAN.♬
CHANG CHANG
CHANG
LUPAAAAN.♬
FIRST OF ALL, KENTARO ...
LUPIN IS GREAT ... ♬
CHANG-A-CHANG
CHANG-A-CHANG
LUPIN IS MOOOO-NGREL!
HOW MUCH LONGER IS HE GONNA FREELOAD HERE...
IF I WAIT UNTIL HE CAN STAND ON HIS OWN TWO FEET AS A "MUSICIAN," I'M GONNA GO NUTS.
♬ WHEN I WANT TO EAT, I EAT. WHATEVER I WANT TO DO, I DO.♡ I'M ALIVE. HALLELUJAH. JUMP!! ♬ ♡
HEY HEY!
HEEEY.
WOO HOO.
SHUT UP, ALREADY. STOP SINGING SUCH STUPID SONGS SO LOUD!!
I WONDER IF HE EVER PLANS TO WORK SOMEWHERE ELSE...
WOW ...

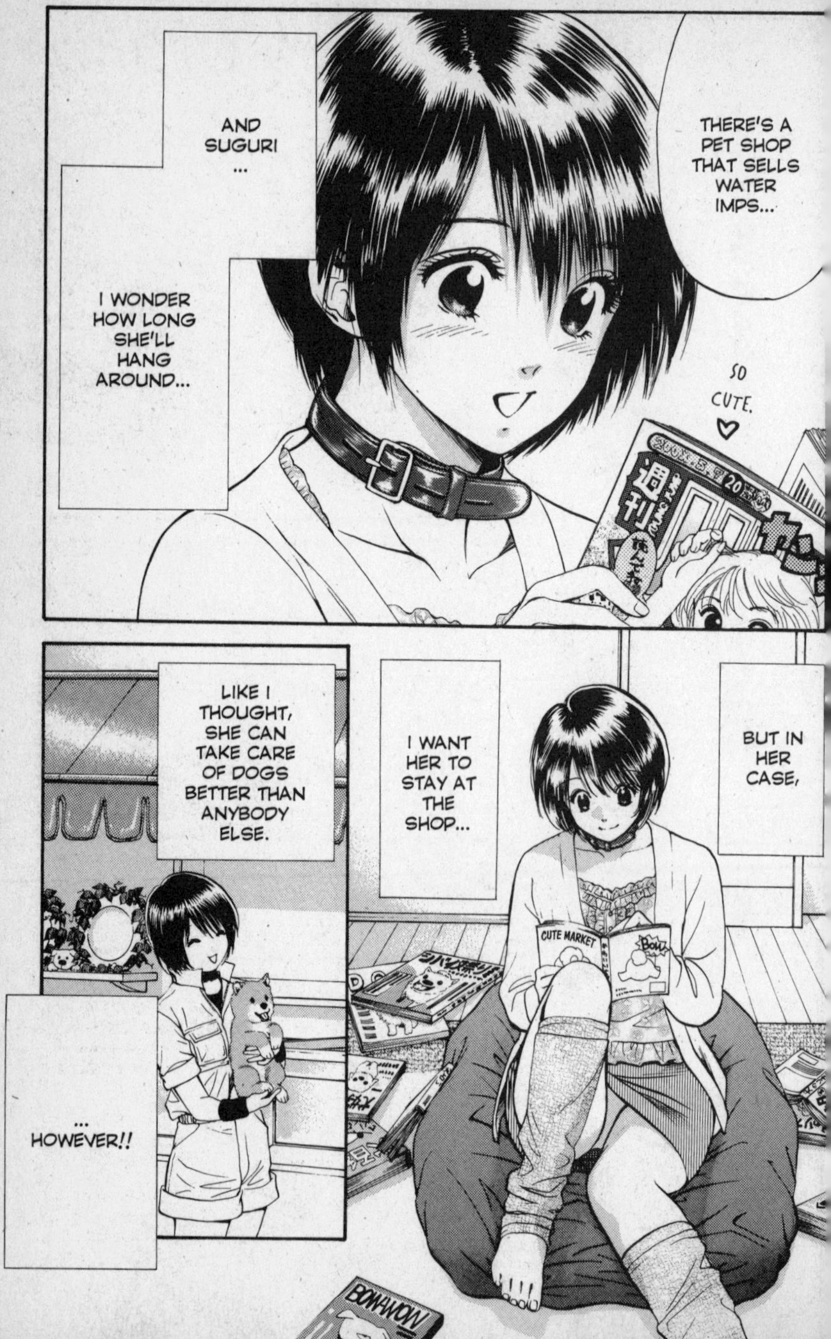
THERE'S A PET SHOP THAT SELLS WATER IMPS...
SO CUTE. ♡
AND SUGURI ...
I WONDER HOW LONG SHE'LL HANG AROUND...
BUT IN HER CASE,
I WANT HER TO STAY AT THE SHOP...
CUTE MARKET
BOW
LIKE I THOUGHT, SHE CAN TAKE CARE OF DOGS BETTER THAN ANYBODY ELSE.
... HOWEVER!!
BOWWOW

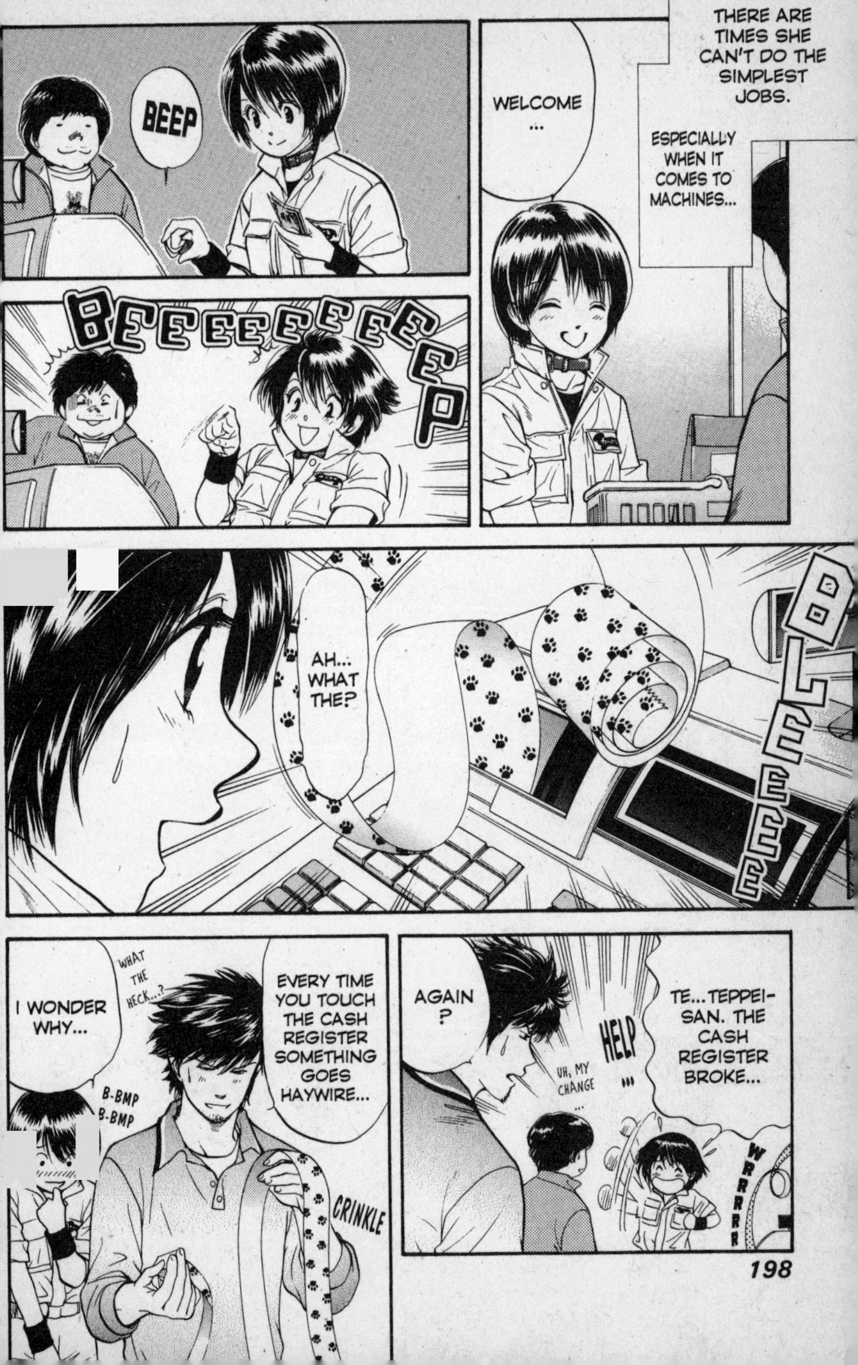
THERE ARE TIMES SHE CAN'T DO THE SIMPLEST JOBS.
ESPECIALLY WHEN IT COMES TO MACHINES...
WELCOME ...
BEEP
BEEEEEEEEEP
BLEEEEEE
AH... WHAT THE?
TE...TEPPEI-SAN. THE CASH REGISTER BROKE...
WRRRRR
HELP ...
UH, MY CHANGE ...
AGAIN ?
EVERY TIME YOU TOUCH THE CASH REGISTER SOMETHING GOES HAYWIRE...
CRINKLE
WHAT THE HECK...?
I WONDER WHY...
B-BMP B-BMP

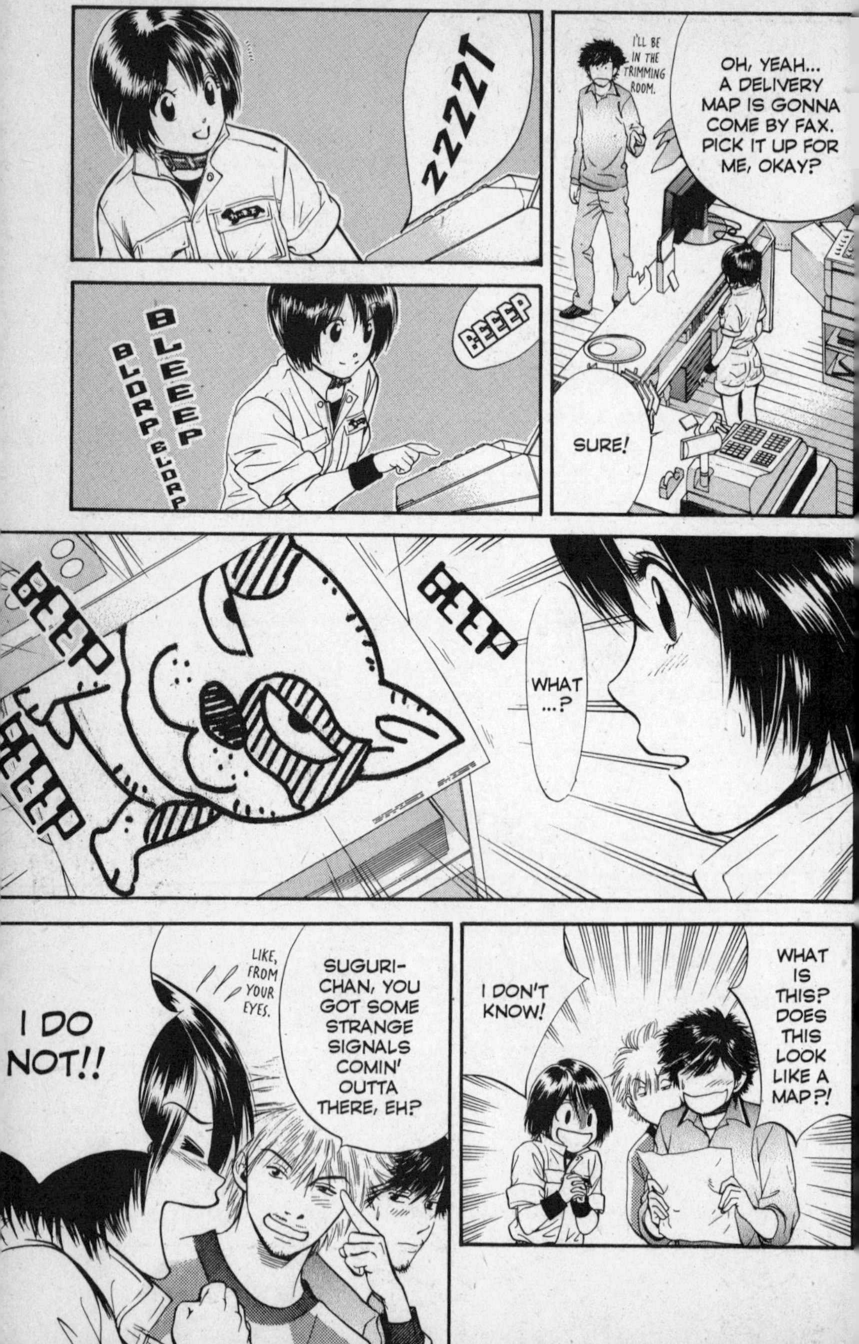
OH, YEAH... A DELIVERY MAP IS GONNA COME BY FAX. PICK IT UP FOR ME, OKAY?
I'LL BE IN THE TRIMMING ROOM.
SURE!
ZZZZT
BEEEP
BLEEEEP
BLDRP BLDRP BLDRP
WHAT ...?
BEEP
BEEP
BEEEEP
WHAT IS THIS? DOES THIS LOOK LIKE A MAP?!
I DON'T KNOW!
SUGURI-CHAN, YOU GOT SOME STRANGE SIGNALS COMIN' OUTTA THERE, EH?
LIKE, FROM YOUR EYES.
I DO NOT!!

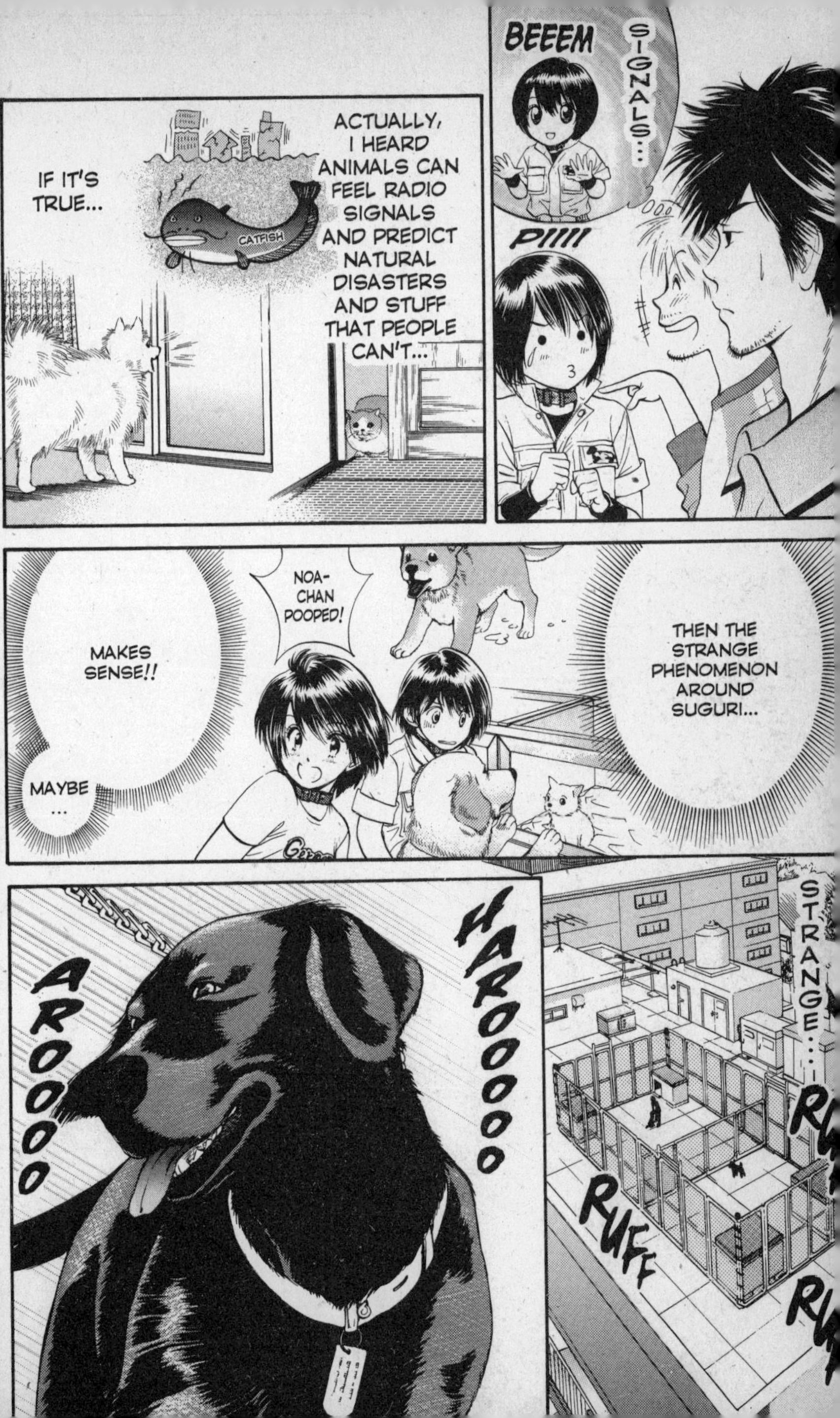
BEEEM
SIGNALS...
PIIII
ACTUALLY, I HEARD ANIMALS CAN FEEL RADIO SIGNALS AND PREDICT NATURAL DISASTERS AND STUFF THAT PEOPLE CAN'T...
CATFISH
IF IT'S TRUE...
THEN THE STRANGE PHENOMENON AROUND SUGURI...
NOA-CHAN POOPED!
MAKES SENSE!!
MAYBE ...
STRANGE...
RUFF
HAROOOOOOO
AROOOOO

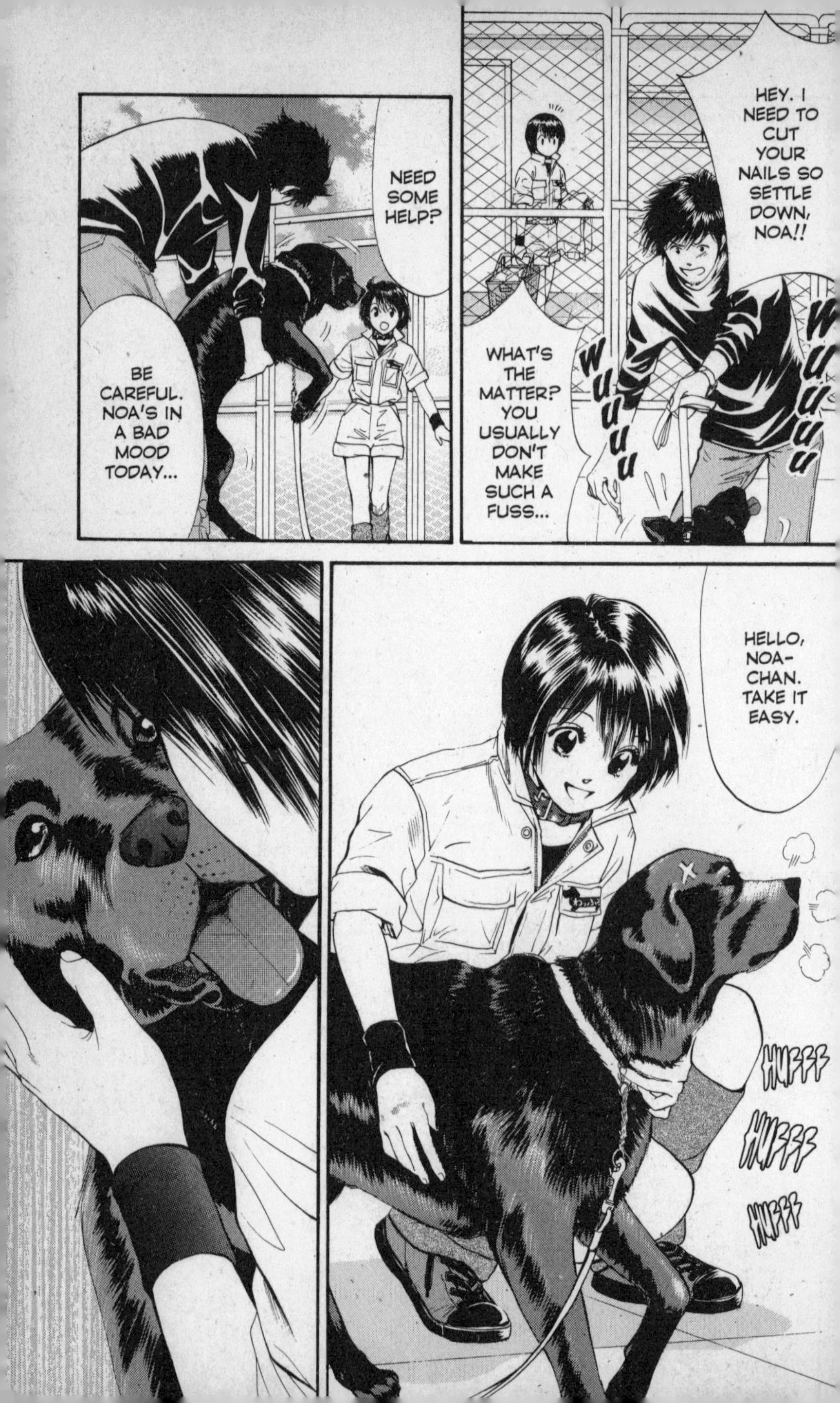
HEY. I NEED TO CUT YOUR NAILS SO SETTLE DOWN, NOA!!
WUUUUUUU
WHAT'S THE MATTER? YOU USUALLY DON'T MAKE SUCH A FUSS...
WUUUUU
NEED SOME HELP?
BE CAREFUL. NOA'S IN A BAD MOOD TODAY...
HELLO, NOA-CHAN. TAKE IT EASY.
HUFFF
HUFFF
HUFFF

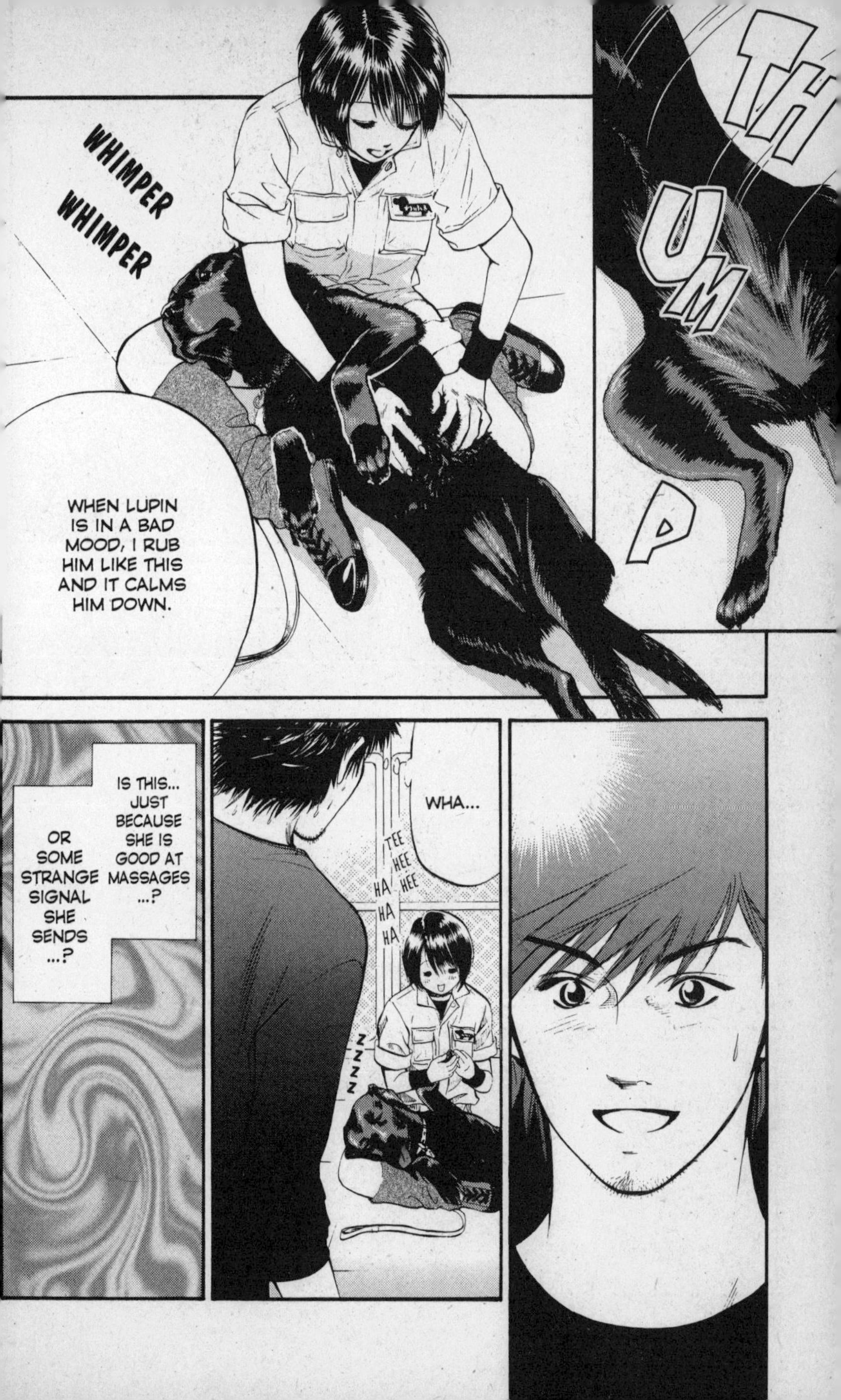
THUMP
WHIMPER WHIMPER
WHEN LUPIN IS IN A BAD MOOD, I RUB HIM LIKE THIS AND IT CALMS HIM DOWN.
WHA...
TEE HEE HEE
HA HA HA
ZZZZ
IS THIS... JUST BECAUSE SHE IS GOOD AT MASSAGES ...?
OR SOME STRANGE SIGNAL SHE SENDS ...?

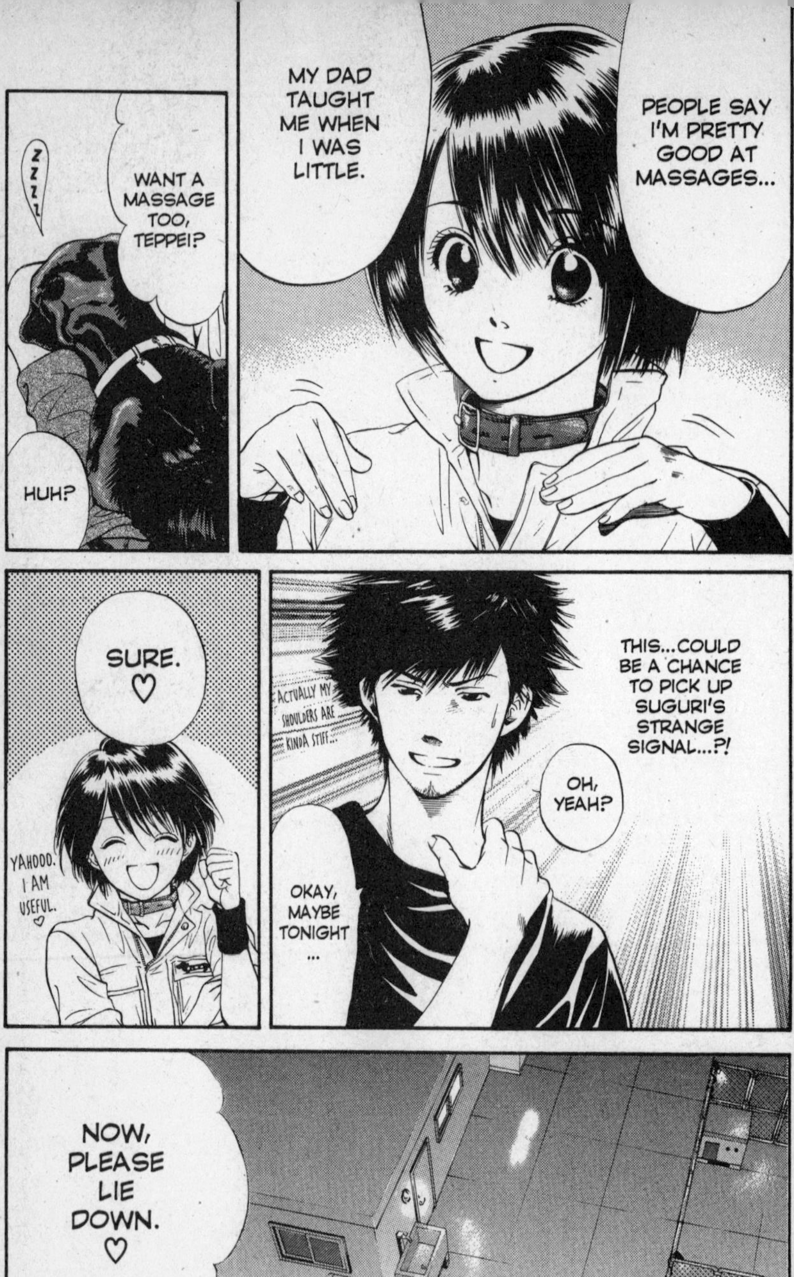
PEOPLE SAY I'M PRETTY GOOD AT MASSAGES...
MY DAD TAUGHT ME WHEN I WAS LITTLE.
WANT A MASSAGE TOO, TEPPEI?
ZZZZ
HUH?
THIS...COULD BE A CHANCE TO PICK UP SUGURI'S STRANGE SIGNAL...?!
OH, YEAH?
ACTUALLY MY SHOULDERS ARE KINDA STIFF...
OKAY, MAYBE TONIGHT ...
SURE. ♡
YAHOOO. I AM USEFUL. ♡
NOW, PLEASE LIE DOWN. ♡

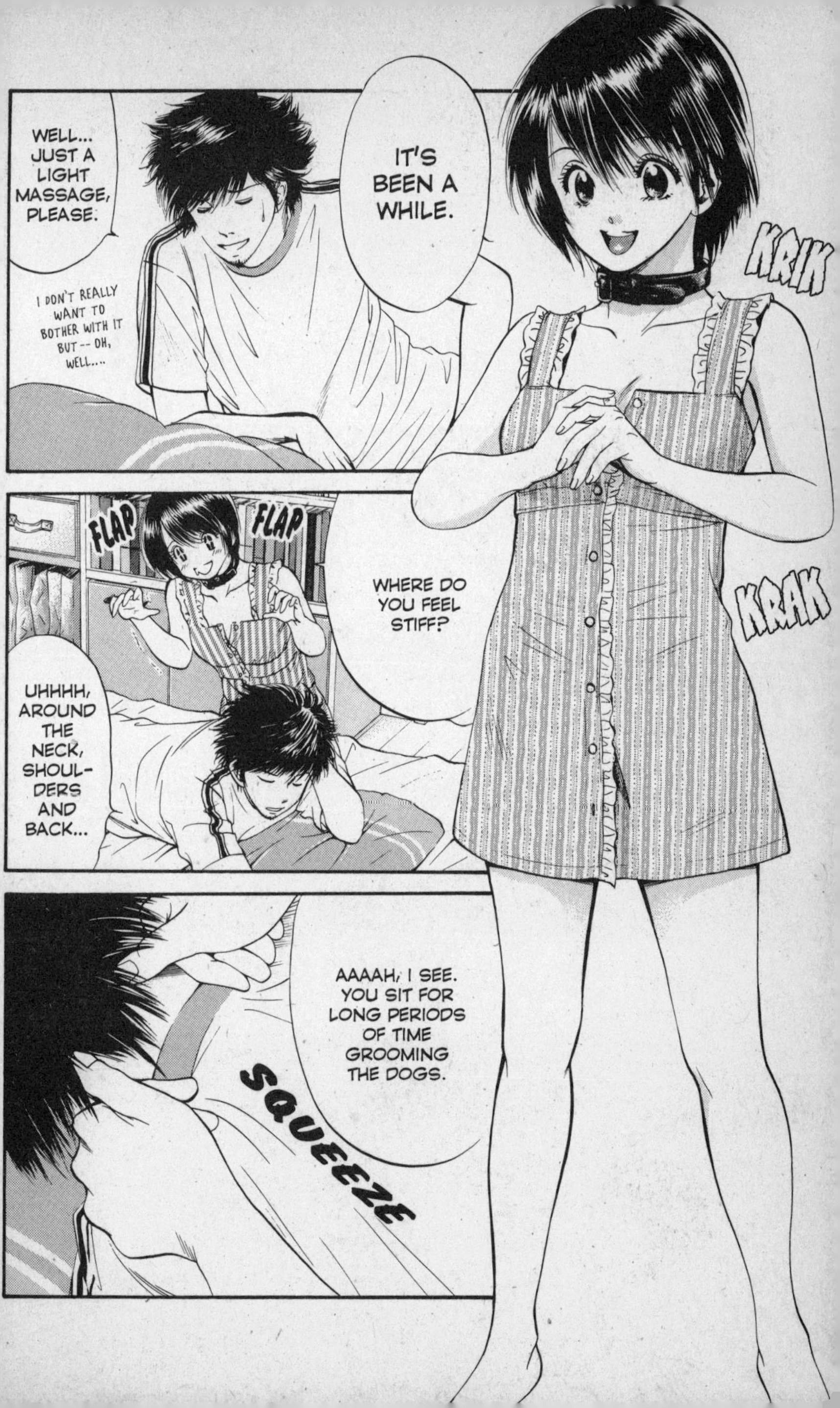
IT'S BEEN A WHILE.
KRIK
KRAK
WELL... JUST A LIGHT MASSAGE, PLEASE.
I DON'T REALLY WANT TO BOTHER WITH IT BUT -- OH, WELL....
FLAP
FLAP
WHERE DO YOU FEEL STIFF?
UHHHH, AROUND THE NECK, SHOUL-DERS AND BACK...
AAAAH, I SEE. YOU SIT FOR LONG PERIODS OF TIME GROOMING THE DOGS.
SQUEEZE

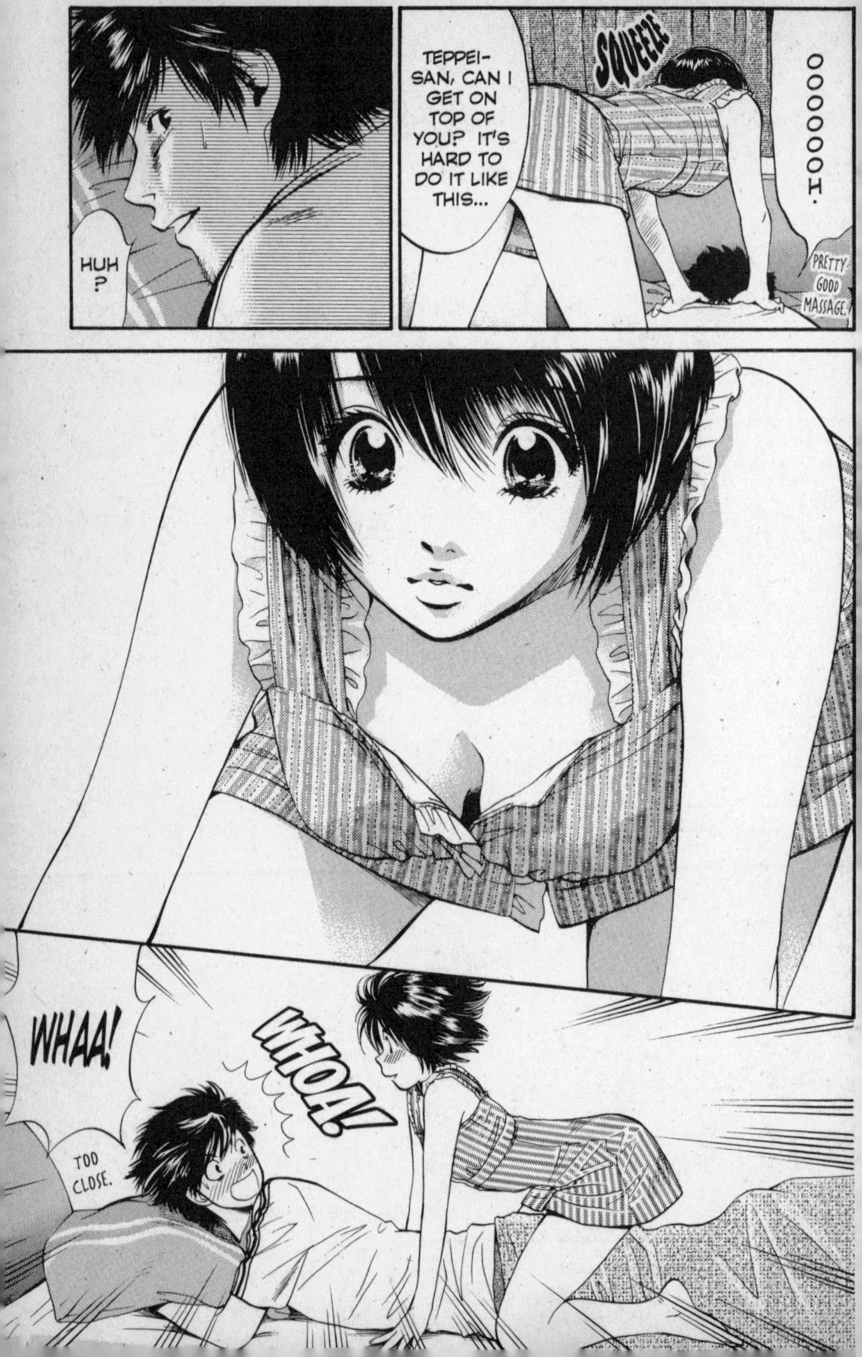
OOOOOOH.
SQUEEZE
TEPPEI-SAN, CAN I GET ON TOP OF YOU? IT'S HARD TO DO IT LIKE THIS...
PRETTY GOOD MASSAGE.
HUH?
WHOA!
WHAA!
TOO CLOSE.

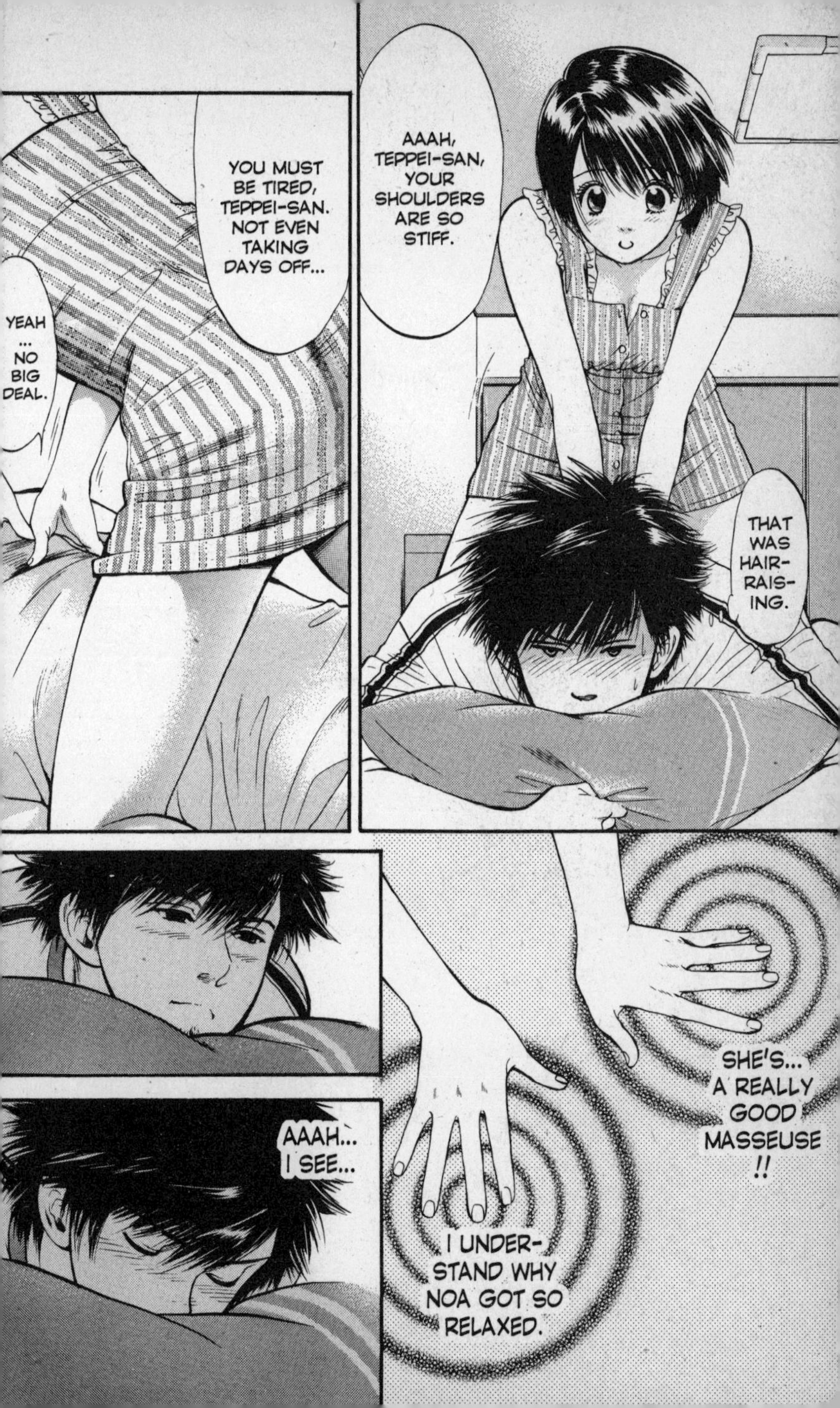
AAAH, TEPPEI-SAN, YOUR SHOULDERS ARE SO STIFF.
THAT WAS HAIR-RAISING.
YOU MUST BE TIRED, TEPPEI-SAN. NOT EVEN TAKING DAYS OFF...
YEAH ... NO BIG DEAL.
SHE'S... A REALLY GOOD MASSEUSE!!
I UNDERSTAND WHY NOA GOT SO RELAXED.
AAAH... I SEE...

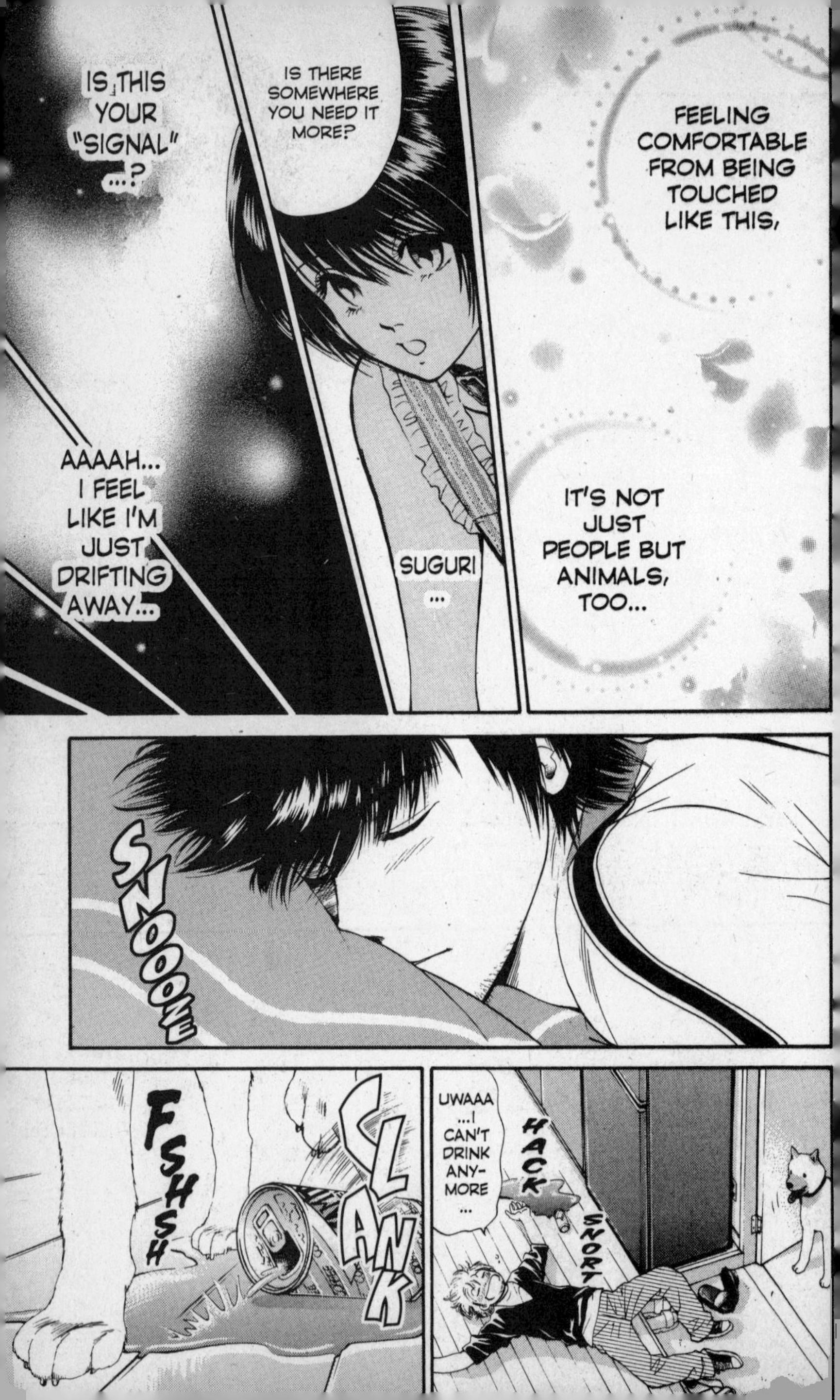
FEELING COMFORTABLE FROM BEING TOUCHED LIKE THIS,
IT'S NOT JUST PEOPLE BUT ANIMALS, TOO...
IS THERE SOMEWHERE YOU NEED IT MORE?
SUGURI ...
IS THIS YOUR "SIGNAL" ...?
AAAAH... I FEEL LIKE I'M JUST DRIFTING AWAY...
SNOOOZE
HACK
UWAAA ...I CAN'T DRINK ANY-MORE ...
SNORT
CLANK
FSHSH

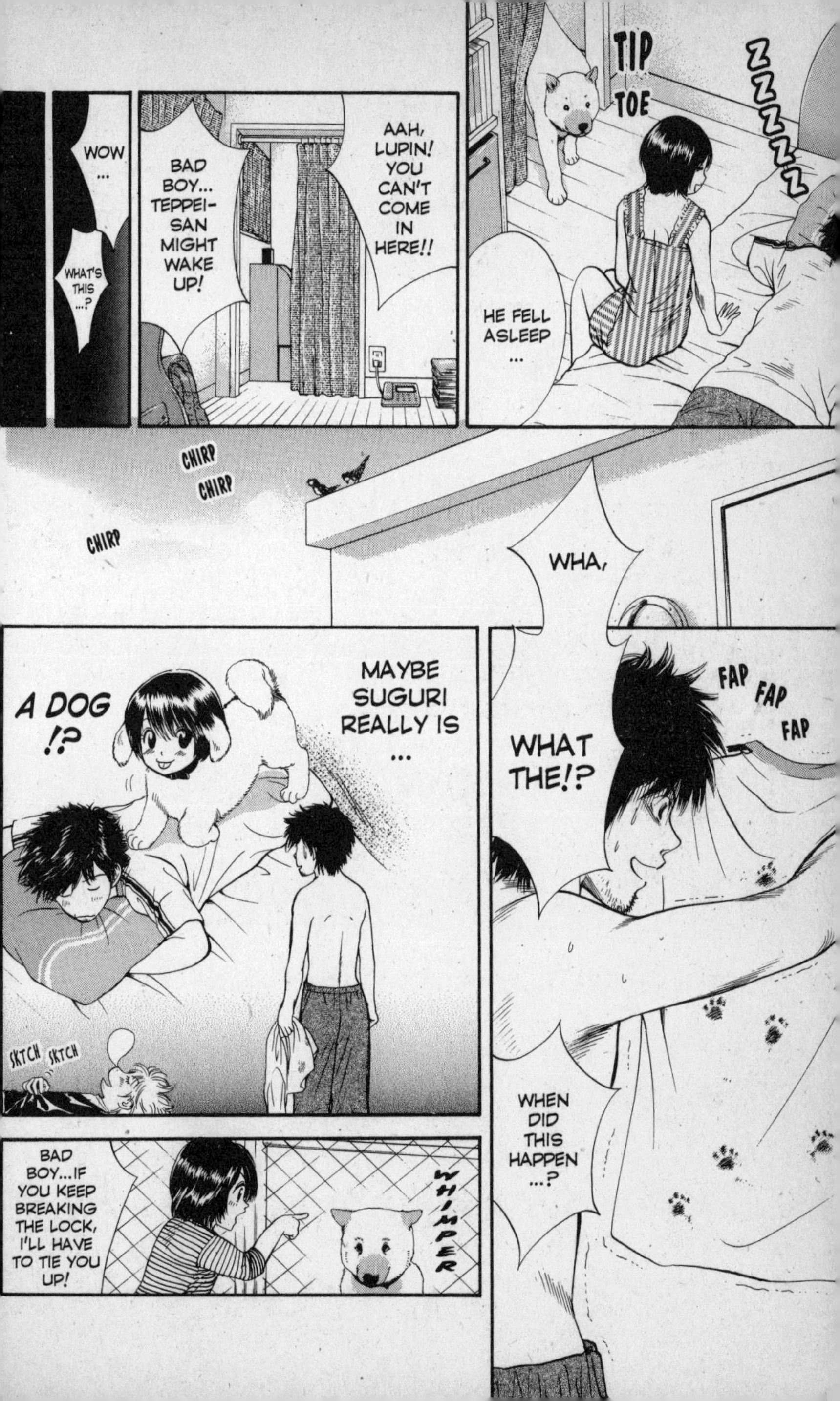

ZZZZZ
TIP TOE
HE FELL ASLEEP ...
AAH, LUPIN! YOU CAN'T COME IN HERE!!
BAD BOY... TEPPEI-SAN MIGHT WAKE UP!
WOW ...
WHAT'S THIS ...?
CHIRP
CHIRP
CHIRP
WHA,
WHAT THE!?
FAP FAP FAP
WHEN DID THIS HAPPEN ...?
MAYBE SUGURI REALLY IS ...
A DOG !?
SKTCH SKTCH
BAD BOY...IF YOU KEEP BREAKING THE LOCK, I'LL HAVE TO TIE YOU UP!
WHIMPER

Nonfiction baka theater

Not hearing things clearly

I'm going for out for Ippuku.
Fwip
What?
Seppuku!?
Super Helper Katosan
End of year
Hmm... New Year's Cards...
What should I do this year...?
Hey, Mom?
Super Chief and Straight Man @ Mamicchi
For dinner... how about tempura?
Rumble
What? Tokoroten!?
Super punctual hunger clock
It's just natural.
What a shame.
No it isn't!!

Did you enjoy "Inubaka" volume one? An unprecedented pet boom is going on in Japan and you can see all kinds of dogs all over town. I live by myself now and I'm not allowed to have pets, so I can't have dogs either.
But last summer, a cute white dog came to my parents' house.
It's called a Japanese Pomeranian. It's a very rare dog. I had two mutts before but this is the first time I've had a finely bred dog.
It's very clever and good-looking and I'm looking forward to watching it grow up. In this comic I wrote about dog poo from the very beginning, but if you have a dog you'll become friends with poo, too (lol).
No time to complain about it being disgusting. If you have a dog, you know very well...

Anyway, what's in store for "crazy for dogs" Suguri!? Stay tuned!

GOING FOR A SMOKE BREAK IS CALLED "IPPUKU"

"SEPPUKU" MEANS "HARA-KIRI" OR RITUAL SUICIDE

TOKOROTEN IS A NOODLE MADE FROM SEAWEED

Inubaka
Crazy for Dogs
Vol. #1
VIZ Media Edition

Story and Art by
Yukiya Sakuragi

Translation/Hidemi Hachitori, Honyaku Center Inc.
English Adaptation/Ian Reid and John Werry, Honyaku Center Inc.
Touch-up Art & Lettering/Kelle Hahn
Cover and Interior Design/Hidemi Sahara
Editor/Ian Robertson

Managing Editor/Annette Roman
Editorial Director/Elizabeth Kawasaki
Editor in Chief/Alvin Lu
Sr. Director of Acquisitions/Rika Inouye
Sr. VP of Marketing/Liza Coppola
Exec. VP of Sales & Marketing/John Easum
Publisher/Hyoe Narita

Published by VIZ Media, LLC
P.O. Box 77010
San Francisco, CA 94107

10 9 8 7 6 5 4 3 2 1
First printing, February 2007

www.viz.com
store.viz.com

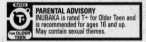